D1546286

DISPELLING THE DARKNESS

༁ྃ། །མགོ་སྨྲ་རུ་གྲུ་མ་ལྡི་ལི་ལོ་རོ་ཞེས་ཁུབ་པ་ལེས་སྤུབ་པའི་ མོ་དུ་ཀྱེ་མ་ཁས་པ་རྣམས་པ་མྱེ་ན་སྤུ་མ་
དུ་སྤོང་ཕོ་ཀྱི་ལྤུབ་པའི་ངོ་མས་ཁྲུ་བ་བཀྱེན་ལ་སོ།།

༈ ༄༅། །ཕྱག་མ་མེ་མེར་ཆེ་ངག་དག་རྣ་སྲེ་ཉ་མེད། །བོ་རྡོ་ཀྱིས་གཟི་གཉིས་མི་པང་ཚེར་ཨས་མེད། །མ་དག་པོང་
དཔ་ཕྲ་ལྤུར་ལེ་མི་མང་། །ཞེས་སྐྱོན་དུ་རྡོ་ཉི་ཀྱིས་བྱུག ། པ་ངེ་ནག་ནས་ལ་ས་ནོ་སྣ་གཟམ་ལས།། ཅེ་
འོད་ཟེར་ནག་ལ་འཁར་ལ་རྣམས། །ཁ་ལྤུ་ལེས་པུ་ཐོ་བ་ཞིན་ནོ་མ་ཉེད། །མ་ཕར་རྣ་ཏུ་ཏུ་རང་རོ་ལ་མ་རྣ།
།འཇམ་རྣམ་གཉིས་ཀྱིས་རི་པོ་རོ་ཉིན་བོ་བཞིན། །ཁ་ལ་རོ་རོ་མེད་ཅེ་ཕྱེགས་རྨེ་མེ་མེད། །ཕྲུམ་རྣ་མེར་རོ་ཉི་ཏེ་ཆེན་
པའི་མ་དག །རོ་ལི་རྗེ་ལས་ལོ་པོར་དུ་མོ་ངོ་རེ་ཉིས་ནུ། །སྲུག་དོ་ལས་མེད་པ་རོ་འི་ཉི་རུ་ཉིས་ཀྱུབ། །བོ་རེ་ཀྱུན་ཀྱི་ཉུབ་
ནའོ་རྣ་ཀྱི་མ་ཉི། །ཞེས་ལ་ར་ཕི་ན་སུ་སོ་ལེ་སུ་རུ་ཀྱི་མཚར། །སྦུགུ་ཕྱེ་ལོས་ཞི་མེ་ཉོ་ནོག་ཚང་ཇ་ཏེ།། དོ་
ལ་ཀྱུ་ནམས་གནོན་ཕ་ཉིང་ནབས་ན་ཞེ་དུ། །རབ་ཁ་ཕྱེ་ལོ་ས་གཉིས་མེད་ནོ་སེལ།། མ་དག་སྨེན་པ་ནའི་རྣགས་རང་ཏོ་
མ་སྤུན། །རོ་ལ་ཉེས་ནག་ཕྱེ་ར་རང་དུ་ལས།། །དག་ཏོ་ཉི་ལྡག་པ་ན་ས་སྤུ་འོ་ཨོ། ར་ང་མཁའ་ནེ་འི་ཀྱུར་མ་
སྤུན་འཚོ་ལ་ལོ།།   །སྲེས་མེད་ནའི་ནེ་ནུ་མེ་ཁོ་ནག་ཏོ་ཀྱི་ས་ནཱི། །ཁ་ཆུག་རོ་ནུན་པ་ས་རྣས་དག་ཀོ་ངོ་
ཏུ་ནོ། །འབྱིས་པ་པ་ཉོ་ཉིས་ནའི་མི་རོ་ནོ་ཏེ། །གོ་ཏ་ སར་རྣ་རོམ་ས་ལ་ལ་ཕ་ང་ནུ་ར་ཏེ། །དོ་ཏུ་ཉིས་ཀྱུ་ན་ཁྱུ་ཙ་ཏཱ་
ཅེ་ས་སོ་ཏོ། །ལམ་ར་ཏུ་ཉི་ཉི་ནེ་ན་སྤུ་ལ་ས་མེ་ན། །ཀ་ལ་ཉི་ཉིས་འཇིམས་ཏེ་ཆིམ་ས་ཉུ་ནས་ས་ཕ་ས་ར་ནོ།
།སྦུ་ལ་ས་ནེ་ནོ་ཞི་ན་ནོ་རོ་ལ་ཞིན་ནརབ་འབོ་ཕི་ཉེར། །ཞམ་ནའི་མེ་ད་ར་ཀྱུ་ར་ནྤུ་ས་མེ་ནོ་ཉུ། །ནོ་ལ་ཁྱི་ལ་
ཀྱུ་ཙུ་གནོན་བར་ཀྱུར་ཀྱུ་རང་ནས། །ནོག་ག་ཕི་ཆེ་ས་ཀྱི་འཁར་ཏུ་ཉི་ར་ཏེ། །ཕུ་ཏ་ལ་ཕི་ལེ་ཉ་ར་ར་མཚན་ས་
ནེ། །ར་ང་ནེ་འབས་པ་ར་ང་ད་ཕ་ཏུ་བུལ། །ཀ་ཉ་ར་འཇོ་མས་པ་ལ་མས་ལོ་ན་ནའི་ཕ་ལ་ས་ག་མ་ཀ་ས། །སོ་ཏེ་ཏེ་
ཉ་ལ་ནེ་འཕྱེ་མ་ཏོ་ནེ་འོ་ང་འཕ་ར་ཏུ་ཉེར། །ཇ་མེ་ར་ས་ཆེན་ཀྱི་ཕུག་རྐྱུ་ལ་ས་པ་ར་མ་ཏོར། །ཉེ་ལས་ སྤུད་ལ་རོ་
ཉེ་ས་ཉེ་རབ་ས་འད་ངྀ། །ཀ་ནོ་ཉིས་ན་ས་མི་མེད་ར་ད་ག་ཏི་ཙ་བས་ར་ཏུ་ཉིས། །ཕ་ས་ཕ་ག་ར་ཉམ་ས་ག་ཙོ་བར་
ས་ཏུ་ཉ་ར་འི་ཉེར། །ཇ་ས་ལ་ར་ད་ག་ཉ་རྣམ་ས་ཀྱི་སྤུ་ར་པ་ས་ཏོ། །ཞུ་ལ་ས་སྐུ་ད་ག་ཉོ་ཏུ་ཉེ་ཕ་སོ་ཁས་འི་ཏེ།
།རབ་ར་ག་ག་ས་མི་ལེ་ས་ཀྱུ་ཉུ་ཏུ་ན་ར་རྣམ་ས། །ཞ་ན་ར་ཉི་ཀྱི་ཉི་ས་ན་ས་པའི་ཙ་ར་ཏུ་ཉེ་ས་ཏེ། །ཕྱུ་ན་ས་
ག་ནམ་ས་མེ་ཉེན་ མེ་ཚ་ལ་ས་མི་རྣམ་ས་ལ། །ཕེ་ནམ་ས་སྤུ་ད་ཐམ་ས་ཉ་ན་སྤུ་ལས་ལུ་ལུ་ལྤུ། །ཁ་ཉི་ད་རོ་ས་
སྤུ་རྣམ་ས་ལ་ཤ། །ཀ་རྡོ་ར་རྣམ་པ་ར་འབྲྀག་པ་ས་གྲོ་ནས་པོ་འི་ཏེ། །ར་ད་ད་ར་ནམ་ལ་ང་མེ་ཉཔ་ང་ར་ར་
དྤུ། །མི་ག་ནང་ངོ་ནམ་ས་ཀྱི་ནུ་ཀྱུ་ཙུ་སྤུག་ས་པ་རྣམ་ས། །ཕྱི་རྣམ་ས་ན་ད་ཕུ་ལ་པ་ར་མེ་ནེ་ད་ར་པའི་ཕྀ་ར། །ཞ་མས་
ས་རབ་ར་ཙུ་ཉི་ག་ཙ་ལ་ལུ་རབ་ར། །ཕྱུ་ཏེ་ཏེ་ཏོ་ག་ས་ར་རབ་ས་ལ་ བ་ཉི་སྤུ་ཉེ་ས་ལུ་ས། །ར་ང་ནི་ཕ་ག །
ག་ཏོ་ཀྱུ་ན་ར་ནྤུ་ར་ར་མ་ཏོ། །ར་ད་ལ་ས་ལྤུ་ལ་མེ་ད་ཉ་རྣ་ པ་ས་མ་ས་ཙུ་དི། །ཕི་ལེ་ནས་ཉོ་མེ་ད་ན་སྣ་ མ་ས་ཙུ།
གནས་ར་ཀྱུ་རི་སྤུ་ར་ཙ་ན་མ་ས་འི། །སྤུ་ཀྱི་ས་ལ་ཕོ་ནས་ན་ ལ་ང་ནེ་མ་འི་མ་ད་ཉ། །ཕུ་ག་ཙ་ན་རྣམ་ས་ཀྱི་རོ་ག་ལ་ཉོ་ད་ར་ར་ཙོ་དེན།
།མི་རྣམ་ས་ཉ་ད་ལ་ཕྱེ་ག་ས་རཱ་མི་མ་ནའི་ཉེང་། །ཕྱུ་ལས་རེ་ཕོ་ར་ཕི་ར་ཉོ་ད་ ཉི་ར་ཏ་ད་རྨ། །ཉུ་ག་ཀྱུ་ལ་ས་ད་ག་ཀི
མེ་ཀུ་ར་རྣམ་ས་ཙ་ན་ཉ། །ར་ཉོ་པ་ར་ར་ཀྱུ་ན་ཉའི་སྤུ་ག་ཉ་ལ་ས་རྣམ་ས་ཉ། །རྣ་མ་སྤུ་ར་ད་ཉེན་ནའི་རྣ་མ་ང་།
སོ་ག་ས་ར་ང་། །འབུ་ས་ཕུ་ར་ཀྱུ་འི་ནེ་ས་ཉོ་ག་ར་མི་ག་ལ་མ། །མ་ཏི་སྤུ་ར་མཆེ་ར་ར་ནུ་བ་ང་ ང་མ་ལུ། །
།ཕུ་ག་ས་མེ་ད་པ་ར་རྟོ་ག་ས་པ་ར་ནས། །ཕི་ལ་ས་རུ་པ་ད་ཆེན་ཉ་རུ་རྒྱུ་ན་ཕའི་ཉྀ། །ཀ་ན་ར་ཉི་ས་ན་སྤུ།
ར་མེ་ད་པ་འི་ཀྱུ་ར་ཀྱུ་རྨས་རྣ་ས་ཏ། །ཀ་ན་འ་ར་ར་ད་ག་ར་ཉི་ནེ་ཉི་རུ་ནའི་ཉི། །ཀ་ན་ཉི་ཀྱུ་ས་ན་ཉུ་
རོ་མེ་ད་པ་འི་ཀྱུ་ར་ཀྱུ་རྨས་རྣ་ས། །ག་ན་ས་ན་ར་རོ་ད་ཉ་ན་ད་མ་ན་འི་སྤུ་ན་ས་ལུ་ར་རྣམ་ས། །ར་ད་ག་ན་ད་པ་ ལོ་ཉ་ར་
མེ་མས་ལེ་ལ་ས་ན་ད། །ཞི་ན་ར་ས་སྤུ་ག་ནསྤུ་ན་ཙོ་ར་ན་ས་བ་ལ་ས་ར་ལ་ཁ། །ཕུ་ར་དུ་ན་བ་ལ་ས་ག་ཙ་ཉི་ཀ་ཀུ་ཉ་ཙ་
ཏུ། །ཕུ་ག་ས་ར་ཏེ་ར་ཏེ་ཉེ་ས་ ཉ་ནe ་ཉ་ར་ས་དུ་ཉི་ར་ཏ་ད་གོ་ལ། །ཕྱུ་ས་སྤུ་ག་ར་ཅི་ར་རྣ་ས་ཟ་ཉོ་ག་ར་ལུ་ག་ར་ཉོ་ད།

DISPELLING
the
DARKNESS

*A Jesuit's Quest
for the Soul of Tibet*

൙

DONALD S. LOPEZ JR.

THUPTEN JINPA

HARVARD UNIVERSITY PRESS
*Cambridge, Massachusetts
London, England*
2017

Frontispiece: The first page of *Inquiry concerning the Doctrines
of Previous Lives and Emptiness*. Image reproduced with kind permission of the Archivum Romanum
Societatis Iesu (ARSI), Rome.

Library of Congress Cataloging-in-Publication Data
Names: Lopez, Donald S., Jr., 1952– author. | Thupten Jinpa, author. | Container of (expression):
Desideri, Ippolito, 1684–1733.
Title: Dispelling the darkness : a Jesuit's quest for the soul of Tibet /
Donald S. Lopez Jr., Thupten Jinpa.
Description: Cambridge, Massachusetts : Harvard University Press, 2017. |
Includes bibliographical references and index.
Identifiers: LCCN 2016033438 | ISBN 9780674659704 (hard cover : alk. paper)
Subjects: LCSH: Desideri, Ippolito, 1684–1733—Criticism and interpretation. | Desideri, Ippolito,
1684–1733. Works. Selections. English. 2017. | Jesuits—Missions—China—Tibet Autonomous
Region—History—18th century. | Desideri, Ippolito, 1684–1733—Travel—China—
Tibet Autonomous Region.
Classification: LCC BV3420.T5 L67 2017 | DDC 261.2/43092--dc23
LC record available at https://lccn.loc.gov/2016033438

Contents

❧

Introduction   1

1. Introduction to *Inquiry concerning the Doctrines of Previous Lives and Emptiness*   30

2. Selections from *Inquiry concerning the Doctrines of Previous Lives and Emptiness*   78

3. Introduction to *Essence of the Christian Religion*   150

4. *Essence of the Christian Religion*   192

    A Final Thought   251

    Appendix 1: Topical Outline (*sa bcad*) of the *Inquiry*   255
    Appendix 2: Subjects of the *Inquiry*   259
    Appendix 3: A Latin Version of the *Inquiry*   273

    Notes   277
    Acknowledgments   293
    Index   295

DISPELLING THE DARKNESS

Introduction

෴

On May 30, 1721, Ippolito Desideri, a Jesuit priest from Tuscany, arrived in Nyalam, the last Tibetan village before the border with Nepal. Five months earlier he had received a letter from Rome ordering him to leave Tibet. He made his way to the border, where he dispatched appeals to the Vatican imploring the Holy Father to allow him to continue his work in Tibet. While he awaited a response that never arrived, he continued writing what he considered his most important work, a refutation, composed in scholastic classical Tibetan, of the central Buddhist doctrines of rebirth and emptiness. Desideri carried this manuscript with him back to Rome, where it languished in the Jesuit archives, read neither by the Tibetan audience for whom it was intended, nor by anyone else. This book is a study of that text.

Ippolito Desideri had not been the first Roman Catholic missionary to Tibet, nor would he be the last. The Portuguese Jesuit Antonio de Andrade (1580–1634) established a mission in Tsaparang, in far western Tibet, in 1625. Despite early success, it lasted only a decade as a functioning mission.[1] In 1627 two other Portuguese Jesuits, Estavão Cacella and João Cabral, traveled from Bengal to Bhutan, where they were received by the Tibetan ruler there; Cacella would eventually travel to Shigatse in the Tsang province of Tibet. In 1661 two Jesuits living in Beijing, the Austrian Johann Grueber and the Belgian Albert D'Orville, were ordered back to Rome. The usual sea route was blockaded by the Dutch and so they set out overland, from Beijing to Goa, traveling through Tibet and stopping in Lhasa for two months, arriving on October 8, 1661. D'Orville died in Agra, but Grueber made his way to Rome. His account of Lhasa served as the basis for Athanasius Kircher's inaccurate and hostile description of Tibetan Buddhism in his 1667 *China Illustrata.*

Although Desideri was not the first European missionary to visit Tibet, he is the most famous. His fame derives from two sources. The first is the lengthy "relation" (or *relazione*) that he composed after his return to Italy, a work known by the abbreviated title *Notizie Istoriche del Thibet (Historical Notices of Tibet);* the full title of the work is *Notizie Istoriche del Thibet e memorie de' viaggi e missione ivi fatta dal P. Ippolito Desideri della Compagnia di Gesù dal medesimo scritte e dedicate (Historical Notices of Tibet and Memoir of the Journeys and Missions Undertaken by Fr. Ippolito Desideri of the Society of Jesus, Written and Dedicated by the Same).* This work lay unknown for more than a century. It was discussed for the first time in English in Cornelius Wessels's 1924 *Early Jesuit Travellers in Central Asia, 1603–1721,* where "Hippolyte Desideri" is one of seven Jesuit travelers. In 1932 the Italian explorer and scholar Filippo de Filippi (1869–1938) published an English translation of the *Historical Notices,* bringing Desideri's text to an Anglophone audience for the first time. However, readers were unaware that de Filippi had mixed and matched among several editions of the text and had omitted large sections, including those in which Desideri condemns Tibetan Buddhism. The work received its first proper scholarly study in the 1950s, when the great Italian Tibetologist Luciano Petech (1914–2010) published an annotated critical edition of the Italian text. It was only in 2010 that the *Historical Notices* received a full and accurate translation and study in English, in Michael Sweet and Leonard Zwilling's *Mission to Tibet: The Extraordinary Eighteenth-Century Account of Father Ippolito Desideri, S.J.* This magisterial work contains not only a full and annotated tradition of *Historical Notices* but also a detailed biography of Desideri and a study of the rather complicated formation of his famous text.

The other great source of Desideri's fame is that he wrote a number of works in Tibetan. In 1732 the Propaganda Fide confirmed its grant of the Tibet mission to the rival Capuchin order and barred the publication of any writings from the Jesuit mission. As a result, Desideri's Tibetan works re-

mained largely unknown until they were discovered in the Archivum Romanun Societatis Iesu (ARSI) by Cornelius Wessels, who reported the existence (he could not read Tibetan) of four of the texts in his 1924 work. *Essence
of the Christian Religion* (translated here) was mistakenly catalogued in the
Japanese section of the Jesuit Archives and was only discovered in 1970. Four
of these works were translated into Italian by Giuseppe Toscano, SX, and
published between 1981 and 1989.[2] The first discussion of them in English
is found in a 1990 essay by Richard Sherburne, SJ, entitled "A Christian-
Buddhist Dialog? Some Notes on Desideri's Tibetan Manuscripts."[3] (It will
be clear from the translations included in the present volume that the answer
to the question in the title of his essay is no.) *Inquiry concerning the Doctrines
of Previous Lives and of Emptiness,* the work that Sherburne calls, accurately,
Desideri's *opus magnum,* has never been translated in whole or part until the
present volume.

Thanks to recent advances in Anglophone studies of Desideri, we now
have a full and accurate translation of his *Historical Notices,* we know a great
deal about his life, and we understand the Jesuit academy of the early eighteenth century of which he is a product.[4] What we lack are English-language
translations of his Tibetan works. The present volume is a first attempt to
remedy that situation. Two of his works, his *Inquiry concerning the Doctrines
of Previous Lives and of Emptiness* and his *Essence of the Christian Religion*
are translated here, the first in part, the second in full. How these texts
were chosen will be described below. Before turning to that, let us begin
with Desideri's life.

THE LIFE OF DESIDERI

Desideri's life has been recounted in detail elsewhere;[5] we will provide only
a brief outline here. He was born in the town of Pistoia in Tuscany on
December 20, 1684. He entered the Jesuit order in 1700, studying at the
Collegio Romano, proceeding through the curriculum in rhetoric and philosophy. In 1710 he began the study of theology, excelling to the point that
he was asked to teach logic the following year. In 1712 he requested permission to become a missionary. After audiences with Pope Clement XI and with
Cosimo III de' Medici, he made his way to Genoa, where he sailed for India
on November 23, 1712. Braving high seas and Turkish pirates, the ship made

port five months later in Goa, the Portuguese colony on the west coast of India and one of the headquarters of the Society of Jesus in India. Assigned to the Tibet mission, he traveled by sea from Goa to Surat, then proceeded to Delhi, where he met the Portuguese Jesuit Manoel Freyre. Together they set off for Lahore, then into the Himalayas to Kashmir, then to Ladakh, the westernmost Tibetan domain, arriving in its capital, Leh, on June 25, 1715. They remained in Leh for fifty-two days, during which time Desideri began his study of the Tibetan language. The two priests were made welcome in Ladakh, so much so that Desideri wished to found the mission there, but Father Freyre, who was his superior, insisted that they continue eastward to Lhasa. They departed on August 17; the journey of about 700 miles (as the crow flies) required seven months. The priests were able to survive the difficult journey thanks to the protection of a Mongol noblewoman who allowed the two priests to join her armed caravan. They reached Lhasa on March 18, 1716.[6]

After just a month in Lhasa, Father Freyre decided to return to India, leaving Desideri alone, by his own account the only European and the only Christian in Tibet (although there were both Armenians and Russians in Lhasa). Tibet was ruled at that time by a Mongol king, Lhazang Khan, and Desideri was summoned to the court. According to Desideri's account of their meeting, the khan was impressed by the Tuscan's determination to teach Tibetans the route to heaven and his declaration that he wished to remain in Tibet for the rest of his life. His esteem for Desideri apparently increased when Desideri provided him with medical assistance. Lhazang Khan had been poisoned some years earlier and still suffered from its effects. Desideri offered him a dose of theriac, a panacea that contained some sixty-four ingredients, including opium, which provided the khan with a restful sleep.[7]

On January 6, 1717, less than a year after his arrival, he presented the khan with an exposition of Christianity, written in Tibetan. This is generally regarded to be the text found among Desideri's Tibetan writings called *Dawn, Signaling the Rising of the Sun That Dispels the Darkness (Tho rangs mun sel nyi ma shar ba'i brda).*[8] The khan, himself a Buddhist, proposed a debate between Desideri and a learned Tibetan monk, but suggested that Desideri and the Capuchin missionary, Francesco Orazio della Penna (who had arrived in the meantime), first undertake further study. In July 1717, Desideri moved to Shidé (Bzhi sde) monastery in Lhasa, and then, in

August, to Sera, a monastery of some 5,500 monks on the outskirts of the city and one of "three seats" of the Geluk sect. His notes from his studies, preserved in the Jesuit archives in Rome, trace his course through a young monk's textbooks on elementary logic through to the masterworks of the tradition, including the *Lam rim chen mo, The Great Treatise on the Stages of the Path to Enlightenment,* by the founder of the Geluk sect, Tsong kha pa (1357–1419), a work that Desideri describes as "a profuse, admirable, clear, elegant, subtle, clever, methodical, and most accurate compendium of everything pertaining to that sect."[9] As we shall see, Tsong kha pa's work would serve as Desideri's primary source as he sought to refute the basic doctrines of Buddhism.

Desideri's studies at Sera were interrupted by war. A rival faction of Mongols invaded Lhasa in December 1717, assassinating Lhazang Khan and pillaging the city. Desideri fled east to the Capuchin residence in the province of Dakpo. There he continued his studies until the Capuchins (who had had a mission in Lhasa from 1707–1711 and had returned in October 1716) finally received a decree from the Propaganda Fide in Rome confirming that Tibet had been assigned to the Capuchins "to the exclusion of every other order."[10] They presented Desideri with the letter on January 10, 1721. He left Lhasa on April 28, 1721, reaching Kathmandu on January 20, 1722. He continued on to India, where he would remain for five more years, finally returning to the city of his birth on November 4, 1727.

Desideri arrived in Rome in the wake of the Chinese Rites Controversy and in the midst of the Malabar Rites Controversy. In both, the Jesuits were criticized for their efforts to accommodate local practices (ancestor worship in China and caste distinction in India).[11] Although such charges were not made against the Tibet mission, the Capuchins claimed that their failure to successfully evangelize Tibet was due to the errors of the Jesuits who had preceded them there; they had particularly harsh words about Desideri. The last years of Desideri's life were consumed with composing often tedious defenses of his work, as well as the remarkable account of his time in Tibet, the *Historical Notices.* He died in Rome on April 13, 1733.

Desideri was not the first Christian missionary, or even the first Jesuit, to study the doctrines of Buddhism in order to refute them. In an effort to place his works in some context, let us briefly survey other Jesuit encounters with Buddhism.[12]

JESUITS IN OTHER BUDDHIST LANDS

In the popular imagination, each of the Asian lands seems to have its paradigmatic missionary, the name that comes to mind when the Roman Catholic missions are mentioned. For Japan, it is Francis Xavier; for China, it is Matteo Ricci; for Indochina, it is Alexandre de Rhodes; for Siam, it is Guy Tachard. For Tibet, it is Ippolito Desideri. The fame of these figures, however, sometimes obscures the remarkable efforts of others, such as Alessandro Valignano in Japan, Nicolas Trigault in China, Cristoforo Borri in Vietnam, Nicolas Gervaise in Thailand, and Francesco Orazio della Penna in Tibet.

The success of a mission is often measured by the number of converts to the Christian faith. The mission that Francis Xavier initiated in Japan eventually gained many converts, until the brutal suppression by the Tokugawa shoguns. By the late seventeenth century, there were hundreds of thousands of converts to Christianity in China. A different measure of success might be the influence that the missionaries had at the respective royal courts of their mission fields. Here, the Jesuit mission to China was clearly the most successful, with a succession of priests appointed to various positions at the Qing court. One notes, however, that among the many things the Jesuits could offer the emperor, heaven seems to have been the least interesting to his court. Instead they were interested in more worldly matters—maps, clocks, telescopes, music, and painting. We recall that Ricci translated four books of Euclid's *Elements* into Chinese, that Tomás Pereira built a pipe organ in Beijing and gave music lessons to the Kangxi emperor's children, that Giuseppe Castiglione painted equestrian portraits of the Qianlong emperor.

By these various measures Desideri appears to have been an utter failure. He made very few converts. He did not translate any European works into Tibetan. He may have had an audience (or two) with the ruler of Tibet, but his presence seems to have been tolerated rather than valued. Ricci debated with Buddhist monks and his works were read by Chinese scholars. To date, no reference has been found in any Tibetan source indicating Desideri's presence, much less his influence, during the almost seven years he spent in Ladakh and Tibet. Instead Desideri's fame derives above all from the fact that he developed deep learning in the doctrines of Tibetan Buddhism and then sought to refute them, not in Latin but in the idiom of Tibetan Buddhist scholasticism, demonstrating a mastery of both form and content unmatched by his brethren who sought to proclaim the faith in the languages of Asia.

In 1551 the Jesuit missionary to Japan, Juan Fernández (1526–1576) sent a report on the religion of Japan to Francis Xavier. As Matteo Ricci and his brothers in China would be, the Jesuit missionaries in Japan were initially regarded as Buddhist monks who had arrived from Tenjiku, the Japanese Buddhist term for India. This caused a considerable sensation among the various Japanese Buddhist sects, who sent representatives to meet monks from the land of the Buddha's birth and ask them questions about Buddhist doctrine. Many of these monks came from the Zen sect, known then, as it is today, for its bold negations of just about everything. Hence, the Jesuits learned from them (as they translated from Japanese into Spanish) that "there is no soul and that when man dies, everything dies, because what came from nothing returns to nothing."[13] As a consequence, the Jesuits in Japan were far less exercised about the question of reincarnation than Ricci, and later Desideri, would be. For the Jesuits in Japan, the pernicious Buddhist doctrine was nothingness (*mu* in Japanese) and emptiness *(kū)*. In his report to Francis Xavier, Fernández wrote, "They admitted that this is so, saying that it is a principle from which all things come; men, animals, and plants, and that all created things have this principle in them. . . . This principle, they say, is neither good nor evil, involves neither glory nor punishment, and neither dies nor lives, so that is a non-being."[14] From the Jesuit perspective, therefore, they not only denied the existence of God, they denied the existence of any kind of first principle, or at least a first principle that was not nothing. Desideri would return again and again to this theme.

At the end of the sixteenth century, a further attempt would be made by a Roman Catholic missionary to refute the doctrines of Buddhism, not in Japan but in China. It was Matteo Ricci in his famous *The True Meaning of the Lord of Heaven (Tianzhu shiyi)*. As we shall see, his understanding of Buddhist doctrine and his efforts to refute it were far less sophisticated than Desideri's.[15]

The fascinating evolution of Ricci's text is too complicated to recount here; a few points bear noting, however.[16] It began as Ricci's revision of a catechism composed by his fellow Jesuits Michele Ruggieri and Piero Gomes, with the title *The True Record of the Lord of Heaven, A New Compilation from India (Xinbian xizhuguo tianzhu shilu)*, first published in 1584. This subtitle was not meant to indicate that the Jesuits had a headquarters in Goa. At the beginning of their mission, the Jesuits sought to represent themselves as Buddhist monks (including shaving their hair and beards); in China at the time, "the West" *(xiyu)* meant India. This text by Ruggieri and Gomes was a relatively standard catechism (adapted for the Chinese), declaring in sixteen chapters that there is one God, that he is the creator of heaven and earth, that the soul is eternal, that God is the judge, that he dispensed the Ten Commandments and later came to earth to teach a new law. In the work, the missionaries referred to themselves as "monks from India" *(tianzhu seng)*.

In the years that followed, Ricci and his fellow Jesuits came to recognize the low regard in which Buddhist monks were held by many Chinese scholars. They therefore requested, and received, permission to grow their hair and beards and exchange the robes of a Buddhist monk for those of a Chinese literatus. Between 1591 and 1594, Ricci translated into Latin the "four books" of the Confucian tradition—the *Analects* of Confucius, the *Mencius,* the *Great Learning,* and the *Doctrine of the Mean.* Whereas he regarded Buddhism as a form of idolatry fraught with superstition and error, he saw in the Confucian classics not an alien religion but a kind of natural law that was compatible with, and thus could serve as a foundation for, the propagation of Christianity. He would argue that to truly practice Confucian self-cultivation, one must believe in God, and he sought passages in the Confucian classics that he could cite to make that case. In October 1596 he completed the first draft of *The True Meaning of the Lord of Heaven.* Published more than a century before Desideri began writing his *Inquiry* and likely unknown to him, it is nonetheless a work that resembles Desideri's *Inquiry* in a number of ways.

The first, and most obvious, is that the two Jesuits seek to use the scriptures of the heathen to support the doctrines of the Church. In addition to the "four books," Ricci also uses passages from the "five books"—the *Classic of Poetry,* the *Book of Documents,* the *Book of Rites,* the *Book of Changes,* and the *Spring and Autumn Annals*—to support his arguments. Desideri was faced with a far larger canon and made extensive use of it. The second similarity is that both authors used the device of the interlocutor (something common to the catechism genre). However, whereas Ricci remained close to the conversational style familiar from Europe, Desideri adopted the conventions of Tibetan scholastic debate.

In addition to form, there are also two important similarities in content. Both the Jesuit nobleman from hilly Macerata in western Italy and the Jesuit patrician from Tuscany sought to refute the Buddhist doctrines of emptiness and rebirth. We will consider Desideri's arguments in detail in the chapters that follow. Here we can briefly review the arguments put forth by Ricci in *The True Meaning of the Lord of Heaven*.

As Desideri would do a century later, Ricci begins by declaring his commitment to reason and a request to his interlocutor to dispute anything that is unreasonable. "Everything which reason shows to be true I must acknowledge as true, and everything which reason shows to be false I must acknowledge as false. . . . To abandon principles affirmed by the intellect and to comply with the opinions of others is like shutting out the light of the sun and searching for an object without a lantern."[17] But like Desideri, Ricci employs some cultural chauvinism as he begins to make his case, explaining that Christianity, which he calls "this doctrine about the Lord of Heaven," is something that all the great nations of the east and west know and uphold. "But the scholars of your esteemed country have seldom come in contact with other nations, and are therefore unable to understand the languages and culture of our regions and know little of their peoples."[18]

Apart from some disparaging remarks about the character of the Buddha (something that Desideri refrains from, at least in his Tibetan writings), Ricci's refutation of Buddhism focuses on two doctrines: emptiness and rebirth. His discussion of emptiness is brief; he does not demonstrate anything more than a vague understanding. Indeed, he equates the Daoist nothingness *(wu)* with the Buddhist emptiness *(kong)* and mocks the notion that something that does not exist can give rise to what does exist. Ricci writes, "Those who live below heaven value the real and the existing and despise the non-existent. When we speak of the source of all phenomena we are clearly speaking of that, the value of which is beyond comparison. How then can one employ despicable words like 'voidness' and 'nothingness' to represent it? . . . A thing must genuinely exist before it can be said to exist. What does not genuinely exist does not exist. If the source of all things were not real and did not exist then the things produced by it would naturally also not exist. . . . How can things which are essentially nothing or void employ their voidness and nothingness to cause all things to come into being and continue to exist?"[19]

The Madhyamaka school of Buddhism, whether in India, Tibet, or China, does not describe emptiness as the primordial source of all things, as "nothingness" is described in works like the *Daodejing*. However, the problem of the production of something that does exist from something that does not exist is a perennial problem in Madhyamaka thought, one that Desideri would explore in his own refutation of emptiness, a task that he undertakes with both a deeper understanding of Buddhist doctrine and a greater philosophical sophistication than Ricci displays in *The True Meaning of the Lord of Heaven.*

Ricci's attack on the doctrine of reincarnation is more interesting than his brief discussion of emptiness; again, it is very different from that of Desideri. Writing for a Confucian audience, he focuses on the ethical rather than the logical problems. As Roman Catholic missionaries to Asia would do consistently, Ricci attributes the doctrine of reincarnation to Pythagoras, who, he reports, was outraged when he saw evil men prosper and thus proclaimed that the consequences of their misdeeds would occur in their next life, when they were reborn as animals whose forms would reflect their human failings; the tyrannical would be leopards, the arrogant would be lions, the licentious would be pigs, thieves would be foxes. After the death of Pythagoras, his idea found little support among the ancients. "But just then the teaching leaked out and found its way to other countries. This was at the time when Śākyamuni happened to be planning to establish a new religion in India. He accepted this theory of reincarnation and added to it the teaching concerning the Six Directions [that is, the six destinations of rebirth: as gods, demigods, humans, animals, ghosts, and hell beings], together with a hundred other lies, editing it all to form books which he called canonical writings."[20] These books made their way to China. Before considering the errors of the doctrine, Ricci demeans its source, explaining that India is a small place that lacks civilization and standards of moral conduct. "The histories of many countries are totally ignorant of its existence. Could such a country adequately serve as the model for the whole world?"[21]

Furthermore, there was no sin when the Lord of Heaven first created humans and animals and hence no need for reincarnation. Did he change their souls to allow reincarnation when sin entered the world? (This allusion to the Garden of Eden would likely have been lost on Ricci's Chinese readers.) And why would the prospect of rebirth as an animal be a disincentive to the sinful? The bloodthirsty would be happy to have the fangs and claws of a tiger. A thief would be happy to have the stealth of a fox.

In *The True Meaning of the Lord of Heaven,* Ricci also offers arguments in favor of the killing of animals and the eating of meat, arguments that are based largely on Confucian principles of filial piety and appropriate family relations. He attributes the Buddhist prohibitions against doing so to the belief in reincarnation; Buddhists are reluctant to kill animals because those animals might have been their human parents in a former life. But if they harbor such fears, why do they have no compunction about making an ox pull a plow and whipping a horse that is pulling a cart? If animals had been one's parents in a former life, not only would farming be improper, people could not wed for fear of marrying their former parents. He concludes his argument against reincarnation and in favor of killing animals with a more Christian approach, describing the world as created by the Lord of Heaven for man's use, with the sun and moon providing illumination, colors to please the eye, and music to please the ear. Fruits and vegetables are harvested for food and trees are cut down for firewood. Birds and animals were also created for use by humans. The hides of animals provide clothing and shoes and their tusks can be made into utensils. Their flesh is made to be eaten. If this was not the intention of the Lord of Heaven, why did he make it taste so good? (This might be regarded as the vegan's koan.) Animals have been killed and eaten by the sages of all nations throughout history without compunction. The Golden Rule applies only to humans.

A somewhat more positive, and accurate, description of the Buddhist doctrine of emptiness is found in the writings of Cristoforo Borri, a Jesuit missionary to Vietnam, a region that was called Cochin China at the time. The chapter entitled "A Short Account of the Sects of Cochin-China" begins with "a great metaphysician of the kingdom of *Siam,* whose name was *Xaca,* much ancienter than *Aristotle,* and nothing inferior to him in capacity, and the knowledge of natural things." This single phrase is the most positive valuation of the Buddha in all the accounts of the Roman Catholic missions of Asia. Borri goes on to explain the origins of the doctrine of emptiness.

He once went up to the top of a mountain, and there attentively observing the moon, which rising in the darkness of the night, gently raised itself above the horizon to be hid again the next day in the same darkness, and the sun rising in the morning to set again at night, he concluded that moral as well as physical and natural things were nothing, came of nothing, and ended in nothing. Therefore returning home, he wrote several books and large volumes on the subject, entitling them, "Of Nothing"; wherein he taught that the things of this world, by reason of the duration and measure of time, are nothing; for though they had existence, said he, yet they would be nothing, nothing at present, and nothing in time to come, for the present being but a moment, was the same as nothing.

His second argument he grounded on the composition of things; let us instance, said he, a rope, which not being naturally distinguished from its parts, inasmuch as they give its being and composition, so it appears that the rope as a rope is nothing; for as a rope it is no distinct thing from the threads it is composed of, and the hemp has no other being but the elements whereof its substance consists; so that resolving all things after this manner into the elements, and those to a sort of *materia prima* and mere *potentia,* which is therefore actually nothing, he at last proved, that the heavenly things, as well as those under the heavens, were truly nothing! . . .

He inferred, that all these things being nothing, they took their origin as it were from a cause not efficient but material, from a principle which in truth was nothing but an eternal, infinite, immutable, almighty, and to conclude, a God that was nothing, and the origin of this nothing![22]

Borri's story of the Buddha's conclusion that everything is nothing (which might be recast in more proper Buddhist terms as everything is empty) is not found in Buddhist accounts, perhaps deriving instead from Borri's own considerable skills as an astronomer. However, the example of the rope is found in Buddhist literature, where an object is sought among its parts—in this case, a rope is sought among the strands that constitute it—and is not found. This absence of the object is its emptiness. The example of the rope also evokes the Buddhist example of the "rope-snake," a coiled rope in a dark corner that is mistaken for a snake, leading to fear and flight on the part of the perceiver. On closer inspection, it is found that the snake is merely a rope, and that the emotions and actions precipitated by the error in perception were entirely baseless; there never was a snake in the corner. This example is sometimes provided as a metaphor for the various forms of attachment and aversion that dominate emotional life, all founded on ignorance, that is, the mistaken belief that the objects of experience are real. The more profound philosophical point that is often made in the case of the "rope-snake" is that just as the snake is nowhere to be found among the parts of the rope, the snake is also nowhere to be found among the parts of the snake. The only difference between the snake and the rope is that what is called a snake can perform the functions of a snake, whereas a rope cannot. This notion—that

that which is empty can nonetheless possess causal efficacy—is a point of continued contention in the history of Buddhist philosophy, and one that Desideri would also contest.

However, we would do Father Borri a disservice if we saw in his words only vague allusions to and gross caricatures of points of Buddhist philosophy. More importantly, we must also see the thought of Aristotle (as interpreted by St. Thomas Aquinas), the philosophical foundation of all the great Jesuit missionaries to Asia. Thus, Borri speaks of an analysis of the rope that reduces it to its threads, its threads are reduced to hemp, and hemp is reduced to the basic elements of air, earth, fire, and water. In Aristotle, and in Aquinas, those elements in turn are composed of *materia prima,* or prime matter, a kind of pure materiality, devoid of substance and form. As such, it does not have any concrete existence, but instead is pure potency, "mere *potentia*" in Borri's words. For Aristotle, prime matter is nonetheless real, in the sense of being the potency for substances to change into determinate things. Xaca, as Borri calls the Buddha, arrived at a different conclusion, that prime matter is in fact nothing, and hence declared that everything in heaven and earth is nothing. It is likely for this reason that Borri describes him as "much ancienter than *Aristotle,* and nothing inferior to him in capacity, and the knowledge of natural things."

Borri also alludes to Aristotle's four causes: the material cause, the formal cause, the efficient cause, and the final cause. In the simple case of a statue, these would be: marble from which the statue is made, the creature or thing depicted in the statue, the sculptor, and the end or purpose for which the statue is made. For Aquinas, both the efficient cause and the final cause are God. According to Borri, the Buddha declared that all things "took their origin as it were from a cause not efficient but material, from a principle which in truth was nothing but an eternal, infinite, immutable, almighty, and to conclude, a God that was nothing, and the origin of this nothing." That is, the Buddha did not posit the existence of a creator God, or any other efficient cause, declaring instead that everything is simply a transformation of the material cause—the substance that undergoes change—and that that substance was nothing.[23]

Desideri describes the doctrine of emptiness in similar terms, but sees it as the most pernicious of Buddhist doctrines because it makes the existence of God impossible. The logical consequence of emptiness—that everything is dependent and that there is nothing beyond this realm of dependently originated things—leaves no room for any notion of a preexistent and absolute reality. The radical implications of such a view for theism were not lost on Desideri. Left unchallenged, any rational discourse on God would be impossible. He writes: "The fundamental error of the Tibetans' sect and the source of all other false dogmas they believe is their positive, direct, and express denial of the existence of any being in itself, uncreated and independent, and of any primary and universal cause of things. The malice of the infernal enemy was able to perpetrate such a shrewd and subtle trick that he has not only concealed the extreme monstrosity and irrationality of this error with pretty tinsel, but on top of that has succeeded in giving it such a veneer and façade as to make it appear to those people as a subtlety of the most elevated and purest understanding, the culmination of a sanctity and perfection that cannot be achieved in any other way, and the only door immediately leading to true happiness and eternal bliss, although it is an error that more than any other is totally opposed to these goals."[24]

DESIDERI'S TIBETAN WORKS

The Roman Catholic missionaries to Tibet generally held the Tibetans in high regard, with Francisco Godinho, an early Jesuit missionary to western Tibet, going so far as to declare that the Tibetans were not idolaters and had knowledge of the trinity.[25] Desideri would reject arguments of Christian influence and considered Tibetans to be idolaters, but better idolaters than those of Hindustan who worship vice and passion. "It is true that the blind Tibetans do not worship any divine being (at least explicitly and directly), but they have chosen to exclude from all the objects they accept and to whom they burn incense anything they would deem more worthy of disapproval and reproach than of honor and reverence."[26] In a manual he wrote for missionaries, he praises the Tibetans' commitment to reason again and again, finding in the Tibetan monasteries an extensive literature and a sophisticated scholastic tradition. He writes, "Apart from the fact that these people customarily employ themselves in the daily exercise of dialectics, formal argumentation, and doctoral studies of their universities, their books (and they possess great libraries) are extremely subtle, abstract, and sophistic, and the system of their false religion is very wide-ranging, abstruse, and abstract, and to understand it well requires no ordinary ability. To all this I should add that although the Tibetans are quite amenable to listening with good will, they are not superficial or credulous; they want to see, weigh, and discuss everything in great detail, with logical reasoning; they want to be convinced and not to be instructed."[27]

Desideri concluded that preaching the Gospel alone would be insufficient to win converts in Tibet. The edifice of their doctrine had to be demolished. And he concluded that that edifice rested on two pillars: the doctrine of rebirth and the doctrine of emptiness, doctrines that he regarded as particularly pernicious because each prevented belief in the existence of God. His strategy was to compose a work, written in Tibetan, employing Tibetan Buddhist vocabulary in the Tibetan Buddhist scholastic genre, and citing Tibetan Buddhist texts in support of his arguments. His hope was that he could convince the scholars of Tibet, through argumentation, that the doctrines of rebirth and emptiness were false. And because of the great deference that the Tibetan laity showed to their scholars, if the scholars could be convinced, the people would follow. As he wrote in his missionary manual, "The religious, as scholars accustomed to logical discourse, will listen, understand the force of arguments, object, and discuss, and taken by reason will allow themselves to be convinced, and their surrender will easily bring about the surrender of the laity."[28]

It was our intention to translate in its entirety what Desideri considered to be his most important composition, the text that he continued to work on as he waited in vain for permission to remain in Tibet, the text whose title signals his identification of the two foundations of Tibetan Buddhism: *Inquiry concerning the Doctrines of Previous Lives and Emptiness, Offered to the Scholars of Tibet by the Star Head Lama called Ippolito (Mgo skar gyi bla ma i po li do zhes bya ba yis phul ba'i bod kyi mkhas pa rnams la skye ba snga ma dang stong pa nyid kyi lta ba'i sgo nas zhu ba)*. In the pages that follow, we shall refer to it simply as the *Inquiry*. Let us begin with what we know about its composition.

In a letter to the pope, dated February 13, 1717, some eleven months after he arrived in Lhasa, Desideri wrote, "Here I had composed two books, the first of which refutes the error that each can be saved in his own religion *(legge)*, showing that there is only one way to salvation and that all the other ways are eternal damnation. And in the second I refute the diabolical error of transmigration, and this in two sections: the first against the transmigration of the wicked, the second against the transmigration of the good."[29] The first work may or may not be *Dawn, Signaling the Rising of the Sun That Dispels the Darkness.* The second work may be something that Desideri wrote in Italian.[30] By 1718, however, he had begun work on his massive refutation of rebirth, written in Tibetan.

Tibetan Buddhist texts were traditionally written on long narrow leaves of paper, modeled on the palm-leaf manuscripts of Sanskrit texts that were brought from India and translated into Tibetan. Many Tibetan texts survive in manuscript form, but texts that achieved wide currency would be carved onto wooden blocks, in relief and backwards, to produce xylographs or woodblock prints. With each side of each page of a text requiring a separate block, a number of important monasteries had extensive warehouses for the storage of the blocks. The pages of a book, whether manuscripts or block prints, were not bound but instead were wrapped in cloth. The page number was written vertically on the left side of the front of each page. Two of Desideri's works, *Dawn, Signaling the Rising of the Sun That Dispels the Darkness (Tho rangs mun sel nyi ma shar ba'i brda)* and *Essence of the Christian Religion (Ke ri se sti yan gyi chos lugs kyi snying po)* are written on oblong pages in this style.

The *Inquiry* is different. Desideri obviously carried with him or otherwise had delivered to him from India a supply of "signatures," that is, large sheets of European paper that would be folded to produce pages. These units would eventually be sewn together and bound in a book. The signatures used by Desideri were folded so that each produced eight folios or sixteen pages.

Desideri used twenty-nine such signatures for the *Inquiry,* providing him with 232 folios or 464 pages. Following the Tibetan convention, the page number appears in Tibetan on the front (but not the back) of each folio, such that the last Tibetan page is 232. The pages are large (34.5 cm. long and 19 cm. wide) generally with thirty-five lines per page. They are written in a clear and careful capital *(dbu can)* script, either by a copyist or, more likely, by Desideri himself.[31]

It is difficult to say with certainty when Desideri wrote the book, but one can say when much of it was copied. Beginning with the first page, Desideri provides the date in the upper left-hand corner for each of the first nineteen signatures, meaning that a date appears every eight folios, beginning on folio 1 and ending on folio 145.[32] The number of days between each signature, or eight folios, varies considerably, from as few as eight days to as many as thirty-seven. There may be some significance in the fact that the first and last dates (June 24, 1718, and June 24, 1719) are one year apart. What is certainly significant, although what it signifies remains unclear, is that Desideri's dating of the signatures ends on June 24, 1719, but the text continues for another ten signatures or eighty folios without dates. The handwriting appears to be consistent throughout the text.

At the end of December 1717, Desideri left Sera for Dakpo, where the Capuchins had a small hospice, or lodging. It is there that he wrote, or at least began to write, the *Inquiry*. As he recounts in his *Historical Notices:*

> At Dakpo Khyer, where I had peace and quiet, I resumed my usual way of life, continuing my study of other books of this sect necessary to my work, and gradually completing the book refuting the errors of these people that I had earlier begun.
>
> This book of mine is divided into three volumes. In the first volume I refute the errors that make up the intricate labyrinth of belief in metempsychosis according to the system specific to this people. In the second volume I reject their other main error, that is, Tongbà-gnì, the treatises on which, as I've already indicated, are very long and very intricate. In these, their lawgiver, with the most subtle deceit, leads his followers to atheism, wherein the possibility of an uncreated, self-existing being who is the creator of the world is completely excluded, all under the attractive guise of elevating the spirit, eradicating the passions, purifying the soul, and inculcating detachment from oneself and all things, culminating in total passionlessness. In the third and shortest volume, I set out the very same teachings contained in our Christian doctrines and standard catechisms, in part using proofs and in part suggesting them indirectly with brief reasons, using a method and style appropriate to a Christian community that is not yet mature and well schooled in doctrine but is young and in the process of formation.
>
> The first and second books are entirely in a style of argumentation and disputation that follows the forms and methods of the Tibetans themselves. In both of these books the numerous arguments and reasons, though framed in ordinary language, are almost always taken from their own principles, beliefs, and authors, and from the books that they hold to be canonical and irrefutable. The third book is in the form of a dialogue, with some argumentation at those places where it is necessary. Many people asked me for copies of this last book before I left the mission.[33]

Desideri's description does not accord exactly with the works that remain. The first treatise to which he refers is likely the *Inquiry*. However, although both the title of the text and its topical outline (*sa bcad*, translated in Appendix 1) indicate that he will consider the doctrine of rebirth ("previous lives") and the doctrine of emptiness, the work ends long before the refutation of rebirth is complete. It never turns to the doctrine of emptiness. The second book to which he alludes could be *Origin of Sentient Beings, Phenomena, and So Forth (Sems can dang chos la sogs pa rnams kyi 'byung khung)*. Or it is possible that the second and third books are in fact one, the *Essence of the Christian Religion*, which is in two parts. The first is a relatively brief refutation of the doctrine of emptiness; whether this is the work to which Desideri refers remains unclear. The second half of the text is the third book to which he refers, which is indeed a catechism in the form of a dialogue. It is only the second half of this text that seems to merit the title *Essence of the Christian Religion*.

Desideri provides another description of his Tibetan works in chapter 19 of book 4 of the *Historical Notices,* where he writes:

> For the welfare and furtherance on the mission established by me in the kingdoms of Tibet, I wrote in that language and still have with me in Rome (1) a small book on the unity of the true Law of salvation in which the belief that everyone can find salvation in his own law is shown to be false; (2) a lengthy volume in refutation of the belief in, and complicated system of, metempsychosis; (3) another volume directed at the views of the Tibetans demonstrating the existence of a being in itself and of a first cause of everything, employing natural reason and arguments based upon their very own principles; (4) and finally, a new catechism adapted to the understanding of those who are hearing about the Christian religion for the first time.[34]

Here, the first work may or may not be *Dawn, Signaling the Rising of the Sun That Dispels the Darkness,* the second is the *Inquiry*, the third is likely *Origin of Sentient Beings, Phenomena, and So Forth,* and the fourth is clearly *Essence of the Christian Religion.* It is noteworthy that in neither description does Desideri mention his fifth Tibetan work, the unfinished *Definite Goodness (Nges legs).* The term "definite goodness" has a technical meaning in Tibetan Buddhism, signifying liberation from rebirth. Desideri renders it, plausibly, as *summum bonum,* devoting the text to arguments for the existence of God, that the doctrine of God does not contradict the doctrine of emptiness, and that the *summum bonum* is not to be found in Buddhism.[35]

Desideri notes that many people asked him for copies of the catechism. However, no copies survive, raising once again the question of Desideri's influence in Tibet and on Tibetan Buddhism, despite his own report that the impact of his books was significant. By the fall of 1719, the political situation in Lhasa was sufficiently stable that he felt he could safely return to Lhasa. In September 1719, some two months after the last recorded date in the *Inquiry* (June 24), Desideri traveled to the capital and remained there until February 1720. Describing his reception, he writes:

> I had just returned to Lhasa from Dakpo Khyer when the Tibetan doctor of religion who had been my language teacher—and with whom I had corresponded from time to time, informing him of what subjects I was writing about—very eagerly requested copies of them from me. After having carefully read and considered them, he praised them profusely and expressed much astonishment, declaring that he himself was not capable of writing a work equal to it, much less of responding to my strong logical arguments. These works had gained such widespread notice that soon there was a constant stream of people coming to my house, especially doctors of religion and professors from both the monasteries and the universities, especially from the two largest ones, Sera and Drepung (Breê-bung), asking to see and read these books. Their universal opinion and judgment was that they needed to choose some of their most distinguished and erudite lamas to examine my work and determine the specific passages that they could not refute, and to put into writing and present me with those other passages for which they could find counterarguments so that I could resolve these and clearly elucidate the truth.[36]

Again, given the lack of any confirmation of his success, either in the form of Tibetan accounts or in the form of additional surviving copies of the text, one is left to wonder how best to evaluate Desideri's claim.

In his *Historical Notices*, Desideri reports that he was working on the text up to the time that he left Tibet. Writing of his activities in Nyalam (a town near the border with Nepal, which Desideri calls by its Nepalese name Kuti) in late September 1721, he writes, "At that time I was also occupied in adding some chapters to my book refuting the errors of metempsychosis and reading some of the principal Tibetan books most relevant to that task."[37] He would leave Tibet on December 14.

By all indications, Desideri considered the *Inquiry* to be his most important Tibetan composition. Near the end of his *Historical Notices,* Desideri calls on future missionaries to "use every care to procure from every region the principal books of each false religion and the books refuting them written and disseminated up to the present day by zealous and virtuous workers."[38] Among Desideri's Latin writings, we find what appears to be the beginnings of his translation of the *Inquiry* into Latin. It is a work entitled *Explanation of the Book Written in the Tibetan Language in Refutation of the Pythagorean Doctrine of the Transmigration of Souls according to the Tibetans' System* (see Appendix 3).[39]

With this overview of Desideri's Tibetan works, let us turn to the studies that led to their composition.

DESIDERI'S BUDDHIST EDUCATION

It is clear from his *Historical Notices* that Desideri had an extensive knowledge of Tibetan Buddhist belief and practice, including such things as the Tibetans' reverence for the Dalai Lama as a human manifestation of Chenresik (Avalokiteśvara, the bodhisattva of compassion). A good deal of such knowledge could have been gained through observation and conversation. However, we see in his Tibetan writings (as well as in the *Historical Notices*) that Desideri also had an extensive and sophisticated understanding of Tibetan Buddhist philosophy and doctrine, something that could be gained only through sustained textual study by someone who had mastered a large and complex technical vocabulary. What is not clear, from either the *Historical Notices* or his Tibetan works, is how Desideri gained such understanding. We know from the report of the Capuchin missionary Francesco Orazio della Penna that early on Lhazang Khan assigned one Yonten Pelsang (Yon tan dpal bzang) to teach the two priests, and we know from Desideri's own report that he studied at Sera monastery, moving there in August 1717. Apart from this we have no information, either from Desideri or from contemporary Tibetan sources, about his studies. Some insight, however, is provided by the notes that Desideri kept of his studies.[40] These notes allow us to trace the development of his understanding of specific

Buddhist doctrines, doctrines that he decided that he must both master and refute in his mission to evangelize Tibet.

The first set of notes (preserved in Goa 74), dated July 1, 1717, while Desideri was still at Shidé, shows that Desideri began his studies where a young monk begins his study of Buddhist logic, in a genre of works known as "Collected Topics" *(bsdus grva)*. Here the student learns such things as the principle of contradiction, the principle of identity, and the law of the excluded middle. Desideri's notes begin with the topic of color and proceeds to *gzhi grub* ("established bases"), which introduces many of the standard categories of Buddhist epistemology, and then to the topic of the relation between the definition and the definiendum. The notes, written in the *umé* *(dbu med)* script (probably not by Desideri), appear to be drawn from oral instruction rather than from a particular text. The forms and conventions of Tibetan debate that Desideri learned would be put to use in the *Inquiry* as he built his arguments against the Buddhist concept of rebirth.

On September 14, 1717, after having moved to Sera, Desideri began taking notes on the text that, more than any other, would shape his understanding of Tibetan Buddhism, as well as his condemnation of it: Tsong kha pa's *Great Treatise on the Stages of the Path to Enlightenment (Byang chub lam rim chen mo)*, a work that encompasses the entire Buddhist path, from taking refuge in the three jewels to the realization of emptiness.

Desideri seems to have carefully studied the topical outline *(sa bcad)* of Tsong kha pa's large text, copying out its major headings and then adding the corresponding page numbers to make a table of contents, something that Tibetan texts traditionally lack. This is interspersed with notes in Italian, which indicate the topics that most interested him. For example, he writes extensive notes on the distinction between the provisional *(neyārtha)* and definitive *(nītārtha)*, important hermeneutical categories.

Among the many chapters in Tsong kha pa's text, Desideri dwelled at length on the chapters on karma and rebirth, which set forth how positive actions result in happiness and negative actions result in suffering, leading to rebirth in the good realms of gods and humans and the evil realms of animals, ghosts, and hell beings. It is this doctrine that Desideri seeks to refute in the *Inquiry*. Tsong kha pa cites many Indian texts, and Desideri lifts many of the quotations in the *Inquiry* directly from *The Great Treatise*. However, in some cases he went on to find the original text in the Tibetan canon (not an easy task, even for a trained Tibetan scholar), scan the pages to find the original passage, and then copy out longer quotations from the text, quotations that Tsong kha pa did not use. On the topic of karma, he also located a sūtra that Tsong kha pa does not mention, the *Differentiations of Actions (Karmavibhaṅga, Las rnam par 'byed pa)*. Many of the passages found in Desideri's notes in Goa 74 would later appear in the *Inquiry*.

Desideri also took extensive notes on the section in *The Great Treatise* that deals with the realms of animals, ghosts, the hells, and the specific misdeeds that lead to rebirth there. Again, he went to the canon, found Tsong kha pa's quotes and copied out long passages, which he used in the *Inquiry*. Among the texts he copied were the *Sūtra on Limitless Lives (Tshe mtha' yas pa'i mdo)* and the *Sūtra Setting Forth the Causes and Effects of Good and Evil (Legs nyes kyi rgyu dang 'bras bu bstan pa'i mdo)*. He seems to have been particularly struck by the story in the *Sūtra on Repaying Kindness (Drin lan gsab pa'i mdo)* in which the future Buddha, during a lifetime in hell, shows compassion for a fellow denizen of the infernal realms. Desideri copied the entire story from the fourth chapter of the sūtra, citing it in both the *Inquiry* and the *Historical Notices*.[41]

In order to understand the workings of the law of karma, one must understand how afflictions *(kleśa)* motivate negative deeds. Desideri thus took detailed notes from Tsong kha pa's presentation of the nature of these afflictions, their causes, their functions, as well as their antidotes.

Desideri's notes, however, do not focus entirely on the topics of karma and rebirth. Goa 74 also contains the names of various Indian units for the measurement of time and distance as well as units of matter. In the *Inquiry*, he would use these to demonstrate what he saw as the philosophical incoherence of the notion that time has no beginning.[42]

Not all of the notes that he took, however, found their way into the *Inquiry*. He took lengthy notes (some six and a half pages) from the relatively obscure *Sūtra on the Flowering of the Bhagavan's Wisdom ('Phags pa bcom ldan 'das kyi ye shes rgyas pa'i mdo)*. There are also large sections of the well-known *Perfection of Wisdom in Eight Thousand Stanzas*, copied in cursive writing by a skilled hand, likely not Desideri's. Neither of these sources would play an important role in his arguments.[43]

That Desideri moved from a young monk's textbook on logic to taking detailed notes from Tsong kha pa's *Great Treatise* in just two months' time suggests that he had a Tibetan scholar as a tutor, at least initially, to help him navigate the vast world of Tibetan Buddhist thought. Then, with that compass in hand, he would set out on this own. Still, throughout the *Inquiry,* Desideri's reliance on Tsong kha pa, whose system he sought to refute, was pervasive, going so far as to present as his own Tsong kha pa's advice on which texts to study. Quoting Tsong kha pa verbatim, he instructs his reader, "Hence, using what has been explained as illustrations, you should look at *Mindfulness of the Excellent Teaching,* the *Sūtra of the Wise and the Foolish,* the *Hundred Actions Sūtra,* the *Hundred Bodhisattva Stories,* the prefaces in the discipline, and other scriptures as well to develop an intense and enduring certainty. Take this to be a goal of crucial importance."[44]

We find, then, that Desideri did not simply translate Christian prayers into Tibetan or declare the truth of Church doctrine. Instead, he learned the theological grammar and adopted the religious sensibility of Tibetan Buddhist clerics, using their own vocabulary, their own doctrines, and their own philosophical conventions, and even their own scriptures to defeat them, at least from his perspective. Had a Tibetan Antonio ever read Desideri, he might have remarked, "The devil can cite Scripture for his purpose."

DESIDERI'S TIBETAN STYLE

By any standard, Desideri's *Inquiry* is a remarkable work of Tibetan letters, made all the more remarkable because it was not written by a Tibetan. In its extensive vocabulary, its knowledge and adaptation of the conventions of classical Tibetan, in its command, and creative use, of a broad range of Buddhist works, it remains unsurpassed among works by Europeans writing in Tibetan; works from the Capuchin mission, which may have been comparable to Desideri's, do not survive.[45] Other foreigners, including Mongolians and Chinese, composed important works in Tibetan, but only after many years of study in the monastic colleges of Tibet. The fact that the number of works by Europeans is admittedly small does not diminish the importance of Desideri's achievement. Indeed, it enhances it, for it testifies to how difficult it is for a foreigner to even undertake such a task. In the commentary on the *Inquiry,* we note Desideri's skill in composing Tibetan verse, how the opening stanzas follow the literary conventions of the salutation verses, the statement of the intention and purpose of the text, and the exhortation to the reader to heed the author's words.

Desideri's prose has a conversational tone, reminiscent of a genre known as *zin bris* (often translated as "notes"), texts compiled from notes taken at an oral teaching by a lama. A similar conversational tone, but in a specifically dialogical style, is found in a genre of debate texts called *mtha' dpyod* (literally "analysis of the limits"), a literary style that Desideri encountered in his studies and that he uses extensively in his own writings. This is one of the most technical of the many styles of Tibetan Buddhist prose, with long and complex sentences. Desideri's ability to write in this style may have been aided by the fact that he had learned a similar style that was employed by the Italian scholars of Baroque period. Indeed, we find this style in Desideri's Italian-language drafts of his Tibetan works.[46] We have sought to reproduce this style in our translation, maintaining the multiple clauses and the lengthy sentences.

Desideri also mastered the abbreviations used in Tibetan texts to save space—something that was not particularly common in mainstream Tibetan texts—abbreviations such as *semn* for *sems can* ("sentient being") and *thamd* for *thams cad* ("all").

Despite Desideri's literary achievement, however, no Tibetan reader of the *Inquiry* would regard it as a work of high literary quality. It is evident from the opening verses that the author is unschooled in Tibetan *belle lettres,* which requires, at least for authors after the thirteenth century, a mastery of metaphor, derived particularly from the influential Sanskrit text *Mirror of Poetics (Kāvyādarśa).*[47] Furthermore, there are enough oddities in the *Inquiry* to immediately identify the author as a foreigner.[48]

Desideri's idiosyncratic Tibetan seems to suggest that he composed the text himself, without the assistance of a Tibetan scholar. There remains the question of whether the manuscripts themselves were written in Desideri's own hand or whether he employed a scribe. Both of the texts translated here are written in *uchen* (capital), a script normally used for woodblock printing; the cursive *umé* is more common for letter writing and less formal documents. There is no question that his *Essence of the Christian Religion* was written by a professional scribe and in a format suited for traditional woodblock printing, although the text seems never to have been printed. The *Inquiry* is more ambiguous, but a strong argument could be made that Desideri wrote it in Tibetan himself. The entire text of more than four hundred pages is written in a single hand over a period of almost three years; although Desideri's account books occasionally mention payments to a scribe, it seems unlikely that a single scribe would have remained with him for such an extended period of time. Furthermore, the handwriting is almost identical to that found in Desideri's extensive notes on Tsong kha pa's *Great Treatise* during his careful study of the work in 1717. The fact that the text is written in capital *uchen* script is a further indication that it is the work of a foreigner; Tibetan authors generally composed their works in the cursive script and later had the manuscript transferred into the capital script for woodblock printing by a professional scribe. Learning to read and write Tibetan characters in capital *uchen* is easier than mastering the cursive script, as any student of Tibetan can attest. If Desideri had used a scribe, one would expect to see corrections and annotations in a different hand; however, the corrections that occur, as well as the occasional marginalia, appear to be by the same hand. Despite these indications, without further evidence the question of whether Desideri wrote the Tibetan script of his *Inquiry* must remain unresolved.

TRANSLATING DESIDERI'S *INQUIRY*

Our original intention was to translate the *Inquiry* in its entirety. However, when we began translating, it became clear that this would be impossible to accomplish in a single volume. The precise length of such a translation is difficult to calculate accurately because of fluctuations in the size of the handwriting over the 464 large pages. However, a fair estimate would be 400,000 words in English, without notes or commentary, in a work that requires many notes and much commentary. To provide a full translation of the *Inquiry* with notes and commentary would require at least five large volumes.

With a full translation infeasible in the short term, a number of options remained. The first was to translate none of the text and instead provide our own summary. This had the advantage of presenting the entire work, at least in terms of its arguments, but had the disadvantage of sacrificing an accurate presentation of Desideri's mastery of Tibetan Buddhist scholastic philosophy (and of its formidable vocabulary). It would also prevent us from presenting Desideri's intricate, and often tortuous, arguments, as well as his strategic use of passages from Buddhist scriptures to make his Christian points. We therefore decided against a summary, but offer two appendices that fulfill this purpose in their own way. The first is a translation of the topical outline *(sa bcad)* of the entire text, the traditional Tibetan listing of headings and subheadings ("with regard to the first, there are four"). This table of contents is found in Appendix 1.

In addition, Desideri provided his own organizational markers not typically found in Tibetan Buddhist texts. In the left-hand margin he places a single *yig mgo* (a double *yig mgo* is traditionally used to mark the start of a new section in a text) with a number under it. These tend to correspond to a line in the text that has a sentence beginning with "furthermore" *(gzhan yang)*. Desideri numbers these up to 76, ending on folio 158b (page 316) and thus far from where the text ends. However, because Desideri marked these points in the text, presumably to indicate a change in subject, we have translated each of these sentences (and often a number of following sentences) in order to provide a somewhat more informative sense of the text as a whole than that found in the traditionally spare topical outline. These are found in Appendix 2.

Having concluded that some portions of the text should be translated, the question remained of how many portions and of what length, given the length constraints for this volume. A fuller sense of the text could obviously be provided by offering many short passages, selected from throughout the text. However, experiments in this direction yielded snippets that were hard to follow and that failed to provide a clear sense of the structure of Desideri's arguments. It was also difficult to decide which passages to select from his massive unfinished text.

We decided in the end to provide two large selections, of roughly equal length, one from the very beginning of the text and one from deep into the text. This strategy allowed us to present some of Desideri's arguments in full, in the length he intended and the length they deserve, while also leaving enough space in the book for us to comment on each of the passages, explaining his arguments as well as the Buddhist doctrine he assumes that his learned Tibetan reader commands.

The first passage is the opening pages, where Desideri seeks to convince the Tibetan Buddhist reader that the long text, one written by a non-Buddhist that seeks to refute Buddhism, is worth reading. Desideri clearly crafted this section with great care, paying close attention to both the form and the content. It contains some of his best poetry, as he seeks to follow the conventions of a Tibetan Buddhist text. The argument he provides begins with something of a defense of interreligious dialogue *avant la lettre,* yet a dialogue whose purpose is conversion. Unlike the proponents of comparative religion in the nineteenth and twentieth centuries, he had no interest in illuminating the category of religion. Unlike the proponents of interfaith dialogue of the twentieth century, he had no interest in promoting sectarian harmony. Desideri understands, rather, that in order for him to convince the Tibetans of the glories of Christianity and the errors of Buddhism, he must first convince them of the need to study another religion, even a religion that they consider inferior to their own. As he proceeds through this section, the terms that he uses to describe Tibetan Buddhism become increasingly harsh.

As we discuss in the commentary to the text, one of Desideri's strongest objections to the Buddhist doctrine of rebirth is the claim that it has no beginning. This is clearly something that Desideri must refute, for if rebirth has no beginning, there is no first cause, and therefore no need for God. After the introduction to the text, Desideri embarks on a lengthy attack on the notion that rebirth has no beginning. This section was far too long to include and is quite difficult to follow without extensive explanation of how Desideri uses the conventions of Tibetan scholastic debate (including wordplay). We chose a section from later in the text, the point at which Desideri's hypothetical opponent challenges Desideri to explain why, if there is no rebirth, incarnate lamas can remember their past lives and even correctly identify items that belonged to their predecessors. Desideri provides a detailed, and fascinating, refutation of this claim.

To gain some sense of the mass of Desideri's *Inquiry,* the reader will note that the two substantial sections provided here translate slightly more than eight percent of Desideri's Tibetan text.

THE *ESSENCE OF THE CHRISTIAN RELIGION*

The *Inquiry* is an unfinished work. Indeed, judging from the topical outline Desideri provides, it was far from finished, even at 464 pages. Desideri does not complete the refutation of rebirth nor does he even begin to consider his second target, the doctrine of emptiness. His refutation is found instead, and at first sight rather improbably, in his *Essence of the Christian Religion.* This work, of unknown date, is a manuscript of fifty folios, written in traditional xylograph form on pages 26 cm. long and 17.5 cm. wide (the pages are

rather short and squat by Tibetan standards), in a clear capital script by a
skilled hand (likely a scribe) with ten lines proportionally spaced on each
page, except for the first page, where there is a larger script, as is sometimes
the case in Tibetan works. The first twenty-two of the folios are devoted to
a refutation of emptiness. In order to provide some sense of how Desideri
would go about refuting this most famous of Mahāyāna doctrines, we
decided to translate this portion of the text. The remainder of the text is the
catechism to which Desideri alludes, with an ostensibly jarring shift in tone,
away from the high philosophical discourse of the refutation of emptiness
to a more pastoral tone in the catechism, where a "seeker of the essence of
wisdom" asks a series of questions that are patiently answered by a *"paṇḍita,"*
a scholar. The seeker of wisdom begins by conceding that he has now seen
(presumably through the refutation of emptiness) that his own religion is
false and thus he asks for instruction in the true faith. The contents of the
catechism are of course familiar to anyone with a basic knowledge of Roman
Catholic doctrine. The interest in the text lies elsewhere: Desideri's creative
use of Buddhist vocabulary to convey Christian doctrine. *Essence of the
Christian Religion* is translated here in its entirety.[49]

℘ ℘ ℘

Desideri's fascinating description of his time in Tibet and of the Tibetan
religion, and his masterful command of the intricacies of Tibetan Buddhist
doctrine, its vocabulary, and its literary conventions have rightfully won him
the admiration of many, with some seeing him as the forefather of the field
of Tibetan Studies. Whether such an assessment is deemed accurate or not,
at least two facts must be remembered. The first is that Desideri was a missionary. As he brings his lengthy *Historical Notices* to a rousing close, he
writes: "There, all crowded together, are Guinea and Ethiopia, Monomo-
tapa [Mutapa in Africa], Socotra [part of modern Yemen], Brazil, Marag-
none [Maranhão in modern Brazil], Malabar, Mogul, China, Japan, and a
hundred other distressed kingdoms and empires in Africa, Asia, America, who
are unceasingly showing to God errors refuted, superstitions abolished,
millions of hellish demons smashed, unholy temples beyond number demolished, kings baptized, peoples converted, churches built, and Christian
communities established, and everywhere among nations without number,
splendid victory monuments and triumphal arches erected to the Catholic

faith, due to the labors, hardships, fervor, blood, and lives of so many zealous missionaries."[50] Despite the obvious affection he felt for Tibetans and the admiration he felt for Tibetan scholars, there can be no doubt from reading what he wrote for his fellow Jesuits or from reading what he wrote for Tibetans that he considered Tibetan Buddhism to be a false religion that doomed the Tibetan people to perdition.

The second point to recall is that, by almost any measure, Desideri was a failure. His converts were few, his presence in Tibet seemed to warrant no mention whatsoever in Tibetan writings, where much is written, and he returned to Italy to find not the acclaim that he felt he deserved but a certain ignominy. Although he seems to have enjoyed good relations with his Capuchin compatriots in Tibet, upon his return to Rome he brought a lawsuit against them. This led to charges and countercharges, including impugning each other's language skills, at the end of which the Propaganda Fide simply reaffirmed the Capuchins' rights to Tibet.[51]

Indeed, we are left to wonder whether his failure is one reason for his fame. We know that members of the Capuchin mission also wrote works refuting points of Buddhist doctrine and also wrote catechisms in Tibetan. But because they remained behind in Tibet, with some dying there, their works have been lost; they were not carried out of Tibet for posterity, as Desideri did with his own works. If Desideri had stayed in Tibet, as he wished, the Tibetan works that we have today might not have survived. But he was forced to leave Tibet, taking his Tibetan works with him, leaving them unread by the Tibetans for whom they are intended, but read by twentieth and twenty-first century scholars, bringing him great fame.

The spiritual politics of the time must be understood in order to understand Desideri and his works, in Italian and in Tibetan. But if we set those aside for the moment, we are left with a remarkable achievement. In the upper left-hand corner of the first page of the *Inquiry,* he wrote the date June 24, 1718. He had first encountered the Tibetan language when he arrived in Leh, the capital of Ladakh on June 25, 1715, just three years before. This would be akin to a Tibetan monk making his way from Lhasa to Rome without knowing Italian or Latin, and three years after his arrival writing a 400-page refutation of Aquinas's *Summa Theologica,* in Latin. It borders on the miraculous, as if Desideri were speaking in tongues.

CHAPTER ONE

Introduction to *Inquiry concerning the Doctrines of Previous Lives and Emptiness*

ɕ੭

The opening pages of the *Inquiry* represent a fascinating and important text in their own right. Desideri seeks to capture the attention of Tibetan readers, trying to convince them of the importance of reading a text that (to his mind) successfully refutes two of the most important and deeply held doctrines of their Buddhism: rebirth and emptiness. Thus, before he begins his refutation of rebirth, Desideri provides what we will call the preamble. He offers his own poetry, in a range of styles on a range of subjects, while making a sustained argument for what today would be called "comparative religion." We will consider each of the sections of the preamble in turn. We begin with the title of the text.

Lacking a separate title page, these words are written across the top of the first page: *Inquiry concerning the Doctrines of Previous Lives and of Emptiness, Offered to the Scholars of Tibet by the Star Head Lama called Ippolito (Mgo skar gyi bla ma i po li to zhes bya ba yis phul ba'i bod kyi mkhas pa rnams la skye ba snga ma dang stong pa nyid kyi lta ba'i sgo nas zhu ba).* Several words in the title deserve comment, beginning with the first word in English and the last word in Tibetan. The word is *zhu ba*. Its most common meaning is "question" in the honorific form, not in the sense of seeking information but in the sense of requesting something from a superior, such that "entreaty" and "petition" are suitable translations. Desideri is politely asking the scholars of Tibet to listen to his arguments against rebirth and emptiness, using the word "offered" (*phul,* the honorific form of the verb "to give"). Because most of the text consists of those arguments, we have chosen the word "inquiry." He refers to these two doctrines by their standard terms in Tibetan, literally "former births" *(skye ba snga ma)* and emptiness *(stong pa nyid),* calling them "doctrines" *(lta ba,* literally "views" in the sense of philosophical views). He phoneticizes his given name, Ippolito, into Tibetan. And while he addresses his text to the "scholars" *(mkhas pa)* of Tibet, he refers to himself not as a scholar but as a lama, perhaps seeking to signal both his clerical identity and his prestige.

The adjective that he uses for himself requires some discussion; he refers to himself literally as "star head" *(mgo skar).* One of the terms that was used in Tibet to describe Turkic Muslims and, later, Russians and Armenians was "white head" *(mgo dkar),* derived from the Chinese term for Uighurs, who wore white turbans. In the title Desideri uses a homonym, such that the term means "star head" instead of "white head." This does not appear to be a spelling error or a mistake by a copyist; later in the text he refers several times to "the religion of the star heads," clearly referring to Christianity.[1] As the nineteenth-century American hymn says, "As I went down in the river to pray, studying about that good old way, and who shall wear the starry crown, good Lord, show me the way."

THE OPENING POEM

Desideri's *Inquiry* begins with a series of poems, distinguished by both their subject matter and their style; in classical Tibetan poetry, the lines of a single poem have the same number of syllables but different poems have different numbers of syllables; one's skill as a poet is measured in part by the ability to write good poetry in poems of varying line length, with the stress falling on the same syllable in each line of the stanza.[2]

A Tibetan Buddhist text typically begins with what is literally called an "expression of worship" *(mchod brjod),* a kind of homage or invocation. It can be something simple, but often is quite elaborate, composed in verse, and is considered the place in the text where the author displays his skills as a poet. The being to whom homage is paid may be a buddha, a bodhisattva, a deity, or a human teacher. That person may be single or multiple; it is common, for example, for the homage to be paid to a lineage of teachers, beginning with the distant past and ending with the author's own teacher.

The object of Desideri's homage, written in verses of nine syllables, remains unnamed, something that is not unusual. A Tibetan reader of the homage would likely suspect that it is directed to the Buddha himself. Addressed in the second person, as is common for the genre, he is described with a range of standard Buddhist phrases, such as "the sole lord worthy as refuge" and "the sun whose light pervades all," and his compassionate deeds on behalf of suffering sentient beings are extolled. The hymn, however, is not directed to the Buddha. It is directed to Jesus Christ.

There are hints of this early on. "Not relying or depending on another yourself, / All that exists depends on you." This seems to contradict the famous Buddhist doctrine of dependent origination *(pratītyasamutpāda)*, according to which even the Buddha depends on causes and conditions. But the Buddhist reader would likely not pause over this passage, assuming that it means that the Buddha did not rely on a teacher in his last lifetime, finding the path to nirvāṇa through his own efforts. The next stanza says, "Gently but firmly you created all that is." Again, this would likely be read as a reference to the doctrine that when a buddha is enlightened, he creates his own world, his own "buddha field" *(buddhakṣetra),* as the arena for his teachings.

Even passages that seem clearly Christian when the object of the homage is known might pass unnoticed under the Buddhist eye. For example:

> You did not see unbearable suffering as a burden;
> You saw it as a crown.
> Accepting these with love and asking to undergo them,
> Venturing your body and life you gave away your flesh, blood, body,
>   and life.

In the *jātaka* stories, the stories about the Buddha's former lifetimes (of which there are more than five hundred in the Pāli collection), there are numerous accounts in which the bodhisattva gives up his life, whether he is an animal or a human, for the welfare of others. Among the various collections of these stories, the *Garland of Birth Stories (Jātakamālā)* by Āryaśūra, thirty-four stories in verse, was particularly popular in Tibet; Tsong kha pa established the tradition of teaching this text during the great Prayer Festival *(Smon lam chen mo)* in Lhasa each year.[3] In one story, the bodhisattva encounters a starving tigress, so hungry that she is about to devour her own cubs. He commits suicide by jumping off a cliff, his body providing food for the tigress. In another, as a king, he allows five vampires to drink his blood (the five are later reborn as his first five disciples). In still another, he cuts flesh from his own body to feed a hawk that is pursuing a dove. The hawk requires more and more flesh, and the bodhisattva is left with just his skeleton.

Even a passage that makes a direct reference to Christian doctrine might pass unnoticed. In the early church there were important debates about the relationship between God the Father and Christ the Son, including whether they were of different substances, similar substances, or identical substances. The First Council of Nicaea in 325 declared that they were of identical substance, or *homoousios* in Greek, that God and Jesus are consubstantial and co-eternal. This council and the Council of Chalcedon declared that Jesus had two natures, one divine and one human, and that these were not two parts of his person but were each completely present in a state of *hypostasis,* making him fully God and fully human. Any learned Christian of the early eighteenth century (who could read Tibetan) would have seen allusions to these doctrines in this stanza of Desideri's poem:

> To compassionately search out and lead
> Those who enter evil paths without dread or fear,
> Wandering toward the abyss and toward danger,
> You lovingly appeared in this world
> As a single being who, without abandoning your indestructible nature,
> Came to be united with a human nature.

A Buddhist reader would likely see here an allusion to the two bodies of the Buddha: the *dharmakāya* or "truth body," regarded in the Mahāyāna as a kind of eternal principle of enlightenment, and the *rūpakāya* or "form body," the physical body of the Buddha that appears in the world for the benefit of sentient beings.

In this long poem that opens the *Inquiry,* there are perhaps only two stanzas that would give a Tibetan reader pause. This is the first:

"The savior, the glorious leader is pierced on the right."
My mind is fully focused on this fact,
With stainless and unshakable sincerity.
Because his extinction is not known
I offer praise, eulogy, and worship.

In this stanza, Desideri coins the term *sgrol mdzad,* literally, "one who performs liberation," almost certainly his term for "savior," but one that would not look out of place to a Tibetan. The next phrase, "glorious leader," would be familiar; the Buddha is often referred to as the one who leads beings out of *saṃsāra.* It is "pierced on the right" that would seem odd. Desideri is clearly referring to the spear wound on Jesus's right side, received during the crucifixion. Tibetan readers would of course miss this allusion, causing one to wonder why, among the many attributes of Jesus, Desideri would choose this one. The answer may lie in the sound of the Tibetan words as much as in their meaning. "Pierced on the right" is *g.yas bzug* in Tibetan, pronounced *ye-suk.* Thus, another reading of the line, which again a Tibetan reader would miss, would be "The savior, the glorious leader, is called Jesus."

Continuing to the fourth line, by saying of Jesus, "his extinction is not known," Desideri is contrasting Jesus and the Buddha, but again the comparison would likely be lost on Tibetan readers. A buddha is said to have two types of knowledge: the knowledge of extinction (*kṣayajñāna* in Sanskrit, *zad shes* in Tibetan) and the knowledge of non-arising (*anutpādajñāna* in Sanskrit, *mi skyes shes* in Tibetan). These are technical terms referring to the fact that the buddha (or an *arhat*) knows (1) that the destructive emotions *(kleśa)* that cause suffering have been completely destroyed, extinguished, and hence are extinct, and (2) the knowledge that, having been destroyed, they will never arise again. Hence, the Buddha knows extinction in this technical sense, and he also knows extinction because he passes into nirvāṇa, which is often described as the extinction of suffering and rebirth. Desideri is proclaiming the superiority of Jesus to the Buddha, because, being eternal, he will never know extinction. Again, Buddhist readers would not be puzzled, imagining that it is an allusion to the limitless life span of the Buddha, proclaimed in such works as the *Lotus Sūtra.*

The other dissonant passage in the poem, and the one most likely to give a Buddhist reader pause, is this:

In order to free us from defilement,
Each day you transform your blood
Endowed with the power to cleanse and completely dispel
All impurity from every mind.

For the Christian reader this is obviously a reference to the miracle of transubstantiation that occurs each day with the celebration of the Eucharist, where bread and wine are transformed into the body and blood of Christ. Yet even here the Tibetan Buddhist reader might not be deterred, knowing that in the vast tantric pantheon, there are all manner of wrathful deities drinking blood from skullcups.

Desideri ends his long hymn to Jesus with words that are thoroughly Buddhist, evoking the most fundamental of Buddhist practices:

My mind is not satisfied by description.
I go for refuge to him from the depths of my heart,
With my body, speech, and lucid mind.
I humbly bow down to him.

In this beautifully composed poem, then, Desideri speaks in code. It is a testament at once to his knowledge of Buddhist imagery, his skills as a poet, and his powers of dissimulation that he was able to create such an eloquent *double entendre,* a poem that could be read as Buddhist by a Buddhist and as Christian by a Christian without either suspecting the other meaning. At the same time it is a testament to the scope and malleability of the Buddhist and Christian vocabularies, allowing each to unwittingly accommodate the other.

THE SECOND POEM

In the second poem, the form, the tone, and content change markedly. Desideri speaks directly to the imagined readers of the *Inquiry:* the scholars of Tibet. It is a short poem of shorter lines (seven syllables each). The tone is one of fawning hyperbole, a familiar mood in Tibetan verse. He begins by stating that the fame of Tibetan scholars has spread around the world and that when he learned of their existence he was overcome by an irresistible urge to meet them and thus endured "the hundred thousand hardships" to cross the ocean and travel through many lands to reach Tibet. Upon his arrival, his wish to meet the Tibetan scholars only grew stronger, but he was impeded, this time not by distance, but by language. He could not speak Tibetan and so his wish could not be fulfilled. Now apparently that obstacle has been overcome, yet the number of learned scholars in Tibet is so great that it is impossible for him to meet them all, to pay his respects and ask his questions. This book, the *Inquiry,* therefore, is meant to serve that purpose. Among the conventions of Tibetan composition, this part of the poem would be the "promise to compose" *(rtsom par dam bca' ba),* a statement, in verse, of the author's intention to compose the work that follows. It is intended to help bring about the work's completion, although it did not do so in this case. Nowhere in this poem does Desideri state the true purpose of his journey to Tibet and of the text he will compose: the conversion of the Tibetan people to Christianity.

THE THIRD POEM

The third poem, continuing in the seven-syllable form, seems directed, not to an ethereal figure (whether Jesus or the Buddha) or to the generic "scholars of Tibet," but to a specific Tibetan, apparently a person of power living at the time of Desideri's mission. The question is: who?

The poem begins with *e ma ho,* an expression of wonder and delight, and then with these words, continuing in this vein for many stanzas:

> You are the ridgepole of Tibet most firm,
> You are the lamp of Tibet blazing bright,
> You have become the jewel of Tibet,
> I bow my head at your feet.
> Pray care for me with compassion.

One might imagine that it is directed to Lhazang Khan, the Khoshut Mongol who ruled Tibet at the time of Desideri's arrival, to whom Desideri had presented his first Tibetan composition, and whom Desideri regarded as his patron. But Lhazang Khan had been killed by the Dzungar Mongols when they sacked Lhasa in December 1717. It was this invasion that caused

Desideri to flee to the Capuchin hospice in Dakpo, where he began to compose the *Inquiry*. The language Desideri uses is reminiscent of the metaphors, images, and epithets that Tibetans traditionally use when describing the Dalai Lama, and it is possible that Desideri in fact had the Dalai Lama in mind.

In 1706, with the apparent support of the Qing emperor, Lhazang Khan deposed the Sixth Dalai Lama, who is remembered especially for his love poetry, and sent him under armed guard to China. He died or was murdered en route, although there is a legend that he survived and lived out his life incognito.[4] Lhazang Khan declared another monk to be the true Sixth Dalai Lama, a claim rejected by the Tibetans. Shortly thereafter, a child in eastern Tibet was identified as the Seventh Dalai Lama, an identification that the Qing emperor himself acknowledged in 1715. Thus, with the assassination of the Lhazang Khan and the deposing of his Sixth Dalai Lama, the stage was set for the triumphal entrance of the Seventh Dalai Lama into Lhasa. This would not occur until the autumn of 1720. Yet it is likely that Desideri would have known of his existence in 1718 and would have been eager to make his presence known to the new king and to present him with his *Inquiry*. As he writes:

In order to make this entreaty
Of utmost importance in your presence,
I have come from a great distance.
Looking upon me with eyes of kindness,
You have held me with love and compassion
As if they were your two hands.

So mustering my courage in your presence
I offer you various arguments,
Specifically in the form of inference,
On two topics: former lives
And the emptiness of intrinsic existence.

Yet Desideri had not been held by the Seventh Dalai Lama with love and compassion, as he had been—at least in his own telling—by Lhazang Khan. This raises the possibility that Desideri had composed the opening poem prior to the death of the man he considered his kind patron, including it as he began copying out the text on June 24, 1718. Regardless of the personal identity of the object of his prayer, Desideri's extravagant hope, it seems, was that he could convert the ruler of Tibet to Christianity, or "the pure and stainless truth" as he calls it throughout the text, leading in turn to the conversion of the Tibetan people.[5]

> If you are pleased to follow
> The pure and stainless truth,
> Your qualities will be abundant
> And through blessings of the transcendent
> May you attain all that is auspicious.
> May you be transported to the shores of salvation,
> The supreme essence of all aspirations.

THE FOURTH POEM

After all of the extravagant praise of the preceding verses, in the fourth poem Desideri offers his first criticism of Tibetan scholars, beginning:

> These days those who strive for the quality
> Of understanding the fields of knowledge well
> Are mostly weak in their efforts
> And unskilled in the essentials of practice.

Such a lament is in fact a familiar sentiment in Tibetan Buddhist literature and is often expressed at the beginning of a text. A common theme in Buddhist literature is that we live in a degenerate age, that the more time that has elapsed since the Buddha passed into nirvāṇa, the more difficult it is to follow the path, due to a deterioration in the intelligence and dedication of Buddhists. A work will therefore often begin by explaining that it has been composed in consideration of the sad state of current practice, while appealing to that small group of readers who are not so benighted as to be unable to benefit at all from what the author has to offer. For example, at the beginning of Tsong kha pa's *Great Treatise on the Stages of the Path to Enlightenment,* a work that Desideri studied carefully before beginning the *Inquiry,* we find these verses:

These days those who strive at yoga have studied few [of the classic
    texts]
While those who have studied much are not skilled in the essentials of
    practice.
They tend to view the scriptures through the eyes of partisanship,
Unable to use reason to discriminate the meaning of the scriptures.[6]

We see again that Desideri has learned the conventions of Tibetan Buddhist literature well, to the point of plagiarizing Tsong kha pa, something
that occurs again and again throughout the text. And we see again that he
puts those conventions to use for his own purposes, giving them his own
coded meaning. This is clear from his use of the term translated as "biased"
in the translation of Desideri (and as "partisanship" in the passage from
Tsong kha pa above). The Tibetan term is *phyogs re,* literally meaning something like "one side" and hence "incomplete," and by extension, "biased."
Desideri, following Tsong kha pa, refers to those whose eyes are "biased" in
this sense. For Tsong kha pa, this prevents them from correctly determining
the meaning of the scriptures. Desideri makes a more powerful claim:

Those with only biased eyes
Lack the power of mind to distinguish
White and black, religion and irreligion;
They are completely bereft of religion.

"White and black" *(dkar nag)* in Tibetan Buddhist literature signifies
good and evil; dharma can mean Buddhism, religion more generally, and
ultimately, the truth itself. Desideri's claim will be that Buddhism, renowned
as the dharma, is not the dharma, because it is not the true religion. But
those whose eyes are biased are unable to see this because their eyes have
not seen the alternative, the religion that is true. In the pages that follow, he
will provide a detailed argument for the importance of learning about other
religions. He only hints at this in this fourth poem, implying that stasis leads
to stagnation and that it is through stimulation, even agitation, that beneficial change occurs. Borrowing from the final stanza of the opening prayer
of Tsong kha pa's most famous text, Desideri ends the poetry portion of the
preamble with another standard element of a Tibetan Buddhist text, a request to listen, that is, to read what follows.

Therefore those who have clear intelligence,

Who are not obscured by the darkness of prejudice,

Who seek salvation from the abyss of fears

That destroys the mind itself,

Who seek to reach the shores of definite goodness;

May those fortunate beings

Listen with single-pointed attention.

THE CASE FOR COMPARATIVE RELIGION

In the long prose section that follows, Desideri anticipates by a century and a half Friedrich Max Müller's famous dictum of comparative religion, "He who knows one, knows none."[7] Müller was making a broad point about the value of studying other religions, whereas Desideri will ultimately urge the Tibetans to study just one other religion. But before he does that, he must first make the general case. And so he begins:

> Here, having seen that, among all the fields of knowledge, the knowledge of religion is of very great importance, one must understand the very great importance of removing, as if with an antidote, such faults as having ears that are biased when listening to a religion and having eyes that are biased when studying a religion. Regarding the religions of others, I can conclude without difficulty that looking at what is written and listening to what is explained will be sources of joy and delight to the minds of the learned in this Tibet.[8]

Desideri goes on to argue that there is little point in a cursory study of all religions other than one's own and that it is equally pointless to attempt to examine all of the specific doctrines of a single religion in a short period of time. Rejecting these two approaches, he will present a single religion, "the stainless, perfect, excellent, and supreme religion of the star heads." Furthermore, he will not present all of their doctrines, but instead "will explain it by elaborating—from the perspective of [the doctrines of] previous lives and the emptiness of intrinsic existence—on just two cherished articles of belief of that perfect and steadfast teaching." He does not identify these two articles of faith in this text, but he does so in the *Essence of the Christian Reli-*

gion. They are the doctrine of the trinity and the doctrine of the incarnation, or, as Desideri writes there, "the miraculous way that the highest has three natures and the way of the supreme guide Jesus Christ's act of kindness in being born as a human; he came into the world and died for the sake of all humans." And although he will say so later, he does not say that he will refute the doctrines of rebirth and emptiness but only that he will present the two Christian doctrines in terms of rebirth and emptiness.

But first he must cultivate his audience, a cultivation that begins with a caution. He says that those who have long been living in darkness (by which he means the Tibetans, but does not say so) are intimidated by light, averting their eyes in fear that it will harm them. In the same way, the narrow-minded and biased are intimidated by the light of another religion, fearing that to learn about it will be a violation of their own faith. In order to dispel such fears, he presents a long argument for the value of studying another religion.

Again following Buddhist literary conventions, Desideri uses many analogies to support his case. Each land has its own culture: its own cuisine, style of dress, and language. Yet through trade, one is able to acquire things from other cultures that are a source of benefit and happiness. The best musician knows how to play many instruments, the best physician knows many remedies, the best honey comes from the flowers of many trees.

At the same time, two things may be superficially different but share much in common, just as Tibetans are of different sizes and shapes but speak the same language and eat the same food. In the same way, two religions (by which he means Buddhism and Christianity) may differ in some ways, but they are similar in many of their doctrines and practices.

Thus, to encounter another tradition that accords greatly with one's own tradition and to understand them both is like having two butter lamps burning in a single room, or one gold or silver ring shining with the light of two diamonds. Again, if a tree receives the appropriate amount of water from separate sources—rainwater and water from a stream—its roots will grow large, and the tree will be more and more firmly fixed in the earth. In the same way, by moistening one's mind with the complete instructions and essential points of one's own religion as well as another religion that accords with it, one's body, speech, and mind will become most conducive to religion and one will, like a thick nail, abide with a firm aspiration to religion.

A traveler who becomes lost benefits greatly by meeting a group of people traveling to the same destination. In the same way, one gains great confidence from the knowledge that learned men from other lands have set out on the path to the single goal of all religions, what Desideri calls "the ultimate destination of the supreme reality of definite goodness" *(nges legs dngos mchog gi mthar thug pa'i don)*. "Definite goodness" is a technical term in Tibetan Buddhism and is often paired with "high status" *(mngon mtho)* as the two goals of religious practice, with "high status" referring to rebirth as a human or god, and "definite goodness" meaning liberation from rebirth. Desideri's implication is that Buddhism and Christianity share the latter, and higher, goal. (We should recall that in an earlier work he composed in Tibetan, a work that he entitled "Definite Goodness," Desideri argued that such goodness is found only in Christianity.)

However, Desideri faces a problem, one that he recognizes. All religions proclaim their own superiority. Buddhism is no different in that regard, and in Tibet there had long been the claim that the Land of Snows was a special realm, where all the teachings of the Buddha were preserved and practiced. Tibetan scholars were also well versed in the traditional history of Buddhism in India, where generations of Buddhist teachers, beginning with the Buddha himself, had demonstrated the superiority of Buddhism to the myriad religions and philosophical schools of ancient India. With the superiority of Buddhism so clearly proven and the supremacy of Buddhism in Tibet so long established, what is to be gained by studying another religion that is, almost by definition, inferior to Buddhism? Desideri has an answer:

> Even if the other's religion that one listens to or studies is not only inconsistent with one's own religion but is a degraded view, sows misdeeds, and is completely degenerate, [listening to or studying it] is a cause of benefit and joy to the mind of a learned one. For example, even though silver, iron, copper, wood, clay, and so forth are deficient and degenerate compared to gold, among these some can be used as currency to purchase gold, some as a tool and means to discover gold, some to cleanse all the stains and impurities of gold, and some to help mold the gold into whatever ornament one desires, such as earrings, by actually making the gold pliant and malleable; a craftsman can turn [gold] into any ornament he desires.

He seems to be saying that although iron and wood are inferior to gold, iron and wood can be turned into a shovel, allowing one to find more gold. At this point in the argument, he implies no criticism of Buddhism whatsoever. In fact, he seems to concede its superiority to all other religions. His strategy at this early stage of the text is merely to convince Tibetan scholars that it is worth their time to read the pages that follow. He thus appeals to the ideal of the bodhisattva, so powerful in Tibetan Buddhism, implying that it is the duty of the bodhisattva to study other religions because when he has studied them, he will feel great compassion for those beings who are bereft of religion. In Desideri's words, "He will then exhort himself and pray from the depths of his heart, without despair and weariness, to make the light of the perfect truth, excellent and sublime, of the stainless and thoroughly pure religion shine upon the minds of these people." The long and effusive phrase "the light of perfect truth, excellent and sublime, the stainless and thoroughly pure religion" *(chos lugs dri ma med pa rnam par dag pa bden pa yang dag 'od zer mchog dam pa)* appears throughout Desideri's text in various forms. It always means Christianity. His point, still only implied at this point in the text, is that one who is truly concerned for the welfare of the people of the world must instruct them in the truth, and the truth is to be found in its most perfect form in Christianity. But at this stage of his argument, he is not prepared to make such a declaration. He argues instead that the value of the true religion is enhanced by the study of a false one, just as placing a dark form behind clear glass creates a pleasing color. The rich and healthy become complacent in their good fortune, only striving to maintain their happiness when they encounter the impoverished and the afflicted. In the same way, "some people who abide in the most excellent religion" may nevertheless become complacent and forgetful, only dedicating themselves to their religion when they encounter those who wander blindly, "completely bereft of the dharma." A skilled physician can turn poison into an antidote.

Furthermore, it is not the case that false religions have no good qualities whatsoever. The bark of sugarcane is bitter, but when it is crushed, the sweet essence is revealed. In the same way, "the rough bark of irreligion, falsity, and evil tenets can be completely discarded. The mind of the learned will take only the well-crushed essence that benefits the mind and will joyfully partake of the sweet taste again and again." Ultimately, however, in order for the truth to be fully recognized and appreciated, one must also be aware of the existence of falsehood; the light of a fire can be seen only in the presence of darkness. "Thus, without their opposite, one cannot refute the other, and one will never find the freedom in which the darkness of ignorance is dissipated, the thornbushes of evil tenets are burned and consumed, and the filth of irreligion is cleansed."

To this point in the text, Desideri has been relentlessly positive in his portrayal of Tibet, its people, and its religion. He has come as a supplicant, asking only that the scholars of Tibet, whose renown had reached Europe, pay heed to what he has to say about the religion of the star head people, arguing for the benefits of its study, even if it is inferior to the religion of Tibet. For the reader who knows Desideri's ultimate motivation, his code is clear. Yet in the surface of the words there is nothing that is not respectful, even ingratiating.

In the next section, his tone changes markedly as he explains "the benefit of discarding the evil path and entering the good path." He begins by mocking the provincialism of the Tibetans, that if they would travel outside Tibet, then their exalted view of their land as "unrivaled, pleasing, and perfect" would change. Indeed, the farther one travels from Tibet, the more marvelous the lands.

> If they were to arrive in Nepal or Kashmir and see sights they had never seen before, the flames of their attachment [to Tibet] that had burned so brightly before would dim. If they continued farther on the road and their eyes were delighted by the vast land of India with sights adorned with many pleasurable things, then all the attractive characteristics of Tibet exaggerated in the past would disappear without a trace. Going from the south in a great ship farther and farther, [they would reach] the other side of the great ocean. To the east is China, a land that produces jewels and pleasures. To the west are the lands of the star heads, where there are displayed precious qualities, manufacturing, jewels, and wonders of all types. If their minds are engrossed in the various sites that are the heart of the world, they must perceive and be convinced that this birthplace, this Tibet, is a very unappealing, very unattractive, and very painful place.

The same can be said for religion. For those who know only their own religion, it may seem superior, but only because they know nothing about (and Desideri uses his stock phrase for Christianity) "the other's religion that is stainless, superior, pure, and most excellent." This is a dramatic shift in tone; he is no longer extolling the study of another religion because it leads to a greater appreciation of the superiority of one's own religion. Now the comparison reveals that one's own religion, Buddhism, is in fact inferior to the religion of the other, Christianity. To make his point, Desideri begins to catalog some of the flaws of the religion of Tibet.

In his *Historical Notices,* written for a very different audience, Desideri could characterize Tibetan religion as a vast system of "errors and idolatrous superstitions."[9] He is more selective in his criticisms here, as he identifies where Christianity—always referred to as "the other's religion" *(gzhan gyi chos lugs)*—is superior to Buddhism. First, he says that if one dispassionately examines the other's religion, one will find that in the area of ethics—in the language of Buddhism, "what is to be adopted and what is to be discarded"—there is no fault to be found. And although the religion of the Tibetans has a similar system of ethics, many Tibetans do not follow it. In addition, even among those practices sanctioned by Buddhism, some are clearly sinful. Presumably referring to Tibetan protector deities and the tantric practice of invoking wrathful deities, he says that the Tibetan worship of ghosts and demons is an abomination. Presumably referring to certain wrathful tantric rituals, he writes, "Evil spells, curses, vengeance rites, and so forth have been thoroughly proven by the intelligent to be terrible sins. Yet they are not only sanctioned by one's teacher, they are part of one's training and are explained in the scriptures." When Tibetans understand this, their attachment and loyalty to their religion, grown strong simply through the force of habit, will begin to fade.

It is clear from both his Tibetan and his Italian writings that Desideri found great fault in the doctrine of karma. At first sight this seems surprising. It is a system of ethics, of "what is to be adopted and what is to be discarded," that lists ten sins: killing, stealing, sexual misconduct, lying, divisive speech, harsh speech, senseless speech, covetousness, harmful intent, and wrong view. Depending on how one interprets the last item of the list, there seems to be nothing to which the Christian cleric would object, and indeed it does not appear that this is what is irksome to Desideri. Instead, what he finds abominable is that the virtues and sins performed in this world also bear their fruit in this world as all manner of mundane pleasures and pains. That is, the Buddhists do not heed the Gospel of Matthew (6:19–20), where we read, in the Douay-Rheims version, "Lay not up to yourselves treasures on earth:

where the rust, and moth consume, and where thieves break through and steal. But lay up to yourselves treasures in heaven: where neither the rust nor moth doth consume, and where thieves do not break through, nor steal." When Desideri describes the doctrine of karma for his Italian audience, he writes:

> They propound and establish as a universal principle that all agreeable things such as leisure and enjoyment are the fruits of virtue and the good works of living beings and all painful things such as affliction and trouble are penalties and punishments for living beings' deeds. They hold this principle to be so all-encompassing that they regard it as a loathsome and intolerable blasphemy to say that even the slightest and barely perceptible annoyance, such as lightly bumping a hand or foot and suffering an almost imperceptible pain, is caused by anything other than a prior blow committed by that same person.[10]

Here in his Tibetan text, he is only slightly more restrained, using a Buddhist vocabulary to say that the Buddhist system, by claiming that the pleasures of the mundane world are the result of virtuous actions done in the past, promotes attachment to those pleasures, which in fact are not pleasures but are sources of terror. The Buddhist who has analyzed this "will see that their own tradition has no real salvation of any kind and that it is impossible to eliminate the fault of squandering all the perfect virtues." This will lead to a deep sense of sadness in the Buddhist, who will lament, "Alas, although mired up to my head in a swamp of rotting corpses, a swamp that smells like excrement, I think that I live in a place where all precious things are gathered. What greater self-delusion and stupidity could there be?" Again, Desideri uses his Buddhist allusions well; one of the four "neighboring hells" in the standard cosmology is called "swamp of corpses."

As further proof of his skill, Desideri then switches into verse to employ classic Buddhist metaphors for delusion. A standard tenet of Buddhism, emphasized especially in the Yogācāra and Madhyamaka schools, is that things do not exist as they appear, that they seem to be real but in fact are not. For example, the *Diamond Sūtra* famously declares:

> View all conditioned things as like
> Stars, cataracts, butter lamps,
> Illusions, dewdrops, bubbles,
> Dreams, lightning, and clouds.

The Madhyamaka master Buddhapālita wrote, "The Bhagavan set forth the categories of illusion, echo, reflection, mirage, dream, ball of foam, water bubble, and plantain tree as examples of the fact that conditioned phenomena lack self."[11] Each of these metaphors is subject to extensive elaboration and commentary. A magician is able to use a spell to create an illusion, causing his audience to see a pebble as a horse, an elephant, or a beautiful woman. The reflection of the moon in a still pond appears so real that a monkey hangs down from a branch to try to grab it but falls into the water and drowns. A woodsman seeks the heartwood of a plantain tree, but after peeling away the layers finds that it has no essence. Desideri clearly learned these metaphors, as well as the philosophical context in which they are employed in Tibetan Buddhism. But he put them to an entirely different use: as metaphors for the deceptive nature of the religion of the Tibetans. And in an act of particular literary bravado, he begins the verses with two lines from one of the most beloved Buddhist texts in Tibet, Śāntideva's *Engaging in the Bodhisattva Deeds (Bodhicaryāvatāra)*, where at 4.23, referring to the rare good fortune of being reborn as a human with access to the teachings of the Buddha, the poet writes:

> If, having found such leisure
> I do not cultivate virtue
> Nothing could be more mistaken than this;
> Nothing could be more foolish than this.

Desideri changes only one word, "than this" *('di las)* to "than me" *(dbag las)*, but completely changes the meaning, having the Buddhist declare his shame at being deceived by Buddhism. Desideri then takes four stanzas from the eleven stanzas of the *Samādhirāja Sūtra* that are cited by Tsong kha pa in his *Great Treatise on the Stages of the Path to Enlightenment* to illustrate the doctrine of no self. In each stanza, Desideri again radically changes the meaning and intention of the Buddhist text to serve his purpose. He does so by simply changing the last line in each stanza from "Know that all phenomena are this way" to "So too is my tradition devoid of truth." It is not all phenomena that are devoid of essence; it is Buddhism.[12]

> There is no one more mistaken than me.
> There is no one more foolish than me.

Magicians conjure forms,
Horses, elephants, and chariots;
Just as they do not exist as they appear;
So too is my tradition devoid of truth.

Just as the moon's reflection appears at night
In water that is clear and without waves,
Yet the water moon is empty and cannot be grasped;
So too is my tradition devoid of truth.

Just as at noon in the summertime,
A man traveling and afflicted by thirst
Sees a mirage to be a body of water;
So too, mine is irreligion, devoid of truth. . . .

Just as a man goes to a moist plantain tree
Because he wants its core,
Yet everywhere, inside and out, there is no core.
So too is my religion devoid of a core.

At this point Desideri abandons any attempt to code his message. Yet he maintains his command of a Buddhist vocabulary, describing what the Buddhist must do:

Thus, having encountered the other's religion that is pure, stainless, superior, peerless, and excellent, through the power of listening to it and studying it well with the clear eyes of faultless intelligence, without obscuration by the darkness of prejudice, the heart of the learned, like waking from the dullness of the sleep of ignorance and regaining mindfulness, will understand directly that the religion they upheld before has defects everywhere. Their mind tormented by pain, they will realize that, without wishing to and unknowingly, they have drunk an evil poison, and they will vomit it out with great effort. They will recognize with certainty that, spurred by grave error, they have completely lost the path that accords with their own welfare, and will endeavor to turn away from the evil path and enter the good path.

The Buddhist who rejects his false religion and accepts the stainless and pure religion of the other should be prepared to suffer abuse and rebuke from the ignorant followers of the false religion. In that case, he should not heed their criticisms but instead resolve to dedicate himself to the true religion until he dies. Furthermore, death may come at any time. At this point Desideri makes another bold rhetorical move, paraphrasing the chapter on death and impermanence in Tsong kha pa's *Great Treatise,* where one is instructed to contemplate three facts: death is certain, the time of death is uncertain, and at the time of death nothing is of benefit except religion. Desideri repeats these almost verbatim and even uses some of the same citations from Buddhist scriptures that Tsong kha pa employs. Here, the advice is offered to the Christian convert, as if to say: because death can come at any moment, there is no reason to be concerned about criticism from others. But he is also making another point. To Tsong kha pa's three facts—that death is certain, the time of death is uncertain, and at the time of death nothing is of benefit except religion—Desideri seems to add: and it must be the true religion.

In short order, then, Desideri has argued for the value of studying a religion that is different from one's own; that this value extends even to the study of religions inferior to one's own because it increases one's faith and conviction; and that this value extends especially to the study of a religion superior to one's own because it leads one away from evil and to the good.

One might imagine that at this point Desideri would launch into his critique of Buddhism and of the doctrines of rebirth and emptiness. However, he continues his argument for the value of studying another religion with a section that he calls, "How to See the Other's Religion in a Wise Way." He begins by discussing the importance of the study of religion in a general way, without specifying whether it is one's own or another's religion, whether it is Buddhism or Christianity. He employs the familiar Buddhist agricultural imagery of the seed and the soil, saying that religion is the seed from which all virtue grows. He thus sets forth what he calls "the three recognitions" (borrowing Tsong kha pa's "three recognitions"—of oneself as a sick person, the dharma as the medicine, and the teacher as the physician): seeing religion as a seed, oneself as the soil, and that living in accordance with religion leads to a happiness beyond any worldly happiness; he calls that happiness "definite goodness" *(nges legs),* a technical term that, as noted above, typically refers to liberation from rebirth, either as an *arhat* or as a buddha.

Desideri provides an interesting sequence of causation that seems at odds with basic Buddhist doctrine. He states that the seed that is religion produces sprouts of both virtuous and non-virtuous deeds, implying that religion (presumably in the generic sense) can motivate non-virtuous activities. These sprouts ripen in turn into "benefits and faults," meaning experiences of pleasure and pain. That is, the fruits, pleasure and pain, grow from the sprouts of virtue and non-virtue, and the sprouts of virtue and non-virtue in turn grow from the seed of religion. Without the sprout the fruit cannot grow, and without the seed the sprout cannot grow. He writes, "When the growth of sprouts of virtue or non-virtue and the ripening of benefits and faults as the fruition of virtue and non-virtue never occur, then it follows that the two types of deeds and the two types of fruit that are based upon a mindful awareness that serve as a kind of life-force called 'mind,' 'mental faculty,' or 'consciousness,' become totally non-existent." That is, there can be no experience of pleasure and pain ("the two types of fruit") without virtuous and non-virtuous deeds ("the two types of deeds"), and these in turn depend, not on what in Buddhism would simply be the mental consciousness *(manovijñāna)* that is neutral in itself, its moral valence depending on various mental factors *(caitta)*, but instead on what Desideri calls "mindful awareness" *(dran shes)* or simply "mindfulness." Although technically this is also neutral, the usages of such a term in Buddhism tend toward cases of mental virtue. Furthermore, Desideri says that it is "like a life-force *(srog)*," and that this life-force is given various names, such as "mind" *(sems)*, "mental faculty" *(yid)*, or "consciousness" *(rnam par shes pa)*. He seems intent on putting these three basic Buddhist terms in quotes, using a phrase *(zhes bya ba)* that can also mean "so-called." He appears to imply that the true referent of these various Buddhist terms is the Christian soul.

Desideri goes on to explain that what is called the mind, mental faculty, or consciousness is the soil into which the seed of religion will be planted and it is therefore important to first prepare the ground, both by clearing away those things that would prevent its growth and by providing those things that would promote its growth. Before turning to that, he distinguishes between humans and beasts. Animals seek only happiness in this world and make no preparations for the world beyond; they know nothing of religion, and so they do not plant the seeds of virtue nor do they reap its fruits. In order to be superior to beasts, humans seek happiness beyond this world, and they should judge religions accordingly. He writes:

Whether the religion that one listens to and studies is one's own or another's, to the extent that the fruit of religion that it presents is entirely the worldly happiness shared with beasts, to that extent it is contrary to religious awareness, and one must, through the application of awareness, turn one's mind away from it. To the extent that the religion that one listens to and studies is such that, for whatever mundane happiness one sees, hears about, or thinks of, if a deep sense of revulsion and discouragement arises giving rise to the thoughts "This too is of the world, this too is of the world," "Those are the aims of beasts," "Those are suffering," "This is of no use," to that extent one should hold that religion to be reliable and appropriate.

This kind of statement would have been familiar to Desideri's Tibetan readers. In this section he is drawing heavily from Tsong kha pa's *Great Treatise,* which is based on a typology of religions and religious practitioners that Tsong kha pa drew from Atiśa, the Bengali master who came to Tibet in 1042. In a work called *Lamp for the Path to Enlightenment (Bodhipathapradīpa),* he placed religious practitioners into three categories: those who seek happiness within *saṃsāra* (through rebirth as a human or a god), those who seek to escape *saṃsāra* themselves (by becoming an *arhat*), and those who seek to liberate all beings from *saṃsāra* (by becoming a buddha). Tsong kha pa organizes his entire text around this typology, with the lowest level of religious practitioner being one who seeks happiness in the next lifetime and acts in such a way as to achieve it. That is, someone who merely seeks happiness in this lifetime does not qualify as a religious practitioner. In order to qualify as a religious practitioner of the lowest rank, one must recognize the workings of the law of karma, accumulating virtue and avoiding non-virtue in an effort to be reborn as a human or a god in the next lifetime. Furthermore, Buddhist texts often distinguish Buddhism from other religions by stating that through the practice of other religions, one may be reborn as a human or a god (including as a god of the exalted reaches of the Formless Realm), but it is only through the practice of Buddhism that one can be liberated from birth and death and from the sufferings of *saṃsāra.*

Desideri is clearly writing with an understanding of this typology, and at first sight he appears to be describing religion in a manner that is consistent with it. On closer inspection, however, we note that he states, "To the extent that the fruit of religion that it presents is entirely the worldly happiness shared with beasts, to that extent it is contrary to religious awareness, and one must, through the application of awareness, turn one's mind away from it." For Desideri, only those religions that promote a deep sense of revulsion for the world qualify as religions. When he writes that such people should think, "This too is of the world," he is evoking the famous passage in I John 2:16, "For all that is in the world, is the concupiscence of the flesh, and the concupiscence of the eyes, and the pride of life, which is not of the Father, but is of the world." From this perspective, Desideri would consider only persons of medium capacity and of great capacity to be religious (in Buddhist terms, those who seek liberation as an *arhat* or a buddha) and only those traditions that set forth the path to permanent liberation from *saṃsāra* to be true religions. He would therefore expel from the ranks of the religious those who live virtuously in order to have a happy rebirth. As we shall see, one of Desideri's chief criticisms of Buddhism, one of the several reasons he sees it as a false religion, is that it teaches that the practice of virtue results in happiness in the world; or put in Buddhist terms, that according to karmic theory all feelings of mental and physical happiness in the world are the result of virtuous deeds performed in the past. But this distinction would likely go unnoticed by the Buddhist reader in a text where the vocabulary and imagery are so familiarly Buddhist.

Desideri continues with the agricultural metaphor, saying that in order for a seed to grow, the soil must be free from various defects. In the same way, in order for the seed of religion to take root, the mind must be free of various impediments, such as forgetfulness, misunderstanding, and worldly attachments. As long as such impediments are present, someone who encounters the true religion will derive no benefit from it. Instead, one needs unwavering focus on the essential points of the religion and the strong conviction to understand them with precision, unsullied by worldly concerns.

Desideri turns next to the topic that occurs at the beginning of Tsong kha pa's *Great Treatise:* the proper way to listen to the teachings. He again draws heavily on Tsong kha pa, listing the same three conditions for listening (impartiality, intelligence, and interest) and using some of the same quotations from Indian works that Tsong kha pa employs, especially those that particularly serve his purpose. For example, Tsong kha pa cites a passage from Bhāviveka:

The mind tormented by prejudice
Will never find tranquility.[13]

In glossing this line, Tsong kha pa says that "prejudice" is attachment to one's own religion and hostility toward the religion of others. This fits perfectly into Desideri's argument and thus he repeats Tsong kha pa's statement almost verbatim. He concludes this section with a poem in five and a half four-line stanzas. One of those stanzas, from the *Samādhirāja Sūtra,* is taken verbatim from Tsong kha pa; a second stanza is a substantial rephrasing, for Desideri's purposes, of a stanza from Śāntideva's *Engaging in the Bodhisattva Deeds* (5.109) that Tsong kha pa also cites. He closes the section with a prose paraphrase of yet another of Tsong kha pa's citations from an Indian text, this one from Candragomin:

Our minds are constantly confused;
We have been ill for a very long time.
What is achieved by lepers
Who have lost their arms and legs and only occasionally take medicine?[14]

Desideri writes, "Just as one or two doses of medicine do nothing for a leper who has lost his legs and arms, in the same way, for a mind strongly stricken and long afflicted by the grave illness of wrong views, impure tradition, and irreligion, it is not sufficient to practice the points of the stainless and pure religion only once or twice. Thus, they analyze all the essential points of such a path with discriminative wisdom and strive persistently like a flowing stream." Desideri is finally coming to the end of his preamble and moving toward the heart of his text: his prolix refutation of rebirth. He must justify the need for a sustained commitment to the stainless and pure religion; anything less will not suffice. Occasional doses of medicine will not save the limbs of the leper.

For Desideri such commitment should take a specific form: debate. And so he sets a final task for himself before he begins his refutation: to establish the importance of debate. From one perspective, this should be a simple task. Formal debate over points of doctrine had been introduced into Tibet during the "later dissemination" *(phyi dar)* of Buddhism into Tibet that began in the late tenth century. The formalized debate that Desideri witnessed (and perhaps participated in) during his time at Sera monastery had been developed by Chapa Chökyi Sengé (Phyva pa Chos kyi seng ge, 1109–1169).

The Tibetan term he uses is *rtsod pa,* a word typically translated into English—especially in the context of its stylized monastic form—as "debate," although it also means "dispute," "argument," and "quarrel." In order for Desideri to remain in accordance with the Tibetan style that he had used so skillfully thus far in the text, he would need to provide canonical—that is, Indian—sources to support his argument. Yet because the term carries these rather negative connotations, and because this particular form of debate (although traced back to India) had its own distinctively Tibetan form, there were no paeans to debate for Desideri to cite. Undaunted, he becomes more bold in his attempts at adaptation.

Among the six perfections *(pāramitā)* that bodhisattvas cultivate over the long path to buddhahood, the first is the perfection of giving *(dānapāramitā)*, which has three types: the giving of material gifts, the giving of fearlessness, and the giving of the dharma. Desideri goes on to enumerate sixteen benefits of the gift of the dharma: one will be endowed with a good memory, insight, intelligence, and steadfastness, one will not be vulnerable to Māra, and so on. Desideri rather baldly claims that these sixteen benefits of giving the gift of the dharma are also the benefits of debating about religion. However, he lacks an Indian passage to support this. Undeterred, he creates one. In his *Great Treatise,* Tsong kha pa cites three stanzas from Āryaśūra's *Garland of Birth Stories (Jātakamālā),* stanzas that praise learning (literally "listening" or "hearing," *śrutam* in Sanskrit). Desideri takes this passage and simply substitutes "debate" for "learning." Hence, "Debate is the lamp dispelling the darkness of ignorance," and so forth. This begins a long section of poetry in praise of debate: it "saves one from drowning in the sea of illusion," it is "the central pillar of the path," it is "the guide to the place of salvation."

These verses are but a prelude to a long section of interspersed prose and poetry on the five benefits of debate. The first benefit is that debate allows one to easily understand the central points of a religion. In this regard Desideri claims that debate is superior even to the classical Buddhist triad of listening, contemplation, and meditation in its power to allow one to grasp what one had not grasped before. Again adapting a stanza from the *Groups of Utterances (Udānavarga),* he writes:

Through debate one understands phenomena;
Through debate one dispels delusions;
Through debate one discards the meaningless;
Through debate one attains the perfections.[15]

For the second benefit of debate, Desideri turns to the imagery of the senses, as he would in his *Historical Notices* when he praised the idolatry of Tibet over the idolatry of Hindustan,[16] and as he had at the beginning of this text, where he humbly argued that another religion, although inferior to one's own, was still of some value in helping one to appreciate the superiority of one's own religion, just as base materials like wood and iron could be used to make a shovel to extract gold from the earth. Here, the gold that has been extracted from the earth is not immediately pleasing to the eye. It must be cleaned and polished to be captivating. He continues:

> Although the eye repeatedly looks at a vast feast of food and drink of a hundred flavors, with the best and most perfect flavors, if that food is not chewed by the two rows of teeth and swallowed, such things as encountering the flavor, experiencing the flavor, continuing to experience the flavor, and having experienced the flavor will not occur. In the same way, although the religion of others that the learned have listened to, read about, and examined may be stainless, pure, and superior, listening, contemplation, and meditation are like the eye looking at it repeatedly; if one does not chew it with the two rows of teeth and swallow it with the method of honest debate about religion, one will be unable to experience the delicious and complete flavor of such a tradition. And if one does not repeatedly burn and wash it again and again with the fire and water of debate, then the mind of the learned will not be overwhelmed and encompassed by the radiance and brilliance of the various qualities that exist in that religion, its incomparable charm, and the limitless things that uncontrollably captivate the mind.

It is as if a certain violence is required to reveal the truth, as gold is heated with fire and delicious food is chewed by the two rows of teeth. The three traditional forms of wisdom—those that arise from listening, from contemplation, and from meditation—are like looking at food. Just as food must be tasted using the teeth, so the true flavor of a religion is revealed only through debate. As he adds in verse, medicine is made by pounding plants, music is made by beating drums, and the best of religions must be struck hard with the flint of debate in order to produce a brilliant light.

The violent metaphors continue with the third benefit of debate. This time, Desideri provides no poetry, perhaps because the metaphor is not common to Indian or Tibetan Buddhism. In those traditions, especially in the Mahāyāna, the rhetoric is one of infinite expansion, with rays of light extending to all corners of the universe, the Buddha's wisdom extending to all objects of knowledge, his memory extending to an infinite number of past lives. Imagery of cutting, of severing, of limiting are certainly found; the webs of illusion are rent, the roots of ignorance are severed, the bonds of *saṃsāra* are broken. What is cut is that which must be destroyed. For Desideri, however, cutting is necessary for growth. He speaks of a flowering fruit tree that is weakened by growth, its strength sapped by uncontrolled spreading. For it to grow strong and bear flowers and fruit, it must be pruned. In the same way, when studying another religion, the mind must not be allowed to range uncontrolled from one topic to the next; "on all occasions of listening to and examining the other's religion, superior and pure, if one becomes excited due to attachment to one's own tradition, or one's mind's ability to remain on its object is interrupted and it is uncontrollably drawn to other pleasing objects, or the mind is distracted away from its object, then all these diffusions should be stopped by the power of debate, as with a pruning knife."

The rhetoric of withdrawal, limitation, and control occurs most often in Buddhism in the context of instructions on meditation, particularly in instructions on the state of concentration called serenity *(śamatha)*. Desideri would have been familiar with this vocabulary from his reading of Tsong kha pa's *Great Treatise on the Stages of the Path to Enlightenment,* which devotes a long section to the topic. Here, somewhat strangely, as he continues to extol debate, he moves from the language of the vineyard to the language of the meditation retreat. There is a famous meditation instruction: tie the elephant of the mind to the object with the rope of mindfulness.[17] That is, when the mind wanders from its object of concentration, mindfulness—the recognition that it has wandered—will lead the mind back to its object, attaching it there. As he had done in the case of the gift of the dharma, Desideri rewrites this statement by replacing the key term with the term "debate." He writes, "With the rope of debating about religion one will be able to tightly tie one's mind to the object of the other's religion." He introduces more of the vocabulary of meditation, describing the dangers of lethargy and sloth, when the mind becomes sunk too deeply into its object. In Tsong kha pa's instructions on serenity meditation, the antidote to this lethargy is a form of meta-attention called introspective awareness, which involves monitoring one's mental and physical state. Again Desideri makes his substitution. "Again, for example, by using a grindstone, all the rust that had formed on swords and so forth can be removed and the iron will be clear and sharp, useful for cutting. In the same way, by using honest debate about religion like a grindstone, one grinds away the mind itself, which is afflicted by being sunk or absorbed in sloth and slumber, and the way the mind is focused on its object."

The fourth benefit of debate is not specified by Desideri. Instead, he provides a long poem, filled with metaphors of manipulation, refinement, and purification, concluding with these lines:

Likewise a debate that is not weak
On the subject of a stainless, true, and pure religion
Increases the joy in the heart of the learned.
When walking in the darkness of night,
The circle of the moon seems ever more attractive;
When the darkness of false debate is awakened by honesty,
Religion will captivate the mind ever more.

The fifth and final benefit of debate is again not identified. Again, Desideri provides more poetry, where the person who debates is called a lamp that dispels the darkness of evil philosophies. Like the cold wind of autumn that dispels dark clouds, debate dispels the clouds of wrong views. Evoking the famous *siṃhanāda,* the "lion's roar" of the Buddha that silenced all of his opponents, he describes the debater:

With the sound of the lion's roar of a lofty mind,
He will subdue the brains of the entire world,
The stainless faith, the supreme religion,
Through his kindness, will spread to all directions.
The skill of such a person among all the learned
Will be held as a crown ornament by the unbiased.

True to the tropes of Tibetan philosophical rhetoric, Desideri concludes his preamble with a standard statement. "Fearing excessive words, I have gathered the essential points. They can be known in detail elsewhere." Exactly where that "elsewhere" might be is something that he does not specify. It is doubtful that he intended some place in the Tibetan canon.

And so Desideri concludes the remarkable preamble to his great unread work. Its purpose is to set the stage for the refutation of rebirth that constitutes the bulk of his text; it takes up only eight folios of the 232 folios of the text. Yet Desideri clearly felt that it was essential, and he crafted it with great care, attending closely to both its form and to its content.

Desideri turns next to the topic announced in the title, *Inquiry concerning the Doctrines of Previous Lives and Emptiness.* Before describing the genre he adopts and the content of his arguments, it is important to have some sense of the Buddhist doctrine of rebirth, especially as it was understood in Tibet in the first decades of the eighteenth century. In addition, it is important to have some sense of Desideri's understanding of the doctrine of rebirth.

The doctrine of rebirth is held with a general consistency across the schools and regions of the Buddhist tradition; there is not a wide divergence of doctrine between the Mahāyāna and non-Mahāyāna schools or between Southeast Asia and East Asia, as there is with the doctrine of emptiness, for example. The Sanskrit terms that are typically used are *punarbhava* (literally, "existence again"), *punarjanman* or *punarjāta* ("birth again"), and *jāti* (simply, "birth"). Each of these terms is rendered rather literally into Tibetan, where another term also appears: *skye ba snga phyi,* which means "former and later births." In the title of his *Inquiry,* Desideri uses the term *skye ba snga ma,* "former births," to refer to the doctrine of rebirth.

According to the classical Buddhist doctrine, upheld in Tibet, all unenlightened beings in the universe, known as "common beings" *(pṛthagjana),* have been reborn in the past and will be reborn in the future, until they achieve liberation from rebirth, which is the ultimate goal of Buddhist practice. Until that time they will wander in the realm of rebirth called *saṃsāra,* which is composed of six realms: those of gods, demigods, humans, animals, ghosts, and the denizens of hell, with the heavens of the gods and the hells having elaborate divisions and subdivisions. They are reborn in a particular realm as result of their former deeds *(karma).* Thus, the cycle of rebirth has no end until one finds the path to escape from it, a path that the Buddha set forth in his first sermon. Given Christian notions of heaven and hell, Desideri and other Jesuit critics of Buddhism were not particularly exercised by the notion that one's deeds in this life will determine one's fate in the next life, although, as we saw in Matteo Ricci, they objected to the idea that a human could be reborn as an animal. They were far more troubled by perhaps the most philosophically vexing element of the doctrine of rebirth: that the cycle of rebirth has no beginning.

Although there is a standard creation myth in Buddhism (preserved in the *Aggañña Sutta* in the Pāli canon and retold with some variation in other sources), that myth describes only the creation of a new world system after a previous world has been destroyed. It does not describe the creation of the universe, or the beginning of the process of rebirth. Indeed, according to Buddhist doctrine, a new world system is created by the past deeds of the beings who will eventually come to inhabit it.

One often sees reference to the Buddha's "noble silence," and there is a famous list of fourteen questions (or ten in the Pāli listing) that the Buddha declined to answer; they are called *avyākata* in Pāli, meaning "unexpounded" or "indeterminate." It was in response to such questions that the Buddha famously asked whether a man shot by a poisoned arrow would spend time pondering the height of the archer and the kind of wood used for the arrow, or whether he would seek to extract the arrow before its poison killed him. Likening these fourteen questions to such pointless speculation, he called them "a thicket of views, a wilderness of views, a contortion of views, a vacillation of views, a fetter of views. It is beset by suffering, by vexation, by despair, and by fever, and it does not lead to disenchantment, to dispassion, to cessation, to peace, to direct knowledge, to enlightenment, to Nibbāna."[18] The first of these questions is: Is the world eternal? When the Buddha was asked this question, he remained silent. When he eventually spoke, he said that such questions were not to be answered, either because they could not be, or because the questions were wrongly framed and the product of mistaken assumptions, such that any answer would be misleading.

The Buddhists explicitly reject the idea of a God who is the creator of the universe and of the creatures who inhabit it. They set forth instead a cycle of birth, death, and rebirth that has no beginning, created only by the former deeds of the beings who inhabit the cycle, an infinite series of contingent causes producing contingent effects, as philosophically frustrating as such a doctrine might be. Perhaps one reason the doctrine of rebirth is not set forth with the philosophical detail that one finds, for example, in the doctrine of no self is that the doctrine of rebirth, at least in its general contours, appears to have been inherited by the Buddhists; with the important exception of the Lokāyatas or Materialists (literally "Worldlings"), the competing philosophical schools mentioned in Indian Buddhist texts seem to uphold, or at least not reject, the doctrine of rebirth.

"Proofs" of rebirth would appear only in later Indian Buddhist literature. The argument, in brief, is based on the strict Buddhist causal dualism of mind and body, according to which, although matter and mind can serve as each other's "cooperative condition," it is impossible for one to be the substantial cause of the other. Therefore, each moment of consciousness (of any of the six types of sentient beings) is the product of the previous moment, extending back in time to the moment of birth and (for womb-born beings such as humans and animals) to the moment of conception. Because the semen of the father and the "blood" (in Buddhist terms) of the mother are both matter, they cannot produce consciousness. The consciousness that enters the combined drops of semen and blood must therefore come from a previous moment of consciousness, and hence from a previous lifetime.

As a Christian thinker, Desideri would obviously not dispute the dualism of body and mind (or body and soul), but the doctrine of rebirth more generally presented profound problems for Christian doctrine. Desideri saw the system of rebirth as absurd, lacking Aristotle's unmoved mover and first cause. For Aquinas, the unmoved mover is God. Indeed, four of his five arguments for the existence of God rest on the conclusion that there must be a first cause. And in his essay *On the Eternity of the World (De Aeternitate Mundi),* Aquinas specifically rejects the notion of something eternal that was not created by God: "If someone holds that something besides God could have always existed, in the sense that there could be something always existing and yet not made by God, then we differ with him: such an abominable error is contrary not only to the faith but also to the teachings of the philosophers, who confess and prove that everything that in any way exists cannot exist unless it be caused by him who supremely and most truly has existence."[19] Buddhists hold that the cycle of rebirth is eternal and is not created by God.

We will turn soon to how Desideri argued against the Buddhist position when he wrote in Tibetan for a Tibetan Buddhist audience. Before doing so, we should consider briefly how he explained the doctrine of rebirth in Italian to a Roman Catholic audience. We should begin by noting that his initial understanding was mistaken; in a letter to a fellow Jesuit written in Lhasa on April 10, 1716, two years before the date on the first page of the *Inquiry,* he writes about the Tibetans: "No sort of meat is forbidden to them;

they do not hold to the doctrine of the transmigration of souls, and do not practice polygamy; three points in which they differ from idolatrous natives of India."[20] In a passage from his *Historical Notices* written years later, Desideri, despite his unveiled contempt, demonstrates both an accurate and detailed understanding of the mechanisms of karma and rebirth:

> Although the Tibetans are idolaters and pagans, their sect is very different in its customs and doctrines from that of the pagans of Asia. While it is true that they took their religion from the ancient pagans of Hindustan, that is, Mogul, the ancient books and customs have passed out of usage in Hindustan owing to the passage of time and the introduction of newly concocted fables and new beliefs. What is more, the Tibetans, owing to their subtle intelligence and continual speculative activity, have rejected much that was opposed to the logic of ordinary human discourse and have only embraced those points that can more easily, due to a certain appearance of goodness, deceive human understanding, which by itself is forsaken and completely unilluminated by the pure, invincible, and supernatural light of the true enlightened faith. Therefore, the Tibetans have deviated from their own teachers, and at present the Indians and the Tibetans have philosophical schools that differ from each other, and they follow dissimilar religions.
>
> The main and fundamental error from which springs, or better expressed, under which all the errors of the false Tibetan sect are subsumed, is the nefarious error of metempsychosis or the transmigration of souls, which the Tibetans themselves declare to be a tangled and inextricable vortex and an endless and bottomless sea owing to the infinity of notions and fantastical difficulties of which they pretend it is composed; but, in perfect truth, it would be much more fitting to describe it as a highly intricate and inextricable labyrinth and an endless and bottomless sea owing to the vast and extremely tangled combination of errors with which that fundamental error has been blindly compounded and of which the principal and most significant are the following.
>
> (1) They assert that the world and everything in it, living beings and their origin, that is, the continual course of transmigration, have existed *ab eterno* [from the beginning of time], so that beginning with the present birth of any particular being and following it back through an infinite series of prior births, one can never arrive at a birth that could be proven to be the first one.

(2) They do not accept fate, as Democritus does, namely that all things animate and inanimate originate by chance through a blind and random movement of erroneously imagined particles. Neither do they accept with Plato and Aristotle that the world, living beings, and everything in the world is created by God; nor do they accept in any way any primary, universal, uncreated, and independent cause upon which all things depend. On the contrary, they positively and directly deny and reject both fate and the existence of any entity uncreated in itself that would be the lord and creator of the universe.

(3) They assert that the world, considered universally in its totality and as a whole, and everything contained in it is caused exclusively by the actions of living beings, and that every birth of every particular living being was, is, and will be caused by the virtuous or sinful actions committed by that particular living being in previous lives. Thus it would follow that the actions of living beings existed prior to those beings themselves, which is an obvious absurdity. To extricate themselves from this they say that the real absurdity consists in the false notion of conceiving living beings as existing prior to their actions. They add that this absurdity is based on another and even more absurd belief, that every living being has a unique birth that can be proven to be that living being's first, a position they tenaciously deny and reject.

(4) First, they divide whatever has been, is, or will be into the actions of living beings and the fruits of those actions. Secondly, they subdivide the actions of living beings into white or good deeds and black or bad deeds, and the fruits of those deeds into good things and afflictions, that is, into pleasant things, such as leisure and enjoyment, and painful things, such as affliction and trouble.

(5) They propound and establish as a universal principle that all agreeable things such as leisure and enjoyment are the fruits of virtue and the good works of living beings and all painful things such as affliction and trouble are penalties and punishments for living beings' deeds. They hold this principle to be so all-encompassing that they regard it as a loathsome and intolerable blasphemy to say that even the slightest and barely perceptible annoyance, such as lightly bumping a hand or foot and suffering an almost imperceptible pain, is caused by anything other than a prior blow committed by that same person.

(6) They associate the pleasant things of leisure and enjoyment with the births of pleasant and happy living beings and the enjoyments, leisure, and good things connected with such births. Similarly, they associate painful things and trouble with the births of distressed living beings and the pains, afflictions and troubles connected with such births.

(7) In the same way, the good and evil deeds of living beings are subdivided. There are good deeds that result in good births and good deeds that result in good things and leisure in succeeding births, whether in good births or bad. The same is the case for evil deeds in that some result in a painful birth and some result in affliction, pain, or trouble in succeeding births, whether they are good or bad.

(8) Pleasant births with leisure, which according to them are the fruit of good actions, are divided into three classes: birth as a Lha [*lha,* or god], that is, in a state of great happiness and pleasure but one that is transitory and with a definite end; birth as a Lha-ma-in [*lha ma yin,* or demigod], that is, in a state between that of a human and a Lha; and lastly, birth as a human being.

(9) Painful and troublesome births are similarly divided into three classes: birth as a brute animal, that is, a beast; birth as a Itaa [*yi dvags,* or ghost], which I will explain later; and birth in Hell.[21]

Based on this (quite accurate) understanding of the Buddhist doctrine of rebirth, Desideri embarks on his refutation of it in the *Inquiry.* We immediately notice an abrupt change in style. He moves from what might be called an expository style to an argumentative style, adopting the conventions of a genre of Tibetan Buddhist literature called the *mtha' dpyod,* a term that literally means "analysis of the limits" but that might be translated as "critical analysis." Such works are typically divided into three sections: (1) the refutation of the other person's system *(gzhan lugs dgag pa),* (2) the presentation of one's own system *(rang lugs bzhag pa),* and (3) the elimination of any objections that the opponent might raise about one's own system *(rtsod pa spong ba).* In the topical outline *(sa bcad)* that Desideri provides for his text, all three of these elements are present. The first part, the refutation of the opponent's position, generally takes the form of a syllogism *(prayoga, sbyor ba)* or a consequence *(prasaṅga, thal 'gyur).* A syllogism, or more accurately, an enthymeme (a term that Desideri himself uses in the *Historical Notices* to describe Tibetan debate), consists of a subject, a predicate, and a reason, in the form: "The subject, A, is B, because of C." This form is often used in setting out one's own position. A consequence also consists of a subject, predicate, and reason, but in the form, "It follows that the subject A, is B, because of C." This form is often used to point out unintended consequences, including fallacies and absurdities, in the opponent's position.

As we consider Desideri's refutation of rebirth, each of the three sections—the refutation of the Buddhist position, the presentation of his own position, and the rebuttal of objections that the opponent might raise—would offer particular insights, showing how he would go about refuting rebirth; how he would go about setting forth Christian doctrine on creation, virtue, grace, salvation, heaven, and hell; and the Buddhist objections that he would imagine. Sadly, among the three sections in Desideri's table of contents—the refutation, the presentation, and the rebuttal—he does not finish even the first, although he appears to be reaching the end. The final sentence in the text is a subheading, which reads, "Second, conclusion of the refutation of the other's system on the topic of former and later lives, showing that a great many points in the texts of the opponent are unreliable and impure, like the collapsed relying on the collapsed. Specifically, there are twenty [such points]. With regard to the first." It seems that Desideri never wrote the section presenting his own system or the rebuttal of objections; the refutation of emptiness is entirely missing. As we will see in Chapter 4, some of what he might have said about his own system and about emptiness can be inferred from *Essence of the Christian Religion,* which begins with a refutation of emptiness and then goes on to present a summary of church doctrine, including such topics as creation, salvation, heaven, and hell. That summary, however, is presented as a catechism, in the form of a dialogue between a Christian teacher and a Tibetan who has renounced Buddhism, lacking the kind of philosophical rigor of the "critical analysis" *(mtha' dpyod)* genre that Desideri employs in the *Inquiry.*

There, Desideri will typically make statements in the form of a syllogism or consequence, with one syllogism or consequence leading to another. When the hypothetical opponent speaks, it is generally in one of two forms. He may say, "That does not follow." This is one of the acceptable responses that an opponent can make in a Tibetan Buddhist debate, saying *ma khyab,* literally, "There is no pervasion" or "There is no entailment." Specifically, such a response is objecting to one of the elements of syllogism or consequence by saying, "It does not follow that whatever is the reason is necessarily the predicate." In the first debates that young monks learn, one will say, "The subject, the color of a white conch, is white, because of being a color." Although the statement that the color of a white conch is white is correct, the opponent objects, "That does not follow," meaning that "It does not follow that whatever is a color is necessarily white." The phrase "If you say that it does not follow" occurs throughout Desideri's text. The other interjection of the hypothetical opponent comes in the form of a question or statement, marked by "If you say . . ." or "If you think . . ."

Desideri begins his refutation of rebirth with this declaration: "If you Tibetans employ from your own tradition a correct inferential reasoning familiar to the other party [i.e., the opponent], then it follows that no birth of any sentient being has the quality of being beginningless, because the birth of any sentient being that has already been born does not have the quality of being beginningless." The phrase "correct inferential reasoning familiar to the other party" is a technical term in Buddhist logic. Here, "inferential reasoning" refers not to the internal process of drawing an inference in one's own mind but to the statement of an inference that has a subject, a predicate, and a reason. Such an inference is "correct" if the relationships among those three components of the inference are valid. The term "familiar to the other party" *(parasiddha, gzhan grags)* means that when stating one's position to an opponent, the opponent must be both familiar with the elements of the statement and in general agreement about their nature and relationships. The term is used in discussions of debates between Buddhists and non-Buddhists and receives particular attention in the context of the question whether there can be a "commonly appearing subject" *(chos can mthun snang)* when a Madhyamaka debates with a non-Madhyamaka. Desideri seems to be using the term to tell his Tibetan opponents that if they indeed insist that, in a debate between a Buddhist and a non-Buddhist, the Buddhist must state his position in terms that are known to the opponent and are willing to proceed with the debate on those conditions, then Desideri is going to use the reasoning that is familiar to him, as the other party, to refute the Buddhist claim that rebirth has no beginning.

Desideri's initial argument against the Buddhist claim exploits the ambiguity of the classical Tibetan language where, without the use of qualifiers, there is not always a clear distinction between an abstract noun and a specific noun. In this case, the term "birth" *(skye ba)* can refer to both the general process of rebirth and to the specific birth of an individual person. When it is asserted in Tibetan Buddhism that birth has no beginning, it means that the process of rebirth has no beginning in time and that the sequence of rebirths of an individual also extends back in time without a beginning. When Desideri says, "It follows that no birth of any sentient being has the quality of being beginningless, because the birth of any sentient being that has already been born does not have the quality of being beginningless," he is saying that it does not make sense to say with regard to a living person that their birth is beginningless (*thog ma med pa,* literally "without beginning"), because for that person, their birth has a beginning because it has already begun; it began when they were born. It follows, Desideri says, that the only person for whom it is accurate to say that their birth is beginningless is someone who has not been born; their birth is without beginning because it has not begun. This argument is not particularly compelling, but this kind of wordplay is quite common on the debating courtyard of a Tibetan monastery.

Desideri develops a related argument against the doctrine that rebirth has no beginning, again playing on the meaning of the word *skye ba,* which can mean both "birth" and "production," declaring that the notion of birth and the notion of prior existence, both of which the Buddhists seek to maintain, are incompatible. Drawing on the Buddhist theory of causation, Desideri argues that birth entails something that did not exist in the past coming into existence in the present; the Tibetan term *sngar med gsar skye* means "the new production of what did not exist in the past." Therefore, it is illogical to hold that birth has no beginning, because birth is by definition the coming into existence of what did not exist before. Following the famous Madhyamaka strategy of using the opponent's own doctrines to demonstrate the fallacy of those doctrines, Desideri cites a passage from Candrakīrti's *Entrance to the Middle Way* (*Madhyamakāvatāra* 6:8c–9), one of the "five texts" (*gzhung lnga*) of the Geluk academy. In this passage Candrakīrti is criticizing the doctrine of self-production in the Sāṃkhya school of Indian philosophy, according to which only something that already exists in the cause can be produced:

> If it originates from itself it will have no benefit at all;
> Moreover it is illogical for that which had already arisen to re-arise.
> If one conceives what has already arisen to arise once again,

The arising of sprouts and so on will never be obtained here,
And the seed will continue to reproduce until the end of all existence.
In what way can the sprout ever bring about the cessation of the seed?

Desideri argues that if Buddhists hold that birth has no beginning, they must hold that it is preexistent; the logical fallacies that the Buddhists ascribe to the Sāṃkhya position are equally present in their own.

In the next selection translated from the *Inquiry,* Desideri sets aside his attack on the Tibetan claim that birth has no beginning to consider another famous, and less philosophically ponderous, claim put forth in support of the doctrine of rebirth: that some people remember their past lives. Such reports are found throughout the Buddhist world but they play a particular role in Tibetan Buddhism, where they are used to identify the next incarnation of what is called an "incarnate lama" *(sprul sku).* After a high lama (including the Dalai Lama but also many other high lamas) dies, his followers seek to locate his next incarnation. One of the tests that they use is to present the young child with the possessions of the previous lama (such things as teacups and rosaries), together with a similar item, and ask the child to select the correct item, that is, the item that had belonged to him in a previous life.

It is noteworthy that Desideri takes up this more quotidian proof for rebirth. Some background to his decision to do so is found in his *Historical Notices,* where he discusses this phenomenon at some length; he was clearly fascinated by it. Indeed, he devotes three chapters to the topic. The first is entitled "Of the Grand Lama, Chief of This Religion." With regard to the identification of possessions, he writes, "During these examinations and interrogations, the boy will declare that in his previous life such and such a thing happened, that his confidants were so and so, that he often used certain books whose shape and other details he would specify, say where this or that vestment is in a chest locked in such and such a fashion, and in this same way he will give many specific details."[22] The second chapter is called "Persuasive Reasons Why the Above-Mentioned Creation of a New Grand Lama Is the Direct Work of the Devil," and the third chapter is "Reply to the Arguments of Those Who Judge the Above-Mentioned Deception to Be the Artifice of Men and Not of the Devil." It is a sign of his grudging respect for the incarnate lamas he had encountered that he can only attribute their existence to the supernatural and sinister. He notes, for example, that

the place "where the above-mentioned fraud occurs is Tibet, a civilized, pop-
ulated country with sharp-witted people. This is not a question of fooling
some ignoramuses among the common folk but of deceiving whole peoples
of different languages and countries, skillful and feared governors, vigilant
judges, and an absolute sovereign king who would take his revenge on all
those who might try to raise someone to a throne so close to his own by
means of fraud and factionalism."[23]

In addition, these children are impressive. He describes a three-year-old
boy, unable, as Desideri says, "to tell the difference between his wet nurse's
husband and his own father."[24] And yet the child "does not make any errors
in his responses, nor does what he says prove inconsistent, nor is he caught
in any lies concerning the evidence and proofs that he gives of his previous
life in the world. This is not a trick that his mother or nurse could have taught
him or that any men could, however their great cleverness in pretense and
promptness in fabrication."[25] This is not just true of the Dalai Lama. "All of
them manage in the same way to behave with a certain external composure,
gravity, and dignity proper to holy persons, which causes great astonishment.
Because as soon as the young man is called lama we see him suddenly
endowed with an almost superhuman spirit, taking on the dignity and re-
serve proper to a priest."[26]

For our purposes, then, in his *Historical Notices* Desideri sees the phenomenon of the incarnate lama, not as proof of rebirth, but instead as proof of
the Devil at work in Tibet. He takes a more philosophical approach in the
Inquiry, without mentioning the Devil, at least by name.

The translation of this section begins with the hypothetical Tibetan opponent conceding that Desideri's previous argument (not included in the
translation) has been correct: that it is untenable to claim that virtuous deeds
necessarily result in rebirth as a human (among the six realms of rebirth
as a god, demigod, human, animal, ghost, or denizen of hell). Next, the
opponent puts forth another, rather more "empirical" argument in support of rebirth: that lamas remember their past lives, as evidenced by the
fact that lamas are able to correctly identify possessions that belonged to
their previous incarnations.

Desideri defers a direct response to this claim about memories of past lives,
approaching it instead in a roundabout way. He begins by returning to his
point that there is no certainty that virtuous deeds done in the past will result in rebirth as a human; his implication is that if a lama remembers his

possessions from his previous life, it would have to have been the case that he was a human in his previous life, and was reborn as a human in his next life because he has performed the virtuous deeds that result in human birth. Desideri argues that this cannot be assumed. He cites a number of Buddhist texts in support of his point, noting that, up to the moment of death, all manner of factors may intervene to determine the next lifetime, in both positive and negative ways. In Buddhism in general, the state of mind at the moment of death is said to be of great importance. Each sentient being carries with them a large store of seeds that serve as the primary cause for an entire lifetime. It is not the case that at the time of death, the deeds done in that life are weighed, with scales tipping toward either a good birth or a bad birth. Instead, a single deed serves as the primary cause of an entire lifetime, and that deed may have been done in any lifetime in the past. It is said that it is the state of mind at the moment of death that determines which one of those seeds from this infinite store fructifies as the next lifetime.

The Buddhist texts that Desideri cites make it clear that there are various antidotes—things like regret, confession, and the promise to refrain from an action in the future—that can defuse the power of negative deeds, so much so that a deed that would have resulted in rebirth in hell in the next lifetime can be reduced to a headache in this lifetime. In the same way, negative factors can weaken the potency of a virtuous deed to lead to a happy rebirth. Desideri writes, "A person with the power to distinguish between good and bad may perform and accumulate perfect deeds from the time they are born. However, as long as they are alive and until the final moment of death has passed, there is no certainty as to whether they will take delight and pleasure in what is virtuous in such a way that they do not discard or turn away from them, or whether they will weaken virtue and the capacity of the seeds of virtue. It must be concluded that as long as one is alive and until the final moment of death has passed, there is no certainty as to whether one will attain a pleasant fruition or one will undergo limitless suffering after one's death."

Desideri next turns to the relationship between the persons of the former and later lifetimes. Are they the same or different? He has his Tibetan opponent concede that they are neither the same nor different ultimately, but that they are the same conventionally. Desideri dismisses this immediately, saying that if two things are conventionally the same, they must be present at the same time, and that is clearly not the case for the persons of the former and later lifetime. In support of this, Desideri cites a number of texts in which the Buddha says that he was such and such a person in a former life; hence he was not the same person. He is even able to cite Nāgārjuna's *Verses on the Middle Way* (*Mūlamadhyamakakārikā* 27.3) in support of this: "It is not tenable to say, / 'I arose in the past.' / What arose in former lives / Is not this same [person]." Indeed, Desideri moves rather quickly through the claim that the persons of the former and later lives are the same in order to move to the alternative, that they are different. Here, he attacks two of the fundamental claims of Buddhist karma theory.

In Tibetan presentations of karma, four general characteristics are enumerated: (1) that deeds are definite *(las nges pa),* that is, that virtuous deeds produce happiness and non-virtuous deeds produce suffering; (2) that deeds are increasing *(las 'phel che ba),* that is, that the store of karmic seeds is constantly growing; (3) that deeds done are not lost *(las byas pa chud mi za ba),* that is, that deeds do not lose their karmic potency over time, so that a deed done millions of lifetimes in the past can still have effects in the future; and (4) that one does not encounter deeds that one did not do *(las ma byas dang mi phrad pa),* that is, that one does not experience the effects of deeds done by others. Desideri will argue that if the person of the past life and the person of the present life are different, the last two pillars of Buddhist karma theory are untenable.

He rather quickly dismisses the claim that deeds are not lost, saying that we must understand a deed to be "lost" when the effect of the deed does not appear where the deed was done. This would mean that the effect would need to be experienced in the same lifetime in which the deed is done, something quite contrary to Buddhist karma theory; for Desideri it is a consequence of asserting that the person of the past life and the person of the present life are different. If they are in fact different, then the deed done by the person of the past life is lost if it is experienced by someone else.

He uses the same argument against the notion that one does not experience the effects of deeds that one did not do. If the former person and the present person are different, and one claims that the present person experiences the effects of deeds done by the former person, then the present person does indeed experience the effects of deeds he did not do. Desideri writes, "When one analyzes whether or not one encounters [the fruition of] deeds one did not do, one must analyze whether or not the doer of the deeds accumulated in the past appears where one encounters the fruition of the deed that was accumulated in the past. In that case, if you assert that the self at the time of the former lifetime and the self of the present are different, and assert that the former self does not experience the fruition but the later self enjoys the fruition of the deeds done by the former self, then you must assert that one does encounter [the fruition of] deeds one did not do." He has his Tibetan opponent try to avoid this problem by saying that the two persons are different but their continuum *(rgyud)* is the same. Desideri resorts to Madhyamaka reasoning, complete with quotations from Nāgārjuna and Candrakīrti, to dismiss this.

It is at this point that Desideri turns to the question of memories of former lives. As we shall see, he does not deny that incarnate lamas accurately describe the possessions of those said to be their former incarnations. Instead, he denies that such descriptions derive from memory. Beyond this, he finds it rather unseemly that something as banal as identifying a teacup owned by a dead lama would be put forward as proof of a religious doctrine. Indeed, he finds it un-Buddhist. And so he begins this section with two poems. The first seems to be his own composition. It pretends to be the words of an incarnate lama who, although apparently already liberated from the rounds of rebirth, returns from the dead to reclaim his possessions, rather than have them go to his next incarnation. He writes:

My clothes and furniture and pleasing things,
Returning, there is none I will not find again.
Bring these to my presence, the one with power.
If disputed, it is certain that strife and war will arise.

The last line may be an allusion to disputes that arose when there were rival claimants to the title of the previous lama's reincarnation. Desideri witnessed one of the most famous cases of this in Tibetan history, when Lhazang Khan deposed the Sixth Dalai Lama and named his own candidate (who may have also been his son) as the "true" Sixth Dalai Lama.

Desideri skillfully follows this poem with another, a passage from the *Lalitavistara,* a famous biography of the Buddha, in which the Buddha himself declares that death steals everything one possessed; they will never be found again.

Still, Desideri acknowledges the special status of incarnate lamas, and uses this to argue against their memory of former lives. He presents an accurate account of how Tibetans describe incarnate lamas: as saints who have, with great effort, memorized and mastered all of the fine points of the dharma, devoting all of their lives and all of their energies to understanding "without error what is to be recognized, what is to be abandoned, what is to be actualized, and what is to be cultivated by those who wish to attain the supreme goal that beings can achieve." Yet when they are reborn as humans in the very next lifetime, they retain no memory of what had been the focus of their entire life, remembering instead a few trivial possessions. He asks rather mockingly, "Did you or did you not comprehend and take to heart the essential points of such things as cultivating faith, obeisance, offering, confession of sins, rejoicing [in the virtue of others], imploring [the buddhas and bodhisattvas] to turn the wheel of the dharma, requesting [them not to pass into nirvāṇa], and dedication [of merit]?" He is referring to the standard seven-branched service that begins almost every Tibetan Buddhist ritual and which all lamas know by heart. Somehow, the newly born lama seems not to remember it. Indeed, his amnesia of the dharma is so complete that he must begin his training again. Desideri reports, again accurately, the standard Tibetan response: that the process of human birth is so traumatic that everything is forgotten. In that case, Desideri responds, if the newborn child cannot remember his past studies, how could he remember his past possessions?

Desideri next turns to another Buddhist argument for memories of past lives. In his *Entrance to the Middle Way*, Candrakīrti uses an Indian folk belief as a metaphor for memories of former lives. A hut with a thatched roof has a vessel of yogurt inside. There is a dove living on the thatched roof of the hut. Although the dove never sets foot inside the hut, its footprints appear on the surface of the yogurt. Candrakīrti uses this to explain the memory of former lives, but his main point is that despite the fact that everything is empty of intrinsic nature, this does not preclude the possibility of change, something that Candrakīrti calls "inconceivable." Desideri embarks on a lengthy exegesis of the metaphor, not so much challenging the feasibility of the footprints appearing in the yogurt, but spelling out how the elements of the metaphor map onto the Buddhist epistemological categories, focusing especially on the eighteen elements *(dhātu, khams)*, the six objects, the six organs, and the six consciousnesses. His point is that if such a metaphor is used to argue that the present person remembers the possessions of the past person, then it must be used to argue that the present person remembers the learning of the past person.

Desideri next turns to his argument that it is possible for a person to accurately describe the possessions of a dead person without actually remembering them, that is, the surface fact of the accurate description does not entail that the explanation given for the accuracy of the description is valid. Here, Desideri resorts to the well-known Buddhist example of the magician's illusion, in which a magician recites a mantra that causes a pebble to appear as a horse or an elephant. The animal is equally seen by the magician and the audience. However, the audience believes the appearance to be true while the magician knows that it is false. In the same way, one can concede the accuracy of the description without conceding that the accuracy derives from memory of a former life. Indeed, it is possible to say something that is accurate that is also a lie. Citing Candrakīrti, Desideri gives the example of a person who accuses a thief of being a thief, without having seen the person steal.

Desideri then goes to the next step, saying that the description cannot be accurate because the description is not based on the knowledge of the speaker. Desideri is willing to concede only the words of the description. He does not acknowledge their accuracy or the reason given for their accuracy. Where, then, do the words come from? We recall that in the *Historical Notices,* Desideri was reluctant to ascribe the behavior and memory of incarnate lamas to trickery or fraud. He does not dispute reports of the dignified demeanor of toddlers or their ability to accurately locate hidden possessions of a previous lama. He argues instead that such marvels are the work of the Devil. He does not mention the Devil in the *Inquiry.* Yet rather tellingly, in discussing the ability of the present person to remember the possessions of the past person, he gives the example of someone who is possessed by a demon and is able to speak in languages they do not know. He writes, "Thus, for example, a person possessed by an evil spirit speaks in various different languages and they are perceived by the ear consciousness. Although those words are uttered from his mouth, not only is it untenable that he is learned in various different languages, one must assert that it is untenable that he is speaking in various different languages."

Desideri returns to what he sees as the greatest flaw in the claim for memories of past lives: the inability of the person of the present to remember the

Buddhist doctrine that the person of the past devoted his life to learning. If rebirth as a human is the fruition of deeds of perfect virtue, then the fruition itself must not contradict perfect virtue. His implication is that the memory of the doctrine would be consistent with perfect virtue, while the memory of one's former wealth would not be. If there is a contradiction between the cause (the deed of perfect virtue) and the effect (the memory of material possessions), this can only be further proof that the person of the present is unrelated to the person of the past. One of Desideri's aims, of course, is to argue for the existence of an immortal soul, a soul that carries with it both virtue and sin. And so he adds, almost in passing, a criticism of the Buddhist doctrine of emptiness: "Regarding the person who accumulates deeds of perfect virtue, without his intrinsic nature serving as the means for sowing and planting the seeds that yield the fruition of perfect virtue, the virtues of body, speech, and mind will not arise, and, without the arising of the virtues of body, speech, and mind, the person who accumulates deeds of perfect virtue does not come to be established. Therefore, wherever the person who accumulates deeds of perfect virtue is observed, the lack of intrinsic nature of the person who performs deeds of perfect virtue does not exist."

At this point in the text, Desideri adopts a new strategy to attack the Tibetan belief in reincarnation. He sets aside the rhetorical form of critical analysis, with its dense labyrinth of syllogisms, and resorts to a form of cultural imperialism, declaring that the Tibetans' belief in reincarnation cannot possibly be correct because no one else in the world believes it; it is an eccentric view held by a tiny portion of the world's population. He begins with a request from a Tibetan, described as "an impartial and capable person, led and guided by the rope of various pure tenets and solid and irrefutable reasons, who is unclouded by the darkness of prejudice." This person states that, given the vastness of the world and variety of the people who inhabit it, it would be wrong to conclude that everyone in the world is incapable of distinguishing what is reasonable from what is unreasonable. He goes on to say that in some parts of the world, people tell stories about previous lives, and so the belief in former lives becomes part of their religion. Yet everywhere else in the world, people believe in the rewards of virtue, without telling stories about past lives. Indeed, the belief in past lives and the claim that one can remember those lives are "abodes of error and perversions of the perfect faith." He appeals to the Christian priest, the "star head lama," who has far more experience of the world, to "act with kindness to all in the snowy land by clearing away all the stains of doubt and misconception and teaching the articles of the unmistaken faith."

In response, Desideri provides something of a geography lesson, explaining that there are four continents: Europe, Asia, Africa, and America. Europe is "the main one and is wondrous." The religion there is "the excellent religion of the star heads." Asia has five religions: that of the star heads, that of the Jews, that of the Muslims, that of the *ācāryas* (presumably Hinduism), and "the system of Tibet, China, and Nepal," by which Desideri likely means Buddhism, a term that would not be coined in Europe until the next century. In Africa some follow the religion of the star heads and some follow the texts of the Muslims, but most people are pagans. Desideri uses the term *mu stegs pa* (*tīrthika* in Sanskrit), a term used in Buddhist texts to describe non-Buddhists, especially Hindus. In America, "the excellent religion of the star heads is very widespread and there are also many pagans."

Desideri declares that nowhere in Europe, Africa, or America does anyone believe in the cycle of rebirth and no one tells stories about past lives, "lying about how they can remember and describe their earlier experiences as if they were coming here from other worlds." We might note in passing that Matteo Ricci had made a similar argument against rebirth more than a century earlier in his *True Meaning of the Lord of Heaven* (written in Chinese). There Ricci notes that someone who had lived a previous life should be able to remember it, but Ricci reports that he has never met anyone who does. When his Chinese interlocutor objects that there are many stories in Daoist and Buddhist texts of those who do, Ricci dismisses this as the work of the Devil and notes that it is significant that such claims only occur in Buddhist countries; in other countries, from ancient times to the present, great sages have been able to memorize thousands of books but none of them can remember a single event from a previous life. If one cannot remember one's previous existence as an animal, why would the Lord of Heaven have created reincarnation as a means of discouraging sin?[27] Despite the similarity of the arguments, there is no evidence that Desideri knew Ricci's work.

Desideri goes on to explain to his Tibetan audience that the peoples of the other continents have a completely different view of the pleasures and sufferings of the world. The Buddhists believe that the pleasures of the world are the result of virtues performed in the past, and that the sufferings of the world are the result of non-virtues. However, everyone else in the world believes that the pleasures of the world are causes of suffering and are to be renounced, and that the sufferings of the world are opportunities for goodness and are to be welcomed. Furthermore, they believe that when one dies, one goes to the next world, never to return, and that the next world is eternal (unlike the heavens and hells of the Buddhists). "The inconceivable number of persons who follow the three religions of the star heads, the Jews, and the Muslims and who live in or rule the many lands and islands of this part called Asia do not agree with each other on a great many articles of faith. Nonetheless, understanding that the pleasures and sufferings of this world of the living are the causes of virtue and non-virtue and that it is untenable that they be the fruition of virtue and non-virtue, they hold that the wandering in *saṃsāra* is a misconception of childish common beings disturbed by the sleep of ignorance and is a perversion of the perfect faith." If Tibetans believe that those who perform acts of virtue are reborn as humans in Tibet and tell stories of their past lives, then they must believe that those who perform acts of virtue are also born as humans in other lands. Yet no one born as a human in those other lands tells stories of their past lives. It is therefore untenable that Tibetans do so. If the footprints of doves are found in vessels of yogurt in the thatched-roof houses of Tibet, then the footprints of doves should be found in vessels in the thatched-roof houses of other countries. They are not. The memory of former lives is thus contradicted by logic, despite the accounts of those lives being heard by a conventional sense consciousness. The scriptures that assert that one is born as a human as a result of deeds of perfect virtue and that assert that those who are reborn as humans remember their past lives, are "polluted by external and internal causes of error and are established as having the quality of being unworthy of trust, like the collapsed relying on the collapsed." Desideri concludes this section with a poem of his own composition. It ends with the exhortation, again paraphrasing Śāntideva, "Do not sleep at the time of learning; / Dispel the darkness of ignorance."[28]

❧ ❧ ❧

Desideri's *Inquiry concerning the Doctrines of Previous Lives and Emptiness, Offered to the Scholars of Tibet by the Star Head Lama called Ippolito* is a remarkable work, one fully deserving a multivolume project that would include a fully annotated translation and commentary. The two excerpts provided here can only provide a flavor of the full work.

The reader will note the extensive and creative use he makes of Tsong kha pa's *Great Treatise on the Stages of the Path to Enlightenment,* a work that Desideri revered and had mastered. He draws most of his exposition of Buddhist doctrine from this work. In addition, he uses the Indian works that Tsong kha pa cites, and he uses them to refute rather than uphold that doctrine, sometimes by using the exact passages themselves, sometimes by adapting them for his own purposes. It would be mistaken, however, to assume that Tsong kha pa was his only source. His own notes from his studies contain long passages from various sūtras, passages that Desideri drew from other texts.

The style of the work is that of the Tibetan scholar-monk, displaying an impressive command of its vocabulary and conventions, including long passages of original poetry. Indeed, the work displays a level of learning difficult to imagine in a foreigner who had arrived in Ladakh just three years before, knowing no Tibetan; one must wonder whether he received assistance. Yet what Tibetan scholar would aid a foreigner in refuting the doctrine of rebirth? We are left unable to account for how Desideri did it and must, at least for the moment, devote our energies to appreciating what he did.

CHAPTER TWO

Selections from *Inquiry concerning the Doctrines of Previous Lives and Emptiness*

❧

Inquiry concerning the Doctrines of Previous Lives
and Emptiness Offered to the Scholars of Tibet
by the Star Head Lama Called Ippolito

[INVOCATION]

There is nothing superior or higher than you, unrivaled, unequaled,
Inexpressible, inconceivable, without measure or end,
Utterly without cessation, reversal, or change,
Naturally free of defect and fault.

Not relying or depending upon another yourself,
All that exists depends upon you.
You know all that exists, just as it is.
For you, everything is ever equal.

Gently but firmly you created all that is.
Impartial to all, you are without bias.

Unrivaled, you are the lord of great compassion.
Happiness, goodness, and all virtues
Are naturally present in you, with no need to cultivate them.
You are the innate source of all happiness.
You are the ultimate form of happiness, as you are of goodness.
You are the sole lord worthy as refuge, worthy of worship.

As my mind, clear, stainless, and unmoving,
Is completely fixed and settled on you,
I offer eulogy and praise that know no end.
I go for refuge to you from the depths of my heart,
With my body, speech, and lucid mind.
I humbly bow down to you.

To rouse from sleep and dispel all darkness
Of all the beings forever beclouded by the gloom of delusion,
Mindlessly sleepwalking in their ignorance,
You act as the sun whose light pervades all.

To compassionately seek out and lead
Those who enter evil paths without dread or fear,
Wandering toward the abyss and toward danger,
You lovingly appeared in this world
As a single being who, without abandoning your indestructible
    nature,
Came to be united with a human nature.

To those sunk in the mud of false religions,
Constantly indulging in misdeeds,
To those locked in the prison of vile views,
You extend the hand of the peerless true religion
In order to compassionately unbind them and lead them out.
You are forever free of fear,
Yet you know how to free others from fear.

In order to cure those tormented
By dangerous diseases incurable by others,
Wrong deeds like desire and hatred,
You became a physician for us common beings.

You became a rain cloud of blessings
Quelling the ever burning flames
Of pride, jealousy, and lust, so difficult to douse.

For those humans who neither know nor seek the source of refuge,
You are like a mother, because you give birth to all good deeds,
You are like a wet nurse, because you give the milk of virtue,
You are a friend, because you turn back all harm.

You are never tainted by impurity.
We are ever stained by impurity.
In order to free us from defilement,
Each day you transform your blood
Endowed with the power to cleanse and completely dispel
All impurity from every mind.

Ever inseparable,
All qualities of goodness reside in you.
Unsullied by fault, never endowed with defect,
You strive for the sake of the sinful,
Without bias toward any human,
Your great compassion impartially enters into them.

The faults that arise as their fruit,
And the potencies that produce the fruition
Of the sinful deeds created
In all humans of the three times;
In order to utterly purify and completely remove these
From the root with nothing remaining,
Like a wound without the slightest scar,
You took on the burden that others could not bear.

In order to benefit others, you regarded oppressive sufferings
As tools for your own happiness.
You did not see unbearable suffering as a burden;
You saw it as a crown.
Accepting these with love and asking to undergo them,
Venturing your body and life you gave away your flesh, blood, body,
    and life.

[1b] Through the kindness of giving up your body and your life
You completely destroyed the inexhaustible sins of the world,
The forces of the demon.

You open the excellent door
To the city of the attainment of all goodness,
Delivering those who follow you
Into the abode of all goodness.
You are the sole lord, guide of all humanity.

Nowhere is there another like you,
Abiding as protector of all humanity,
Because childish beings do not seek your protection
They fall into a frightening place.

You give relief to the destitute.
You are the place of refuge for those who come to have faith,
Who are capable of hope and are heedful.
Seeing the afflictions of those beings who are most oppressed,
In order to dispel all their sufferings,
You always have great compassion for all.
There has never been a place where it did not come forth.

For those whose faith comes from the heart,
What degeneracy is there from which they cannot be delivered?
To those who have devotion,
What goodness and glory is not granted?
Because they have taken you as their refuge, what need is there to
    speak?

Through merely contemplating this,
Marvelous virtue and perfect joy are born,
One's intellect becomes more strong, one's mind becomes more pure,
And then all blessings arise.

"The savior, the glorious leader is pierced on the right."
My mind is fully focused on this fact,
With stainless and unshakable sincerity.
Because his extinction is not known
I offer praise, eulogy, and worship.

By meditating upon the greatness
Of his peerless and captivating deeds,
His unsurpassed virtues, and so on,
Through his wonders, we are drawn to him.

My mind is not satisfied by description.
I go for refuge to him from the depths of my heart,
With my body, speech, and lucid mind.
I humbly bow down to him.

[PREAMBLE]

The news that in this Tibet there are countless scholars,
So versed in the various fields of knowledge,
Has spread in all directions,
Across great oceans and to different lands.

As soon as this touched my ears,
My mind was tormented by wonder;
A great desire arose in me, uncontrollable and
    unstoppable,
To see them with my own eyes,
To gaze insatiably at those scholars of this Tibet.

My mind became focused, free from doubt,
And once decided,
My intention remained as solid as a diamond,
Incapable of being destroyed
By the hundred thousand hardships and obstacles of the long voyage.

So without laziness, from the west
I crossed from one end of the ocean to the other,
Traveling through many lands,
Until I reached Tibet, the essence of the journey.
Having arrived, my desire to meet [the scholars] increased.
Yet, like a simpleton, I did not understand the language
And so my wish was not fulfilled.

At present, I cannot meet in person
Each and every scholar [in Tibet]
To pay my homage and offer entreaties.
I offer at your feet, with a single-focused intention,
My entreaties and praise in a brief form.

E MA HO!
You are the ridgepole of Tibet most firm,
You are the lamp of Tibet blazing bright,
You have become the jewel of Tibet,
I bow my head at your feet.
Pray care for me with compassion.

You are like a great star shining on Tibet,
You are like the precious heart of Tibet,
You have become the jewel ornament of Tibet,
I offer this entreaty in your presence.
Pray forbear my arrogance.

You are the treasury of Tibet most precious,
You are the source of happiness in Tibet,
You have become the eyes, heart, and life of Tibet;
As I speak your praise,
I look with upturned eyes.
Pray show me your loving smile.

Your speech is suitable for all,
It creates joy in the learned,
It expands the minds of the medium,
It clears the eyes of the lowly,
Completely dispelling the darkness of doubt.
It is the most excellent medicine for all beings,
Captivating the mind of those who listen.

Your mind is like a cloudless sky,
Its nature clear and soft.
Goodness flows from it and descends.
Blazing with the light of wisdom,
It is like the sun that illuminates all. [2a]

Compassionately benefiting others,
It is like the moon dripping with ambrosia.

Your qualities are most wondrous,
Adorned with the ornaments of qualities.
When described, all that is praiseworthy is gathered in you;
When praised, all that is amazing is gathered in you.

You are like the light of moon or sun,
So clear and bright.
Without difficulty, as if directly,
You easily bring meaning to the mind.

You are like the ocean that is difficult to fathom.
Your way of knowing is to seek the depths.
Not knowing how to remain in the middle;
You delight in reaching the depths of knowledge.

You are like an eagle,
Leaving behind the lowly earth to rise into the sky.
Leaving behind the variety seen in the world,
You strive for the profound meaning.

You are like a general, skilled in combat,
Standing proud in the face of his enemy.
You are like the sharpest weapon
Carefully cutting through all doubt.
You are like a powerful elephant,
Endowed with steadfast strength and great force.
You are like a knot tied in silken thread,
Soft and tight combined in one.
You are like stainless moonlight
That touches the golden mountains in autumn.

Among the qualities of your wisdom resides
The whiteness of good deeds unlike all others,
Like a waterfall in the rainy season,
Growing stronger and stronger, filling the ocean.

With great diligence, never interrupted,
Your qualities continue to grow.

Like a garden where various flowers grow,
Their fragrance filling the four directions,
All corners of the world
Are filled with your fame.

Like a powerful monarch seated
On a throne arrayed with jewels,
The happiness of Tibet rests
On your qualities, O Wise One.

In order to make this entreaty
Of utmost importance in your presence,
I have come from a great distance.
Looking upon me with eyes of kindness,
You have held me with love and compassion
As if they were your two hands.

So mustering my courage in your presence
I offer you various arguments,
Specifically in the form of inference,
On two topics: former lives
And the emptiness of intrinsic existence.

Without the eyes of bias,
Utterly renouncing such things as
Enmity born from the faulty eyes of partisanship,
But with the clear eyes of intelligence,
Look carefully with your mind and analyze
All of these most important points.
If you are pleased to follow
The pure and stainless truth,
Your qualities will be abundant
And through blessings of the transcendent
May you attain all that is auspicious.
May you be transported to the shores of salvation,
The supreme essence of all aspirations.

These days those who strive for the quality
Of understanding the fields of knowledge well,
Are mostly weak in their efforts
And unskilled in the essentials of practice.[1]

Hearing about the fields of knowledge, their ears are biased;
Seeing the fields of knowledge, their eyes are biased.
They have no essence, only conceit.
They have no perception, only clouded vision.

Because their ears are biased,
They lack the power to distinguish truth and falsehood;
They lack a path that will please the learned;
They are wrapped in thick darkness.

Those with only biased eyes
Lack the power of mind to distinguish
White and black, religion and irreligion;
They are completely bereft of religion.

How can crops grow in a field
That cannot be cleared,
That cannot be tilled?
Useless, it will produce no fruit.

A motionless body of water,
Moving neither up or down
Is bereft of qualities;
Soon it will be stagnant.

A body whose postures are limited
Is bereft of pleasure
And afflicted by illness.
When it is disturbed, it will decline and die.

With different metals, sticks, and tools
Farmland can be tilled and transformed;
Those who strive to clear the land
Produce abundant crops.
When they find iron, copper, gold, silver, lapis, and turquoise,
And other precious stones
They polish and perfect them.[2]

Ships change their course
When they encounter changing obstacles

Such as reefs, rocks, and sea monsters.
However, a captain among the merchants,
Skilled in steering the ship in a different direction
Saves his life and the merchants,
And reaches the other shore.

Therefore those who have clear intelligence,
Who are not obscured by the darkness of prejudice,
Who seek salvation from the abyss of fears
That destroys the mind itself, [2b]
Who seek to reach the shores of definite goodness;
May those fortunate beings
Listen with single-pointed attention.[3]

Here, having seen that, among all the fields of knowledge, the knowledge of religion is of very great importance, one must understand the very great importance of removing, as if with an antidote, such faults as having ears that are biased when listening to a religion and having eyes that are biased when studying a religion. Regarding the religions of others, I can conclude without difficulty that looking at what is written and listening to what is explained will be sources of joy and delight to the minds of the learned in this Tibet. Yet to look at all the different religions of others or at all of the essential points of a specific religion that one values with just a blink of an eye is like not looking at all. Thus, abandoning the idea of looking at [all the] other religions, I will erect in the presence of the illumined intellects of Tibetan scholars an object for their examination: the stainless, perfect, excellent, and supreme religion of the star heads. I will explain it by elaborating—from the perspective of [the doctrines] of previous lives and the emptiness of intrinsic existence—on just two cherished articles of belief of that perfect and steadfast teaching.

For example, those who always live in a place in the midst of dense darkness become accustomed to it over a long time. If that place were to be pervaded in a single instant by a perfect light, very clear and very bright, they would fear that they were being harmed and, unable to bear the illumination of the perfect light, they would strive hard with their hands, turning their eyes away, to keep from being touched by it. In the same way, those afflicted with the fault of having eyes that are biased when studying a religion become accustomed over a long time to only listening to and studying one religion. When their eyes of intelligence are touched by the very bright light of another cherished religion that is stainless, perfect, excellent, and supreme, most of them will experience fear and anxiety, worrying that they are committing such faults as false understanding and false views at odds with [their own] religion. The thought will arise in them to block with strenuous efforts this very bright light and pure illumination and they will turn the eyes of their mind away from it by all possible means. Thus, to overcome such baseless doubts and fears, I offer in the presence of the scholars, renowned for their knowledge and [recognized as] authoritative in this Tibet, this entreaty from the perspective of another religion. This has four parts:

I.   The benefits of studying others' religions
II. How to see the other's religion in a wise way
III. Demonstrating how, having studied the other's religion, there is benefit in debating about one's own religion
IV. Actual debates on the essential points of so-called previous births[4]

I. THE BENEFITS OF STUDYING OTHERS' RELIGIONS

For example, although there are many different types of clothing, language, script, food, and drinks in many different lands, over the generations people have viewed these [lands] as a cause for accumulating various articles of comfort, jewels, and riches and as causes for obtaining much benefit and happiness. In the same manner, although each of the many different religions has different views, conduct, and meditative practices, to listen to or study these in a wise way is a cause of gaining much benefit.

The Benefit of Becoming Thoroughly Learned in Religion

For example, the ear of someone who has experienced the sounds of stringed instruments, wind instruments, drums, and cymbals is versed in the sounds of music. Similarly, the eye of someone who has looked carefully at colors such as white, red, yellow, green, blue, and so on, is versed in color. A physician who is carefully trained in the many different methods of healing, such as purgatives, emetics, curatives, and ointments, is versed in the areas of healing. The honey collected from the various essences of different flowers has the most excellent and pleasing taste. [3a] Likewise, the mind of one who listens to, studies, and analyzes one's own and others' religions with the ears and eyes of intelligence will be adorned with incomparable knowledge of religion.

The Benefit of Creating an Entirely Firm Mind in Order to Directly Experience Religion

For example, although all Tibetans are different in terms of their physical size and facial shape, there is great conformity in such things as language, script, food, drink, and clothing. In the same manner, although two different religions may differ in one or two ways, they are able to accord greatly with each other in such things as philosophical views, what to accept and reject among virtuous and non-virtuous deeds, and how to meditate. Thus, to encounter another tradition that accords greatly with one's own tradition and to understand them both is like having two butter lamps burning in a single room, or one gold or silver ring shining with the light of two diamonds. Again, if a tree receives the appropriate amount of water from separate sources—rainwater and water from a stream—its roots will grow large, and the tree will be more and more firmly fixed in the earth. In the same way, by moistening one's mind with the complete instructions and essential points of one's own religion as well as another religion that accords with it, one's body, speech, and mind will become most conducive to religion and one will, like a thick nail, abide with a firm aspiration to religion. Again, travelers set out on an unfamiliar road on a journey that leads to a distant destination. When one is traveling alone, from time to time one will be afflicted by the agony of doubt that one has gone off onto a different winding road, not the right road that leads straight to one's desired destination. But if one sees many other travelers traveling like oneself to the same final destination, one's mind is uplifted and gains confidence. Without any sense of wavering in one's mind, one will befriend the other travelers one has met on the road and seek their company. Similarly, religion is the path that leads to the ultimate destination of the supreme reality of definite goodness, the sole object of aspiration of this auspicious human existence. Thus, by listening to and fully studying others' religions, one will understand that a great many learned ones of other countries have set out on the path to the ultimate destination of the supreme reality of definite goodness. In doing so, the mind of a learned one will gain deep and clear conviction in the path they have chosen and create a stable faith based on conviction; all the pains, such as uncertainty, doubt, and fear, will be pacified.

The Benefit of Creating a Strong and Powerful Sense of Joy in Religion by Engaging in Appropriate Religious Deeds and Infusing One's Mind with Religion

Even if the other religion that one listens to or studies is not only inconsistent with one's own religion but is a degraded view, sows misdeeds, and is completely degenerate, [listening to or studying it] is a cause of benefit and joy to the mind of a learned one. For example, even though silver, iron, copper, wood, clay, and so forth are deficient and degenerate compared to gold, among these some can be used as currency to purchase gold, some as a tool and means to discover gold, some to cleanse all the stains and impurities of gold, and some to help mold the gold into whatever ornament one desires, such as earrings, by actually making the gold pliant and malleable; a craftsman can turn [gold] into any ornament he desires. Similarly, even if one concedes that the other religion that one listens to or studies is most degenerate compared to one's own, a learned one who engages in such listening or studying will reflect, "At times, the minds of incalculable people are bereft of religion and are constantly enveloped in dense darkness," and will be utterly moved to compassion. He will then exhort himself and pray from the depths of his heart, without despair and weariness, to make the light of the perfect truth, excellent and sublime, of the stainless and thoroughly pure religion shine upon the minds of these people. Taking the virtue he himself has performed as an example, he will gather all roots of virtue together and dedicate them with a strong intention of *bodhicitta*[5] so that they will never become exhausted. On other occasions, [3b] he will contemplate the fruit of the negative deeds caused by the afflictions and misdeeds of others and create an unbearable sense of shame and remorse for his own afflictions and misdeeds. With the wisdom of discriminative awareness he meditates again and again on the defects of these [afflictions], creating a sense of pain and sadness. Using this awareness, he turns away from the forces of darkness and purifies them. On other occasions, seeing those who live in what is false and irreligious, without faith, passing their time without purpose, he recognizes that, "Though I abide in truth and religion, having come under the power of laziness, I am like one who goes to the island of jewels and returns empty-handed." Like one who awakens from the stupidity of sleep, things of supreme significance will arise in him, such as the realization that the practice of religion is of great meaning, the qualities of faith, positive deeds and their fruit, and the benefits of the practice of study, reflection, and meditation. Through contemplating these benefits again and again with the wisdom of discriminative awareness, his mind will come to be moistened and clear. With this awareness, his mind will turn toward and take joy in goodness, and his mind will be moistened with virtue. Like gold that is made soft and malleable, the heart of the learned one will come ever closer to the principal religious deeds.

Also, for example, through the means of placing a dark object behind a glass, there newly appears upon the surface of the glass a clear and superior light that is more pleasing than before. Also, when a skilled artist repeatedly paints shaded lines in a variety of colors—white, red, yellow, green, and blue—it creates something amazing that is beautiful to behold and pleasing, and the painted forms come to have an unrivaled appearance, inducing joy and pleasure to the eye. In the same way, one needs to listen to and study both the stainless perfect religion and false wrong religions, like placing true and false, white and black face to face, as if they compete with each other. Through the method of rubbing away the surface, in the presence of minds and practices of the learned, the stainless and pure religion will newly emerge in a way that is much more beautiful, pleasing, and worthy of being cherished. The mind of the learned naturally takes joy in such a religion and upholds it as their crown ornament. To the best of their knowledge and ability, they will deeply admire and revere it with fervor and strength for a long time.

Also, for example, some who have an excellent complexion, a pleasing form because of a good physique, who have few injuries or are free of illness, who have great power in their activities, whose wealth is unmatched, who have many friends and relatives and a large circle, such people rely on the causes of happiness as if they were ceaseless. The longer they become accustomed to them, the more their perception of those objects of joy and happiness as pleasurable and pleasing begins to fade. If they were to see with their own eyes many lowly poor people without wealth or protection, bereft of food, drink, and clothing; many common people afflicted by impaired sense organs and severe diseases; and various wretched people unbearably tormented by pain, their perception of their own good and peerless fortune, with few injuries, lack of illness, and strength, stability, and wealth, will grow in the strength of its joy and its constancy. Promising to strive to protect and increase them without reversal, they will come to understand that to the extent that they strive for those things, they will find happiness. In the same way, some people who abide in the most excellent religion that is completely stainless, utterly pure, and superior, listen to, think about, and meditate on all the excellent points of the teaching and the complete instructions. As a result, the longer they become accustomed to it, the more they suffer discouragement, their fervor weakens and completely declines, and they squander themselves through such things as forgetfulness. However, if they were to see all the people enveloped in inconceivable laziness and darkness who, because they abide in impure religions and are completely bereft of the dharma, are possessed by the harm of the afflictions[6] and wander like a sighted person who has gone blind into regions of the immeasurable and inexhaustible flaws of the afflictions [4a], they will come to recognize that compared to those abiding in irreligion, it is inappropriate to be lax in one's service to a pure religion.

Thus, first, being mindful of the qualities of one's own religion, one should cultivate happiness and rejoice in it, like a beggar who finds a treasure. Next, even for the utterly perfect religion, it depends on practicing in accordance with precepts on what is to be adopted and what is to be rejected. This too should be followed on the basis of a strong and firm will to protect [the precepts]; one will create a wish to do so through long contemplation of the faults of not protecting them and the benefits of protecting them.

> Free from discouragement and endowed with effort,
> One attains what has not been attained
> And protects what one has attained without losing it.
> There is nothing that cannot be attained or accomplished.

> Passing days and nights in fruitful ways,
> You will never be deficient in gathering good qualities.
> With goals superior to the ways of men,
> You will flourish like a summer flower.

Thus, through medical science, one who is skilled in medicine and knows how to make medicines turns a virulent poison into a remedy against poison. In the same way, through reasoned analysis that skillfully listens to it and studies it, even a poisonous religion, impure, false, and malignant, can be completely turned into a collection of positive qualities, goodness, and benefit. Also, for example, although the bark of a sugar cane tree lacks any flavor or potency, it is known that there is still a soft core within, which is where one finds the pleasing and delicious flavor. The intelligent person gives up the pleasure of eating the bark and always strives to find the superior core within. In the same way, in the teachings of all the impure false religions there is a bad and rough bark on the outside. However, when they are placed into a great device that skillfully listens to them and studies them, if they are crushed the way that sugarcane is crushed, one will find their essence, which is many eloquent statements, truthful presentations, correct and reliable tenets, and strivings for goodness; the rough bark of irreligion, falsity, and evil tenets can be completely discarded. The mind of the learned will take only the well-crushed essence that benefits the mind and will joyfully partake of the sweet taste again and again.

Again, for example, fire defeats firewood, water defeats flames, flames defeat all dense darkness, and dense darkness completely defeats all types of material objects [by making them invisible]. In the same way, the bright light of the great power of perfect truth, which is pleasing and naturally captivates the mind, will destroy and defeat all the dense darkness of falsehood, the blazing flames of superior tenets will destroy and defeat all the thornbushes of evil tenets, and the cool clear water of stainless religion will destroy and defeat all the filth of irreligion. Also, for example, such pairs—light and darkness, fire and wood, cool water and filth—remain separate. Thus, without their opposites, one cannot harm the other, and darkness, thorn trees, and filth can never be defeated. In the same way, truth and falsehood, superior tenets and evil tenets, and religion and irreligion are heard and seen by individual people; they come into contact with their individual ears and eyes separately. Thus, without their opposite, one cannot refute the other, and one will never find the freedom in which the darkness of ignorance is dissipated, the thornbushes of evil tenets are burned and consumed, and the filth of irreligion is cleansed. Therefore, if a learned person who abides in the perfect religion that is stainless, steadfast, peerless, and supreme were to listen to and study another religion that is imperfect, a false teaching and an evil twisted path of irreligion, it is appropriate for such fortunate persons to generate *bodhicitta* before long, and with a strong motivation to serve others' welfare, strive to be a competent person who takes on the burden of benefiting others.

> Seeing beings debased in the thick darkness of ignorance,
> He will come to be the sun shining with powerful waves of light. [4b]
> Seeing beings fallen into flames of suffering, blazing without control
> In a world of thick clouds of the smoke of ignorance that plagues beings,
> With a sense of urgency of someone whose forehead is aflame,
> He will come to [help beings] swiftly attain the inexhaustible and highest
>   fruition.

The benefit of discarding the evil path and entering the good path is the following. For example, some Tibetans have never been outside Tibet and have never heard the language of any other country. They will have attachment and loyalty to this Tibet, their birthplace, and on many occasions will strongly believe that it is a land that is unrivaled, pleasing, and perfect. If they were to arrive in Nepal or Kashmir and see sights they had never seen before, the flames of their attachment [to Tibet] that before had burned so brightly would dim. If they continued farther on the road and their eyes were delighted by the vast land of India with sights adorned with many pleasurable things, then all the attractive characteristics of Tibet exaggerated in the past would disappear without a trace. Going from the south in a great ship farther and farther, [they would reach] the other side of the great ocean. To the east is China, a land that produces jewels and pleasures. To the west are the lands of the star heads, where there are displayed precious qualities, manufacturing, jewels, and wonders of all types. If their minds are engrossed in the various sites that are the heart of the world, they must perceive and be convinced that this birthplace, this Tibet, is a very unappealing, very unattractive, and very painful place.

In the same way, for those who have never listened to or studied traditions other than the religion labeled as famous in their own land, if they are not obscured by the darkness of prejudice and were to encounter, with the mind and eyes of the learned, the other's religion that is stainless, superior, pure, and most excellent, [they will understand that] first, from the perspective of what is to be entered into and avoided, what is to be adopted and discarded among the virtuous and non-virtuous actions, the other's religion has no fault whatsoever. Thus, [they will see] that in their own tradition, although there are many points on how to abandon sins, among the people who abide in such a teaching, there are some who put them into practice and abandon them and some who do not. Also, in general, to regard as worthy of refuge and worship ghosts and demons who are not worthy of refuge and worship and who are far inferior even to humans and who harm humans is something that is to be utterly abandoned, is utterly abominable; it is heinous and terrible, causing great displeasure to the one worthy of worship and refuge. People give a place to this in their own tradition, like a sighted person who has gone blind. Evil spells, curses, vengeance rites, and so forth have been thoroughly proven by the intelligent to be terrible sins. Yet they are not only sanctioned by one's own teacher, they are part of one's training and are explained in the scriptures. When this is fully analyzed with reasoning, they will see very clearly and without obscuration that such a tradition, which they uphold, has the nature and characteristics of irreligion. In this way, their attachment and loyalty and so on, based on having grown accustomed to it, respecting it, and holding it in esteem, will diminish and be pacified.

Then, from the perspective of the fruit of performing virtuous and non-virtuous deeds, [they see that] the other's religion completely lacks any faults of contradiction or being contrary to reason. They will see the fault of their own tradition for generating thoughts that greatly increase grasping for all objects of attachment by saying that the fruit of virtuous deeds are the pleasures of the mundane world, [which are in fact] a source of terror, similar to hell; those who perform such virtuous deeds have the flaw of acting like beasts. Having carefully analyzed this, they will see that their own tradition has no real salvation of any kind, and that it is impossible to eliminate the fault of squandering all the perfect virtues. Then, like someone awaking from sleep, they will understand more and more clearly that such a religion, which they have upheld, other than being postulated by an internal obscured mind, completely lacks all qualities and characteristics of a perfect religion. Then, with a deep sense of sadness, it is certain they will have such thoughts.

"Alas, just like a sighted person who has gone blind, I have stood at the mouth of this great abyss with no fear. With the height of arrogance I have steadfastly remained until right now acting as happy as a child. Like someone duped by a magical spell, I have become mindless.

"Alas, although mired up to my head in a swamp of rotting corpses, a swamp that smells like excrement, I think that I live in a place where all precious things are gathered. [5a] What greater self-delusion and stupidity could there be?

"Alas, I have drunk the poison made from deception, falsehood, and irreligion, that destroys both virtue and a pure heart, an evil more virulent than the poison of a snake, which only causes the death of the body. I now completely understand that these are the excellent medicines that have the power to completely cure all the diseases of this mind." So I say:

> There is no one more mistaken than me.
> There is no one more foolish than me.[7]

> Magicians conjure forms,[8]
> Horses, elephants, and chariots;
> Just as they do not exist as they appear;
> So too is my tradition devoid of truth.

> Just as the moon's reflection appears at night
> In water that is clear and without waves,
> Yet the water moon is empty and cannot be grasped;
> So too is my tradition devoid of truth.

> Just as at noon in the summertime,
> A man traveling and afflicted by thirst
> Sees a mirage to be a body of water;
> So too, mine is irreligion, devoid of truth.

> Whether or not there is water in the mirage
> Foolish sentient beings want to drink it.
> But they cannot drink water that is not real.
> So too there is no benefit from this religion.

> Just as a man goes to a moist plantain tree
> Because he wants its core,
> Yet everywhere, inside and out, there is no core.
> So too is my religion devoid of a core.

> If, despite having realized these things,
> I would foolishly squander my life in idleness,
> Soon, when the time of death approaches,
> A great sorrow will befall me.[9]

If I burn forever in the fires of hell
Difficult to bear, impossible to stop,
The fire of pointless remorse will burn without end;
There is no doubt I will feel mental pain forever.

Without virtuous acts and the path of religion,
Transcendence of the world cannot be attained in the future.
What is inside me, the wasteful one?
Fool, do not fall asleep right now.

Thus, having encountered the other's religion that is pure, stainless, superior, peerless, and excellent, through the power of listening to it and studying it well with the clear eyes of faultless intelligence, without obscuration by the darkness of prejudice, the heart of the learned, like waking from the dullness of the sleep of ignorance and regaining mindfulness, will understand directly that the religion they upheld before has defects everywhere. Their mind tormented by pain, they will realize that, without wishing to and unknowingly, they have drunk an evil poison, and they will vomit it out with great effort. They will recognize with certainty that, spurred by grave error, they have completely lost the path that accords with their own welfare, and will endeavor to turn away from[10] the evil path and enter the good path. They will turn away from the impure and false teaching and the side of irreligion, and without procrastination, they will generate a strong and powerful awareness, authentic and from the depths of their heart, a yearning admiration with their body, speech and clear mind for the other's religion, stainless and pure. If they worry that various harsh words and criticism, such as "irresolute" and "vow breaker" might come from ignorant, unlearned worldly people inspired by the sleep of ignorance, they should contemplate the following to put their minds at ease.

For example, when one wants to know whether or not there is some stain on one's face, like a smudge, one knows by looking in a mirror; the learned person removes the stain without listening to words that delight the unlearned and dirty. In the same way, [one should think,] "I shall look into the unsullied mirror of this pure religion of the other and definitely identify the flaws of the tradition I loved before, a teaching that is impure, false, a deception of a demon, and a path to hell. I shall not listen to the criticism of the ignorant and unlearned, worldly people inspired by the sleep of ignorance. I shall remove my previous faults and shall follow this pure religion without wavering and with a stainless mind until I die."

Furthermore, consider that it is through seeing impermanence that worldly people see that one must go to the next world, with no certainty as to when one might die. At the time of death, except for religion, nothing whatsoever is of benefit, [5b] and except for irreligion or negative deeds, nothing whatsoever can cause harm. Also, no matter how much you are loved by your family and friends, even if your large clan surrounds you [at death], you cannot be guided by even one of them. No matter how impressive your pile of wealth, you cannot carry even the smallest particle with you. If you must discard even the flesh and bones you have had from birth, what need is there to speak of anything else? Thus, [one should think,] "A time will definitely come when all the marvels of this life will abandon me, and I too will have to cast them aside and go to the world beyond." Consider that this might occur today, and think of how at that time only religion will be your refuge, protector, and ally.

> Cities, kingdoms, and surrounding lands,
> Oceans, the sun, moon, and the stars,
> And these embodied beings will burn.
> If not even their ashes will remain,
> What need is there to speak of humble humans?
>
> Among the many beings seen in the morning,
> Some are not seen in the evening;
> Among the many beings seen in the evening,
> Some are not seen in the morning.[11]
>
> Like ripe fruit falling,
> If, like this, people no longer exist,
> What need is there to speak of people's words?
> Know this and act well.
> Who in the world listens to the insane?
> Though they may criticize you, be at ease.
>
> When the fruit of your deeds ripen
> And the Lord of Death leads you away,

Apart from your virtues and sins,
All the people stay behind,
Nothing will follow after you.

Never to be seen or heard again,
At that time, not even your name remains,
Unpleasant worldly words will be carried by the wind.
What need is there to speak of things like criticism?

Therefore, contemplate these things.
Act wisely and well.
Who in the world listens to the insane?
Though they may criticize you, be at ease.

To summarize these points, in general, through reading about and listening to another's religion, there is the benefit of becoming very learned about religion. Through listening to another's religious tradition that accords with one's own tradition, there is the benefit of generating a very firm conviction to immediately practice religion. Through studying another's religious tradition that does not accord with one's own tradition and is very corrupt compared to one's own tradition, there is the benefit of becoming closer to religious deeds and stirring one's mind, producing a powerful sense of joy in religion. Through listening to and studying well another's religion far superior to one's own, that is stainless, pure, superior, and the best and excellent, there are such benefits as abandoning evil paths and entering the good path.

II. HOW TO SEE THE OTHER'S RELIGION IN A WISE WAY

This has three parts:

1. Generating the three recognitions
2. Abandoning the three defects of a soil
3. Cultivating all three conditions of listening

1. Generating the Three Recognitions

Having the Recognition of Religion as a Seed

For example, without there being a single seed in the world, not even a single sprout would grow, and without the growth of a single sprout, not a single fruit would ripen. Without the growth of a single sprout and the ripening of a single fruit, all these sentient beings sustained by them would become non-existent. Similarly, without there being a single seed known as religion, not a single sprout of virtue or non-virtue would grow. Without the growth of a single sprout of virtue or non-virtue, there would be no ripening of benefits and faults as the fruition of virtue and non-virtue. When the growth of sprouts of virtue or non-virtue and the ripening of benefits and faults as the fruition of virtue and non-virtue become utterly non-existent, then it follows that the two types of deeds and the two types of fruit that are based upon a mindful awareness that serve as a kind of life-force, called "mind," "intellect" or "consciousness," become totally non-existent. Because these points are entirely correct, in general, it is correct that one should recognize one's own or another's "path" or "religion" as like a seed.

Having the Recognition of Oneself as the Soil

For example, in worldly terms, that which is to be ploughed, leveled with a rake, and tamed with water, fertilizer, and heat, and which, along with the seed, serves as the cause for sprouts and so on, is called the soil. In the same way, [one's mind,] which is to be ploughed by means of the three recognitions, [6a] to be leveled by means of eliminating the three defects, and which must be tamed, as with water, fertilizer, and heat, through the power of establishing all three conditions of listening, can serve as a cause—along with the seed of listening to and studying religion—for the sprouts of a perfect virtue. Thus, you should conclude that it is most appropriate to have the recognition of what is called the mind, intellect, or consciousness of any human as being like the soil of religion.

Generating the Recognition That the Benefits of Living in Accordance
with Religion and Doing Good Deeds Are Unique to Humans Compared
to Beasts, and That the Highest Reality of Definite Goodness, Far Superior
to All Worldly Happiness, Is Like the Fruit

For example, to the extent that one recognizes the great importance of the fruits that are gathered in autumn, to that extent one will understand the great importance of planting seeds in the spring. In the same way, to the extent that one understands the great importance of the fruits of living in accord with religion and doing good deeds, to that extent one must understand the great importance of the seed of religion that must be planted in one's mind through hearing and seeing. Again, for example, in [the ability] to sustain their lives, when beasts, who do not till the soil for a single type of food, are compared to humans who till the soil, humans are far superior to beasts. Similarly when humans strive merely to achieve happiness and overcome suffering, because this exists in beasts as well, [these humans] are like beasts.

> An ox whose mind craves a mouthful of grass
> That grows at the edge of a deep pit,
> Falls off the cliff without obtaining it;
> One who desires happiness of life in this world is the same.

Now, it is necessary for humans to be thoroughly and completely in accord with religion and constantly strive day and night to perform good deeds. Therefore, merely the achievement of happiness and the overcoming of suffering in the world is a fruition achieved by the performance of virtue. Thus, for beasts, even the knowledge of religion is totally non-existent; what need is there to mention the practice of religion. Humans must become superior to beasts. Therefore, one must generate the recognition that the benefits of listening to and studying a religion and of living in accordance with a religion and doing good deeds is unique to humans compared to beasts, and that the highest reality of definite goodness, far superior to all worldly happiness, is like the fruit. Thus, one must understand listening to and studying religion to be of very great meaning. Therefore, in all situations of listening to and studying religion, one must cultivate an aspiration able to move one's mind for a long period of time strongly toward such a fruit. Whether the religion that one listens to and studies is one's own or another's, to the extent that the fruit of religion that it presents is entirely the worldly happiness shared with beasts, to that extent it is contrary to religious awareness, and one must, through the application of awareness, turn one's mind away from it. To the extent that the religion that one listens to and studies is such that, for whatever mundane happiness one sees, hears about, or thinks of, if a deep sense of revulsion and discouragement arises giving rise to the thoughts, "This too is of the world, this too is of the world," "Those are the aims of beasts," "Those are suffering," "This is of no use," to that extent one should hold that religion to be reliable and appropriate. And through the application of such awareness one must recognize it as suitable to be considered unrivaled, sublime, most excellent, that which is chosen by those with intelligence and learning, and the crown ornament.

2. Abandoning the Three Defects of a Soil

If the ground has always been used as a road for travelers, or although it lacks roads, if it has many stones, rocks, and gravel, is rough and has no luster, a rocky dry place with no streams, lakes, or springs, or although it lacks stones, rocks, sand, and gravel, if it is filled with stumps, thornbushes, and so on, then even if one were to plant seeds in that soil, they will either be stepped on by travelers or taken by birds and so on, and will not produce green sprouts. Even though sprouts grow, lacking water, they will not produce the necessary growth, maturity, and so on. If they have water, although they may grow for a little while, [6b] they will be destroyed by the stumps and thornbushes growing around them; it would be pointless [to plant them there].

In the same way, although one may have listened to and studied religion, because of sinful friends who lead one astray or impediments made by demons, one might waste the opportunity through forgetfulness and so on. Or, having listened to and studied religion, although one has cultivated conviction, the happiness and joy of admiration, and faith in that religion, lacking the root of immovable and unchangeable confidence, one might grasp it wrongly or form a flawed motivation. Or, although lacking those faults, because of the rocks and thorns of not abandoning worldly entanglements, seeking material possessions, wealth, distractions, striving to find happiness and remove suffering only up to one's death, the best of all harvests of conviction, strong happiness and joy, and the faith that one has found will be completely destroyed. Having become afflicted, if the fruits of trusting in the perfect religion and abiding correctly in good conduct are ruined each day, studying religion will have no great purpose. Thus, one must be free of those.

The antidotes to these three [faults] are the following. By far the most important of all states of mind is to listen to and study all of the essential points of a pure religion with a mind completely isolated in its unwavering focus on virtue. Contemplating this, [one should develop] a one-pointed wish to understand all the essential points, discarding all the rough stones, many rocks, and the gravel of attachment to one's own experience, aversion to others' experience, and pretense, arrogance, pride, and conceit, free from the faults of prejudice and of changing the tenets of one's own system without abandoning them. One should draw conviction from the depths and have the desire to encounter the root of the stainless and pure religion. One should earnestly submit one's mind to listening to, carefully studying, and thoroughly analyzing the other's religion. With a forceful and attentive mind that is not merely words and promises, one should distinguish well between truth and falsehood, proven and unproven, causes of error and causes of certainty, pure religion and irreligion. One should draw forth a perfect conviction in the stainless truth and the pure religion and a strong awareness; with the great effort able to subdue the mind for a long time, one should train oneself to find steadfast conviction. One should not look at all at the experiences of foolish worldly people, their activities, their entanglements, their distractions, their pleasures, and their benefits from material possessions. Instead, without any obstruction, one should raise the mind and develop a faith of conviction that is unwavering, clear, and pure, seeking the definite goodness that is the perfect end, which is the essence and the fruit of a religion that is stainless, pure, superior, peerless, and excellent. Such a person will strive with an undistracted mind, focused single-pointedly only on obeying all the essential points of such a religion and on good deeds both day and night.

3. Cultivating All Three Conditions of Listening

What are the three?

> Impartial, intelligent, and interested,
> Such a listener is a suitable vessel for hearing.[12]

"Impartial" means not being prejudiced. If one is [prejudiced], one is obstructed by it; because one will not see the positive qualities [of what one is listening to] and one will not find eloquent points.

The mind tormented by prejudice
Will never find tranquility.[13]

Being prejudiced means being attached to one's own tradition and having aversion for the other's religion. Therefore, the learned, endowed with intelligence, when listening to and studying the other's religion for the first time, should be like a scale that is neither high nor low, free from all prejudice that is partial toward either oneself or the other.

If one thinks, "Is this enough?," although one may be impartial, if one lacks a mind powerful enough to distinguish between eloquence or authenticity and ineloquence or artifice, one is not a suitable vessel. Therefore, one must possess the intelligence to understand these two; with it, one discards the essenceless and takes the essence. Therefore, the learned, endowed with intelligence, listen to and study the other's religion and then compare and analyze each essential point of their own tradition and the other tradition, [7a] and on all occasions of investigation with reasonings, like the two sides of a scale that is balanced in weight, with a pure mind free of attachment and aversion, they should train themselves to find steadfast certainty about harmful things that are to be seen as faults, such as falsehood, delusion, deceit, demonic obstacles, false seeds, untrue fruit, and evil paths that lead to suffering and error, and they should thus turn their mind away from them. They should aspire completely and as if powerlessly with body, speech, and a clear mind for all the essential points of the stainless truth, all that is proven to be real, definite goodness, the supreme reality, the good path that leads without the slightest delusion or deceit, the pure, peerless, and excellent religion.

If one thinks, "Are these two enough?," even if these two are present, if one does not begin to abandon [the false religion] and cultivate [the true religion] in accordance with what one has understood, one is still a suitable vessel. It is therefore necessary to have greater interest.

Having encountered the utterly pure religion,
Spend your time in practice and make it bear fruit.

One who has found the true religion
But does not abandon the sinful religion
Is more foolish than the person
Who fills a bejeweled gold vessel with vomit.[14]

Having found the peerless and supreme religion,
You should diligently seek what is meaningful.
He who is heedless and abusive,
His learning and knowledge will have no great use.

Those who delight in the stainless teaching,
And practice it with body and speech,
Are patient, loved by friends, and guard their senses.
They shall attain the perfection of learning and knowledge.

Though I have explained the excellent religion,
If you do not put it into proper practice upon hearing it,
You will be like the sick man carrying a bag of medicine.
His sickness cannot be cured.

Beset by laziness and not taking medicine,
What is achieved by uttering mere words of mantras?
Does hearing or reading a medical text
Help someone afflicted by sickness?[15]

Therefore, just as a sick person cherishes the medicine prepared by the physician, the learned endowed with intelligence and great interest will see the great importance of all the essential points and instructions of a religion proven by reasoned analysis to be stainless and supreme. Having done so, they will cherish them with much effort and will not waste time through the laziness of procrastination and the forgetfulness of the weak. And just as the sick person, seeing that without taking the medicine prepared by the physician his illness cannot be cured, and so takes it, in the same way one will practice with persistence, seeing that if one does not put into practice the essential points of the peerless, stainless, and utterly pure religion, one cannot destroy the afflictions and cannot travel away from dangers. Furthermore, just as one or two doses of medicine do nothing for a leper who has lost his legs and arms, in the same way, for a mind strongly stricken and long afflicted by the grave illness of wrong views, impure tradition, and irreligion, it is not sufficient to practice the points of the stainless and pure religion only once or twice. Thus, they analyze all the essential points of such a path with discriminative wisdom and strive persistently, like a flowing stream.

III. DEMONSTRATING HOW, HAVING STUDIED THE OTHER'S RELIGION, THERE IS BENEFIT IN DEBATING ABOUT ONE'S OWN RELIGION

In general, all sixteen benefits of giving the gift of the dharma, which is the giving of the non-material dharma and does not seek profit and honor and does not involve material things like fame, are benefits of engaging in debates about religion. What are the sixteen? One will be endowed with (1) memory, (2) insight, (3) intelligence, (4) steadfastness, (5) wisdom, (6) one will gain realization that transcends the world, (7) one's anger will be pacified, (8) the darkness of ignorance will dissipate, (9) demons will not find vulnerabilities, (10) the unfriendly will not find vulnerabilities, (11) one's friends will not be separated from you, (12) one's words will be credible, (13) one will be fearless, (14) there will be much mental happiness, (15) one will be praised by the learned, and (16) one's gifts of the dharma will be memorable.[16] If one enjoys contemplating the benefits of debating about religion in general: [7b]

Engaging in debate, he becomes faithful[17]
And becomes steadfast in his joy.
Creating wisdom, ignorance ends.
He attains the perfection of knowing all phenomena.

Debate is the lamp dispelling the darkness of ignorance;
The best wealth, it cannot be taken by thieves;
The weapon that destroys the enemy of ignorance;
The best friend that bestows the eye of wisdom.

The friend who does not change though you become poor;
The medicine against delusion that does you no harm;
The best army defeating the army of grave error;
The best fame, the best glory, the best treasure.

In a gathering, it delights the learned;
It enhances the minds of those of medium intelligence;
It removes all the cataracts of the least intelligent;
At the end of a debate, one should take the practice to heart.
It easily rescues one from the fortress of the faithless.

Foster debate like a forerunner;[18]
It guards and enhances all the qualities;
Removing doubt, it rescues from the rivers;
Debate marks the city of joy.

Debate removes agitation and makes the mind lucid;
It eliminates pride and is the root of respect;
Debate is the best wealth, the best friend, and the best leg;
Like a hand, it is the root for gathering virtue.

Debate awakens one from sleep and deluded drowsiness;
It saves one from drowning in the sea of delusion;
It shows the good path to those who have entered evil paths;
It frees one locked in the prison of irreligion.

Debate is the central pillar of the path;
Like the full moon, it spreads the quality of bright dharma;
Like the bright sun, it shows the direction of peace.
To both enemy and friend it is like a mountain.

Like the ocean it endows one with an unshakable mind;
It takes care of one like a guardian or a ferryman;
Debate is the refuge from false leaders;
It reveals the pleasant and unpleasant paths;
It binds one with auspicious conduct;
It is the guide to the place of salvation.

If one develops heartfelt admiration for the benefits of debate between religions, one might like to consider them in brief. I will explain the special benefits divided into just five. What are the five?

One will easily understand what has not been attained;
It demonstrates directly the qualities of religion;

It removes laxity and excitation and increases the mind's focus;
It increases the joy of the mind contemplating religion;
With religion, it defeats evil speech.

The first benefit is this. Although one may listen to, think about, and meditate upon religion, without relying upon honest debate about religion, one will not find the intention that identifies the points of the religion with firm certainty. Although one might find it, it would require much time and great hardship. Relying on forceful debate about religion, one will easily understand.

Through debate phenomena are understood;
Through debate one dispels delusions;
Through debate one discards the meaningless;
Through debate one attains the perfections.[19]

If one enters a covered house,[20]
A house veiled in darkness,
There are things inside it
But a person with sight cannot see them.

In the same way, although the learned here
Possess the eyes of intelligence,
Until they debate they will not know
The qualities of sin and virtue.

A person with sight
Sees forms with a lamp,
In the same way, with debate one will know
The qualities of virtue and sin.

Debate is the measure of the learned;
Debate is like petals for the learned;
Debate is like the chariot of the learned;
Without difficulty one quickly understands the points.[21]

The second benefit is this. When one looks at gold and silver that have newly come out of the earth, they do not attract the eye. But if they are re-peatedly heated with fire and washed with water by an expert smith or a smith's apprentice in accordance with the smith's crafts, the eye that is agitated by the great brilliance of gold or silver that captivates the eye and mind cannot be satisfied in looking at it and the mind uncontrollably longs for its wonder. Although the eye repeatedly looks at a vast feast of food and drink of a hundred flavors, with the best and most perfect flavors, if that food is not chewed by the two rows of teeth and swallowed, such things as encountering the flavor, experiencing the flavor, continuing to experience the flavor, and having experienced the flavor will not occur. In the same way, although the religion of others that the learned have listened to, read about, and examined may be stainless, pure, and superior, listening, contemplation, and meditation are like the eye looking at it repeatedly; if one does not chew it with the two rows of teeth and swallow it with the method of honest debate about religion, one will be unable to experience the delicious and complete flavor of such a tradition. And if one does not repeatedly burn it and wash it again and again with the fire and water of debate, [8a] then the mind of the learned will not be overwhelmed and encompassed by the radiance and brilliance of the various qualities that exist in that religion, its incomparable charm, and the limitless things that uncontrollably captivate the mind.

Whether an ointment fragrant with the best incense,[22]
Or censors using a single incense,
When set alight by a human,
There is a fragrance never experienced before.

If clothes and so forth
Are sprinkled with the fragrance of the best perfume,
When touched by the warmth of a strong sun,
All four directions are filled with the scent.

The more a medicinal plant is beaten with a hammer,
The more the scent of the medicine spreads everywhere;
It is only through blowing, beating, and playing,
That the melody of music is heard.

The more a person strikes with the flint
And hits the firestones,
Fire emerges, rising up,
Illuminating all around with bright light.

In the same way, when the best of religions
Are struck hard against the flint of debate,
All its qualities appear before one's eyes.
Having appeared, it uncontrollably captivates the mind of all.

The third benefit [of debating about one's religion] is this. For example, when a flowering fruit tree is allowed to grow and spread as much as it can, then the unlimited growth of the branches and leaves will consume the tree's strength and its potency will be exhausted; the flowers and fruit will be very few or [the tree] cannot form anything more than a few flowers and fruit. In the same way, in all cases of listening to and studying the other's religion that is stainless, pure, and superior, if one allows one's perception of each of its parts and essential points to occur as it will, due to the power of attachment to one's own tradition, one's mind will not be peaceful and will spread outward and there will be unlimited branches of blindness induced by excitement and leaves of blurred perception and error. It will not be possible for the mind to form the flowers and fruit of pure understanding as well as the recognition and good understanding of the characteristics of the religion. But if the tree with its growing and spreading branches, rather than growing uncontrollably, has most of its excessive branches and leaves pruned, then the tree's potency that previously escaped without bearing fruit will be conserved inside and it will bear fruit. In the same way, on all occasions of listening to and studying the other's religion, superior and pure, if one becomes excited due to attachment to one's own tradition, or one's mind's ability to remain on its object is interrupted and it is uncontrollably drawn to other pleasing objects, or the mind is distracted away from its object, then all these diffusions should be stopped by the power of debate, as with a pruning knife. By doing so, the mind is conserved inside and will be placed in pure *samādhi* and *śamatha* on the other religion. If that is done, then, with the rope of debating about religion one will be able to tightly tie one's mind to the object of the other's religion. Then due to the force of that mind that is unable to spread outside, the soft and delicious fruit arising from perfect and complete comprehension as well as identification and good understanding of the characteristics of that other religion will undoubtedly emerge.

Furthermore, for example, if the iron of a sword becomes rusty, the iron is not clear and it is not useful for cutting. Similarly, at times of listening to and studying the other's pure religion, if the mind is afflicted by being sunk or absorbed in sloth and slumber, then like a blind person or like someone in the dark, or like someone whose eyes are closed, the object will not be clear to the mind, as if it has fallen into darkness. When the mind loosens the way it apprehends its object, because it will not apprehend it clearly or firmly, although there may be small degrees of clarity, the object will not be apprehended with great clarity. There will arise a heaviness of body, a heaviness of mind, an unserviceability of body, and an unserviceability of the mind to thoroughly analyze with strength, all of which are aspects of ignorance. Therefore, just as one needs to restore the two properties of clarity and sharpness to a rusty iron sword, in the same way, when the mind is oppressed by sloth and slumber, not apprehending its objects clearly and becoming lax, without being content with mere clarity of the object or the mere lucidity of the subject, stopping the decline in the mind's apprehension, one needs both factors: [8b] clarity of the object and focused apprehension. One needs to both lift up the mind and focus its apprehension [of the object].

Again, for example, by using a grindstone, all the rust that had formed on swords and so forth can be removed and the iron will be clear and sharp, useful for cutting. In the same way, by using honest debate about religion like a grindstone, one grinds away the mind itself, which is afflicted by being sunk or absorbed in sloth and slumber, and the way the mind is focused on its object. By doing so, one will be able to perceive most clearly each of the parts and all of the essential points and qualities of the other's religion, which is stainless and superior, and develop admiration for it. In these ways, the mind of the learned, using the wisdom of critical investigation, becomes suitable to analyze the parts, essential points, and qualities that it wishes to analyze. Through identifying those, it comes to full conviction regarding the characteristics of purity of the other's religion.

The fourth quality [of debating about one's religion] is this.

A blazing fire stirred by the wind[23]
Spreads through the entire forest.
Inextinguishable, it grows more intense.
A ship driven by the winds at sea
Leaves this side behind and travels across.
At the shore of the ocean it reaches dry land.
A rider galloping on a saddled steed
Is lofty and faster than the wind;

He reaches his destination without turning back.
Pillars attached to beams with nails,
Like an immovable rock, are like a mountain.
Undisturbed by athletes, they remain solid.
When beaten by a smith, iron, copper, and so forth
Become pliant, radiant, with various pleasing shapes,
Turning into whatever vessel one might want.
Silver washed with water and burned with fire,
When looked at captivates the mind and pleases the mind insatiably,
Its whiteness spreading everywhere.
With a diamond, indestructible even by iron,
A crystal cut from a rocky cliff anywhere high or low
Can be turned into a mirror conjuring all forms.
When struck by the morning sun,
Flowers blossom and spread wide;
But in the radiance of the snow they close and cannot bear to be seen.
Extracted beer boiled and boiled with fire
Comes to lose all its coarse tastes
And moves ever closer to its potent and delicious essence.
A bow pulled tight with an arrow
By the greatest archer;
Irreversible, it will forcefully hit its mark.
Likewise a debate that is not weak
On the subject of a stainless, true, and pure religion
Increases the joy in the heart of the learned.
When walking in the darkness of night,
The circle of the moon seems ever more attractive;
When the darkness of false debate is awakened by honesty,
Religion will captivate the mind ever more.

The fifth benefit [of debating about one's religion] is this.

He who engages in religious debates without weakness
Is a person who will create a mind that is an excellent treasure,
Serving as a lamp to dispel the darkness of ignorance.
By casting a lamp into pitch darkness,
All darkness is dispelled.

In the same way, the dense darkness of evil tenets
Is quickly dispelled by the lamp of debate.
He who engages in religious debates constantly
Will clear the supreme eyes of all the world;
He will act as the sun destroying all blindness.
Just as when snow is long assailed by the rays of sun
It completely melts away,
So when long assailed by the rays of debate,
Unable to bear its brilliance, errors cease.
He who engages in religious debates forcefully
Is a person who strives to benefit the world,
Like a wind rising in the sky.
Just as the cold strong winds that rise in autumn,
Dispel all dark clouds gathered in the four directions,
So when the great powers of debate rise
The clouds of wrong views are dispelled.
He who engages in religious debates well,
The learned one, chief among the people,
Is the helmsman who guides the ship from hidden obstacles.
Just as a skilled helmsman guides the ship,
From encountering sea monsters and hidden mountains,
Sailing himself and saving others,
So he who strives to steer with debate
Those who have met the misleading religion of demons
Achieves his own welfare and guides others.
He who engages in religious debates in a direct manner
Is the eye that sees all the foundations of truth.
A person worthy to be held as a crown jewel
Will remove all the stains of misunderstanding,
Wrong ideas, as well as doubt
About the stainless truth and the pure religion.
He will plant faith anew in those who have lost it,
And increase it in those who have lost a little.
With the stream of perfect debate
He will cleanse the stains caused by wrong ideas,
Making religion and truth free from the stains.
All those who uphold falsehood having disappeared, [9a]

When all those have gathered and assembled
Who increase the foundation of unmistaken faith,
Then all opponents who hold the evil tenets of heathens
Will be destroyed and defeated by the dharma.
With the sound of the lion's roar of a lofty mind,
He will subdue the brains of the entire world.
The stainless faith, the supreme religion,
Through his kindness, will spread to all directions.
The skill of such a person among all the learned
Will be held as a crown ornament by the unbiased.

Fearing excessive words, I have gathered the essential points. They can be known in detail elsewhere. With this the introductory section of *Inquiry concerning the Doctrines of Previous Lives and Emptiness, Offered to the Scholars of Tibet by the Star Head Lama Called Ippolito* is complete.

ຕ໐ ຕ໐ ຕ໐

[131b32] The opponent says, "Now, as you have already explained, it is untenable that a person who performs deeds of perfect virtue is born as a human after their death through the fruition of the deeds of perfect virtue. Why is it, then, that the statements of earlier and later lamas or persons are in complete agreement and that a later person describes and remembers without error all of the possessions that were owned by the earlier person?"

[132a] Answer: To speak in that way is most illogical because it is illogical to conceive and to say that what is uncertain is certain; to speak in that way is a case of conceiving and saying that what is uncertain is certain. That follows because to speak in that way is a case of conceiving and saying that it is certain that [the person] will attain a pleasant fruition after their death; until the final moment of death has passed, it is uncertain whether they will attain a pleasant fruition or they will attain an unpleasant fruition. That follows because as long as a person who has the power to distinguish between good and bad is alive and until the final moment of death has passed, it is not certain whether they will attain a pleasant fruition or they will experience an unpleasant fruition. That follows because as long as a person who has the power to distinguish between good and bad is alive and until the final moment of death has passed, they have control over whatever they want

and are capable of applying themselves to either virtue or non-virtue. If you say that that does not follow, it does follow, because if, as long as a person, who has the power to distinguish between good and bad is alive and until the final moment of death has passed, has control over whatever they want and are capable of applying themselves to either virtue or non-virtue, then as long as a person, who has the power to distinguish between good and bad is alive and until the final moment of death has passed, has control over whatever they want and are capable of applying themselves to either virtue or non-virtue, it is not certain whether they will engage firmly, unchangingly, and irreversibly in deeds of perfect virtue or they will involve themselves in negative acts. And if that is not certain, you must assert that until the final moment of death has passed, it is not certain whether they will attain a pleasant fruition or they will experience an unpleasant fruition. These must be fully proven even in the opponent's own scriptures. If you ask why, I will give the reason through both stating examples and applying the meaning concerning the uncertainty of experiencing an unpleasant fruition until the final moment of death has passed. The *Differentiation of Actions* [*Karmavibhaṅga*] says:

There is karma that if one possesses it one will be born as a hell being and will complete the entire life span of a hell being [before] going to the [next] life. What is such karma? It is the karma of someone who performs and accumulates the deeds of a hell being, but is not ashamed of having performed the deed, does not regret it, does not renounce it, does not confess it, does not admit it, does not refrain from it later, but takes delight and pleasure in doing it again.[24] There is karma that if one possesses it one will be born as a hell being and, completing half of the life span of a hell being, will go to the [next] life. What is such karma? It is the karma of someone who, having performed and accumulated the deeds of a hell being, avoids it, turns away from it, condemns it, confesses it, admits it, rejects it, renounces it, and refrains from it later. Then there is karma that if one possesses it, one will go to the [next] life as soon as one is reborn as a hell being. What is such karma? It is the karma of someone who, when they perform and accumulate the deeds of a hell being, is ashamed of having done the deed, and when they regret it, condemn it, confess it, and admit it, they make a vow, saying, "I will not do it in the future." Even if they were to be born as a hell being, as soon as they are born [in hell], they go to the [next life].[25]

The statement in the sūtras and the *vinaya,* "Karma is not lost, even in a hundred eons," refers to not cultivating antidotes, such as the power of repair; if it is cleansed with antidotes such as the power of repair, it is said that even [karma] that is certain to be experienced is purified. [Haribhadra's] commentary on the *Perfection of Wisdom in Eight Thousand Stanzas* says, "If one approaches the antidotes, those things that have the quality of obstacles can be completely eliminated through a powerful antidote, like tarnish on gold, for example. It should be understood that everything, such as the obstructions to the true dharma, are explained in this way. [132b] If this were not the case, it would contradict logic and would contradict many sūtras. Even [what the sūtras] call '[karma] that is certain to be experienced' is explained by this. One should determine that [what the sūtras] call '[karma] that is not certain' is karma whose fruition is occasional, if the cultivation of the antidote is not complete."[26] Thus, confession, restraint, and so forth act to weaken the capacity for fruition [of negative karma] even though other conditions are encountered. In the same way, it is said that having wrong views and anger destroy roots of virtue.[27] [Bhāviveka's] *Blaze of Reasoning (Tarkajvālā)* says:

> Wrong views and harmful intent weaken virtue. Antidotes such as condemnation, restraint, and confession weaken the power of non-virtue. Even when the collection of conditions already exists, the capacity of the seeds of virtue and non-virtue are weakened. Thus, where would any fruit come from? Without the collection of conditions, when the time changes, [the fruition of the deed] never comes forth at all. As it is said, "Through upholding the excellent dharma, even sins that are certain to be experienced will be experienced in this life." And, "Furthermore, deeds that lead to the evil realms are turned into just a headache by this." If you ask, "If there is a fruition which becomes just a headache, how is that a complete removal [of the negative fruition]?" The complete fruition of sinful deeds is to undergo the sufferings of hell. Through these [antidotes], one does not undergo even the smallest of the sufferings of hell. How could this not be a complete removal? Because things such as headaches arise, how could there be no fruition whatsoever?[28]

Thus, in that opponent's scripture itself, with regard to the purification of sins, the causes of undergoing great suffering in the next world become causes of undergoing small suffering, or they are purified and become just a headache in the present body. In the same way, [sufferings] that must be experienced for a long time become shortened or do not need to be experienced at all. Furthermore, from the perspective of whether the power of the purifier is great or small and such factors as the completeness or incompleteness, strength or weakness, and long or short duration of such things as the power of the antidote, there is no consistent certainty. In that case, even in the opponent's scriptures, there are virtuous powers of repair that weaken and destroy non-virtues and the capacity of the seeds of non-virtue. In the same way, one must assert that there are non-virtues that weaken and destroy virtue and the capacity of the seeds of virtue. Therefore, for example, as long as a person who has the power to distinguish between good and bad is alive and until the final moment of death has passed, they have control over whatever they want and are capable of applying themselves to either virtue or non-virtue. Therefore, as long as they are alive and until the final moment of death has passed, they perform and accumulate deeds that must be experienced as the sufferings of hell. However, one must assert that there is no certainty as to whether they are not ashamed of having performed the deed, do not regret it, do not renounce it, do not confess it, do not admit it, do not refrain from it later but take delight and pleasure in doing it again, or whether they will purify it with antidotes such as the power of repair and weaken the capacity of the fruition. In the same way, as long as a person who has the power to distinguish between good and bad is alive and until the final moment of death has passed, they have control over whatever they want and are capable of applying themselves to either virtue or non-virtue. Therefore, as long as they are alive and until the final moment of death has passed, they may perform and accumulate deeds of perfect virtue. However, one must assert that there is no certainty as to whether they will take delight and pleasure in them in such a way that they do not discard or turn away from them, [133a] or whether they weaken and destroy virtue and the capacity of the seeds of virtue. Also, for example, as long as a person who has the power to distinguish between good and bad is alive and until the final moment of death has passed, they perform and accumulate deeds that must be experienced as the sufferings of hell. However, one must assert that there is no certainty as to whether they are not ashamed of having performed the deed, do not regret it, do not renounce it, do not confess it, do not admit it, do not refrain from it later but take delight and pleasure in doing it again, or whether they will purify it with antidotes such as the power of repair and weaken the capacity of the fruition. Because of that, as long as someone is alive and until the final moment of death has passed, one must assert that there is no certainty as to whether, after they die, they will undergo the sufferings of hell or whether, after they die, they will not have to undergo any of the sufferings that must be undergone. In the same way, as long as a person who has the power to distinguish between good and bad is alive and until the final moment of death has passed, they may perform and accumulate deeds of perfect virtue. However, one must assert that there is no certainty as to whether they will take delight and pleasure in them in such a way that they do not discard or turn away from them, or whether they will weaken and destroy virtue and the capacity of the seeds of virtue. Because of that, as long as someone is alive and until the final moment of death has passed, one must assert that there is no certainty as to whether they will attain a pleasant fruition after they die or whether they will undergo an unpleasant fruition after they die.

Furthermore, for example, in the springtime, fruit has already formed on the fruit trees. However, there is no certainty that enough rain will fall in the summertime and the fruit will grow and ripen, or whether there will be a great drought and it will dry up and disappear. A steadfast ship filled with rare gems and various jewels happily sets out on a great voyage on the ocean. However, there is no certainty as to whether it will easily reach dry land, traveling with any obstacles that might arise removed, or whether, with dry land in sight, a strong wind will rise and [the ship] will be battered by waves, causing it to powerlessly hit the sand and sharp rocks that are obstacles from below, making it break open and sink. In the morning and at noontime, the orb of the sun fills everything with limitless rays of light and pleasant light, without darkness and without clouds. However, there is no certainty whether it will set with complete clarity untouched by such things as black clouds or thick darkness, or whether it will set as if it were invisible, obscured by darkness, with thick darkness and black clouds gathered in all directions.

In the same way, a person with the power to distinguish between good and bad may perform and accumulate perfect deeds from the time they are born. However, as long as they are alive and until the final moment of death has passed, there is no certainty as to whether they will take delight and pleasure in what is virtuous in such a way that they do not discard or turn away from them, or whether they will weaken virtue and the capacity of the seeds of virtue. It must be concluded that as long as one is alive and until the final moment of death has passed, there is no certainty as to whether one will attain a pleasant fruition or one will undergo limitless suffering after one's death.

At this point there is a qualm: Is it the opponent's position to assert that it is improper to posit birth as a human as the fruition that arises from a deed of perfect virtue, or do they tend toward and believe the position that asserts that birth as a human is the fruition that arises from a deed of perfect virtue? [133b] If it is the former, then those who speak in the way referred to earlier by the questioner, while alive and before their death, will be committing the sin of falsehood, which deceives the world. If it is the latter, the same is true of this as well. The definition of falsehood or being deceptive is to portray what is a different state of affairs to be something else; and those who speak in the manner referred to earlier, conceive and teach what is uncertain as being certain. That follows because as long as they are alive and until the final moment of death has passed, there is no certainty as to whether they will attain a pleasant fruition or they will undergo limitless suffering. Those who are alive and before the final moment of death has passed teach that there is certainty that they will attain a pleasant fruition after their death. In that case, not only is what they say untenable as an article of belief, it is tenable to prove that it contradicts logic and is a falsehood, a black deception that deceives the world. Therefore,

Not clouded by the darkness of prejudice,
Those endowed with the clear eyes of intelligence
Do not sleep at the time of learning.

If, however, one analyzes on the basis of how newly born children later speak, that would be illogical. For, according to their own scriptures, there is no assertion that the two selves of the former and later births exist ultimately as either the same or different. Therefore, they must assert that the two selves of the former and later births do not exist even conventionally as the same and as different. And through analyzing such things in terms of sameness and difference, one decides that there are only those two [sameness and difference] and must eliminate a third possibility. Therefore to assert that there is a phenomenon that is neither of those two is nonsense.

You might think, "If, as a start, one asserts that initially, the two selves of the former and later births are conventionally the same, what harm is there?" Those endowed with intelligence will look for the harm that is done to the position that they are the same. If you assert that the self at the time of the previous lifetime and the self of today are established as conventionally the same, then because the self at the time of the previous lifetime does not exist at the present time, and the self of the present time is manifest at the present time, one will have to assert something that is not manifest and something that does exist for direct perception are established as being conventionally the same. To assert that is illogical; this is a presentation that only creates[29] a sense of wonder in an ignorant person.

Furthermore, in the opponent's scriptures, the opponent's teacher says, "In that lifetime, at that time I was King Mandhātr." And, "If you think I was someone else in that lifetime, do not see it in that way."[30] The *Sūtra on Repaying Kindness* says, "The one pulling the fiery chariot [in hell] in that lifetime is me today."[31] And the *Hundred Actions (Karmaśataka)* says, "Through the fruition of that deed of causing discord among the followers of that sage, I boiled in the hells for a great many years, many hundreds of years, and many hundreds of thousands of years."[32] Among the selves of the former and later births, some are the fruition of virtues and some are the fruition of those who did deeds of non-virtue.

The assertion that the selves of the former and later births are established as being the same even conventionally is illogical because if you assert that the selves of the former and later births are established as being the same even conventionally, then you would have to assert that what comes from virtues and pleasant fruition and what comes from non-virtues and unpleasant fruition—happiness, suffering, and so forth—are established as the same conventionally. To assert that is not logical. Furthermore, in the opponent's scriptures, it is untenable that the two selves of the former and later births are established as the same. The protector Nāgārjuna says in the twenty-seventh chapter [of his *Verses on the Middle Way (Madhyamakakārikā)* 27.3]:

> It is not tenable to say,
> 'I arose in the past.'
> What arose in former lives
> Is not this same [person].[33]

[134a] You might ask, "What is the reason one must assert that the two selves of the former and later births are not established as conventionally different?" I will set forth what is said in the opponent's own scriptures. The *Samādhirāja* says:

> Then the Conqueror, without sin and with ten powers,
> Explained this supreme samādhi:
> The realms of existence are like a dream.
> Here, no one dies; there is no death.
>
> Sentient beings, humans, even life is not found.
> These phenomena are like foam and a plantain tree.
> They are like an illusion and like lightning in the sky.
> They are like a moon in water and like a mirage.
>
> There are no humans who die in this world
> And then go to another world.
> Yet the deeds that were done are never lost;
> White and black fruit ripen in *saṃsāra*.
>
> They are not permanent; they are not annihilated.
> Actions are not accumulated and they do not remain.
> Yet having been done, one is not untouched.
> One does not feel deeds done by another.[34]

In view of this, although persons who are born and die cannot be found through analysis, white and black fruitions do arise among illusion-like phenomena. Therefore, it is not the case that having done a deed one is never touched by it, that is, one does not experience its fruition. Regarding the fruition of deeds done by others, it is stated that one will not encounter [the fruition of] deeds one did not do, which will be felt or experienced by other persons.[35]

If, however, you assert that the two selves of the former and later births are established as different just conventionally, then you must assert that it is untenable that (1) deeds that were done are not[36] lost and (2) that one does not encounter [the fruition of] deeds one did not do. Regarding the first, if you assert that the two selves of the former and later births are established as different conventionally, then without the former self being destroyed, [the later self] does not become manifest. If you assert that the fruition of a deed done by the former self is enjoyed by the later self, this will be refuted below. Therefore, here, the experience of the fruition of deeds accumulated in the past would not exist because the self who performed the deed would have ceased before experiencing the fruition and because self and other do not experience each other's fruitions even conventionally. That follows because one does not feel [the fruition] of what is done by another. This is so because [in the line] "One does not feel deeds done by another," it has been stated that you do not accept that something is established as other by its own nature, so what you accepted as being established as the other would be on the conventional level. This means that you have to assert that it is impossible to experience [the fruition of] what others have done. In that case, the later self, which is established as different from the former self, does not experience the fruition of the deeds accumulated earlier by the former self; if the fruitions are not even experienced by the former self, the experience of the fruition must not exist.

Furthermore, it must be understood in this way from the perspective of identifying [what it] means [to say that] deeds that were done are lost. For example, the right hand looks for a pot in the east and does not find it there; the left hand, without looking for it in the west, encounters it there. However, it is tenable that the right hand that looked for the pot in the east lost it. In the same way, the earlier self accumulates deeds at the time of the cause but does not experience the fruition of the deeds it accumulated. Even though you assert that at the time of the fruition, the later self enjoys the fruition of the deeds done by the former self, it is tenable that the deeds done by the former self are lost. If you ask the reason for the example and the meaning, I will explain. When one analyzes whether deeds that were done are lost or not, one must analyze whether or not the experience of the fruition of the deed that was accumulated appears where the doer of the deed appeared. If you assert that the self at the time of the former lifetime and the self of the present are different, and assert that the former self does not experience the fruition but the later self enjoys the fruition of the deeds done by the former self, then you must assert that deeds that were done are lost. This is because if you assert that the self at the time of the former lifetime and the self of the present are different, and assert that the former self does not experience the fruition but [134b] the later self enjoys the fruition of the deeds done by the former self, then you must assert that the experience of the fruition of the deed that was accumulated in the past does not appear where the doer of the deed appeared. That follows because the doer of the deed in the past is not different from the former self; you must assert that the experience of the fruition of the deed that was accumulated in the past does not appear where that which is not different from the former self appears.

With regard to the fault of [the claim that] one does not encounter [the fruition of] deeds one did not do, for example, when one analyzes whether deeds that were done are lost or not, one must analyze whether or not the experience of the fruition of the deed that was accumulated appears where the doer of the deeds appeared. In the same way, when one analyzes whether or not one encounters [the fruition of] deeds one did not do, one must analyze whether or not the doer of the deeds accumulated in the past appears where one encounters the fruition of the deed that was accumulated in the past. In that case, if you assert that the self at the time of the former lifetime and the self of the present are different, and assert that the former self does not experience the fruition but the later self enjoys the fruition of the deeds done by the former self, then you must assert that one does encounter [the fruition of] deeds one did not do. That is because if you assert that the self at the time of the former lifetime and the self of the present are different, and assert that the former self does not experience the fruition but the later self enjoys the fruition of the deeds done by the former self, then you must assert that the doer of the deeds accumulated in the past does not appear where one encounters the fruition of the deed that was accumulated in the past. That follows because the doer of the deed in the past is not different from the former self; you must assert that that which is not different from the former self does not appear where one encounters the fruition of the deed that was accumulated in the past.

You might think that if the self of the time of the former lifetime and the present self were different by way of their own nature, then the fault would exist that one does encounter [the fruition of] deeds one did not do. However, there is no place for such a [fault] to be equally found against the assertion that the two are merely different [on the conventional level].

To respond to that, for example, you assert that the former self and the later self are different by way of their own nature; if you assert that the later self enjoys the fruition of the deeds done by the former self, then you are unable to avoid that one does encounter [the fruition of] deeds one did not do. In the same way, you assert that the former self and the later self are just merely different; if you assert that the later self enjoys the fruition of the deeds done by the former self without the former self experiencing the fruition, then you are unable to avoid that one does encounter [the fruition of] deeds one did not do. The reasons are similar. That follows because, as was set forth earlier, the doer of the deeds accumulated in the past is not different from the former self; if that which is not different from the former self does not appear where one encounters the fruition of the deed that was accumulated in the past, then you must assert that the fault of encountering [the fruition of] deeds one did not do, exists. For example, you assert that the former self and the later self are different by way of their own nature; if you assert that the later self enjoys the fruition of the deeds done by the later self, then you must assert that a lack of difference from the former self does not appear where one encounters the fruition of the deed that was accumulated in the past. In the same way, you assert that the former self and the later self are just merely different; if you assert that the later self enjoys the fruition of the deeds done by the former self, then you must assert that a lack of difference from the former self does not appear where one encounters the fruition of the deed that was accumulated in the past. Thus, [Candrakīrti's] *Entrance to the Middle Way* [*Madhyamakāvatāra*, 6:128] says:

> And in the moments prior to nirvāṇa, because there will be no agent
> Undergoing [the process of] arising and ceasing, its effect cannot be;
> And what is gathered by one will be consumed by another.[37]

[135a] And the twenty-seventh chapter [of Nāgārjuna's *Verses on the Middle Way* 27:10–11] says:

> For if this present self were indeed distinct from the past,
> Then it would exist even if the past were denied.
> And the past person would abide just as it was,
> Or it would be born here without having died.
>
> There would be annihilation [of the past self]
> And then destruction of [the fruits of] actions;
> Then [the fruits] of an action done by one person
> Would be reaped by another. This and similar consequences would follow.[38]

Such [consequences] are set forth with regard to the position that asserts that the former self and the later self are different by way of their own nature. In the same way, there are faults that follow from the position that asserts that the former self and the later self are just merely different. You might say that although the former self and the later self are individual, there are not the faults of deeds being lost and of one not encountering [the fruition of] deeds one did not do, because they are the same continuum. To respond to that, if you assert that individual selves are the same continuum, that is illogical, because here, if you assert that individual selves that disintegrate are the same continuum, then having analyzed whether that continuum itself is established as the same as or different from those individual selves that disintegrate, you must assert that there is no way to avoid a third possibility. If you assert that the individual selves that disintegrate are the same continuum, then you must assert that that same entity itself is not established as the same as those individual selves that disintegrate. The reason for this is stated in [Candrakīrti's] *Entrance to the Middle Way* [6.129ab]:

If you assert, "There is no such fault because it is in the same continuum,"
Objections to the same continuum were already explained in an earlier
    analysis.

And, with regard to how it was analyzed earlier, the same text [6:61] says:

Qualities attributed to Maitreya and Upagupta,
Being distinct, cannot belong to one continuum.
For things that differ from each other through their intrinsic characters,
It would be illogical for these to be part of a single continuum.

If things are established as individual by way of their own character, being two separate continuums, they cannot be posited as the same continuum. As the twenty-seventh chapter [of Nāgārjuna's *Verses on the Middle Way*, 27:16cd] says:

If it is held that the present human is distinct
From the future god, then there can be no continuum.[39]

For example, if individual selves are individual by way of their own character, it is not logical to include them in the same continuum. In the same way, if those selves and their continuum are established as individual by way of their own character, then those selves would have to be established as another continuum that is different from their continuum. To assert that is not logical.

Furthermore, it is not logical to assert that the former and later selves are established as having the quality of disintegration and that the continuum itself of those former and later selves does not have the quality of disintegration, yet that those former and later selves and their continuum are established as the same, because it is not logical to assert that things that are established as having individual characters are not individual. In that case, the continuum of those selves that disintegrate must not be viewed as non-different from those forms that disintegrate, just as the characteristics of the aggregates, such as being suitable as form and being subject to disintegration, are not viewed as non-different from the mind.

If you ask why one must assert that the continuum itself is not established as different from those former and later selves, I will explain. As set forth earlier, the doer of the deeds accumulated in the past is not different from the former self. If that which is not different from the former self does not appear where one encounters the fruition of the deed that was accumulated in the past, then you must assert that the doer of the deeds accumulated in the past does not appear where one encounters the fruition of the deed that was accumulated in the past. And if the fruition of the deed that was accumulated in the past is encountered where the doer of the deeds accumulated in the past does not appear, then one must assert that there are the faults of deeds being lost and [135b] of one not encountering [the fruition of] deeds one did not do. It is asserted that the former self and the later self are individual. If you assert that the continuum of the former and later selves is different from those selves, then the opponent is unable to avoid that deeds done are lost and that one does encounter [the fruition of] deeds one did not do. It is asserted that the former self and the later self are individual. If you assert that the continuum of the former and later selves is different from those selves, then you must assert that the fruition of the deeds that were accumulated is not experienced where the doer of the deeds that were accumulated in the past who is not different from the former self appears, and that the doer of the deeds accumulated in the past who is not different from the former self does not appear where the fruition of the deeds accumulated in the past is encountered. That follows because the continuum of the former and later selves itself and the later self appear where the fruition of the deeds accumulated in the past are encountered. Therefore, the continuum of the former and later selves itself and the later self are not non-different from the former self.

Thus, while it is the opponent's donkey that was loaded with the burden, the opponent would be feeding the horse—which was not given the load—the grass and roasted barley that were meant to be given to the donkey. This means that the opponents, arrogant about their surpassing skill in the essential points of cause and effect, would be insufferably denigrating the supreme and excellent essential points of cause and effect. I have explained these points most clearly.

Furthermore, [imagine] that a lama or other person goes to another world and later [comes back as] a newly born small child and says:

I am already free from the rounds of rebirth;
I have descended from the [pure] realm.
Not like leaves that cannot fall from the trees again;
Not like the currents of a river that do not turn back,
I am already free from the rounds [of rebirth].
As if returning, I have turned back;
I shall meet transmigrators again.
The robber of everything that none can turn away
Is the frightful power of death;
He has not robbed what is mine and could not make me powerless.
The gold and silver that belonged to me in the past,
My clothes and furniture and pleasing things,
Returning, there is none I will not find again.
Bring these to my presence, the one with power.
If disputed, it is certain that strife and war will arise.

This is a way of speaking that is contrary to reason. For as explained earlier, the opponent's system asserts that the selves of former and later births are individually distinct, and must assert that the self of the former birth does not exist at the time of the later birth. If one believes in such a way of speaking, one asserts that the self of the former birth does not exist at the time of the later birth, and must assert that what belonged to the self of the former birth exists at the time of the later birth. That follows because they must assert that what was controlled by the self of the former birth does not become uncontrolled at the time of the later birth. Furthermore, the *Extensive Sport (Lalitavistara)* says:

> At the time of death and transmigration
> One is separated forever from beings that are dear and beautiful,
> One does not return, never to meet them again,
> Like a leaf fallen from a tree, like the current of a river.
>
> Death makes the powerful powerless
> Death takes you away, as a river carries away a log,
> Like an eagle to a serpent, and a lion to an elephant,
> And like a fire to grass, trees, and creatures.[40]

Because the opponents believe these statements, if they develop faith in the words of old and young lamas who have died and been born, then how do they reconcile two essential points that cannot be reconciled?

> Alas, the blind who have eyes in this world
> Are those whose great eye of intelligence is covered.
> They master contradictory nonsense,
> Mindlessly placing their faith
> In deceptions concocted by demons.
> Alas, the blind who have eyes in this world
> Lack the power of awareness to distinguish true and false.

[136a] Now, a questioner expresses a qualm, saying, "A later lama or person describes without confusion and remembers without error all of the possessions that were owned by a previous lama or person. How does this happen?" This is the answer. While appealing to those lamas who describe without error and without confusion all of the possessions that were owned by the previous lama, I shall ask them questions in the following way. When you had appeared previously, at that time you engaged in virtuous deeds and accumulated deeds of perfect virtue without laziness. At that time did you or did you not become skilled in such things as reading and reciting the scriptures, distinguishing their fine points, and elucidating both their words and their meaning without confusion? Did you or did you not comprehend and take to heart the essential points of such things as cultivating faith,

obeisance, offering, confession of sins, rejoicing [in the virtue of others], imploring [the buddhas and bodhisattvas] to turn the wheel of the dharma, requesting [them not to pass into nirvāṇa], and dedication [of merit]? Did you or did you not understand without error what is to be recognized [the truth of suffering], what is to be abandoned [the truth of origin], what is to be actualized [the truth of cessation], and what is to be cultivated [the truth of the path] by those who wish to attain the supreme goal that beings can achieve? So, once again, attaining the fruition of perfect virtue and a fruition of these deeds, when you were born as a human in this lifetime, did you remember these without any error? Did you know all those things clearly, without the eyes of your intellect being clouded in the least by the darkness of forgetfulness? Or, like the feeling of nausea when seeing a ripe boil burst open, were you abandoned by your memory of the past so that you had to newly memorize and learn, without it being effortless, whatever you had memorized, learned, and known at the time of the former life, such as essential points of the teaching, supreme complete precepts, and prayers?

As soon as they hear these points raised, the eminent lamas respond in the following way with a consensus of thought and words. "When we appeared previously, at that time we engaged in virtuous deeds and accumulated deeds of perfect virtue without laziness, with great effort, we memorized the words of the dharma and comprehended all of its meaning without exception. However, at the time of being born as a human in this life, arising from the past deed and having attained a pleasing fruition and an auspicious body endowed with leisure, like entering a house that is covered in darkness, whatever dharma, letters, prayers, essential points of teachings, and excellent complete instructions that one had known in the past do not appear to the mind. Thus, the need definitely arises to newly hear these from someone else and to gradually learn them with great difficulty." This is the answer they so kindly provide.[41]

In that case, it is not correct that a later lama or person remembers all of the possessions that were owned by a previous lama or person because a later lama or person does not remember the individual doctrines that were memorized and previously known by the previous lama or person. If you say that that does not follow, I will explain the reason. In the opponent's scriptures, the feasibility of the memory of past experiences is explained like this. For example, although the feet of a dove that lives on the thatched roof of a house that has a vessel filled with yogurt do not step in the vessel of yogurt, its footprints are seen there. In the same way, they assert that although a person of this life has not gone to the time of a previous birth, it is not contradictory that he remembers his previous experiences [from the former life] here [in this life]. As [Candrakīrti's] commentary on [Āryadeva's] *Four Hundred (Catuḥśataka)*, says:

> We abandon the idea that causes and conditions are the same or different [from each other]. If all that exists is an impermanent stream of compositional factors manifested by specific causes, then it is reasonable to say that the imputedly existing self that has those [compositional factors] as its substantial cause remembers its [former] lives. Things are not established by way of their own character; it is not unreasonable that they encounter the conditions of such aspects and [136b] are changed. Therefore, one should analyze thoroughly the inconceivable quality that things have causes that are not established by their own character. Thus, the footprints of a dove that lives on a roof covered with much thatch on a house that has a container filled with yogurt inside are seen [in the yogurt] as if it were mud. Yet, it is impossible that its feet stepped there.

For more detail, one should look in Candrakīrti's *Entrance to the Middle Way*.[42]

Therefore, in the context of analyzing the example, the opponent sets forth six things: (1) the vessel of yogurt, (2) the thatched roof, (3) the feet of the dove, (4) the feet of the dove on the thatched roof, (5) the footprints of the dove that lives on the thatched roof being left in the vessel of yogurt, and (6) the footprints being seen in the vessel of yogurt at a later time when the feet of the dove are not on the thatched roof. In the context of correlating the example to the actual point, if one applies the six parts of the meaning that very much accord with those six, it must be understood in this way. The vessel of yogurt in this case is consciousness. The well-thatched roof in this case are the five sense organs of the eye, ear, nose, tongue, and body, which are parts of the form aggregate. The feet of the dove in this case are the five objects [of the sense organs]: pleasant or unpleasant forms, sounds, odors, tastes, and objects of touch. The feet of the dove on the thatched roof in this case are the five objects of beautiful and ugly forms, sounds, odors, tastes, and objects of touch being perceived by and touched by the five sense organs. The footprints of the dove that lives on the thatched roof being left in the vessel of yogurt in this case are the five objects, such as pleasant and unpleasant forms, which have been perceived by and touched by the five external sense organs, such as the eye, leaving a feeling of either pleasure or displeasure, like an after image or an after sensation, on the mental consciousness, which is not an external part but is an internal continuum. The footprints being seen in the vessel of yogurt at a later time when the feet of the dove are not on the thatched roof in this case correspond to the five pleasant or unpleasant objects of the earlier time, which are not perceptible by or touchable by the five sense organs of the later time. At this later time as well, the mental consciousness is to be understood in terms of the subsequent recollection of the earlier feelings and experiences.

Therefore, for example, although the feet of the dove have just stepped on the roof, just due to their being on top of the roof, the footprints are left in the vessel of yogurt in which they have not stepped. In the same way, although the five external objects such as form have only been perceived by and touched by the five external sense organs such as the eye, just due to being perceived by and touched by the five external sense organs such as the eye, a feeling of pleasure or displeasure from a previous time is left on the mental consciousness that did not perceive or touch [those objects].

Thus, if one asks, "What is the reason a later lama or person remembers all of the possessions that were owned by a previous lama or person?," the opponents give this answer: "It is because the wealth and possessions that appeared to and were touched by the external sense organs of the lama or person of the previous lifetime had produced some feeling in the mental consciousness at the earlier time." In that case, if you assert that a later lama or person remembers without error and without confusion all of the possessions that were owned by a previous lama or person, then you must assert that a later lama or person remembers without error and without confusion the doctrines that were memorized and known by a previous lama or person. And if it is untenable that a later lama or person remembers the doctrines that were memorized and known by a previous lama or person, [137a] then it must be untenable that a later lama or person remembers without error and without confusion all of the possessions that were owned by a previous lama or person, because the reasons are similar. That follows because you assert that the wealth and possessions that existed in the past and were touched by the external sense organs of the lama or person of the previous lifetime produced some feeling in the mental consciousness at the earlier time and this is the reason a later lama or person remembers all of the possessions that were owned by a previous lama or person. What has been touched by the external sense organs of the lama or person of the previous lifetime in all situations of reading, listening, or memorizing creates in the mental consciousness at the earlier time a feeling that accords with that touch. Furthermore, if the opponent asserts that even though the feet of the dove that lives on the thatched roof of a house in which there is a vessel filled with yogurt do not step in the vessel of yogurt, its footprints are seen there, then what need is there to say that [the opponent] must assert that if the feet of the dove step in the vessel of yogurt, then its footprints are to be seen there?

In that case, when one differentiates the eighteen elements—the eye element, the form element, and the eye consciousness element; the ear element, the sound element, and the ear consciousness element; the nose element, the odor element, and the nose consciousness element; the tongue element, the taste element, and the tongue consciousness element; the body element, the object of touch element, and the body consciousness element; the mind element, the phenomenon element, and the mental consciousness element—then the well-thatched roof is the object of the five external elements of the eye, ear, nose, tongue, and body. The object of the vessel of yogurt that is covered with a well-thatched roof is an object of the five external elements of the eye, ear, nose, tongue, and body and the mental element that is included with them. The object of the feet of the dove that stand on top of the thatched roof and do not step in the vessel of yogurt is the actual object of any of the eye, ear, nose, tongue, and body consciousnesses, and is the object of the five elements of form, sound, taste, odor, and object of touch that are not causes of it being apprehended by the mental consciousness as having signs. The phenomenon element is not a cause of [an object] being apprehended as having signs by any of the eye, ear, nose, tongue, or body consciousnesses. Therefore, the phenomenon element must be understood as being like the feet of the dove that step in the vessel of yogurt without living on the thatched roof.

Thus, if the opponents assert that the forms and so forth that are perceived and felt at the time of the previous lifetime by the external sense organs of the lama or person of the previous lifetime are remembered by a later lama or person without error, without confusion, and without obstruction, then what need is there to say that they must assert that the doctrines that were memorized and known by the lama or person of the previous life-

time are remembered by a later lama or person without error, without confusion, and without obstruction? If it is untenable that the doctrines that
were memorized and known by the lama or person of the previous lifetime
are remembered by a later lama or person without obstruction, then what
need is there to say that it is untenable that a later lama or person remembers without error and without confusion all of the possessions that were
owned by the lama or person of the previous lifetime? Thus, as explained
earlier, regarding the feasibility that a later lama or person does not remember
the individual doctrines that were memorized and previously known by the
lama or person of the previous lifetime, "It must be asserted that it is untenable that a later lama or person remembers without error and without confusion all of the possessions that were owned by the lama or person of the
previous lifetime [137b] because a later lama or person does not remember
the individual doctrines memorized and known by the lama or person of
the previous lifetime." It is correct that the entailment flung here must be
established for the opponent.

If you think, "Would it not be a contradiction to say that it is tenable
that a later lama or person describes without confusion all of the possessions
that were owned by the lama or person of the previous lifetime, but that it
is untenable that he himself remembers all of the possessions that were owned
by the lama or person of the previous lifetime? It is like the contradiction of
asserting that the physical body moves and grows larger yet that body is devoid of life."

To respond to that objection, by understanding that a reflection [of a face
in a mirror] lacks a [real] face, there is no contradiction whatsoever in not
conceiving it to be true as a face but conceiving it to be true as a reflection.
In the same way, there is no contradiction whatsoever in not conceiving it
to be true that a later lama or person remembers all of the possessions that
were owned by the lama or person of the previous lifetime, but conceiving
it to be true that a later lama or person describes without confusion all of the
possessions that were owned by the lama or person of the previous lifetime.
When small children who have not learned language see the reflection of a
face, they play games with it, conceiving it to be true as a face. Older people
who have learned language recognize that those [reflections] do not exist as
a face and lack being a face, yet with regard to their conception of the
mere existence of the reflection that appears as a face, they conceive it to
be true. Or, for example, in the case of an illusion, there is no contradiction

whatsoever in some members of the audience conceiving the [conjured] horse or elephant to be true and the illusionist himself knowing that the horse and elephant are false. In the same way, with regard to a later lama or person describing all of the possessions that were owned by the lama or person of the previous lifetime, there is no contradiction whatsoever in a conventional consciousness not conceiving that it lacks memory that accords with that description, and a reasoning consciousness conceiving that it does lack memory.

Furthermore, for example, the appearance of an illusory horse or elephant is seen by the eye consciousness, and in dependence on the mental conscious-ness determining that the horse or elephant do not exist in the way that they appear, certainty is produced that the appearance as a horse or an ele-phant is an illusory or false appearance. In the same way, the description by a later lama or person of all of the possessions that were owned by the lama or person of the previous lifetime is established to be undeniable for a con-ventional consciousness, and it is determined by a reasoning consciousness that [those possessions] lack being internally remembered in the way that they are described. In dependence on these two [consciousnesses], certainty is produced that the external description is illusory or false. Regarding this, the existence of the description by a later lama or person of all of the posses-sions that were owned by the lama or person of the previous lifetime is not proven by a reasoning consciousness. Its lack of being internally remembered in the way that it is externally described is not proven by conventional valid cognition. Therefore, this is the reason for the necessity of both a reasoning consciousness that investigates whether or not the memory exists in the way that it was externally described, and the conventional mind that conceives of the description itself as existing.

In that case, for example, the description by a later lama or person of all of the possessions that were owned by the lama or person of the pre-vious lifetime is established to be undeniable for a conventional con-sciousness, and it is determined by a reasoning consciousness that [those possessions] lack being internally remembered in the way that they are described. There is no contradiction whatsoever between these two. In the same way, there is no contradiction whatsoever in asserting that it is tenable that a later lama or person describes all of the possessions that were owned by the lama or person of the previous lifetime, and that it is unten-able that he remembers all of the possessions that were owned by the lama or person of the previous lifetime, because the subjects are separate and the objects are also separate.

[138a] Furthermore, [the opponent says, "In that case,] we assert that it is untenable that our later lamas or persons remember all the possessions owned by the previous lama or person. Therefore, we assert that it is untenable that our later lamas or persons describe all the possessions owned by the previous lama or person. But does that violate conventional valid cognition?"

In answer to that, for example, illusionists make conjured forms and conjured humans of various sizes and make them utter various verbal responses to each other. Some small children who see the show think, "The conjured humans are talking to each other." If an older person skilled in language contradicts the small children who are not skilled in language, saying that [the conjured humans] are not [speaking to each other], he is not contradicting conventional valid cognition. In the same way, even though one asserts that it is untenable that our later lamas or persons describe all the possessions owned by the lama or person of the previous lifetime, one is not contradicting conventional valid cognition. For example, at the time of the show, although it is established by conventional valid cognition that various verbal responses occur, it is not established by conventional valid cognition that the conjured humans utter various verbal responses to each other. In the same way, although it is established by conventional valid cognition that various words arise describing all the possessions owned by the lama or person of the previous lifetime, the description by the later lama or person of all the possessions owned by the lama or person of the previous lifetime is not established by conventional valid cognition. If you ask the reason, I will explain.

Someone speaking to a person who has stolen some jewels, without knowing that the person has stolen something, tells a lie, saying, "You stole it." Someone else, who saw the person steal the jewels, says, "You stole it." Both are similar in saying, "You stole this wealth." Yet, although the thief did steal it, one is telling a lie and the other is telling the truth. Thus, [Candrakīrti's] *Clear Words (Prasannapadā)* says, "Driven by dislike, someone blames a person who has in fact committed a robbery, saying, 'He stole it,' without in fact knowing that he did so. Another person accuses [the thief], having actually seen [the crime]. Although there is no difference in the fact, there is a difference in the person who understands it, saying to one,

'You are a liar,' and to the other, 'You are telling the truth.' When the first person is properly investigated, it will lead to ill-repute and [be considered] a misdeed; for the other it will not."[43] It should be understood in this way through using this example.

For example, through analyzing the two true and false statements, it is not sufficient to decide merely "It exists as the speaker said." Nonetheless, if one cannot decide, "The speaker spoke correctly and in accordance with his understanding," then one must assert that one cannot decide, "The speaker spoke truthfully and without falsehood." Therefore, by analyzing whether or not later lamas or persons are describing all the possessions owned by the lama or person of the previous lifetime, it is not sufficient to simply decide, "This and that possession was owned by the lama or person of the previous life, in accordance with whatever words were uttered from the mouth of the later lama or person." Nonetheless, if one cannot decide, "The thing described by words in accordance with whatever words were uttered from the mouth of the later lama or person is an object of his awareness or his discrimination," then one must assert that one cannot decide, "This lama or later person has described all the possessions owned by the lama or person of the previous lifetime." For example, seeing with the eye is not established without relying on the form that appears to the eye. In the same way, the description in words [138b] is not established without relying on the thing that is described in words being an object of awareness or discrimination.

It is not established by conventional valid cognition that all the possessions owned by a lama or person of the previous lifetime are objects of awareness or discrimination of a lama or person of the present. Therefore, although the arising of words describing all the possessions owned by a lama or person of the previous lifetime is established by conventional valid cognition, it must be asserted that the description by the later lama or person of all the possessions owned by a lama or person of the previous lifetime is not established by conventional valid cognition. Thus, for example, a person possessed by an evil spirit speaks in various different languages and they are perceived by the ear consciousness. Although those words are uttered from his mouth, not only is it untenable that he is learned in various different languages, one must assert that it is untenable that he is speaking in various different languages. In the same way, childish common beings apprehend the later lama or person describing all the possessions owned by a lama or person of the previous lifetime. Although the words are uttered from his mouth, not only is it untenable that the later lama or person remembers all the possessions owned by a lama or person of the previous lifetime, one must assert that it is untenable that he describes all the possessions owned by a previous lama or person. Therefore, the opponents' statement, "It must be asserted that a later lama or person remembers all the possessions owned by a previous lama or person because the later lama or person describes all the possessions owned by a lama or person of the previous lifetime," levels at us the faults we have brought against them. Thus, we should throw these objections back at them.

It must be asserted that it is untenable that the later lama or person remembers all the possessions owned by a lama or person of the previous lifetime because one must assert that it is untenable that the later lama or person describes all the possessions owned by a lama or person of the previous lifetime.

[The opponent] might think, "The later lama or person not describing all the possessions owned by a lama or person of the previous lifetime depends on the later lama or person not remembering all the possessions owned by a previous lama or person. And the later lama or person not remembering all the possessions owned by a lama or person of the previous lifetime depends on it being untenable that the later lama or person describes all the possessions owned by a lama or person of the previous lifetime. Therefore, whatever examples and reasons that we state to prove our own position are not established as being similar to what [you have presented] earlier; otherwise there will be the fault of the similarity between the proof and what is being proven."

That is not the case. The later lama or person not describing all the possessions owned by a lama or person of the previous lifetime is not held as a proof of the later lama or person not remembering all the possessions owned by a lama or person of the previous lifetime. Therefore, the later lama or person describing all the possessions owned by a lama or person of the previous lifetime is shown to be untenable because it is shown to be unsuitable as a proof for the opponent's position that the later lama or person remembers all the possessions owned by a lama or person of the previous lifetime. Apart from the fact that the later lama or person not remembering all the possessions owned by a lama or person of the previous lifetime has already been established in dependence on a proof that is different [from the thesis], [139a] it is stated as a proof for why it is untenable that the later lama or person describes all the possessions owned by a lama or person of the previous lifetime.

Furthermore, with regard to the position that asserts that those who perform deeds of perfect virtue are born as humans through the fruition of those deeds after they die, it is asserted that at the time of the later lifetime, the person born as a human does not remember the scriptures that he memorized and learned at the time of his previous life, but at the time of the later lifetime he remembers all of the possessions that he owned at the time of his previous lifetime. This is to be understood and its faults presented. If it is the time of the attainment of the fruition of perfect virtue, it must be a time that does not contradict perfect virtue and that attaches the mind to the object of that [perfect virtue], and it must be a time when the mind is not distracted toward an object that is an obstacle to perfect virtue, because if it is the time of sowing and planting the seed that yields the fruition of perfect virtue, it must be a time that does not contradict perfect virtue and that attaches the mind to the object of that [perfect virtue], and it must be a time when the mind is not distracted toward an object that is an obstacle to perfect virtue. If you say that does not follow, it does follow because the means for sowing and planting the seed that yields the fruition of perfect virtue and the means for enjoying the fruition of perfect virtue must be the same. That follows because if the means for sowing and planting the seed that yields the fruition of perfect virtue does not become the means of enjoying the fruition of perfect virtue, then the means for sowing and planting the seed that yields the fruition of perfect virtue must become wasted. That follows because if the means for sowing and planting the seed that yields the fruition of perfect virtue does not become the means for enjoying the fruition of perfect virtue, then the means for sowing and planting the seed that yields the fruition of perfect virtue must become something that is not suitable to accumulate and has no connection to accumulation.

Furthermore, if it is not the case, then one would have to assert that the person who accumulates deeds of perfect virtue and the person who enjoys the fruition of deeds of perfect virtue are not the same and are different. If you ask the reason, I will explain. Regarding the person who accumulates deeds of perfect virtue, without his intrinsic nature serving as the means for sowing and planting the seeds that yield the fruition of perfect virtue, the virtues of body, speech, and mind will not arise, and, without the arising of the virtues of body, speech, and mind, the person who accumulates deeds of perfect virtue does not come to be established. Therefore, wherever the person who accumulates deeds of perfect virtue is observed, the lack of intrinsic nature of the person who performs deeds of perfect virtue does not exist. If the means for sowing and planting the seeds that yield the fruition of perfect virtue does not become the means for enjoying the fruition of perfect virtue, this means that the person himself who performs deeds of perfect virtue and serves as the means for sowing and planting the seed that yields the fruition of perfect virtue would not become a means for enjoying the fruition of perfect virtue, yet the enjoyment of the fruition of perfect virtue would still exist. In that case, wherever one would have to assert that the enjoyment of the fruition of perfect virtue is observed, it would be possible that the lack of intrinsic nature of the person who performs deeds of perfect virtue would not be non-existent; one would have to assert that the person who accumulates deeds of perfect virtue and the person who enjoys the fruition of perfect virtue are different.

In brief, for example, the sense organ of the eye serves as the means for seeing pleasant forms and serves as the means for enjoying pleasant forms. The ear sense organ serves as the means for hearing melodious sounds and it serves as the means for enjoying melodious sounds. Such things as knowing how much to eat, living in isolation, knowing satisfaction, and mental and physical pliancy serve as the means for practicing the dharma and they serve as the means for enjoying feelings of pleasure now, which arise through practicing the dharma in this lifetime. [139b] In the same way, it must be asserted that such things as not contradicting perfect virtue and, having attached the mind to the object of that [perfect virtue], the mind not being distracted toward an object that is an obstacle to perfect virtue, serve as the means for sowing and planting the seeds that yield the fruition of perfect virtue and serve as the means for enjoyment at the time of attaining the fruition of perfect virtue.

Furthermore, for example, the sprout that arises from a rice seed is rice, the sprout that grows from a barley seed is barley, the sprout that grows from a wheat seed is wheat, and the sprout that arises from a pea[44] seed is peas. In the same way, you must assert that the fruition that arises from the seed of perfect virtue has the character of perfect virtue because, if a sprout does not grow from a seed at a place where it is tenable for the seed to exist, then dense darkness would arise from the tongues of a flame and it would not be possible to avoid anything that is or is not an effect being produced from anything that is or is not its cause. If the fruition that arises from the seed of perfect virtue must have the character of perfect virtue, then the time of the attainment of the fruition of perfect virtue must be the time of the enjoyment of the fruition of perfect virtue. And, with regard to things that have the character of perfect virtue, the enjoyment does not arise except in dependence on the mind being attached to the object of perfect virtue and the mind not being distracted toward an object that is an obstacle to perfect virtue. It must be decided that the time of the attainment of the fruition of perfect virtue is the time of not contradicting perfect virtue and attaching the mind to the object of that [perfect virtue] and is the time of the mind not being distracted toward an object that is an obstacle to perfect virtue. In that case, if you assert that that the person who performs deeds of perfect virtue is born as a human through the fruition of those deeds after he dies, then you must assert that the time when the person who performs deeds of perfect virtue is born as a human through the fruition of those deeds after he dies must be the time that he attains and enjoys the fruition of perfect virtue. Therefore, you must assert that the time when the person who performs deeds of perfect virtue is born as a human through the fruition of those deeds after he dies, must be the time that he enjoys things that have the character of perfect virtue. Therefore, you must assert that the time when a person who performs acts of perfect virtue is born as a human after he dies, must be a time when he does not contradict perfect virtue and attaches the mind to the object of that [perfect virtue] and the mind not being distracted toward an object that is an obstacle to perfect virtue. In that case, you must assert that (1) not contradicting perfect virtue and attaching the mind to the object of that [perfect virtue] and (2) not remembering anything about religion and its essential points that one had memorized and learned earlier are mutually exclusive. And you must assert that (1) not being distracted toward an object that is an obstacle to perfect virtue and (2) remembering without error and without confusion all of the possessions owned at the time of a previous lifetime are mutually exclusive. Therefore, you must assert that (1) a person who performs deeds of perfect virtue being born as a human through the fruition of those deeds after he dies and (2) that person remembering all of the possessions he owned in a previous life but not remembering anything about religion and its essential points that he had memorized and learned earlier are mutually exclusive. You must assert that asserting this is a position that creates amazing delusion and is only frivolous and contradictory talk that does not rest on reason. In that case, in order to prove that a person who performs deeds of perfect virtue is born as a human through the fruition of those deeds after he dies, you are proposing that he remembers his former experiences. What is to be proved is not established because the proof contradicts logic and is not established.

[140a] Here, an impartial and capable person, led and guided by the rope of various perfect tenets and solid and irrefutable reasons, who is unclouded by the darkness of prejudice, says: "In this world there are many different types of humans, such as foolish common beings, the wise, and the superior. Therefore, it is illogical that all of the different types of humans, wherever they are, completely lack the power of mind to distinguish the logical and the illogical, coming under the power of external and internal causes of error, lacking the path that leads to the supreme aim of persons, the goal. In all of the lands that exist on the vast earthly circle of the world, some humans who are about to die and are being born tell common people stories about coming here from other worlds. When they do so, it is tenable that they make it an article of the perfect faith that a person who performs perfect and virtuous deeds will be born as a human after they die as a fruition of those deeds. In some of the lands that exist on the vast earthly circle of the world, some humans who are about to die and are being born tell stories about how they can remember and describe their earlier experiences as if they were coming here from other worlds. However, when, in all of the other limitless and immeasurable lands, they teach about a different fruition that arises later from deeds of perfect virtue and does not contradict reason, without stories about returning here from other worlds, one must understand that [the belief that] after their death, one who has performed deeds perfect of virtue is born as a human through the fruition of those deeds, and that they remember their experiences from the time of their previous life are abodes of error and perversions of the perfect faith.

"However, without considering your body and life, you star head lamas, who have bestowed the great kindness of coming to this Tibet from so far away, seeking to bring about the welfare of others, have carefully examined and minutely analyzed the various lands and the various religions of the various lands. Having told us stories about what things are like in all the other different lands of the vast world in the past and in the present, please act with kindness to all in the snowy land by clearing away all the stains of doubt and misconception and teaching the articles of the unmistaken faith."

In answer to this question: If one were to set forth how the structure of the vast world came about, the vast circle of the earth is composed of two: dry land and the realm of water. If one were to set forth what the circle of the earth composed of dry land and the realm of water is like, it is a vast sphere of earth made from four collected and gathered parts. The first of the parts, which is the main one and is wondrous, is called Europe. It has many large lands and small lands and large islands and small islands. In all the lands and islands, the marvelous ones who stand firm and the persons with incomparable training in all fields of knowledge hold the excellent religion of the star heads to be the crown jewel and abide in it unwaveringly and unshakably with body, speech, and a perfectly clear mind.

The second part is called Asia. Among the great many large lands and small lands and large and small islands are India, Kashmir, Nepal, China, Tibet, Upper Mongolia, Lower Mongolia, and so forth. In all those lands and islands, some follow the excellent religion of the star heads, some the system of the Jews, some the system of the Muslims, some the scriptures of the *ācāryas,* and some the system of Tibet, China, and Nepal. The third part is called Africa. It has a great many large lands and small lands and large and small islands. Among all the lands and islands, some follow the excellent religion of the star heads and some follow the scriptures of the Muslims, [140b] but most of the common people are pagans. The fourth part is called America. It has a great many large lands and small lands and large and small islands. Among all the lands and islands, the excellent religion of the star heads is very widespread and there are also many pagans.

On no land or island among the immeasurable lands and islands of the three parts called Europe, Africa, and America has this wandering in *saṃsāra* become an article of faith. Among an inconceivable and immeasurable number of beings who follow various different religions, not a single person tells stories of returning here from another world at any time of dying or being born. The pleasures of this world of the living are to be understood as the causes and conditions of affliction, non-virtue, and suffering and [those pleasures] are unmistakenly held to be unsuitable as the fruition of true virtue. The various qualities of all the sufferings of this world of the living and particularly the quality of severing the root of the afflictions, the quality of refraining from sin, and the quality of serving as a cause for manifesting virtue and goodness are to be understood. With an attitude of taking on those [sufferings], they are held to have a pleasing quality and to be unmistaken objects to wish for, and it is held that it is clearly untenable that [sufferings] are fruitions that arise from non-virtue. They believe that in this world of the living, at the time of fruition, leaving nothing behind, persons go from this world without coming back, like the leaves from a tree and the currents of a river. And in accordance with what propelled them at the time of the cause, they believe that they will experience a fruition that is endless and inexhaustible in the next world.

The inconceivable number of persons who follow the three religions of the star heads, the Jews, and the Muslims and who live in or rule the many lands and islands of this part called Asia do not agree with each other on a great many articles of faith. Nonetheless, understanding that the pleasures and sufferings of this world of the living are the causes of virtue and non-virtue and that it is untenable that they be the fruition of virtue and non-virtue, they hold that the wandering in *saṃsāra* is a misconception of childish common beings disturbed by the sleep of ignorance and is a perversion of the perfect faith. Among an inconceivable and immeasurable number of beings who follow these three different religions, not a single person tells stories of returning here from another world at any time of dying or being born, and they believe that, in accordance with what propelled them at the time of the cause, they experience a fruition that is endless and inexhaustible in the next world. Thus, in just some of the lands and islands that exist on the vast earthly realm of the world, there are just a few people dying or being born who tell stories, lying about how they can remember and describe their earlier experiences as if they were coming here from other worlds. However, in all of the other limitless and immeasurable lands and islands, immeasurable numbers of beings in this world—except for the very few people who contradict reason and are not like us—unmistakenly teach about and observe a different fruition that arises later from deeds of perfect virtue and does not contradict reason, without any stories about returning here from other worlds.

Therefore, those endowed with the clear eyes of intelligence, unclouded by the darkness of prejudice, must understand that if birth as a human is a fruition that arises from deeds of perfect virtue, [141a] then, for example, it is asserted that those born as humans in the land of Tibet are born there through the fruition of deeds of perfect virtue. In the same way, one must assert that those born as humans in any other lands and islands are born there through the fruition of deeds of perfect virtue. For example, you assert that those born as humans in the land of Tibet are born there through the fruition of deeds of perfect virtue, and you assert that those born as humans in the land of Tibet are those who performed deeds of perfect virtue at the time of a previous life. In the same way, you assert those born as humans in any other lands and islands are born there through the fruition of deeds of perfect virtue. You must assert that those born as humans in any other lands and islands are those who performed deeds of perfect virtue at the time of a previous life. For example, you assert that those born as humans in the land of Tibet are those who performed deeds of perfect virtue at the time of a previous life, and because of that assertion, you assert that among those born as humans in the land of Tibet, some of them remember their previous experiences, describing their previous experience and telling stories about their previous life. In the same way, you assert that those born as humans in other lands and islands are those who performed deeds of perfect virtue at the time of a previous life, and because of that assertion, you must assert that among those born as humans in other lands and islands, some of them remember their previous experiences, describing their previous experience and telling stories about their previous life. And if, among those born as humans in other lands and islands, not even one person tells stories about their previous life, then, because the reasons are similar, it must be untenable that among those born as humans in the land of Tibet, there is even one person who tells stories about their previous life, as if they had come here from another world.

Thus, the assertion that in some country some person tells stories about their previous life, as if they had come here from another world, is contrary to reason. Those endowed with intelligence must understand it in this way: things that are false, have the quality of deception, and are like illusions are not reliable because they are things that exist in one way and appear in a different way. Furthermore, it is illogical to say that what is not non-deceptive is valid because it is illogical that a fool is valid. Therefore, you must assert that the five conventional sense consciousnesses are not valid sources of knowledge with regard to objects that are not directly perceivable; for you must assert that the five sense consciousnesses are not non-deceptive. This is because you must assert that the five sense consciousnesses are false and have the character of being deceptive, and they are like illusions. That follows because to the five sense consciousnesses, things exist in one way and appear in a different way. Therefore, it must be decided that those who hold that [things exist] as they appear to the five conventional sense conscious-nesses are like the blind leading the blind and lack the path that is pleasing to the wise. Therefore, those who do not contradict the path that is pleasing to the wise investigate with reason and analyze the things that appear to the five conventional sense consciousnesses. If the way in which a thing appears to a conventional sense consciousness does not logically contradict the way it abides, then it is possible that the thing [exists] as it appears to the con-ventional consciousness. However, if it is understood that the way in which a thing appears to a conventional sense consciousness logically contradicts the way it abides, one holds unmistakenly that the thing does not exist in the way that it appears to a conventional sense consciousness and that it is a thing that exists in one way and appears in a different way.

Thus, to the eye sense consciousness, the wondrous orbs of the sun and moon appear to be close to the peak of a mountain and to be much smaller than the form of a vast expanse of the ground, that they can neither obstruct nor measure up [to the space on the ground.] In that case, [141b] one de-cides that the wondrous orbs of the sun and the moon appear in one way to the conventional sense consciousnesses and exist in a different way because one understands that it contradicts logic that the wondrous orbs of the sun and moon appear to be close to the peak of a mountain and to be much smaller than the form of a vast expanse of the ground, that they can neither obstruct nor measure up [to the space of the ground].

Now, the opponent asserts that among those born as humans in the land of Tibet, some remember what they experienced in the past as if they had come from an earlier time, describing their previous experience and telling stories about their previous life. [The opponent also] asserts that such things are established by the valid cognition of a conventional consciousness and a reasoning consciousness, or are established just by the valid cognition of a conventional consciousness. If it is the first, that is untenable because, if you assert that it is established by the valid cognition of a conventional conscious-ness and a reasoning consciousness that those who perform deeds of perfect virtue are born as humans through the fruition of those deeds after they die, that they remember what they experienced in the past as if they had come from an earlier time, describing their previous experience and telling stories about their previous life, then [the claim] that those who perform deeds of perfect virtue are born as humans through the fruition of those deeds after they die must be established by the valid cognition of a conventional consciousness and a reasoning consciousness. However, as was set forth earlier, it contradicts logic that those who perform deeds of perfect virtue are born as humans through the fruition of those deeds after they die. If it is the second, that is also untenable because it contradicts logic that those who perform deeds of perfect virtue are born as humans through the fruition of those deeds after they die, that they remember what they experienced in the past as if they had come from an earlier time, describing their previous experience and telling stories about their previous life, and [it is untenable] because it is impossible for something that contradicts logic to be established by the valid cognition of a conventional consciousness. Thus, if it can be established that it contradicts logic that the fire that burns and the fuel that is burned and what is felt and a feeling do not depend on each other, then it is impossible to establish by the valid cognition of a conventional consciousness that fire burns without the fuel being burned and feeling is established when there is nothing to be felt.

Furthermore, for example, although the feet of a dove that lives on the thatched roof of a house that has a vessel filled with yogurt do not step in the vessel of yogurt, its footprints are seen there. In the same way, it is asserted in the scriptures of the opponent that although a person of this life did not go to a previous birth, the previous experiences are remembered here. One must understand how the feasibility of the memory for previous experiences is inferred in the scriptures of the opponent. For example, if you assert that although the feet of a dove that lives on the thatched roof of a house in the land of Tibet that has a vessel filled with yogurt do not step in the vessel of yogurt, its footprints being seen there is established by the valid cognition of a conventional consciousness, then you must assert that although the feet of a dove that lives on the thatched roof of a house in any other land or island that has a vessel filled with yogurt do not step in the vessel of yogurt, its footprints being seen there is established by the valid cognition of a conventional consciousness. And, although the feet of a dove that lives on the thatched roof of a house in any other land or island that has a vessel filled with yogurt do not step in the vessel of yogurt, if its footprints being seen there is not established by the valid cognition of a conventional consciousness, then, although the feet of a dove that lives on the thatched roof of a house in the land of Tibet that has a vessel filled with yogurt do not step in the vessel of yogurt, it must be untenable that its footprints being seen there is established by the valid cognition of a conventional consciousness. In the same way, if you assert that although a person born as a human in the land of Tibet did not go there at the time of a previous birth, it is established by the valid cognition of a conventional consciousness that they remember and describe here their previous experiences, then you must assert that although a person born as a human in any land or island [142a] did not go there at the time of a previous birth, it is must be established by the valid cognition of a conventional consciousness that they remember and describe here their previous experiences. And if it is not established by the valid cognition of a conventional consciousness that although a person born as a human in any land or island did not go there at the time of a previous birth, they remember and describe here their previous experiences, then it must be untenable that it is established by the valid cognition of a conventional consciousness that although a person born as a human in the land of Tibet did not go there at the time of a previous birth, that they remember and describe here their previous experiences. For example, regarding the reason for the feet of a dove being on top of a roof covered with much thatch of a house that has a vessel filled with yogurt inside, if the vessels of yogurt in houses in the land of Tibet are similar to the vessels of yogurt in any other land or island, then you must assert that no reason can be shown as to why in the vessels of yogurt in houses in the land of Tibet the footprint of a dove is seen, yet in the vessels of yogurt in houses in any other land or island, the footprint of a dove is not seen. In the same way, regarding the reason a person who went there at the time of a previous birth in a previous lifetime experienced this or that, if the persons who are born as humans in the land of Tibet in this lifetime are similar to the persons who are born as humans at the time of this lifetime in any other land or island, then one must assert that no reason can be shown why persons born as humans at the time of this lifetime in the land of Tibet, although they did not go there at the time of a previous birth, remember it here and describe their previous experiences, yet persons born as a human at the time of this lifetime in any other land or island, although they did not go there at the time of a previous birth, do not remember it here and describe their previous experiences.

Thus, as has been explained here, in all the other inconceivable and immeasurable [number of] lands and islands that exist in the vast earthly sphere of this world, not a single person has ever existed who remembered and described past experiences and told stories of his previous lives, as if he has come here from another world. In just some lands and islands that exist on the vast earthly sphere of this world, some people who are being born tell stories of their previous lives in the manner of remembering and explaining their past experiences, as if they have come here from another world, and this appears to a conventional sense consciousness. However, having developed certainty that what appears as memories and descriptions are illusions or false appearances in dependence on ascertaining with a reasoning consciousness that the memories and descriptions do not exist as they appear, one must realize that in these contexts, what appears to a conventional consciousness has a quality of falsity and deception, like an illusion.

Furthermore, it is not established by the valid cognition of a conventional consciousness that those who perform deeds of perfect virtue are born as humans through the fruition of those deeds after they die and that, being born there, they remember their past experiences, because those who perform deeds of perfect virtue being born as humans through the fruition of those deeds and that, being born there, their remembering their past experiences, is not an object of a conventional consciousness. That follows because with regard to those who perform deeds of perfect virtue being born as humans through the fruition of those deeds after they die, the "mind" or the "mentation" or the "consciousness" of those who perform deeds of perfect virtue, having given up the aggregates of the previous body, once again enters the womb and takes on the other aggregates of a body in a human place of birth. Therefore, it must be asserted that the "mind" or the "mentation" or the "consciousness" of those who perform deeds of perfect virtue is not established as an object of the five senses. Nor is it an object of the five external senses that the mind of one who performs deeds of perfect virtue, having given up the aggregates of the previous body, once again enters the womb and takes on the other aggregates of a body in a human place of birth. [142b] For example, if a vessel of yogurt that is covered by a roof with much thatch is not an object of the five senses, then it must follow that the footprint of a dove which is left there is not an object of the five senses. In the same way, without the mind of one who performs deeds of perfect virtue being an object of the five external senses, one must assert that his memory of past experiences is not an object of the five external senses. In that case, those who perform deeds of perfect virtue being born as humans through the fruition of those deeds and that, being born there, their remembering their past experiences, cannot depend on any conventional consciousness or reasoning consciousness. Therefore, the scriptures of the opponent which assert that [i.e., rebirth and the memory of rebirth] are not established by any proof or reason and are established as scriptures polluted by external and internal causes of error and are established as having the quality of being unworthy of trust, like the collapsed relying on the collapsed.

> Not clouded by the darkness of prejudice,
> Those endowed with the clear eyes of intelligence
> Do not sleep at the time of learning.
> With the eye of wisdom closed,
> Unable to distinguish what is and is not a fruition of virtue,
> The darkness of ignorance is not dispelled;
> The path of unreliable prejudice and deception is not discarded.
> If one does not enter the path pleasing to scholars,
> One will go to the next world
> Without time to return to correct one's errors
> And will undergo incessant suffering.
> You who are endowed with intelligence, understand this:
> Do not sleep at the time of learning;
> Dispel the darkness of ignorance.

Introduction to *Essence of the Christian Religion*

ငာ

Essence of the Christian Religion is unique among Desideri's five extant Tibetan works. Unlike *Origin of Sentient Beings, Phenomena, and So Forth (Sems can dang chos la sogs pa rnams kyi 'byung khungs)* and *Definite Goodness (Nges legs)*, it is written in the capital script rather than cursive script and presented as a traditional Tibetan xylograph, suggesting that it was intended to be printed and read widely. Like *Dawn, Signaling the Rising of the Sun That Dispels Darkness,* it presents the unique superiority of Christianity, but it does so in far more detail and with a better grasp of the vocabulary and conventions of the classical Tibetan language. Finally, unlike the *Inquiry,* it is complete. It is a manuscript of fifty folios, written in traditional xylograph form on folios 26 cm. long and 17.5 cm. wide (the pages are rather short and squat by Tibetan standards), in a clear capital script by the skilled hand of a scribe, with ten lines proportionally spaced on each page, except for the first page, where there is a larger script, as is sometimes the case in Tibetan works.

The title is *Essence of the Christian Religion (Ke ri se sti yan gyi chos lugs kyi snying po).* This is the only work of Desideri that uses "Christian" in the title. In the title and throughout this work, he renders "Christian" as *ke ri se sti yan,* which would be pronounced *kay ree say tee yen* in the Central Tibetan dialect. In addition, he consistently refers to his religion as "the Christian faith and religion" *(ke ri se sti yaṇ gyi dad lugs dang chos lugs)*. In the *Inquiry*, he is more allusive, referring to Christianity as "the light of perfect truth, excellent and sublime, the stainless and thoroughly pure religion" *(chos lugs dri ma med pa rnam par dag pa bden pa yang dag 'od zer mchog dam pa)*, sometimes shortened to "the stainless and pure religion" *(chos lugs dri ma med pa rnam par dag pa)*. He also refers to it as "the religion of the star heads" *(sgo skar gyi chos lugs)*, where, as discussed earlier, "star head" *(sgo skar)* is a pun on the homophone "white head" *(sgo dkar)*, a Tibetan term for Europeans. In *Dawn, Signaling the Rising of the Sun That Dispels Darkness*, he refers to himself as *sgo skar dpa' 'dri*, a term that does not make sense in Tibetan until one learns from the Italian original of the work that *dpa' 'dri* (pronounced *ba di* in Tibetan) is meant to render *padre*. Hence, a Catholic priest is a "star head padre."

The term in the title translated as "religion" *(chos lugs)* literally means "religious system" or "doctrinal system." It is the standard Tibetan term for a system of doctrines and is used to refer both to Buddhism and to non-Buddhist religions. Finally, the term *snying po* means "essence" or "heart"; it is the same term used to render the Sanskrit *hṛdaya* in what is known in English as the *Heart Sūtra*.

Before turning to the contents of the work, we should consider Desideri's brief references to it. In book 1, chapter 13, of his *Historical Notices*, written after his return to Italy, he relates the story of his composition of his first work (which may or may not have been *Dawn*), which he presented to Lhazang Khan on January 6, 1717. In chapter 15 he describes his time at Dakpo between December 1720 and April 1721, "continuing my study of other books of this sect necessary to my work, and gradually completing the book refuting the errors of these people that I had begun earlier."[1] He describes three books. Of the third, he writes:

> In the third and shortest volume, I set out the very same teachings contained in our Christian doctrines and standard catechisms, in part using proofs and in part suggesting them indirectly with brief reasons, using a method and style appropriate to a Christian community that is not yet mature and well schooled in doctrine but is young and in the process of formation.
>
> The first and second books are entirely in a style of argumentation and disputation that follows the forms and methods of the Tibetans themselves.

In both of these books the numerous arguments and reasons, though framed in ordinary language, are almost always taken from their own principles, beliefs, and authors, and from the books that they hold to be canonical and irrefutable. The third book is in the form of a dialogue, with some argumentation at those places where it is necessary. Many people asked me for copies of this last book before I left the mission.[2]

The third text is *Essence of the Christian Religion.* Although Desideri notes that many people asked him for copies of this last book, none seem to have survived. Elsewhere in his *Historical Notices,* Desideri calls *Essence of the Christian Religion* "a new catechism adapted to the understanding of those who are hearing about the Christian religion for the first time."[3]

In neither of his allusions to *Essence of the Christian Religion* does Desideri indicate that the first quarter of the text (1a1–22b9) is devoted to a refutation of emptiness. It is unclear why Desideri does not mention this; it may be that because he had dealt with emptiness extensively in both *Origin of Sentient Beings, Phenomena, and So Forth* and *Definite Goodness,* he did not need to mention its presence in *Essence of the Christian Religion.* Still, it is important to account for its presence there and for the part it plays in what Desideri calls a catechism. Given the disjunction in topic and style, is it an unrelated preface or is it essential to the presentation of Christianity that Desideri makes for his Tibetan audience? Before considering this question, it would be useful to briefly review what emptiness meant in Desideri's Tibet.

Buddhism is renowned for its doctrine of "no self" *(anātman),* said to have been the subject of the Buddha's second sermon after his enlightenment. According to this doctrine, as elaborated in great detail in India in the centuries that followed, there is no perduring soul or self to be found among the many physical and mental elements that together constitute the person, nothing that persists from lifetime to lifetime. There is no enduring entity that is the doer of deeds and the thinker of thoughts. Indeed, there is nothing among the various elements of the mind and body that lasts longer than an instant. There is instead merely a continuum of mental and physical moments that, because of their continuity and coherence, are mistakenly imagined to be endowed with some permanence. Furthermore, this error—that there is a self where in fact no self exists—constitutes the fundamental form of ignorance in Buddhism, motivating desire for and attachment to what benefits that self and hatred and aversion toward what threatens it. That desire and that hatred in turn motivate the negative deeds of body, speech, and mind that eventually bear fruit in the form of physical and mental suffering, both in the present lifetime and in future lives. Belief in self, therefore, is the root cause of all the suffering in the universe.

The doctrine of no self is held with some consistency throughout the centuries across the Buddhist traditions of Asia, although it receives more emphasis in some times and places than in others. The term "emptiness," although present in the mainstream traditions of Indian Buddhism, is far less central. The Sanskrit term is *śūnyatā*, taking the common adjective for "empty" (*śūnya*, as in the case of an empty vessel) and turning it into an abstract noun with the addition of the suffix *tā*. It is therefore misleading to translate the term as "voidness" or "nothingness." The term appears most frequently and famously in the Mahāyāna sūtras, especially in a genre of texts called perfection of wisdom (*prajñāpāramitā*), which began to appear some four centuries after the Buddha's death. Here we find the famous declaration in the *Heart Sūtra* that "form is emptiness; emptiness is form." Where the term "emptiness" does not appear, it is hinted at in often confounding statements, such as, in the *Diamond Sūtra*: "Any dust of the earth preached by the Buddha has been preached by the Buddha as being without dust. Thus it is called the dust of the earth." The perfection of wisdom sūtras are not philosophical treatises; they more often proclaim emptiness than articulate it in any systematic fashion. That task would fall to Indian commentators.

By far the most famous and influential of the Indian exponents of the doctrine of emptiness was the Indian monk Nāgārjuna, whose life is known for the most part only through legend; scholars speculate that he lived in the second century CE. Many of his works survive, and a number of these deal with the doctrine of emptiness; the most famous is his *Verses on the Middle Way (Madhyamakakārikā)*,[4] a work in twenty-seven chapters, which considers the major constituents of Buddhist thought—including nirvāṇa and the Buddha himself—and demonstrates that even they cannot be found under analysis. For example, in the chapter on motion, he argues that the activity of motion is not to be found on the path already traversed, the path being traversed, or the path yet to be traversed. Nāgārjuna is regarded as the founder of the Madhyamaka or "Middle Way" school of Indian Buddhism, where the middle way is not between the extremes of self-indulgence and self-mortification, as set forth in the Buddha's first sermon, but between the extremes of existence and non-existence. The question of exactly what this meant would provoke much commentary.

Of equal importance was this question: If all phenomena in the universe are empty, what is it that they lack? The most common answer was *svabhāva*, a term that literally means "own being" in Sanskrit, and that is often translated as "intrinsic nature" or "inherent existence." The doctrine of emptiness came to be an extension of the earlier doctrine of no self, with "self" no longer referring simply to a kind of eternal soul, but to a quality of independence and self-sufficiency falsely attributed even to inanimate objects. From this perspective, the ideas of self and no self could be extended from persons to all phenomena in the universe. Indeed, in Madhyamaka works, one finds the terms "lack of self of persons" *(pudgalanairātmya)* and "lack of self of phenomena" *(dharmanairātmya).* Thus, all things, both persons and things, are devoid of self, devoid of any intrinsic nature; the belief that they are endowed with self is ignorance. Such a doctrine provided the foundation for Madhyamaka critiques of various Hindu schools as well as the substantialist tendencies they ascribed to other Buddhist schools. Yet this negative metaphysics provided only critique. In order for the Madhyamaka school to explain the functioning of *saṃsāra,* and the possibility of escape from it, another doctrine was required.

One of the most important terms in early Buddhist thought was *pratītyasamutpāda,* often translated as "depending arising" or "dependent origination." In a number of early accounts of the Buddha's enlightenment, it was his understanding of this doctrine during his meditation in the third watch of the night that brought about his awakening. When the term is used in that context, it refers to a rather elaborate chain of twelve causes and effects, beginning with ignorance and ending with aging and death. Nāgārjuna and his followers used the same term in a more straightforward sense, taking it to mean the fact that everything depends on something else: effects depend on their causes, wholes depend on their parts, and objects of experience depend upon the minds that perceive and name them. Because everything is therefore dependent, nothing is independent, and thus dependent origination serves as a powerful proof of emptiness. Between the extremes of existence and non-existence, emptiness avoids the extreme of existence.

The fact that everything is dependent does not imply that everything is nothing—that things do not exist at all. The quality of dependence, especially when articulated in terms of cause and effect, provides the foundation for the functioning of the world: that a sprout is produced from a seed, that virtuous actions produce happiness in the future, that meditative insight destroys the seeds for future rebirth. Dependent origination avoids the extreme of non-existence.

In Nāgārjuna's writings, dependent origination and emptiness are not only fully compatible, they are in fact the same, with each implying the other. As he states in chapter 24 of the *Verses on the Middle Way* (24:18–19), "We declare that dependent origination is emptiness. It is a dependent designation; just this is the middle way. Because there are no phenomena whatsoever that do not arise dependently, there are no phenomena whatsoever that are not empty." Furthermore, for Nāgārjuna, the very contingency of the world is what makes change and transformation possible. If things were endowed with the autonomy, stability, and permanence that the ignorant imagine them to possess, the world would be static and sclerotic. It is emptiness that makes everything possible.

Desideri's understanding of the doctrines of emptiness and dependent origination was both detailed and accurate, despite the fact that he considered them, or at least "the lawgiver" who taught them (as he calls the Buddha), to be diabolical. As we did to illustrate his understanding of the doctrine of rebirth, we provide a passage from his *Historical Notices* in which he explains the doctrine of emptiness to his Italian audience:

> Their lawgiver says that all our intellectual knowledge and judgments about any object, can be considered in two ways: in a material sense—stretched, as they say—or in a mystical, elevated sense. The former is called Trang ton [*drang don,* "provisional meaning"], the latter Nġnee ton [*nges don,* "definitive meaning"] or, under another name, Ton tambà [*don dam pa,* "ultimate"]. In the first sense he declares the existence of things is apprehended congruent with the ignorance that is common and inherent to all living beings, by virtue of which everything is held to be endowed with that being which appears in it and presents itself to the external senses. In the second sense he says that things are apprehended as non-existent and empty of all being, because in this sense being is not regarded as a pure and material being but only as being through itself, existing independently of any cause and without any connection to anything else, or in the final analysis, existing through its own intrinsic essence and through its own nature.

. . . After ordaining the above, their lawgiver quite purposefully sets out to guide his followers along this very difficult path, teaching and explaining to them this supreme, fundamental principle of his infernal doctrine and diabolical religion by means of wordy, numerous, abstruse, and fallacious treatises. He teaches that nothing exists, that everything without exception is empty of existence and in every way similar to the moon's image that appears in water, to painted fruits and liquids and similar things that not only lack the property of illumination, stimulating the taste or relieving thirst, but do not even have the being that appears to be in them and are entirely empty of any being as moon, fruit, or water.

To these similes and specious examples he adds reasons to prove that all things are empty of existence in themselves. The reason, he says, is that nothing has its own being through its own intrinsic nature and exists essentially on its own. The reason for that, he adds, is that nothing is totally independent because everything is Tên cing breeware-n-giunvà [*rten cing 'brel bar 'byung ba*, "dependently arisen"], that is, there is nothing unconnected, unlinked, and without reciprocal correlation. And if it be, he concludes, that everything considered in the light of its essential nature has some correlation with some term or object, then nothing possesses its own essence absolutely of itself but rather from the term or object with which it is correlated. This is so, because, as he says, firewood is what it is through a necessary correlation with fire and its combustive property, and independent of fire it is not combustible; therefore, if we regard it in its unique and most simple essence without regard to anything else, firewood cannot be called combustible. Indeed, because it is impossible to conceive of its combustibility without conceiving at the same time of some other thing, it is, in its own regard, empty of combustibility and in the highest sense not combustible.⁵

The writings of Nāgārjuna, especially as interpreted by the seventh-century Indian monk Candrakīrti, would become highly influential in Tibet, especially through the efforts of Tsong kha pa (1357–1419), who is regarded as founder of the Geluk sect of Tibetan Buddhism. Tsong kha pa wrote commentaries on Nāgārjuna's *Verses on the Middle Way* and on Candrakīrti's *Entrance to the Middle Way (Madhyamakāvatāra)*, and he wrote at length about emptiness and dependent origination in the "insight" *(lhag mthong)* sections of two of his most famous works, both called *Stages of the*

Path to Enlightenment—one called "great" *(chen mo)* and the other called "medium-length" *('bring)*. Tsong kha pa found deep significance in the compatibility of emptiness and dependent origination, composing a long paean to the Buddha entitled *In Praise of Dependent Origination (Rten 'brel bstod pa)* in which he praised it as the Buddha's highest teaching.

Tsong kha pa was not without his critics. Some saw his emptiness as too radical, arguing instead that the nature of reality, especially its manifestation as the buddha nature *(tathāgatagarbha)*, was endowed with purity and substance. Others saw his dependent origination as too conservative, granting an excessively ontological status to the ephemera of ordinary experience. With the political ascendancy of the Geluk sect that began when the Fifth Dalai Lama was placed on the throne of Tibet in 1642, Tsong kha pa's views gained a new authority and orthodoxy. When Desideri studied Buddhist philosophy, first at Shidé and later at Sera monastery (both Geluk institutions), Tsong kha pa's works were held supreme, and Desideri would study each of Tsong kha pa's works mentioned above.

It was either Desideri's good fortune or his sad fate to take the Gospel to the Buddhist land where the doctrine of "nothingness," so excoriated by his fellows missionaries in Japan and China, was articulated with a philosophical rigor and technical vocabulary unmatched elsewhere in the vast Buddhist world. Based on his writings, it is clear that Desideri understood emptiness better than any of his fellow Jesuit missionaries to Asia. This is evident from the works that he cites, his accurate use of its technical vocabulary, and the style and sophistication of his argumentation. In a fascinating passage in his *Historical Notices,* he explains both his recognition of the importance of understanding the doctrine of emptiness and the rather miraculous way in which he gained that understanding.

> More than anything else, I sought to become familiar with, and thoroughly understand, the most abstract and complex treatises dealing with Tongbàgnì [*stong pa nyid*], or the vacuum. This word is not taken in a material and philosophical sense but in an allegorical one; its logical consequence is the utter denial of an uncreated, independent, inherently existing being, and with that, to absolutely shut the door to any knowledge of God.
>
> What I am going to say may seem difficult to believe, but I can only declare that I am not exaggerating or altering the truth in any way. When it came time for me to study these treatises, the doctor of religion assigned

as my teacher protested that he was unable to explain them to me or help me understand them. Believing that to be only a pretext to prevent me from understanding the subject, I begged and pleaded time and again that he explain them to me. Seeing that I was not convinced, he declared that he was not adequate to the task and that only a few of the most eminent lamas could satisfy me. He offered to take me to the other doctors of religion, and I sought out others on my own, but all of them confessed to me, as had my teacher, that explaining such recondite and complex treatises to me was more than they could do.

But I was determined to understand them, and seeing that I lacked any human help to do so, I fervently placed myself in the hands of God, the father of human reason, for whose glory alone I had undertaken this enterprise. Then, with dedication and composure, I set about on my own to read these books over and over and then review them from the beginning, but this was still fruitless, as they were so obscure. Nevertheless, even with all that, I did not lose heart. I went back and re-read them, and with renewed confidence in God I labored diligently until a small glimmer of light began to dawn that led me, little by little, to the admiration of the doctors of religion, to so perfect an understanding of this highly complex material that I was able to explain it to others as if I were a professor. This gave me an enormous advantage in combating the errors of that sect and in defending our holy religion.[6]

As noted above, it is clear that Desideri's understanding of emptiness, and of Buddhist doctrine more generally, derived above all from Tsong kha pa. His notes from his studies are preserved in the Jesuit Archives, and they indicate that he read Tsong kha pa's major works. In addition, the great majority of citations of Indian Buddhist works that appear in Desideri's writings are passages that appear in Tsong kha pa, and he translated Tsong kha pa's most famous work, *The Great Treatise on the Stages of the Path to Enlightenment (Byang chub lam rim chen mo),* from Tibetan into Italian (a translation since lost). Here we can note that even Desideri's account of how he came to understand emptiness echoes that of Tsong kha pa in his famous *In Praise of Dependent Origination,* a work that Desideri must have read. In this work, Tsong kha pa addresses the Buddha directly:

This excellent system, most marvelous,
Some individuals who are not so learned
Have entangled it in utter confusion,
Just like the tangled *balbaza* grass.

Seeing this situation, I strove
With a multitude of efforts
To follow after the learned ones
And sought your intention again and again.

At such times as I studied the numerous works
Of both our own [Middle Way] and other schools,
My mind became tormented ever more
Constantly by a network of doubts.

The night-lily grove of Nāgārjuna's treatises—
Nāgārjuna whom you prophesized
Would explain your unexcelled vehicle as it is,
Shunning extremes of existence and non-existence—

Illuminated by the garland of white lights
Of Candra's well-uttered insights—
Candra, whose stainless wisdom orb is full,
Who glides freely across scriptures' space,

Who dispels the darkness of extremist hearts
And outshines the constellations of false speakers—
When, through my teacher's kindness, I saw this
My mind found a rest at last.[7]

Desideri's relationship to Tsong kha pa's works is of sufficient importance
to merit its own study.

Let us now turn to *Essence of the Christian Religion.* It is a convention of
Tibetan Buddhist letters that a work should open with a poem, one that
begins with what is called the invocation or literally the "expression of
worship" *(mchod brjod).* Unlike the *Inquiry,* which begins with a lengthy
and beautifully composed poem in several parts and meters, the poem that
opens the *Essence* is a very brief praise to God, in which Desideri stresses

God's independent nature, something that he will argue for in the pages that follow.

Desideri refers to God with the term that he will use throughout the work as the "self-existent jewel" *(rang grub dkon mchog)*, a term that he likely chose with particular care. "Self-existent" (which would be more literally rendered as "self-established") is a technical term in Buddhist philosophy that implies independence, autonomy, and eternity, something that is beyond and untouched by the chain of cause and effect, akin to what in Western philosophy is referred to as "necessary being." In the Madhyamaka school, self-existence is a synonym for intrinsic existence *(rang bzhin gyi grub pa)*. It is also the object of negation *(dgag bya)*, that falsely imagined quality that is to be refuted by Madhyamaka reasoning. It is to be refuted because, for the Madhyamaka school, nothing is endowed with self-existence, everything is empty of self-existence, the belief in self-existence is the ignorance that leads to all forms of suffering, and the understanding of the emptiness or the lack of self-existence is the wisdom that leads to liberation from rebirth and to buddhahood. Desideri is therefore boldly challenging one of the foundations of Buddhist philosophy by choosing the term as the name of God.

The other component of the name of God is *dkon mchog*, usually rendered as "jewel" or "gem." This is *ratna* in Sanskrit, the famous jewel of the "three jewels" to which Buddhists go for refuge: the Buddha, the dharma, and the saṃgha. As was often the case when they rendered Sanskrit terms, Tibetan translators sought to encompass the connotations of the word in their translations. Thus, rather than translating *ratna* as "gemstone," they translated it as "rare-supreme" *(dkon mchog)*, with traditional etymologies saying that the three jewels are called jewels because they are difficult to find and, when found, they are of great value. Desideri was likely less interested in this particular etymology, which he would have known from his studies, than in the fact that he wanted to use the name of the Buddhist object of worship for the Christian God.

The invocation in a Tibetan Buddhist work is typically followed by what is called the "promise to compose" *(rtsom par dam bca' ba)*, the author's pledge to complete the work he sets out to write. Desideri provides this in prose, stating that those who are unable to distinguish what is and is not religion, by which he certainly means the true religion, will fall into hell. Motivated by compassion, he will produce a work that will help others make use of the "essence of wisdom" (a term he will use again in the catechism section of the text) to distinguish between "the religion that is stainless and pure and the religion that is unreliable and false," that is, between Christianity and Buddhism. With this direct and rather perfunctory preamble, Desideri launches his attack.

He begins with a fascinating and apparently original argument based on one of the most famous metaphors in Buddhist philosophy, the reflection of the moon in a lake, the classic example of something that does not exist as it appears. On a clear and calm night, the reflection of the moon appears so clearly on the surface of the lake that the moon itself seems to be floating there. In some versions of the metaphor, this phenomenon has fatal effects, as a monkey reaches down from an overhanging branch to try to touch the moon, falls into the lake, and drowns. The reflection of the moon in the lake is therefore a metaphor for the false appearance of all conventional phenomena in the universe, which appear both to the sense perceptions and to the thoughts of all sentient beings to be intrinsically established, autonomous, and to exist in and of themselves, when in fact they do not; in fact they are empty of any intrinsic nature. This error in perception and conception is highly consequential. Because sentient beings perceive and conceive of the objects of their experience to exist in and of themselves, they develop attachment to some of those objects and aversion to others, with this desire and hatred inspiring all manner of non-virtuous deeds, including murder and theft, which eventually fructify as various forms of mental and physical suffering and as rebirth as an animal, a ghost, or a denizen of hell.

The ontological status of the phenomena of the world is further articulated in Madhyamaka in the famous doctrine of the two truths: the ultimate truth *(paramārthasatya)* and the conventional truth *(saṃvṛtisatya)*, with the former existing as it appears and the latter not. For the Madhyamaka school as interpreted by Tsong kha pa, emptiness is the only ultimate truth. Yet this emptiness is not a single independent reality but the specific absence of intrinsic existence of each phenomenon in the universe, each having its own emptiness. The phenomena that are in fact empty (with the exception of emptiness itself), those phenomena that appear falsely to the minds of ignorant (in the sense of unenlightened) sentient beings, are conventional truths. This category is further divided into real and unreal conventional truths. The former are those objects that, although empty, can perform a function (a vessel can hold water, a table can support a vessel) and those that cannot (one cannot drink the water of a mirage); although such objects are empty, these conventional truths are real in the sense that they can perform a function. The moon reflected in the still lake would be an unreal conventional truth because, although it appears to be the moon, it cannot illuminate the evening sky; it cannot perform the function of the moon.

Desideri is not particularly interested in the fine points of the two truths doctrine nor does he wish to dispute that the phenomena of the world are somehow contingent. His fundamental objection is to the fundamental doctrine of the Madhyamaka school: that because everything is dependently arisen, everything is empty of intrinsic nature, including emptiness. In both his refutation of emptiness here and his refutation of rebirth in the *Inquiry,* his fundamental claim is that creation and hence existence are impossible without one thing that is uncreated and uncaused, and that exists intrinsically, independently, and eternally—that is, that creation and hence existence are impossible without God, the self-existent jewel. As Desideri will argue throughout this first section of the *Essence,* in order for something to be false, there must be something that is true.

To make this point, he takes the famous metaphor of the reflection of the moon in a lake and turns it to his advantage, arguing that the meaning that the Buddhists derive from the metaphor—the deceptive nature of the objects of experience and all that follows from that—is based on the assumption that in order for there to be a false moon in the lake, there must a real moon in the sky. It therefore follows that in order for the doctrine of emptiness to have any meaning, there must be something that is not empty. To argue, as the Buddhists must, that the moon reflected in a lake is a metaphor for the ontological status of the real moon is untenable. He then declares, "In the same way, it must be concluded that your assertion that there is not a single thing that is intrinsically established and your assertion that all persons and phenomena undeniably exist is only meaningless contradictory talk." He returns to the metaphor of the moon later in the text, making his point even more bluntly. "If you assert the existence of all things that are empty of intrinsic nature and established for a conventional consciousness, then you must assert the existence of something supremely excellent which is not the emptiness that is empty of intrinsic nature and which is intrinsically established. Therefore, the more you make learned proofs and engage in detailed analysis, the more the philosophy which holds that there is not even an atom that is intrinsically established is shown to just be a perspective that is unreliable and creates amazing delusion."

As noted above, the hallmark of Madhyamaka philosophy, especially as interpreted by Tsong kha pa, is that nothing is intrinsically existent and that all persons and phenomena exist only conventionally. Desideri is thus declaring from the outset that the doctrine that the Tibetans regard as the foundation of the most profound philosophical school is utter nonsense. It does not seem to be the case that he makes such a bold declaration out of some misunderstanding of the fine points of Buddhist doctrine. Judging at least from his command of the technical vocabulary, it appears that he understands the Buddhist arguments and finds them illogical, as he must if he is to argue convincingly for the existence of God.

He focuses first on the doctrine of dependent origination, observing, correctly, that the Buddhists hold that everything that exists is dependently arisen. Taking this in its most basic sense of things depending on their causes, Desideri notes the infinite regress that this must entail, with the chain of causes and conditions that have produced a person of the present necessarily extending back into the infinite past, because each cause is itself the effect of a prior cause. This is a conclusion that the Buddhists would not dispute, but for Desideri it is untenable. He says that if the road from India to Lhasa is endless, then a traveler who sets out on the road will never reach Lhasa. In the same way, if causation requires actual contact between the cause and the effect and if the chain of causation extends into the infinite past, those causes could never extend forward in time to produce a present effect. "Therefore it would be impossible for the force of those earlier and later causes and conditions to be in contact with the person who is born at the present time, and you would have to assert that it follows that it is meaningless to say that the person of the present time is perceived to be born at the present time." For Desideri, there must be some foundation that is not dependent and is not empty, and upon which the very notion of dependence rests. If, as the Buddhists hold, emptiness is itself empty, it cannot provide that foundation. "This is an assertion that there is no place upon which things rely and depend. Therefore, it must be asserted that this is only meaningless contradictory talk that cannot be upheld." And, he continues, it is illogical to say that everything is empty and emptiness itself only exists in dependence on something else. His point, of course, is that there must be something that is not empty. The very idea of all things having a status of existence that is dependent and contingent must presuppose something that is its opposite, something with intrinsic existence. This is exactly what the Buddhist doctrine of emptiness (at least as interpreted by Tsong kha pa) rejects, a ground or foundation that possesses intrinsic or absolute existence.

Desideri next turns from what he considers the logical fallacies of the doctrine of the emptiness to an argument that might be described as psychological. He states that the human mind has the capacity to imagine something that surpasses a particular object of experience. Indeed, he describes this not simply as a capacity but as an involuntary function, that when the mind experiences something, it also imagines something that is superior to it. This is particularly true of the intelligent, who "are involuntarily discontented, and, through their awareness that what is established as the supreme, the best of the best, without compare is something to be sought, they assert that something that is supreme, the best of the best, without compare, can or cannot be found." It would be illogical to say that dumb animals can find pleasure but intelligent humans cannot and instead are constantly tormented by the suffering of not being able to find what they seek. If the intelligent can imagine perfection, Desideri argues, it must exist. He is presenting an early modern version of the fourth of the famous five proofs for the existence of God put forth by St. Thomas Aquinas, the "argument from degree." In Part One of the *Summa Theologica,* St. Thomas writes:

> Among beings there are some more and some less good, true, noble and the like. But *more* and *less* are predicated of different things according as they resemble in their different ways something which is the maximum, as a thing is said to be hotter according as it more nearly resembles that which is hottest; so that there is something which is truest, something best, something noblest and, consequently, something which is most being; for those things that are greatest in truth are greatest in being, as it is written in [Aristotle's] *Metaphysics* Book II. Now the maximum in any genus is the cause of all in that genus; as fire, which is the maximum heat, is the cause of all hot things, as is said in the same book. Therefore there must also be something which is to all beings the cause of their being, goodness, and every other perfection; and this we call God.[8]

At this point, then, Desideri is simply translating the argument of Aquinas into Tibetan, without using the word "God." As he proceeds, he takes two important technical terms in Madhyamaka philosophy and recasts them for his purposes: the conventional consciousness (*tha snyad pa'i shes pa*) and the analytical consciousness (*rigs pa'i shes pa,* literally "reasoning consciousness"). In Madhyamaka thought, the former refers to either sensory perceptions or mental cognitions that are unmistaken about the conventional status of an object. That is, they correctly perceive the object's features and functions in accordance with worldly conventions. Such cognitions are tainted by ignorance, a deep-seated "innate" grasping, in the sense that they perceive things to intrinsically exist. However, that ignorance does not prevent these cognitions from accurately apprehending their objects and making inferences about them at the conventional level. The critical or analytical consciousness is a mental faculty that seeks to identify the ultimate nature of an object. In the discourse of Madhyamaka, the analytical consciousness is said to search for an object among its parts and not find it; what it finds is the absence of the object, that is, the emptiness of the object. For that reason it is often said that no object can "withstand analysis" by the analytical consciousness.

Desideri presumably understood the traditional meaning of these two terms before he redefined them. For him, a conventional consciousness has a mundane object and an analytical consciousness has a supreme object; up to this point, this conforms to the Buddhist view that what the analytical consciousness finds is emptiness, the ultimate truth. Yet for Desideri, anything that is dependently arisen and empty of intrinsic existence (which would include emptiness itself according to Tsong kha pa) is a mundane object of a conventional consciousness. He explains that the analytical consciousness could never find joy in empty and contingent things. Still, it would be illogical if the analytical consciousness could never find joy. Therefore, the analytical consciousness must seek and find an object that intrinsically exists.

Desideri argues that because there are two types of consciousness—the conventional and the analytical—there must be two types of objects: those that either exist or do not exist conventionally and those that either exist or do not exist ultimately. As plausible as this sounds, it is not something that the Madhyamaka would concede. It is the case that objects either do or do not exist conventionally; those that do not exist conventionally do not exist at all; the water of a mirage would be an example. For the Madhyamaka everything that exists, exists conventionally, and nothing that exists, exists ultimately. Desideri argues that the "wisdom of discriminative awareness" *(so sor rtog pa'i shes rab),* which in this case is a synonym for the analytical consciousness, must find an object that intrinsically exists, at least conventionally. Contrary to what Tsong kha pa would assert, Desideri suggests here, and elsewhere, that if everything lacks intrinsic existence, then nothing exists at all, even conventionally. He does not argue that everything must intrinsically exist. He argues instead that in order for the world to function, at least one thing must intrinsically exist. "If there is not a single thing that exists conventionally and is able to withstand analysis by reasoning, then it must follow that all things without exception that are indisputably established for a conventional consciousness are utterly non-existent. And if you assert that even though things that are indisputably established for a conventional consciousness do not exist ultimately, their existence is nevertheless tenable and that there is an authentic place for presentations of such things as past, present, and future, and cause and effect, then you must assert that there is some excellent object which both conventionally exists and is able to withstand analysis by reasoning."

Desideri sees further implications in the Buddhist claim that there is no entity in the universe that intrinsically exists, declaring that without such a "supreme entity that is conventionally existent and able to withstand analysis by reasoning," persons would not exist because the birth of such beings would be untenable even conventionally. As he does again and again throughout both the *Essence* and the *Inquiry,* Desideri resorts to Aquinas's first argument for the existence of God, the argument for the unmoved mover, to refute both emptiness and rebirth. Indeed, he argues that the very notion of beginningless rebirth, so central to Buddhist doctrine, renders the very term "birth" meaningless. It is an unborn person who is born; if birth has no beginning, then the state of being unborn would also have no beginning. "Therefore, that philosophical system in which the birth of a person exists beginninglessly is illogical because one would have to assert that the unborn state of a person who has not been born exists beginninglessly; the assertion that the birth of a person exists beginninglessly has the fault of contradicting your own position."

As further proof for the existence of something that intrinsically exists—that is, for the existence of God—Desideri argues that everything that exists has its opposite, illustrating this with a long list: earlier and later, formed and formless, learned and ignorant, light and dark, large and small, long and short, and so on. If there is something that does not intrinsically exist, then there must be something that intrinsically exists. In a sense, Desideri is turning the Buddhist's own argument for universal relativity on its head by using it to argue for the need to posit an intrinsically real entity. Reality is composed of contrasts, binary facts—above and below, right and left, and so on—which entails that if there are things that are devoid of intrinsic existence there must at least be one thing that has intrinsic existence. This, he argues, is how reality is structured.

Desideri next turns to another of the classic themes of Madhyamaka philosophy, the relationship between the whole and its parts. In the well-known metaphor of the chariot, this relationship is explored in what is called the "sevenfold analysis": the chariot does not intrinsically exist because it is (1) not its parts, (2) not other than its parts, (3) not the basis of its parts, (4) not based on its parts, (5) not in possession of its parts, (6) not the collection of its parts, and (7) not the shape of its parts. Desideri seems particularly interested in the sixth of these, arguing that the collection of the parts must depend on the parts but that the parts that the collection depends on must be intrinsically established. Otherwise, just as the sequence of cause and effect would extend infinitely back in time in the case of beginningless rebirth, the interdependence of parts would extend infinitely through space. "And if you assert that it must come through an infinite continuum, then, as was demonstrated earlier, it would follow that the collection of those things would be utterly non-existent." He is equally unmoved by the analysis of the "four possibilities of production," according to which something is not produced from itself, from what is other than itself, from what is both itself and other than itself, or from what is neither itself nor other than itself. He concedes that the four possibilities can be refuted but does not concede that this implies that the object is not produced. He writes, "It must follow that without the parts of the chariot, a chariot does not exist. In the same way, it must follow that without a single thing that is established for a conventional consciousness, their collection also does not exist. Therefore, as was set forth earlier, because it is illogical to assert that individual things that are established for a conventional consciousness exist without a beginning point, it is also illogical to assert that a collection of them exists without a beginning point."

As Desideri moves toward the conclusion of his refutation of emptiness, he provides his own example, one that is not drawn from Buddhism. He says that a point on a blank piece of paper, what he calls a drawing of the smallest particle, is not the center of a circle, yet it exists. If, at a later point, a circle is drawn with that point at its center (and he draws such a circle on the page of his text), that point would become the center of the circle. That circle has arisen in dependence on the point, but the point, which existed prior to the drawing of the circle, does not exist in dependence on the circle. Unlike his other examples, Desideri does not explain what follows from this, simply saying, "The meaning is to be understood in accordance with how the example is set forth." His implication seems to be that an object comes into existence in reliance on a preexistent reality, without that reality in turn relying on the object for its existence. God is the still point in the center of the universe, the fundamental point of reference.

He concludes his refutation of emptiness by declaring, "The need to assert something supreme that is intrinsically established has been proven from the perspective of many philosophical positions and reasons. Due simply to the fact that it is intrinsically established, it is not established as a basis that relies and arises dependently upon all the conventionally established things that themselves have the quality of arising in dependence [on something else]. And although it is not established as a basis in that way, it is something that must exist. At a time that has a beginning, the various things that are not established apart from causes and conditions come into existence by the unsurpassed force and capacity of that supreme entity which is intrinsically established and by the benevolent power that brings into existence what did not exist in the past; [things] become manifest in complete reliance and dependence on it." He then declares his intention to prove the existence of that supreme, intrinsically existing entity. Before setting out to do so, he offers a final condemnation of Buddhism, stating that he has shown that it is false that rebirth has no beginning. In that case, it is also false that sentient beings are reborn as a result of their past actions. In that case, the Buddhist theory of causation is false. In that case, the assertion that there is a path leading to a destination is false. "Therefore, the positing of the attainment of the final aim of beings and of a suitable object of refuge is incorrect."

Such arguments were not unknown to Madhyamaka thinkers. At the beginning of chapter 24 of his *Verses on the Middle Way* (24:1–6), Nāgārjuna lays out the objections to emptiness made by Buddhist essentialists. These objections center on the point that, if nothing possesses intrinsic existence and if everything is empty, the entire Buddhist system—of cause and effect, the Buddhist path, as well as the attainment of enlightenment—would be untenable. Desideri makes a more radical point: that, given that he has "demonstrated" that one must admit at least one thing to have intrinsic existence, any system that accepts the doctrine of emptiness is revealed to be false.

In his *Historical Notices,* Desideri states that the Tibetan lawgiver (the Buddha) "led his followers to entirely lose sight of everything that could guide them to the cognition of a true deity; or to state it positively, he led them directly and explicitly to deny the existence of the true God."[9] He asserts that the Tibetans, "led by their false religion positively and directly deny the existence of the true God." To their credit, due to their "naturally sharp intellect," they reject "the false and monstrous divinities of the ancient pagans of Hindustan." Indeed, they prefer "not to recognize any supreme creator of the world with absolute and independent power over it and human beings rather than assent to one in the way that was deceptively proposed to them." The Tibetans did so because of "the inconsistencies, absurdities, and contradictions of their masters."[10]

It is unclear on what basis Desideri makes this claim, because he seems unaware of Buddhist arguments against the existence of God. One of the hallmarks of Buddhist thought through its long history in India was the argument (in various forms) against the existence of a creator deity *(īśvara),* going back to the *Brahmajāla Sutta* of Dīgha Nikāya. Critiques of theism occur in such influential works as the *Mahāvibhāṣa,* the *Abhidharmakośa* by Vasubandhu, the *Tarkajvālā* by Bhāviveka, and the *Tattvasaṃgraha* of Śāntarakṣita, the monk credited with founding the first Buddhist monastery in Tibet. The last three of these works were widely known and studied in Tibet. However, in the Tibetan academy the most important arguments against the existence of God were found in Dharmakīrti's *Pramāṇavārttika.* Like the *Abhidharmakośa,* it was one of the "five books" of the Geluk curriculum and thus was being studied at Sera during Desideri's time there. Desideri would have known the name of Dharmakīrti because he is cited occasionally by Tsong kha pa in *The Great Treatise.*

Tsong kha pa does not discuss the concept of God there, and Desideri did not venture far beyond Tsong kha pa's text. If he had, he would have encountered an influential argument against the existence of a preexistent, independent God, creator of the universe. It occurs in chapter 2 of Dharmkīrti's *Pramāṇavārttika.* Here, one finds a critique of what bears an uncanny resemblance to Aquinas's "argument from design." In Dharmakīrti's text, the proponents of this argument seek to prove the necessity of a prior intelligence that is the primary cause of everything but is itself uncaused.

The gist of Dharmakīrti's critique centers on demonstrating what he views as logical contradictions in such a concept: How can an intelligence that is purported to have created everything and that knows everything be permanent when all of the objects of its knowledge are impermanent? How can there be a connection between a cause, which is atemporal and permanent, and its creations, which are temporal and impermanent? What would it mean to attribute causal capacity to something that has no temporality? How can there be anything that is self-caused when causation by definition requires something to be caused by something else?[11]

Sadly, Desideri seems unaware of these arguments against "the true God." Because he was a proud inheritor of the Thomistic tradition, it would have been fascinating to see how he might have responded to them.

What follows in *Essence of the Christian Religion* is the catechism, which is entirely different in language, style, and substance from the refutation of emptiness that forms the first quarter of the text—so different that one might wonder whether they were composed at the same time. Yet the refutation of emptiness and the catechism are not unrelated. As the conclusion of the refutation makes clear, Desideri feels that he has demonstrated the logical necessity of an uncreated and independent first cause, a cause that, in the language of Madhyamaka, possesses intrinsic existence. If such a first cause exists, then the Buddhist notions of karma, rebirth, the path to liberation from rebirth, and the state of enlightenment that is the goal of that path are all refuted. The three jewels in whom the Buddhist seeks refuge provide no refuge at all. Desideri believes, then, that he has refuted Buddhism, leaving it in ruins. The next step is to build a new citadel.

Up to this point in *Essence of the Christian Religion,* Desideri has employed the model of Tibetan philosophical discourse both in the structure of his arguments and in his vocabulary. At this point in the text, he switches, after a blank space on the page of the text, to a completely different style, that of the Roman Catholic catechism. This was already a well-established genre among the Jesuits, and included such famous works as the *Catechismus Minor* of Peter Canisius. Francis Xavier had composed his own catechism. It was common to use the question-and-answer format to convey the fundamental doctrines and practices of the church, with the answers often intended for memorization. Catechisms were often translated into other languages as tools for conversion. Indeed, the Capuchin missionary Orazio della Penna translated into Tibetan *La Dottrina Cristiana* by the famous cardinal and saint (and opponent of Bruno and Galileo) Roberto Bellarmino (1542–1621); the translation has been lost.

Thus, for this part of the text, the final three-quarters, our focus shifts rather dramatically. Up to this point we have sought to appreciate how Desideri understood the profound Buddhist doctrine of emptiness and the arguments that he constructed, using the language and conventions of Tibetan Buddhism in his attempt to refute it. In the catechism, our concern is quite different. What Desideri is trying to convey, the content of his words, is entirely familiar and unsurprising: the standard Roman Catholic doctrine of his day. Our interest then is not in what he says as much as how he says it, how he uses the Buddhist vocabulary of classical Tibetan to convey the truths of the Catholic Church. As in other catechisms, he proceeds methodically through a standard set of topics—the holy Trinity, the Apostles' Creed, the Lord's Prayer, the Ave Maria, the Ten Commandments, the Six Commandments of the Church, the Seven Deadly Sins, and the Seven Sacraments—providing an explanation of each, translating a wide range of standard Christian terms into Tibetan.[12] But he does not translate all terms; he provides phonetic renderings of a number of Latin and Italian words, not only of proper names but also of specific practices. Thus, we find Tibetan transliterations of Jesus Christ, Mary, Pontius Pilate, Catholic, church, Judea, baptism, repentance, Christian, cross, angel, Advent, Epiphany, Pasqua, Adam, Eve, confirmation, Eucharist, penitence, holy oil, ordination, and matrimony.

The dialogue that Desideri imagines is between a Tibetan who is Buddhist (or perhaps a former Buddhist) and a Roman Catholic priest, although Desideri gives each his own designation. The Tibetan is called "a seeker of the essence of wisdom" *(shes rab kyi snying po 'tshol ba);* we recall that in his "promise to compose" that opens the text, Desideri declares, "Therefore, having created the aspiration that seeks to benefit others, here, for those interested in religion, I will produce [in them] a faultless power of mind that distinguishes good and bad, true and false, by means of the essence of the wisdom that analyzes both the religion that is stainless and pure and the religion that is unreliable and false." The Roman Catholic priest is simply called "the *pandita*," the pundit. It is noteworthy that Desideri does not use the standard Tibetan translation for this term *(mkhas pa),* but instead provides the Tibetan transliteration of the Sanskrit term (one that would have been known to learned Tibetan readers), perhaps in an effort to indicate the foreignness of the authority and to evoke the Tibetan reverence for all things Indian.

The conversation begins where Desideri's claim to have demonstrated the fallacy of Buddhism ends: the seeker of the essence of wisdom asks, "Now, if the religion and the path of us Tibetans are unreliable and incorrect, we who enter such a path will have to undergo only suffering after we die." The pandita, "who develops the power of flawless intelligence to distinguish between true and false and what is good and bad," confirms that Tibetans are doomed to hell because of their belief in a false religion and offers to set forth "the stainless faith and pure religion" known as the Christian religion; Christians are people who have faith in Jesus Christ and uphold his teachings. When the seeker of wisdom asks about faith in Jesus, the pandita explains that there are three kinds of faith. This would have been familiar to a Tibetan reader.

According to a rubric followed in Tibetan Buddhism, faith (*śraddhā; dad pa*) is one of eleven "virtuous mental factors" (*caitta; sems byung*) that are present individually or in combination in a virtuous state of mind. Three kinds of faith are enumerated: the faith of clear admiration, which is a clarity of mind that arises from contemplating the Buddha, the dharma, and the saṃgha; the faith of belief, a firm conviction in the Buddhist doctrine; and the faith of emulation, literally "the wish to attain" (*thob 'dod* or *mngon 'dod*), that is, the desire to achieve those states, such as liberation from rebirth, in which one had previously gained conviction. Desideri was clearly aware of these, and recast them for his purposes, enumerating what he calls the faith of belief (using the identical Buddhist term), the faith of reliance (a term of his own coinage), and the faith that is clear, stainless, and joyful (derived from the first of the Buddhist terms). In good Buddhist style, the first has three elements, the first of which is, "Because the self-existent precious jewel is the peerless sole lord, it is believing in two things: the miraculous way that the highest has three natures and the way of the supreme guide Jesus Christ's act of kindness in being born as a human; he came into the world and died for the sake of all humans."

We see a pattern that will continue throughout the text. Wherever Desideri can find an analogue in Buddhist doctrine to serve in his exposition of Christian doctrine, he makes use of it, as he does in the case of the three kinds of faith, and as he does repeatedly throughout the catechism. Especially in his expositions of good and evil and of virtue and sin (as in the case

of the Ten Commandments), he draws heavily on standard Buddhist doctrine and often does not deviate far from it. His greater challenge comes
where he must describe doctrines that are quite foreign to Buddhism, such
as original sin, where he must resort to a more detailed exposition.

In general, in *Essence of the Christian Religion,* Desideri attempts to adapt
Buddhist vocabulary to convey the fundamental tenets of Christianity in
terms that would be familiar to a Buddhist audience in Tibet. One might
call this a kind of Christian *upāya,* the skillful method of teaching in terms
that the listener can understand, regardless of whether it is literally true.
However, we do not need to seek a Buddhist analogue in this case; such an
approach was laid out by the founder of the Jesuits, Ignatius Loyola, in the
eighteenth annotation of his *Spiritual Exercises:* "The Spiritual Exercises
should be adapted to the disposition of the persons who desire to make
them, that is, to their age, education, and ability. In this way, someone who
is uneducated or has a weak constitution will not be given things he or she
cannot well bear or profit from without fatigue. Similarly, exercitants should
be given, each one, as much as they are willing to dispose themselves to receive, for their greater help and progress."[13]

Desideri's mention of "the self-existent jewel," his word for God, causes
the seeker to ask what that is. Desideri embarks on a long description, noting
that he has already explained (in his critique of emptiness) that there must be
something that is intrinsically established. He goes on to argue that because
this entity is self-existent, it is especially powerful in the past, present, and
future. Hence, the first task for the Buddhist who wishes to embark on the
true path is to meditate "again and again from the depths of the mind on
the existence of something that is intrinsically established." (We should
note that this is the exact opposite of the Buddhist meditation on emptiness
set forth by Tsong kha pa in the "insight" section of his *Great Treatise on the
Stages of the Path to Enlightenment.*) The seeker promises to do so, asking the
paṇḍita to next explain why it is called a jewel. It is important to note that
in translating God as "self-existent jewel" Desideri has coined a jarring phrase
for the sect of Tsong kha pa, combining a term that is well-known as the
object of negation and making it an adjective to describe "jewel," which, as
part of "the three jewels," is one of the most famous and revered terms in
Buddhism. Desideri obviously knows this and plays on it, explaining that
the self-existent jewel is a jewel because it "is worthy of worship and worthy
as a place of refuge." Indeed, in a statement that flies directly in the face

of Tsong kha pa's philosophy, the paṇḍita declares, "Therefore, you should understand that, apart from that which is intrinsically established, everything else that exists is immeasurably small, immeasurably base, and immeasurably faulty in the presence of its intrinsic establishment. Therefore, you should know that, apart from that which is intrinsically established, there is nothing that is worthy of obeisance and worship or worthy as a place of refuge. Therefore, you must conclude that apart from the self-existent precious jewel, the peerless sole lord, there is no other jewel."

Having thus dismissed the Buddhist trinity, Desideri turns to the more difficult task of explaining the Christian trinity in Buddhist terms.[14] He begins by alluding to (without mentioning the source) the medieval story of Augustine walking along the beach and coming upon a child who had dug a hole in the sand. The child was walking down to the shoreline, filling a seashell with water, and then pouring the water into the hole. When Augustine asked him what he was doing, he said that he was pouring the ocean into the hole. When Augustine told him this was impossible, the child replied that it was also impossible for Augustine to understand the doctrine of the trinity. Desideri writes, "For example, if someone thought, 'I am going to pour all the waters of the great ocean into a shallow pit,' he would be no different from a child who has not learned words. In the same way, if I were to think, 'I will teach the immeasurable mode of being of the self-existent sole lord himself, who is inexpressible and inconceivable,' I would be no different from such a child. However, in order to satisfy your mind, I will clarify this article of faith just briefly."

He explains that the self-existent jewel, through the act of knowing itself, creates a reflection of itself that is inseparable from itself, yet the reflection and self-existent nature are two, "with a slight difference in nature." The nature that creates the reflection is called "father" and the reflection is called "son." The father and the son rejoice in each other and through this a third nature is created, called the "unsurpassed pure mind" *(bla med yang dag yid)*, his rendering of "holy spirit" into Tibetan. There is no obvious analogue to the notion of holiness in Buddhism; where the standard adjective in Christianity is "holy," it is often "noble" *(ārya; 'phags pa)* in Buddhism, with noble truths, noble paths, and noble persons. "Spirit" also has no obvious Tibetan translation. The term that Desideri chooses to render "spirit," *yid* (the Tibetan translation of the Sanskrit *manas,* "mind"), is often used interchangeably with *sems* (the Tibetan translation of the Sanskrit *citta,* "consciousness").

Thus, nothing about the term itself is particularly exalted. In an effort to add that connotation, he calls it "unsurpassed" and "pure," but these adjectives are commonly used in Buddhist literature to describe states of mind achieved by enlightened beings.

Desideri insists that despite the existence of the father, son, and unsurpassed pure mind, it is important not to regard them as three jewels (as there are in Buddhism); together they are "a single indivisible unity without a difference in entity." Just as the water from a spring forms a river, and together the waters from the spring and the river form a lake, with all three being water, so the father creates the son and the unsurpassed pure mind comes from the father and son, yet they are all of a single nature. Throughout this discussion, the term that Desideri uses to render "person" in the context of the three persons of the Trinity is *bdag nyid* in Tibetan, a term that literally means "selfhood" or "self-ness," but appears often in the philosophical vocabulary as "entity" or "nature," as in the case of two things (or in this case three things) having the "same nature" *(bdag nyid gcig)*. Continuing with the aquatic metaphor, the seeker of the essence of wisdom proclaims himself to be like a small child who once considered a modest lake to be a vast body of water.[15] Now, through the kindness of the paṇḍita, he has seen the boundless ocean and rejoices in the majesty of the self-existent jewel. He next asks about Jesus. Among the many ways that Desideri might have rendered the savior's name in Tibetan, he chose *g.yas gzu* (pronounced *yesu*), two syllables that mean "right" (in the sense of direction) and "upright" or "honest."

Here Desideri is faced with a particular challenge. In explaining the nature of God, the self-existent jewel, he was speaking in terms that a learned Tibetan monk would understand. Such a monk would reject the possibility of a self-existent being, but he would at least understand the claim. In the case of Jesus, Desideri needs to explain the nature of Jesus, a question that occupied the church fathers in the early centuries of the Common Era. Desideri describes Jesus as inseparable from the self-existent jewel and the unsurpassed perfect mind. Although he himself, like the self-existent jewel and the unsurpassed perfect mind, is timeless, at a point in time he took on a human mind and a human form. And although his unsurpassed nature was different from and unrelated to that human form, "they became one nature without duality and he was born as a human." After he was born, he served the people, taught his disciples, and performed miracles. When he was thirty-three, "he was nailed to the wood of the cross with iron nails and died, sacrificing his life." Desideri attributes two acts of immeasurable compassion to Jesus: coming into the world and dying on the cross (a term that Desideri transliterates as *khu ru ze'i shing*); these two deeds are the object of the first type of faith, the faith of belief. He explains that to commemorate these, many times each day Christians make the sign of the cross; he then gives instructions about how to do so.

When the seeker of the essence of wisdom asks how to generate the faith of belief, the paṇḍita responds, "The twelve main disciples of the glorious and supreme guide Jesus Christ composed twelve statements as a way to generate the faith of belief." Desideri thus provides his translation and rather extensive commentary on the Apostles' Creed. This is the current Vatican version in English:

> I believe in God, the father almighty, creator of heaven and earth. I believe in Jesus Christ, his only son, our Lord. He was conceived by the power of the Holy Spirit and born of the Virgin Mary. He suffered under Pontius Pilate, was crucified, died, and was buried. He descended into hell. On the third day he rose again. He ascended into heaven and is seated at the right hand of the Father. He will again come to judge the living and the dead. I believe in the Holy Spirit, the holy catholic church, the communion of saints, the forgiveness of sins, the resurrection of the body, and the life everlasting. Amen.

Desideri's translation into Tibetan, a translation that he says is suitable for recitation, is three times as long because of the need for him to gloss so many terms whose meaning would be so familiar to a Christian audience. For example, "the communion of saints" becomes "the coming together of the roots of virtue gathered by pure beings." Each of his translation decisions deserves detailed discussion. Here, we can only consider three.

In order to render the phrase "he was born of the Virgin Mary" Desideri writes, "He entered and was formed in the womb of his celibate mother, without being tainted by any fault and was born from the ever good Mary, who was completely without the fault of unchastity." The conception of Jesus as portrayed in the Annunciation is dense in doctrines of immaculate conception (of Mary in the womb of her mother Anne), of original sin, of virgin birth, and of the word becoming flesh. These do not translate easily into Tibetan. Thus, Desideri focuses on Mary's purity and virginity, while evoking the story of the Buddha's conception, which would have been well known to Tibetans. It was also well known to Desideri, who recounts it at some length in his *Historical Notices,* complaining that it is a satanic parody of the conception of Jesus.[16] Desideri refers to the chastity of the mother, using *tshang spyod,* the Tibetan term for *brahmacarya,* "pure conduct" in Sanskrit. Buddhist texts describe the period of the future Buddha's gestation at great length, focusing especially on the purity and splendor of his mother Māyā's womb, so different from the womb of ordinary women, which Buddhist texts describe as a disgusting cesspool. Hence, Jesus enters the womb "untainted by any fault." It is difficult for Desideri to convey Mary's virginity; the fact that he uses two phrases to do so indicates its importance for him, but both, translated here as "celibate" *(tshang spyod)* and "being completely without the fault of unchastity" *(mi tshangs,* literally "impurity") are terms that appear most often in the context of lay and monastic vows of celibacy, without implying virginity. Finally, it is interesting that Desideri calls Mary the "ever good" *(kun tu bzang mo).* In the Nyingma sect of Tibetan Buddhism, with which Desideri had some familiarity, this is the name of the consort of Samantabhadra (which means "ever good" in the masculine), the preexistent and primordial buddha. Desideri is thus able to convey something of the cosmic significance of the Virgin Mary, while confusing the issue of her celibacy; as the consort of Samantabhadra, Ever Good is depicted naked and in sexual union with the primordial buddha.

To render "on the third day he rose again" Desideri writes, "When the third day arrived, the body in which he had died, leaving nothing, came back to life, without having feelings of suffering or signs of decay." Tibetans would imagine that at the death of an enlightened being, that being would rise in a new body, whether an enjoyment body *(saṃbhogakāya)* or a rainbow body *('ja' lus),* not in the body that had died. Thus, Desideri must specify that the body that had died came back to life, and that that body had been completely dead, with no remnant *(lhag med)* of consciousness. It was also important that he specify that although it was a human body that had been subject to suffering and decay three days earlier, it was now free of those.

To render "the resurrection of the body" Desideri writes, "At the end time of the world, all humans will encounter the physical body in which they died in the past and in that, without lacking consciousness, will rise again." In Tibetan Buddhism, a dead body does not generally come back to life under auspicious circumstances. There are *délok* (*'das log,* literally "returned from the dead"), those who claim that they died, went to hell, and then came back to life in order to exhort the living to live virtuous lives. The story of Lady Nangsa (Snang sa), who returns from the dead, is the subject of a famous Tibetan opera.[17] There are also the *rolang* (*ro langs,* literally "raised corpse"), a kind of zombie who is reanimated through black magic to perform nefarious deeds. As noted above, enlightened beings do not return to the bodies they left behind, which in traditional Tibet were either burned, thrown into a river, or chopped up and fed to vultures, with particularly exalted lamas (including the Dalai Lamas) being embalmed and entombed. Thus, it is important that Desideri specify that on Judgment Day the dead will "encounter the physical body in which they died in the past" and that, unlike a zombie, that body will not lack consciousness.

Having provided this translation, Desideri turns to a detailed discussion of each of the elements of the Apostles' Creed, again in the form of the seeker of the essence of wisdom asking questions and the paṇḍita providing answers; it comprises ten folios of this fifty-folio text. And again, this conversation deserves far more comment than can be provided here. He explains *creatio ex nihilo*—a concept that would be quite foreign to a Buddhist—in some detail. He discusses the virgin birth in detail, noting that all humans are born based on, using Tibetan terms, the semen and blood of their parents in a place of lust. In the case of Jesus, the unsurpassed pure mind created a body out of the pure heart blood of Mary and also created a sublime consciousness that united with the body. Then "the self-existent jewel in his nature as the son united the body and mind of that perfect child with himself." To explain Mary's virginity, Desideri states that Jesus was born without a father and that "Mary, the precious mother of our glorious guide, was ever good, never having the fault of unchastity before her son was born, at the time when her son was born, and after her son was born."

The question of how the all-powerful and primordial self-existent jewel could suffer on the cross and die, a question that was also pondered in the early church, leads to a description of the events in the Garden of Eden: "Not long after that, deceived by a demon, the man and woman did not act as they had been instructed and displeased the sole self-existent jewel. Immediately, the self-existent jewel became unhappy with the two original humans and all the humans of their lineage. So, in keeping with that misdeed, he caused such things as suffering, unhappiness, fear, sickness, aging, and death to arise relentlessly, as punishment for not heeding his instructions." The term translated as "demon" is *bdud* in Tibetan, the same term that is used for Māra, "the Buddhist devil," who consistently seeks to obstruct the Buddha and his followers from achieving their aims.

The misdeeds of the descendants of the first man and first woman are so powerful that they cannot be counteracted by virtues, dooming them to hell. It is only through the willingness of the self-existent jewel to take on a human form and suffer and die that the welfare of humans can be fulfilled. If their welfare has been fulfilled by Jesus, the seeker of the essence of wisdom asks, why is it that humans still go to hell and why is it that when misdeeds are committed, they need to be expunged? The paṇḍita explains that Jesus is like a doctor who prepares an antidote for those bitten by a poisonous snake. Those who have been bitten must both ask for the antidote and take it; otherwise they cannot be cured.

The seeker then asks about hell. In Buddhist cosmology there is an extensive system of hells, said to be located deep underground directly below Bodh Gayā, the site of the Buddha's enlightenment. There are eight hot hells, eight cold hells, four neighboring hells, and all manner of trifling hells. A Tibetan reader would thus be undaunted to learn that in the Christian religion, there are four hells: (1) the hell of those who undergo relentless suffering; (2) purgatory, for those who still carry the remnants of their evil deeds; (3) the limbo of children who died before the root defect (*rtsa ba'i nyes sgrib*, as Desideri translates "original sin") can be cleansed through baptism (which Desideri transliterates as *'ba' sde zi mo*); and (4) the limbo of the pure beings of the past. This is the hell into which Jesus descended after his crucifixion and before his resurrection for "the Harrowing of Hell": "The hell called the limbo of the pure beings of the past is for those who have no residue of faults to be purified, yet in the past were not able to go to the place where they would attain the vision of the face of the self-existent jewel in the realm which is the highest aim; [this limbo] is the place where the minds of these pure beings abide in goodness. Jesus Christ, the sole lord who is the peerless guide and savior, went to the realm of hell called the limbo of the pure beings of the past after he died and accomplished their final aim, leading them finally to the place where they attained the vision of the face of the self-existent jewel without end."

In Buddhism, one is reborn as a human or a god as a result of virtuous deeds done in the past and is reborn as an animal, ghost, or denizen of hell as a result of negative deeds done in the past. These deeds, however, whether good or bad, create their effect of happiness or suffering, which then come to an end. Desideri therefore goes to some lengths to explain that all humans are born "as though chained to the root defect" and this defect dooms them to suffering and hell (which, unlike the Buddhist hells, is a state of eternal damnation). Salvation comes through two remedies, which are found only in the Christian religion: baptism and penitence. "Apart from the Christian faith and religion, these two do not exist in any other faith or religion, as illustrated by the example of the sick who do not ask for medicine. Only in the faith and religion taught by Jesus Christ, who is sole lord and savior, is there the blessing that repairs, powerfully defeats, overpowers with limitless great compassion, and eradicates any misdeed." Even in this case of uniquely Christian doctrines, Desideri hews closely to Buddhist doctrine, repeating two fundamental principles of karma theory: good deeds and misdeeds are not wasted, and one does not experience the effects of actions accumulated by someone else.

Indeed, it is important to note that Desideri is not simply translating Christian ideas into Buddhist doctrine; he uses the catechism as an occasion for critique—albeit a much more veiled critique than one finds in the *Inquiry*—of emptiness and rebirth. As we saw above, in his discussion of the nature of God he emphasizes that God is self-existent and eternal, endowed with intrinsic nature. God is not empty. When he discusses the resurrection of the dead, he writes, "Therefore, because at the time of the cause, this present body accompanies the mind, and positive and negative deeds are performed, then also at the time of the effect, this present body accompanies the mind and pleasant and unpleasant effects must be felt." This is a critique of rebirth, according to which the karmic effects of deeds done in a past lifetime, and hence by a past body, may be experienced in a future lifetime, and hence by a future body. For the Christian, the body that performed the deeds will enjoy the rewards of its virtue or suffer for its sins when the body is resurrected on Judgment Day.

The idea of the bodily resurrection of the dead on Judgment Day would have been quite foreign to a Buddhist reader and Desideri describes it in some detail. He allows himself a moment of feigned impatience in this imaginary dialogue when the seeker of the essence of wisdom asks how it is possible that the dead return to life in their old bodies when those bodies have been burned or eaten by animals. The paṇḍita replies, "At the beginning of time, he [God] created the body and mind out of nothing. What need is there to speak of his ability at the end time of the world to bring bodies that have turned into ashes and so on back to their previous forms?"

As noted above, Desideri structures his catechism around the topic of the three kinds of faith: the faith of belief, the faith of reliance, and the faith that is clear, stainless, and joyful. His commentary on the Apostles' Creed concludes the section on the faith of belief; he turns next to the faith capable of reliance. Desideri explains that seven objects are set forth for the purpose of developing the faith of reliance. Those seven objects are found in a prayer that Jesus compassionately composed; "it kindly gathers the milk of the faith capable of reliance for us, whom he cares for like a compassionate mother for her beloved child." This prayer is the Lord's Prayer, which Desideri renders in Tibetan in this way:

O our precious father who abides in the boundless heavens, may your renowned name spread widely and become an object of praise and respect. May your realm be manifested to us. May your intention be manifested in all parts of the earth as it is in the boundless heavens. Please give us today food for each day. We ask that you destroy our debts as we do not make others repay debts. Do not allow us to fall into a place that impedes virtuous thoughts and creates non-virtuous thoughts and please protect us and free us from outer and inner harm and all fears. May this be achieved.

Again, as with the Apostles' Creed, the seeker asks about the meaning of each phrase and the paṇḍita provides an exegesis. It is in this section that Desideri describes heaven for the first time. In commenting on the phrase "May your realm be manifested to us" ("Thy kingdom come"), he explains that through the compassion of the self-existent jewel, his children, "will go to the eternal and uninterrupted attainment, having—without obstruction, without veil, and without obscuration—the vision of the face of the self-existent jewel and that after the destruction of the world, they will achieve the perfect and complete attainment, without disintegration and without change, of the unsurpassed enjoyments of body and mind."

The seeker then asks that the perfect faith be established in his mind. The paṇḍita advises him to develop faith in the self-existent jewel as a place of refuge by remembering two of his qualities: his immeasurable power and his immeasurable compassion (the latter term, "the quality of extending immeasurable compassion to all without bias" is drawn directly from descriptions of the Buddha). This will produce unshakable faith. The seeker then asks, if there is no true refuge other than the self-existent jewel, why do Christians pray to Mary? The paṇḍita explains that "there are formless and inconceivably pure minds called angels and the inconceivable mind of pure beings who have attained the highest aim and have attained the vision of the face of the self-existent jewel." Among these, Mary "is like the attendant of the self-existent jewel, making kind requests for great compassion for the sake of the faithful." The paṇḍita thus recommends the recitation of the Ave Maria, which we recall is, "Hail Mary, full of grace. Our Lord is with thee. Blessed art thou among women, and blessed is the fruit of thy womb, Jesus. Holy Mary, Mother of God, pray for us sinners, now and at the hour of our death. Amen." Desideri renders it in Tibetan, opening the prayer with *kye e ma'o,* an exclamation sometimes found in Tibetan poetry, often as an expression of wonder, here clearly rendering, "Hail":

How wondrous! Through the great immeasurable compassion of the self-existent jewel, precious Mary, you have come to have the physical marks of goodness. O, you are completely permeated by the joy of the self-existent jewel. The self-existent jewel assists you like a friend. Among all women, you are to be praised, and the fruition of your womb, the precious Jesus Christ, is also to be worshipped and praised. O Mary, precious mother of the self-existent jewel, at all times, from now until death, kindly ask for immeasurable compassion for the sake of us sinners. May it be fulfilled now.

The Ave Maria receives no comment and the text moves to the third and final kind of faith, the faith that is clear, stainless, and joyful, and how to develop it. The paṇḍita explains that there are many methods, but the best is to follow the instructions of the self-existent jewel on "what to adopt and what to discard," a standard Tibetan Buddhist phrase for ethical behavior. This leads directly to an exposition of the Ten Commandments. There are various versions, but Desideri would surely have had in mind the version of Augustine: (1) I am the Lord thy God; thou shalt not have strange gods before me. (2) Thou shalt not take the name of the Lord thy God in vain. (3) Remember thou keep holy the Lord's Day. (4) Honor thy father and thy mother. (5) Thou shalt not kill. (6) Thou shalt not commit adultery. (7) Thou shalt not steal. (8) Thou shalt not bear false witness against thy neighbor. (9) Thou shalt not covet thy neighbor's wife. (10) Thou shalt not covet thy neighbor's goods. This is how Desideri renders the Ten Commandments in Tibetan:

> Because I am the self-existent jewel who is your lord, do not take anything other than me as an object of worship and an object of refuge. Do not use my name without purpose. On days that are taught to be auspicious, properly perform the rituals of the auspicious day. Honor your father and your mother. Do not take the lives of humans. Abandon sexual misconduct. Do not steal. Do not make judgments and bear witness falsely. Do not covet anything that belongs to another. Do not generate a mind of desire for a woman who belongs to someone else.

The challenges that Desideri faced, both in translating the commandments and in explaining them, appear less substantial than in the case of the Apostles' Creed and the Lord's Prayer, which included so many theological points. The Ten Commandments are concerned instead with ethics, and each of the ten (with the obvious exception of observing the Sabbath, which Desideri explains rather vaguely) has a direct analogue in Tibetan Buddhist literature. Thus, in his discussions of the commandments against killing, stealing, adultery, and bearing false witness, Desideri is able to draw on Tibetan discussions—such as those found in Tsong kha pa's *Great Treatise*—on the ten non-virtuous deeds of killing, stealing, sexual misconduct, lying, divisive speech, harsh speech, senseless speech, covetousness, harmful intent, and wrong view. Thus, in his discussion of sexual misconduct, he borrows directly from Tsong kha pa's *Great Treatise* the categories of inappropriate partners, inappropriate parts of the body, inappropriate times, and inappropriate places.

Even the first commandment about having no other object of refuge would be at least rhetorically familiar to a Tibetan Buddhist from doxographical literature that argued for the supremacy of Buddhism over other Indian traditions. It is in his discussion of this commandment, and in his discussion against killing, that Desideri makes reference to Tibetan Buddhist practice. Clearly alluding to the reverence that Tibetans show to lamas and the offerings they make to images of deities, he writes, "Those who have faith in living persons, those who have gone from this world to the other world, or in conditioned, impermanent, and dependent things and regard them as a jewel-like object of worship and an object of refuge, those who have faith in, make offerings to, and go for refuge to any other types of demons called ghosts, demons, and *nāgas,* and those who use either mantras or sorcery create the misdeed of not abiding by this commandment as well as a heinous act of great force."[18] On the commandment against killing, Desideri specifies that it refers only to killing humans (and even there, when a king orders the execution of a thief, this does not violate the commandment). Knowing of the Tibetan reluctance to kill animals and even insects because they are sentient beings, Desideri, as Matteo Ricci had in China, explains that animals are created by the self-existent jewel for the use of humans and so there is no sin in killing them. "For example, things such as trees, woolen fabric, and fire are simply things established to benefit humans and for the use of humans. Therefore, cutting down a tree, tearing a piece of woolen cloth, or putting out a fire does not create sin. In the same way, the self-existent jewel, the peerless sole lord who made everything that exists, made all creatures other than humans for the benefit of humans. Therefore, one should decide that the killing of wild animals, [domestic] animals, and birds for food, clothing, medicine, and so forth does not create sin."

At the conclusion of the rather lengthy section on the Ten Commandments, the seeker asks the paṇḍita to summarize what to adopt and what to discard. The answer is unsurprising: to believe in God and to love thy neighbor as thyself. However, these sound quite different in Desideri's rendering, the first insisting, against the philosophical foundations of Buddhism, on the existence of God, and the second evoking, quite consciously, the practice of the bodhisattva. "The two things to adopt are (1) to delight in the unsurpassed qualities of the self-existent jewel, the peerless sole lord, and to generate the faith of joy from the depths of your heart with a clear and stainless mind to your utmost capacity and knowledge, and (2) to cherish all other human beings worthy of being cherished like yourself, as if you exchanged [self and other]." The second of these comes clearly from the practice called "the equalizing and exchange of self and other," whose Indian exposition is found in the eighth chapter of Śāntideva's *Engaging in the Bodhisattva Deeds (Bodhicaryāvatāra).* This practice is discussed in detail in Tsong kha pa's *Great Treatise* as a technique for creating *bodhicitta,* the aspiration to achieve enlightenment for the welfare of all sentient beings. This dissonance between the first and the second elements—one overtly anti-Buddhist, the other overtly Buddhist—resonates throughout Desideri's project.

The seeker next asks what else the Christian must adopt and discard, and in response Desideri mentions the six commandments of the church. These are (1) to attend mass on Sundays and holy days, (2) to fast on fast days, (3) to go to confession at least once a year, (4) to receive communion at least once a year, during the season of Easter, (5) to make offerings to the church, and (6) not to marry at times prohibited by the church. None of this translates easily into a Buddhist vocabulary. In Desideri's version, the first commandment is "On days designated as auspicious days you bow with body and mind and listen to the rite of the offering of the sacrifice to the self-existent jewel, the peerless sole lord." The rules about when one should not marry would be baffling to a Tibetan, with the explanation that one should not marry between the first day of Advent and Epiphany. Desideri even seems to have coined a term for "wedding" in Tibetan, calling it the "feast of taking a bride." In colloquial Tibetan, the word for wedding is *chang sa*, literally "place of beer," likely alluding to the Tibetan custom in which the father of the bride drinks beer offered by the groom's family to signal his acceptance of the marriage proposal. It is not a sacrament. Perhaps sensing the difficulty of explaining all this, when the seeker asks the paṇḍita to clarify the meaning of the six commandments, the paṇḍita replies that these things are explained by the Christian priest on auspicious days. He then employs a common phrase of the Tibetan Buddhist exegete, "Fearing too many words, I will not elaborate beyond that."

Despite the Christian content of Desideri's text, it also follows, at least in broad contours, the format of Tibetan doxographical literature with its tripartite division into the basis *(gzhi)*, that is, the exposition of ontology; the path *(lam)*, the exposition of praxis; and the fruition *('bras bu)*, the exposition of soteriology. Thus, having begun with the nature of God and the holy trinity as expressed in the Apostles' Creed and the Lord's Prayer, Desideri moves to the Ten Commandments and the Six Commandments. In a Tibetan setting, having set forth various positive and negative needs, the effects of those deeds would be delineated. It is at this point, then, that the seeker asks the paṇḍita to describe the fruitions of good and evil deeds. He explains that virtuous deeds have three effects: making oneself pleasing in the eyes of the self-existent jewel, the ability to achieve one's purpose, and the ability to purify defects *(nyes sgrib,* Desideri's word for "sins"). By pleasing the self-existent jewel, he compassionately makes one worthy of attaining the highest aim: the eternal vision of the self-existent jewel in heaven. Knowing the Buddhist doctrine of the transfer of merit, in which virtuous deeds done by oneself can be dedicated to the welfare of others, Desideri notes, "What arises from a good deed and this first fruition of immeasurable compassion is not a shared deed that can be dedicated to others; it is produced for the doer of the good deed alone." The third effect of virtuous deeds is different. Desideri explains that confession has the power to deprive negative deeds of their capacity to lead one to hell, yet confession alone cannot prevent those deeds from causing suffering in this world. In order to completely destroy their capacity to cause any suffering, one must engage in virtuous deeds. Desideri explains, "Because this fruit is a shared deed that can be dedicated to others, it has the capacity to bring benefit for both oneself and others."

The paṇḍita turns next to the fruits of negative actions, explaining that a negative deed is not to obey the commandments of the self-existent jewel, either through not abandoning what is to be abandoned or not doing what is to be done. Here again, Christian and Buddhist rhetoric are mixed in a single sentence. He goes on to say that there are two kinds of negative deeds: the root defect and misdeeds committed by oneself. He then embarks on a second description of the Garden of Eden, this time in more detail. He begins with a summary of the account in Genesis of the creation of the universe, noting that in addition to the heavens and the earth, the self-existent jewel created in the heavens, "inconceivably many great minds that are formless," the phrase that Desideri uses to describe angels.

He next describes Adam *(a ldam)* and Eve *(had va),* enumerating the eight "outer and inner ornaments" with which they were adorned by the self-existent jewel. These include having bodies that were pleasing to the self-existent jewel, being free from sickness, aging, and death, not needing to engage in labor because crops grew without needing to plow the earth and animals obeyed them, and having bodies that never resisted the mind's intention to do good deeds. The second and third of the eight ornaments deserve particular comment: "lacking the obstructions to omniscience, their mental power to distinguish right from wrong was very strong" and "lacking the afflictive obstructions, they had very clear minds endowed with the mindfulness to engage in good deeds and the introspection to be frightened by misdeeds." Desideri could simply have said that they could distinguish right from wrong and that they were naturally inclined to do what is right and avoid what is wrong. This would have been perfectly understandable in Tibetan. However, he chose to introduce two technical terms: the afflictive obstructions and the obstructions to omniscience.

The afflictive obstructions *(kleśāvaraṇa; nyon sgrib)* are destructive emotions such as desire, anger, pride, and ignorance (there are six root afflictions and twenty secondary afflictions). These are the mental states that motivate negative deeds, with those deeds bearing fruit in the form of suffering in this lifetime and future lifetimes. The goal of the Buddhist path as classically formulated is to systematically destroy these afflictions, resulting in liberation from rebirth and the achievement of nirvāṇa. A person who has destroyed the afflictive obstructions is an *arhat.* The obstructions to omniscience *(jñeyāvaraṇa; shes sgrib,* literally "obstructions to objects of knowledge") are far more subtle, causing the world to appear falsely and preventing the simultaneous cognition of all objects of knowledge in the universe. One may be liberated from rebirth without having destroyed the obstructions to omniscience. Because they are more insidious, they are more difficult to uproot. Only bodhisattvas seek to destroy them, and the great length of the bodhisattva path is due in part to the time it takes to do so. The only being who has fully destroyed both the afflictive obstructions and the obstructions to omniscience is a fully enlightened buddha. By choosing to use these terms to describe Adam and Eve, Desideri is implying to the Tibetan reader that the first male and female were buddhas. Yet according to Buddhist doctrine the state of buddhahood is irreversible. There can be no fall. Among the conclusions that might be drawn from Desideri's vocabulary is that the power of the self-existent jewel is so great that he can create beings who are fully enlightened buddhas and that his power is so great that he can deprive them of their buddhahood if they disobey him.

Desideri goes on to explain that the self-existent jewel gave Adam and Eve only one commandment: to obey him. If they do so, they and their progeny will be endowed with the inner and outer ornaments and will later attain inexhaustible goodness in his realm. Should they disobey him, they and their progeny "will become the object of my displeasure and as long as you live in the world you will undergo a great many sufferings, such as unhappiness, displeasure, fear, sickness, aging, and death. After you die, you will not be able to go to my realm and you shall not attain the unsurpassed goodness." Without mentioning the tree of the knowledge of good and evil, the serpent, or the apple, Desideri simply says that, "the first two humans were deceived by a demon, and did not act in accordance with the commandment of the self-existent jewel." This first negative deed doomed them and their progeny, and all humans are born with its taint.

The paṇḍita turns next to the difference between heavy and light misdeeds. He borrows the language of Buddhist ethical theory, explaining that the weight of the misdeed depends both on the intention behind the act (was it done willfully or absentmindedly) and on the object of the misdeed (in the case of stealing, was the object of great value or little value). Identical distinctions are made in Buddhist texts, including Tsong kha pa's *Great Treatise*. The seeker then says, "I have heard that, among the heavy faults, there are some that are very powerful, destroying the pure mind like poison." This leads to an exposition of the seven deadly sins. "There are seven that are called faults that destroy the pure mind and faults that are like the fountain and root of all faults. They are pride, avarice, desire for impure deeds, anger, intemperance in food and drink, envy, and the laziness of mental darkness." As noted above, the Buddhists have their own list of six root afflictions and twenty secondary afflictions. Six of the seven deadly sins have cognates in these two Buddhist lists, with "desire for impure deeds" understood as the deadly sin of lust. The only sin that does not have a direct correlate is gluttony or, in Desideri's words, "intemperance in food and drink," a topic that is addressed in Buddhist literature, often in the context of meditation practice and in the cultivation of the virtue of contentment *(chog shes)*. There is thus a substantial Buddhist literature, especially in the "stages of the path" *(lam rim),* "mind training" *(blo sbyong),* and "minds and mental factors" *(sems sems byung)* genres, which Desideri could draw upon.

And indeed he did. In his *Historical Notices,* he writes, "In conclusion, the most basic and oft-mentioned part of their morality deals with the deadly vices that are the source of all other sins. Although they discuss only five, calling them the five poisons of the soul, nevertheless, when explaining them, they do specify all of our seven deadly sins. . . . They speak very correctly about the nature, cause, effects, and solutions for each of them in very much the way that we Christians do both in our moral philosophy as well as in our books on asceticism."[19] In each case Desideri follows a Buddhist model, defining the fault, describing the other faults that follow from it, and its antidote. He then briefly enumerates the effect of negative deeds, both the root fault, as well as the heavy and light faults.

Essence of the Christian Religion ends with a discussion of the seven sacraments. The seeker asks how to create joy in virtue, fear of the forces of darkness, and the power to cleanse faults that have been accumulated in the past. The paṇḍita explains that humans are incapable of any of these through their own efforts, without the blessings compassionately bestowed by the self-existent jewel. There are specific methods for increasing these blessings and they are called sacraments, of which there are seven. It is noteworthy that at this point in the text, Desideri forgoes any attempt to translate terms in Tibetan; he transliterates both "sacrament" and each of the seven: *battesimo* (baptism), *cresima* (confirmation), *eucharistia* (Eucharist), *penitenza* (penance), *olio santo* (holy oil), *ordine sacro* (holy orders), and *matrimonio* (marriage). In each case, Desideri provides a translation ("baptism is the offering of washing"), a description of the ritual, and the blessings that derive from it. His descriptions of confirmation, extreme unction, ordination, and matrimony are quite brief. Of ordination, he writes, "Except for persons well trained in the things to be known, [others] are not suitable vessels to receive this sacrament. Thus, I will not say more than this here."

However, he discusses baptism, the Eucharist, and penitence in some detail. In addition to their centrality to Roman Catholic practice, each of these has analogues in Tibetan Buddhism. The tantric practice often translated as "initiation" is *abhiṣeka,* which means "ablution." It is also common in tantric rituals for substances to be transformed through the recitation of mantras. And confession is a standard element of Buddhist practice, beginning with the fortnightly confession ceremony performed by the monastic community.

Desideri explains how baptism is to be performed, including the act, the words that are to be said, and the proper attitude of the person being baptized. When performed properly, baptism removes all defects, both the root defect and the defects that one has committed in the past. In addition, "There is the blessing that the mind will become pure in every way, you will become pleasing in the eyes of the self-existent jewel, you will be accepted as a child of the self-existent jewel so that, after death, you become worthy of attaining the final aim. There is the blessing that you will come into the community of Christians, children of the self-existent jewel, and will benefit together in all the roots of virtues of that community." He explains that it should be performed by a priest, but that all Christians should learn how to do so. "If you die without actually receiving washing or not having a genuine wish to receive it, you cannot attain the final aim and go to the realm where you will have a vision of the face of the self-existent jewel. Therefore, Christians bestow washing on small children, who can easily die and do not have the capacity to wish to receive washing."

Desideri's description of the Eucharist, in which "Jesus Christ transformed his body and blood to restore the mental power of the faithful," includes an account of the Last Supper, explaining that in the past the faithful made gifts of flowers and gems to the self-existent jewel. Jesus offered his body, his blood, and his life to the self-existent jewel. Unlike impermanent things like flowers and gems, the self-existent jewel was pleased by Jesus's offering of his body, blood, and mind, which are the same entity as the self-existent jewel. Jesus therefore revealed how humans can make the same pleasing offering to the self-existent jewel through transforming bread into his body and wine into his blood and then consuming them. He explains that the offerings only appear to be bread and wine; they are in fact the body and blood of Jesus. After explaining how to receive the sacrament, Desideri explains, "Through this sacrament being an unsurpassed offering, it brings about the blessing that the self-existent jewel is reconciled with those who have faults and he views them with great immeasurable compassion, weakening and exhausting the power of their faults to bear the fruit of suffering."

In his description of penitence, Desideri explains that two elements are involved, one that must be experienced by the external sense consciousnesses and the other that cannot be. That is, the person confessing his sins must articulate them and the priest hearing the confession must speak the words of absolution. In order for the sin to be absolved, the self-existent jewel, who cannot be experienced by the sense organs, must free the person from the bonds of his misdeeds. Desideri enumerates five elements that must be present for confession to succeed: the recollection of one's misdeeds, regret, resolve not to commit the misdeeds again, a complete confession of the misdeeds, and performing penance. Again, this language would be familiar to a Tibetan Buddhist, where the practice of confession (one of the "seven branches" that precede rituals and meditation sessions) is said to require "four powers": the power of the support, that is, the eminence of the being to whom the faults are being confessed; the power of regret; the power of the resolve not to commit the deed again; and the power of the antidote (usually the recitation of mantra) to counteract the misdeed.[20] Reminiscent of the famous story of Marpa forcing Milarepa to undergo great suffering in this life in order to prevent him from being reborn in hell as a consequence of murders he had committed, Desideri writes that penitence carries with it "the blessing of exchanging the inexhaustible sufferings of hell, without end and without liberation, for other sufferings that can be exhausted." *Essence of the Christian Religion* ends rather abruptly with a brief description of the benefits of the sacraments. "If you can repair faulty deeds and accomplish virtuous deeds through relying on excellent methods such as the sacraments, you will generate a wondrous faith that takes delight in the self-existent jewel. You should generate the faith of belief, the faith capable of reliance, and the faith that is clear, stainless, and joyful, not just in words, but with all of your understanding and capacity. If those do not weaken before you die, you will have already embarked on the path without turning back. It is impossible that you will not reach the end of the path; after you die you will attain the highest aim of attaining the vision of the face of the self-existent jewel."

Although Desideri entitled his magnum opus *Inquiry concerning the Doctrines of Previous Lives and Emptiness,* he did not complete his refutation of rebirth and never began his refutation of emptiness, at least in that text. To provide what is certainly a briefer and perhaps more accessible version of what his argument against emptiness might have been, in Chapter 4 we present our translation of *Essence of the Christian Religion.* And because that text is so much shorter than the *Inquiry,* we have translated the entire text, including Desideri's fascinating attempt to translate, in every sense of that term, the fundamental doctrines of the Roman Catholic Church into the vocabulary of Tibetan Buddhism. For good or for ill, that translation seems to have been read by very few Tibetans. We thus can only wonder how it might have been received.

CHAPTER FOUR

Essence of the Christian Religion

ᕔ

[1a] Unrivaled, lacking all faults,
Established as the nature of all virtues, free of fault,
Relying on nothing, independent, spontaneously present,
Changeless self-existent jewel, the sole lord,
With faith in him and offering praise,
I humbly make obeisance with body, speech, and mind.

If one does not have the strength of mind to distinguish between good food and evil poison, one will meet with death, without living very long. In the same way, if one does not have the strength of mind to distinguish between what is and is not religion, then a human will be no different from a dumb animal and, lacking the causes of liberation, will fall into the abyss of all fears. [1b] Therefore, having created the aspiration that seeks to benefit others, here, for those interested in religion, I will produce [in them] a faultless power of mind that distinguishes good and bad, true and false, by means of the essence of the wisdom that analyzes both the religion that is stainless and pure and the religion that is unreliable and false.

First, if you analyze with an unbiased, honest intelligence free from attachment or hatred, you must understand that, judged on the basis of the assertion that there is not a single thing that is intrinsically established and the view that all existent things are the emptiness that is intrinsically empty, the philosophical system of Tibet is unreliable and false. What is the reason? I will explain. If there is not a single thing that is intrinsically established and all existent things are the emptiness that is intrinsically empty, then you must assert that everything is in every way like the reflection of a moon in very clear water. If I were to demonstrate the fault with this position, it would be this: For example, the assertion that the actual form of the moon, which is not a reflection of the moon, is utterly non-existent [2a] and the assertion that it [the moon] actually exists like the reflection of a moon in water is a mere contradiction. In the same way, it must be concluded that your assertion that there is not a single thing that is intrinsically established and your assertion that all persons and phenomena undeniably exist is only meaningless contradictory talk. Furthermore, if you assert that there is not a single thing that is intrinsically established and that all persons and phenomena of the past, present, and future are emptiness, then let us analyze with reasoning a particular person born at the present time. That particular person must be asserted to be dependently arisen because he is emptiness. In that case, it must be asserted that that specific person is not established without causes and conditions, but relies upon causes and conditions because he is dependently arisen. In that case, not only does that specific person rely on causes and conditions, it must be asserted that his causes and conditions rely on other causes and conditions. This is because you have already asserted that there is not a single thing that is intrinsically established and that all existent things are emptiness; the other causes and conditions upon which the causes and conditions of the specific person born at the present time rely [2b] are themselves dependently arisen and must be asserted to be the emptiness that is intrinsically empty. In that case, if, beginning with the specific person born at the present time, you analyze with reasoning his causes and conditions and then their causes and conditions in sequence, you would assert that causes and conditions must continue back infinitely without end.

If one were to demonstrate the fallacies of this position, it would be thus. For example, one determines undeniably with direct perception that a heavy object definitely can be moved. If you assert that it cannot be moved except through being shifted by the force of another object, then, with regard to the force and capacity of the object that shifts [the other object], you must assert that some part [of the object that shifts] must be in contact with the object to be shifted. In contrast, if you assert that through the force and capacity of the object that shifts [the other object], no part of it is in contact with the object to be shifted, then this will contradict the conclusion that the heavy object to be shifted can actually be moved. This would mean that you would have to assert that there would be no meaning [to the statement that] the object to be shifted actually moves; it would be meaningless. In the same way, if you assert that the specific person born at the present moment does not arise except in dependence on his own causes and conditions, [3a] then you must assert that the force and capacity of the creating causes and conditions must be in contact with some part of the person who is created. And if you assert that some aspect of the capacity and power of the creating causes and conditions is not in contact with the person who is created, then this must contradict your conclusion that the person who is created is undeniably and perceptibly created at the present time.

Furthermore, if, for example, you assert that the road leading from here in Lhasa to the land of India is endless, then you must assert that the road leading from the land of India to Lhasa is also endless. Because of asserting that the road leading from here in Lhasa to the land of India is endless, then it is impossible for a traveler who sets out on the road from Lhasa to arrive in the land of India, making it meaningless. If you assert that, then because you assert that the road that leads to Lhasa from the land of India is endless, it is also impossible for a traveler who sets out on the road from the land of India to arrive in Lhasa, making it meaningless. In the same way, at the point of analyzing with reasoning, beginning with the specific person born at the present moment, his causes and conditions and the causes and conditions of their causes and conditions in sequence, if you assert that those causes and conditions must be an infinite series, then, at the point of analyzing the specific person born at the present time, beginning from the sequence of former and later causes and conditions [3b], then you must assert that those causes and conditions must continue infinitely, and you assert that the sequence of earlier and later causes and conditions must continue infinitely. Therefore it would be impossible for the force of those earlier and later causes and conditions to be in contact with the person who is born at the present time, and you would have to assert that it follows that it is meaningless to say that the person of the present time is perceived to be born at the present time.

Furthermore, you assert that there is not a single thing that it is intrinsically established and that everything is emptiness. In that case, because you have already asserted that, apart from relying and depending on something else, nothing exists, you must assert that emptiness [too] does not exist except in the sense of one thing relying and depending on another. If I were to demonstrate the fallacies of this position, it is thus. For example, if someone is necessarily subservient, then it must be asserted that there is no necessity of subservience without his relying and depending on someone else. In the same way, if the emptiness of intrinsic existence must be perceived to exist, then it must be asserted that there is no necessity of perceptible existence without relying and depending on something else. Or, for example, [4a] you assert that all humans are necessarily subservient, without there being even one lord. You have already asserted the existence of a foundation that arises dependently; this is an assertion that there is no place upon which things rely and depend. Therefore, it must be asserted that this is only meaningless contradictory talk that cannot be upheld.

In the same way, you assert that there is no single thing that is intrinsically established and that all things without exception are the emptiness that is intrinsically empty. You have already asserted the existence of a foundation that arises dependently. This is an assertion that there is no place upon which things rely and depend. Therefore, it must be asserted that this is only meaningless contradictory talk that cannot be upheld.

Now, if you say that I must present completely the reasons for my example and its referent, I will say the following to satisfy you. If you assert the existence of that which arises in reliance and dependence on something else, then it is illogical to assert that it is tenable that the very quality of dependence on another is not established at all anywhere and that there is not even a single thing that is definitely established. If you assert that it is tenable that a thing which arises in reliance and dependence on something else is not established at all anywhere and that it is established in dependence on another thing which is itself completely without establishment, then you will have to assert that the very thing that arises through reliance and dependence must be established in reliance and dependence upon itself. That follows because you cannot prove that the same reason does not apply. That follows because where one is not established, [4b] the other cannot be established either.

Let us apply this to such things as above and below, outside and inside, before and after. If something is necessarily above, it is necessarily empty of intrinsic nature because it is not established as such, apart from it arising in reliance and dependence on something else. Also, if you assert that there is not a single phenomenon that does not have the quality of being above, then you must assert that the quality of being above is established without relying and depending on something else. This is because if you assert that there is no reason for it to be established as that without relying and depending on something else, then you must assert that there is no reason for it to be established as that in reliance and dependence on something else. That follows because where it is not tenable for one to be established, the other cannot be established either. In brief, for example, if you assert that the quality of being subservient is not established as such except in reliance and dependence on another, then it is not correct to assert that there is not a single thing that does not necessarily have the quality of subservience.

In the same way, if you assert that things that are established by conventional valid knowledge are not established except in reliance and dependence on something else, then it must be concluded that it is illogical to assert that there is not a single thing that does not arise in reliance and dependence on something else and that is not the emptiness that is intrinsically empty. Furthermore, if, for example, something is necessarily a thing that arises by being built, then it is not correct to assert that the thing that has the quality of being built is not established as that except in reliance and dependence on something else and that there is not a single thing that does not have the quality of being built. And [5a] if something necessarily has the quality of being low, it is not correct to assert that it is not established as that except in reliance and dependence on something else and that there is not a single thing that does not have the quality of being low. Similarly, if it is tenable that the emptiness of intrinsic nature exists, then it is illogical to assert that it is not established as that except in reliance and dependence on something else and that there is not a single thing that is not the emptiness that is intrinsically empty.

If one were to say, "Show me the subtle reason for the example and its referent," I will explain this in order to satisfy the efforts of the questioner. When a phenomenon that is not the most excellent appears as an object of the mind in terms of apprehending its qualities and apprehending its features, the mind involuntarily comes to imagine something else which is superior to such an object. Thus, when one experiences some pleasure that is not most excellent and is not incomparably supreme, one involuntarily comes to imagine something else which is far superior [to that]. Therefore, the minds of the wise are involuntarily unsatisfied, knowing that what is established as the supreme, the best of the best, without compare is something to be sought. The intelligent are involuntarily discontented, and, through their awareness that what is established as the supreme, the best of the best, without compare is something to be sought, they assert that something that is supreme, the best of the best, without compare, can or cannot be found. [5b] If it is the latter, this is illogical, because it is illogical to assert that those whose minds are endowed with strong intelligence and strong will must be irreversibly and completely tormented by the unbearable suffering of not finding what they seek. Therefore, you must assert that apart from all the things that are established by mere conventional knowledge, that are established as emptiness, and that arise in reliance and dependence on something, some object that is superior to those and is intrinsically established is to be found.

Furthermore, it is illogical to assert that dumb animals can find pleasure yet humans cannot find pleasure. In the same way, in general there are two types of consciousness: conventional consciousness, which has a mundane object, and the supreme analytical consciousness. Therefore, when a conventional consciousness encounters an object that does not bring about the quality of suffering, it does not feel happiness. However, it is correct [to assert] that encountering an object other than those, it can become happy and satisfied. But one must conclude that it is illogical to assert that there is no object whatsoever that the supreme analytical consciousness can find which brings it happiness and pleasure. Therefore, it must be asserted that things that are dependently arisen and established as emptiness are simply not found and not perceived by the analytical consciousness. For that very reason, it must be asserted that, for the supreme analytical consciousness it is impossible for anything that is empty of intrinsic nature to be enjoyed and for [the analytical consciousness] to find happiness in them on the basis of that joy. [6a] Therefore, it must be concluded that it is illogical to assert that there is not a single thing that is intrinsically established.

Furthermore, for example, just as, in general there are two types of consciousness—conventional consciousness and analytical consciousness— so it should be understood that there are two types of objects of consciousness: those that either exist or do not exist conventionally and those that either exist or do not exist ultimately. When any object to be known is analyzed with reasoning, initially it must be decided whether or not that object exists conventionally, because if it is correct that it does not exist conventionally, [the need to] analyze whether or not it exists ultimately using the wisdom of discriminating awareness simply does not arise. Therefore, if it is indisputably proven that there must be one thing that is intrinsically established conventionally, then a philosophical school that proves with reasoning that there is not a single thing that is intrinsically established must be shown to be a philosophical school that is unreliable and deceptive. Therefore, intelligent ones, if you are able to be without attachment or aversion without falling to extremes, focus your mind one-pointedly and listen.

If there is not a single thing that exists conventionally and is able to withstand analysis by reasoning, then it must follow that all things without exception that are indisputably established for a conventional consciousness are utterly non-existent. And if you assert that even though things that are indisputably established for a conventional consciousness do not exist ultimately, their existence is nevertheless tenable and that there is an authentic place for presentations of such things as past, present, [6b] and future, and cause and effect, then you must assert that there is some excellent object which both conventionally exists and is able to withstand analysis by reasoning. You might ask: If there is not a single thing that conventionally exists and is able to withstand analysis, how does this prove that, due to that non-existence, it necessarily follows that everything that is established for a conventional consciousness is utterly non-existent? I will explain this.

If you assert that there is no supreme entity that is conventionally existent and able to withstand analysis by reasoning, then it follows that all persons without exception who are established by a conventional consciousness are utterly non-existent, because if there is no supreme entity which exists conventionally and is able to withstand analysis by reasoning, then it must follow that there is no birth whatsoever of persons who are established by conventional consciousness. This follows because the birth of persons established for a conventional consciousness would obviously be without causes and conditions [and such birth] does not exist even conventionally. If you say that that does not follow, I say that it does follow. For if there is no supreme entity which exists conventionally and is able to withstand analysis by reasoning, then it must follow that the birth of persons established for a conventional consciousness is established simply without causes and conditions. Not only does the birth of such beings not exist ultimately, it is completely untenable even conventionally.

If you say, "Well then, if there is no supreme entity which conventionally exists and is able to withstand analysis by reasoning, why must it follow that the birth of persons who are established for a conventional consciousness is established without causes and conditions?," [7a] I will explain.

Do you assert that the birth of persons who are established for a conventional consciousness is beginningless, without a beginning point, or do you assert that it has a beginning? If you assert the former, it is not correct because in the opponent's scriptures, the birth of the person has an endpoint [i.e., nirvāṇa]. If you say that this does not necessarily follow, it does follow because whenever it is correct that there is an endpoint, there must be a beginning point as well. That follows because you have already asserted that the road that leads from the land of India to Lhasa has an end. It is illogical to assert that the road that leads from Lhasa to the land of India has no end.

Furthermore, if you accept that the birth of a person exists conventionally, then you must accept that [such] birth undoubtedly has a meaning. Therefore the birth of persons who are established for a conventional consciousness does not exist beginninglessly because such birth has a meaning. If you say that that does not necessarily follow, it does follow because if birth has a meaning, then it is untenable to say that it exists beginninglessly. If you ask why this is so, I shall explain the reason. It is illogical for a person who has already been born to be born again. Therefore, if you assert the birth of persons in general, you have to assert that it is an unborn person who has not already been born who is born. Thus, if you assert that the birth of a person is without beginning, you must also assert that the state of a person who has not already been born being unborn exists beginninglessly. [7b] Therefore, that philosophical system in which the birth of a person exists beginninglessly is illogical because one would have to assert that the unborn state of a person who has not been born exists beginninglessly; the assertion that the birth of a person exists beginninglessly has the fault of contradicting your own position. There is also the fault of asserting some kind of mere "birth" that has no meaning.

Thus, according to the second alternative, if the opponent is not to depart from the path that is pleasing to scholars, he must assert that the birth has a beginning. Thus, he must assert that there is nothing that arises dependently without being born. Therefore, he must assert that things which arise dependently have a beginning. If he asserts that, he must concede that there is a situation in which things that are intrinsically empty do not exist primordially. In the situation in which all intrinsically empty things without exception do not exist primordially, he asserts either that something exists or nothing exists.

If you adopt the latter position, this is illogical because when you assert that there is not a single thing that exists beginninglessly, then you are asserting that there is nothing, even with a beginning, that exists. In that case, you fall into the extreme of annihilation because you destroy all presentations of cause and effect. Also, you have already asserted there is not a single thing that exists beginninglessly. If you assert that some things that are intrinsically empty and that are undeniably established for a conventional consciousness have a beginning [8a], then you would have to assert that things that are established for a conventional consciousness are born without a cause. This, however, is illogical. Therefore, according to the first alternative, in the situation in which all intrinsically empty things without exception do not exist primordially, you must assert that something exists. If you assert this, then, in the situation in which all intrinsically empty things without exception do not exist primordially, having proven that you must assert that something exists, then, in that case, through analyzing the existing thing, it must be determined whether it exists intrinsically or not, because it is illogical to assert that it is a phenomenon that is not included in those [two categories] and it is also illogical to assert that it is something that is empty of intrinsic nature. This follows because, in the situation in which all intrinsically empty things without exception do not exist primordially, you have asserted that something exists, and it is illogical to assert that it is something that is empty of intrinsic nature. It follows, therefore, if you assert that there is not even one thing that is intrinsically established, then it must follow that all the things that are undeniably established for a conventional consciousness are utterly non-existent.

You might wonder: I have already asserted that things that are undeniably established for a conventional consciousness do not exist ultimately, and I have [also] asserted that there is a legitimate basis for the presentations of such things as past, present, and future, and cause and effect. [8b] So how would you prove that there must be some most supreme entity that conventionally exists and is able to withstand analysis by reasoning?

Fearing excessive words, I will only discuss this briefly. As explained before, the reflection of the moon in a clear lake appears to be the form of the moon. However, it does not exist as it appears there; it appears as something other than what it is. Therefore, it is correct to say that it is false, having a quality of deception, and that it is not intrinsically established. Similarly, to sense consciousnesses polluted by the afflictions and external and internal causes of error, all things without exception that are established for a conventional consciousness appear to be intrinsically established. However, like the reflection of a face in a mirror that falsely appears as a face without existing as it appears there, they have the quality of being deceptive and must be proven to be the emptiness that is intrinsically empty. Furthermore, for example, if it is correct that the reflection of the moon undeniably exists as it appears in the lake, then one would have to assert the existence of something that is the actual form of the moon and is not the mere reflection of the moon. In the same way, if you assert the existence of all things that are empty of intrinsic nature and established for a conventional consciousness, then you must assert the existence of something supremely excellent which is not the emptiness that is intrinsically empty and which is intrinsically established. Therefore, the more you make learned proofs and engage in detailed analysis, the more the philosophy which holds that there is not even an atom that is intrinsically established is shown to be just a perspective that is unreliable and creates amazing delusion.

[9a] Furthermore, consider the fact that existence itself has an inconceivable number of specific instances. When we analyze them in detail, it would be correct to establish that each of the aspects of existence can be divided into two: the essence and its opposite. Thus, there is earlier and later, formed and formless, learned and ignorant, light and dark, large and small, long and short, near and far, inside and outside, that side and this side, high and low, white and black, clear and murky, beautiful and ugly, pleasurable and painful, pleasant and unpleasant, subtle and coarse, ignorant and knowing, being able to speak and being dumb, religious and irreligious, mundane and supramundane, right and wrong, good and evil, above and below, beginning and end, existent and non-existent, empty and full, hot and cold, warm and cool, harmful and helpful, past and not past, difficult and easy, rare and plentiful, soft and hard, smooth and rough, mountainous and flat, delicious and not delicious, melodious and not melodious, dry and wet, new and old, many and few, faulty and virtuous, heavy and light, having a beginning and not having a beginning, connected and not connected, becoming material and not becoming material, clean and unclean, suitable to do and unsuitable to

do, sweet and bitter. It is correct to establish that such aspects of existence are twofold, the essence and its opposite.

If, through this mode of understanding, you might assert that the position that holds that there is not a single supreme entity that is intrinsically established cannot be accused of being false, how will you be able to prevent this position itself from becoming a proof of its own unreliability? Therefore, please know that the different aspects of existence [9b] are established as twofold, the essence and its opposite. When those with unbiased, honest intelligence, free from attachment or hatred, are determining the aspects of existence from the perspective of whether or not they are intrinsically established, it is correct to establish, for example, that other aspects of existence are twofold, the essence and its opposite. In the same way, with regard to the aspects of existence, if they do not generate the awareness which decides that there are these two—the essence and the opposite—of something that exists in the sense of being intrinsically established and intrinsically empty, then they should generate the awareness which decides that the position that asserts, with regard to existence, that there is not a single thing which is intrinsically established is completely unproven and unreliable.

Furthermore, for example, it can be decided that each of the parts of the body are themselves [material] forms and are related to other forms [that is, other parts of the body]. However, there is also a place to analyze whether or not the collection of those parts is related to some other forms. In the same way, all the things established for a conventional sense consciousness are established to be empty of intrinsic nature for an analytical consciousness. Yet there is also a place to analyze whether or not the collection of those things is established as such. Thus, just as you, the opponent, assert that all things that are established for a conventional consciousness to be the emptiness that is intrinsically empty, do you also assert the collection of those things to be such? Or, just as you cannot assert that the collection of parts are connected to some other thing in the way in which each and every part is connected to other forms [i.e., other parts], [10a] in the same way, do you maintain that although the individual things established for a conventional sense consciousness exist as being reliant on other things and dependently arisen, the collection of those things exists as not relying on other things and as not dependent? If it is the latter, this is something the opponent does not assert. If it is the former, and if you assert that the collection of things that is established for a conventional consciousness to not be established except as relying and depending on another, then it is not correct to assert that the other on which it relies and depends is a thing that is not intrinsically established, because if it is not intrinsically established, it would have to come through an infinite continuum. And if you assert that it must come through an infinite continuum, then, as was demonstrated earlier, it would follow that the collection of those things would be utterly non-existent.

In brief, if you accept [the existence of] these things that are established for a conventional consciousness,[1] you will have to accept [the existence of] a collection of them [as well]. For example, when analyzing individual things, an analytical consciousness is able to refute the four possibilities of arising: that they arise from themselves, from other, from both self and other, or causelessly. However, it is not able to refute the arising of individual things themselves. Similarly, when analyzing the collection of those things, the analytical consciousness is able to refute the four possibilities of arising. However, who would be able to refute its arising [itself]?

Also, for example, it is asserted that the individual parts of a body are material; it is illogical to assert that the body [itself] is not material. [10b] Similarly, just as you assert that individual things established for a conventional consciousness do not have the quality of being produced without causes and conditions and do not have the quality of being produced from self or from self and other, so it is not logical to assert that the collection of those things is not established in that way. For example, although there is no occasion in which individual things are intrinsically produced from another, you do not assert that production from another does not exist even conventionally. Similarly, in the context of a collection, although you assert that being intrinsically produced from another does not exist, it is not correct to assert that it is not produced from another even conventionally.

Now, do you assert that the other from which it is produced conventionally is established as merely different from it or as intrinsically other than it? If it is the first, that is illogical because if it were established as merely different from the collection of everything that is intrinsically empty, it would have to be established as the emptiness of intrinsic existence. Thus, it would be illogical to assert the existence of another emptiness of intrinsic nature apart from the collection of everything that is empty of intrinsic nature. Therefore, if it is the second, you must assert that the other from which this collection is produced merely conventionally is established as intrinsically other from this collection itself. Thus, discard the position that there is not even a single thing that is intrinsically established. You must become our ally.

Furthermore, for example, it must follow that without the parts of the chariot, a chariot does not exist. In the same way, it must follow that without a single thing that is established for a conventional consciousness, their collection also does not exist. [11a] Therefore, as was set forth earlier, because it is illogical to assert that individual things that are established for a conventional consciousness exist without a beginning point, it is also illogical to assert that a collection of them exists without a beginning point. Therefore, you must accept a point at which the collection does not exist primordially. Also, as was set forth before, in a situation in which both individual things that are established for a conventional consciousness and the collection of them do not exist primordially, if[2] you assert that not a single thing exists, then it must follow that those things and the collection of them are utterly non-existent at all times and in all ways. For that reason, in the situation in which there is not a single thing that is established for a conventional consciousness and in which the collection of them does not exist primordially, you must assert that something exists. In the situation in which there is not a single thing that is empty of intrinsic nature and in which the collection of those things that are empty of intrinsic nature does not exist primordially, to assert that there is something that exists that is empty of intrinsic nature is only meaningless contradictory talk. Because of that, the thing that must exist in that situation must be established as the very thing that is not emptiness and is intrinsically established.

Someone might object, saying, "For example, without the observed, the observer cannot exist. In the same way, without that which relies and depends on another, that basis upon which they rely and depend cannot exist. [11b] Also, for example, because without the observed the observer cannot exist, the observer must be established as something dependent that is dependently arisen, a mere emptiness that lacks intrinsic establishment. Similarly, because that which does not rely on another and does not arise dependently does not exist, then that basis upon which it arises dependently must be non-existent. Thus, this proves that it is something dependent which is dependently arisen, a mere emptiness that lacks intrinsic establishment."

This is an objection that does not refute [my position]. In response, I shall give an example and then apply it to the meaning. If, on a piece of paper, one draws a picture of the smallest point, simply by doing that, the drawing of the smallest point is not established in the center of a line drawn in the shape of a circle. Although it is not established in the center of such a circle, who would deny that it can be directly perceived? If, at a later time, one drew a line in the shape of a circle around that drawing of the smallest point ⊙, that drawing of the smallest point would come to be in the center of the line drawn in the shape of a circle. That line drawn in the shape of a circle surrounding the drawing of the smallest particle has the quality of arising in dependence on it, because without the smallest point established in the center of it, it would not exist, and because it does not exist except relying upon and arising in dependence upon its center. It is thus. However, that being the case, the subject, the drawing of the point, [12a] is not established as having the quality of arising in reliance and dependence on the line drawn in the shape of a circle around it because the line drawn in the shape of a circle around it does not exist without that, yet it [the point] exists without that [circle]. The meaning is to be understood in accordance with how the example is presented.

The need to assert something supreme that is intrinsically established has been proven from the perspective of many philosophical positions and reasons. Due simply to the fact that it is intrinsically established, it is not established as a basis that relies and arises dependently upon all the conventionally established things that themselves have the quality of arising in dependence [on something else]. And although it is not established as a basis in that way, it is something that must exist. At a time that has a beginning, the various things that are not established apart from causes and conditions come into existence by the unsurpassed force and capacity of that supreme entity which is intrinsically established and by the benevolent power that brings into existence what did not exist in the past; [things] become manifest in complete reliance and dependence on it. Therefore, the supreme entity that is intrinsically established serves as the basis in reliance and dependence upon which the conventional things that appear before and later arise. However, the conventional things that have the quality of dependent origination and which arise in reliance and dependence on it at a time that has a beginning are not themselves established as having the quality of a basis upon which it relies and depends. For it [i.e., the basis], there is not a single conventional thing, in any way or at any time, upon which it arises at a time with a beginning point; [12b] it exists by virtue of its own character.

I will prove the existence of this original being, who is primary and who is the object of stainless faith. Again, if you were to analyze the Tibetan scriptures with a wisdom that is free of prejudice, without going into detail again, then the assertion that the birth of sentient beings has existed beginninglessly, without a beginning point in time, must be proven to be incorrect and to have a quality of deceit and delusion. This is so because, as was set forth here, all things established for a conventional consciousness are only established at a time that has a beginning point. Therefore, the assertion that the birth of sentient beings comes into being through the power of their past actions is proven to be incorrect as well. Therefore, the assertion that sentient beings take rebirth many times in former and later lives, cycling in *saṃsāra,* is proven to be incorrect. Therefore, the unreliable presentation of cause and effect is proven to be incorrect. Therefore, the positing of the path of beings and of the actual end of that path is proven to be incorrect. Therefore, the positing of the attainment of the final aim of beings and of a suitable object of refuge is incorrect.

"Now, if the religion and the path of us Tibetans are unreliable and incorrect, we who enter such a path will have to undergo only suffering after we die." This is a question asked by a seeker of the essence of wisdom.

[13a] A paṇḍita, who develops the power of flawless intelligence to distinguish between what is true and false and what is good and bad, replied. "When gathering provisions for travel, if you pack only poisons or food tainted by poison, you might embark on the road but you will not be able to reach your destination. You will be afflicted by great illness and you will die helplessly. In the same manner, you Tibetans, because of your adherence to a faith that is thoroughly deceiving and a religion that is fundamentally false, after your death will have to undergo only suffering. To give another example, if an inexperienced merchant were to gather a large quantity of fake gold and travel to an island of jewels [in order to purchase jewels], he would be most unhappy, returning home with empty hands and no benefit. Your faith and religion are like fake gold; at the point of your death, it will be of no benefit and will create only suffering."

Again, the seeker of the essence of wisdom asked: "Show kindness to us, the deceived and deluded. Please show us a stainless faith and pure religion."

The paṇḍita replied: "Know that the Christian faith and religion is worthy of being upheld as a crown ornament. It is flawless, unrivaled, perfect, and completely pure."

[13b] Again, the seeker of the essence of wisdom asked, "Who is it that is called a 'Christian'?"

The paṇḍita replied: "Christians are people who have faith in Jesus Christ, the peerless and supreme guide, and who uphold him as the crown jewel and practice the flawless faith and religion set forth by the sole guide, the lord himself."

Again, the seeker of the essence of wisdom asked: "Please teach us about having faith in Jesus Christ, the peerless and supreme guide, and upholding him as the crown jewel and practicing the flawless faith and religion set forth by the sole guide, the lord himself."

The paṇḍita replied: "You need to generate three kinds of faith, not just in words but from the depths of your mind. What are the three kinds of faith? They are the faith of belief, the faith capable of reliance, and the faith that is clear, stainless, and joyful."

The seeker of the essence of wisdom asked: "How does one generate the faith of belief?"

The paṇḍita replied: "There are three [elements]: cherishing the object in whom the faith of belief is generated, identifying how to generate the faith of belief, and the object upon which the faith of belief in generated. First, what is cherishing the object in whom the faith of belief is generated? [14a] Because the self-existent precious jewel is the peerless sole lord, it is believing in two things: the miraculous way that the highest has three natures and the way of the supreme guide Jesus Christ's act of kindness in being born as a human; he came into the world and died for the sake of all humans."

Again, the seeker of the essence of wisdom asked: "Please expand on the reasons why the self-existent precious jewel is the peerless sole lord and then guide our minds to the meaning of the words of this important article of faith."

The paṇḍita replied: "First, the reason he is called self-existent jewel is this. As was explained earlier, all persons and phenomena that have the qualities of production and disintegration are simply emptiness, like the reflection of a moon in a clear lake, without being intrinsically established. For example, when there is the reflection of the moon in a lake, there must be the actual form of the moon; if there is no actual form of the moon, there cannot be the reflection of the moon. In the same manner, if we who are produced and disintegrate exist, there must be something that is eternal without being produced and disintegrating and is intrinsically established. If there were nothing that is intrinsically established, then we who are emptiness would not exist at all, like the reflection of the moon. Therefore, when you enter the path of the stainless Christian faith, the pure religion, [14b] you first meditate again and again from the depths of the mind on the existence of something that is intrinsically established. You must come to believe this, not simply in words, but with all of your thoughts."

Here, the seeker of the essence of wisdom asked: "After the thick darkness of the night has grown thin and the orb of the sun dawns in a cloudless sky, our eyes are filled with sunlight and we become joyful. In the same way, please dispel the darkness of the unreliable and imperfect system and teach us about the existence of that entity which is intrinsically established. This will create immeasurable joy in my mind, and with no doubt remaining, I will believe. Please, have no worries now; teach me the reasons for calling it 'precious jewel' and clarify the meaning of the word for this special article of faith."

The paṇḍita replied: "The reason for calling it 'jewel' is this. In Tibetan, the word 'jewel' *(dkon mchog)* is understood to be an object that is worthy of worship and worthy as a place of refuge. After you have developed the faith of belief in the existence of something that is intrinsically established, you should meditate again and again, from the depths of your mind, with infallible certainty, that it is an infallible jewel. You must come to believe this, not simply in words, but with all of your thoughts.

"If you examine the reasons for this in detail, it is thus. Making obeisance and worshipping with body, speech, and mind are activities of body, speech, and mind that celebrate and revere the qualities and the all-pervasive power of the object to which obeisance and worship are offered. [15a] Therefore if that object is self-established, all of its unsurpassed qualities and greatness are established by virtue of its own character. With limitless force, it will wield power over the past, present, and future. Therefore, it is worthy of obeisance and worship, and is worthy as a place of refuge. It is called 'jewel' with infallible certainty. Setting forth the reasons, I have clarified the meaning of the words."

The seeker of the essence of wisdom then asked, "Please have the kindness to clarify the meaning of the words, 'peerless guide, sole lord.'"

The paṇḍita replied: "If it is self-existent, all of its qualities and greatness must be established by virtue of its own character as boundless in every way. Therefore, there is not a single quality or greatness superior to it and there is nothing else that is its equal or peer in qualities and greatness; it is peerless, and must be the sole lord. Therefore, you should understand that, apart from that which is intrinsically established, everything else that exists is immeasurably small, immeasurably base, and immeasurably faulty in the presence of its intrinsic establishment. Therefore, you should know that, apart from that which is intrinsically established, there is nothing that is worthy of obeisance and worship or worthy as a place of refuge. Therefore, you must conclude that apart from the self-existent precious jewel, the peerless sole lord, there is no other jewel. [15b] If you develop such faith and if you believe in this cherished special article of faith with all your thoughts, please enter the path of the Christian religion. If you cannot develop such faith, entering an excellent path will have no purpose; after your death great sufferings will befall you."

Here, the seeker of the essence of wisdom asked: "For example, when the orb of the sun dawns in a cloudless sky, it is as if there is nothing left of the light of all the stars that illuminated the night sky; they have disappeared. In the same way, the unexcelled qualities and the immeasurable greatness of the self-existent jewel, the peerless sole lord, has appeared to my eye of faith. The illusory and false objects that I once imagined to be like a jewel due to my deluded and utterly deceived way of thinking have disappeared, with nothing left of their qualities or greatness. I will cultivate from the depths of my heart an unwavering faith in the single and unrivaled self-existent jewel; there is nothing else worthy of worship and worthy as a place of refuge. Please, again have the kindness to now teach us the reasons for saying 'the miraculous way the highest has three natures.'"

The paṇḍita replied: "For example, if someone thought, 'I am going to pour all the waters of the great ocean into a shallow pit,' he would be no different from a child who has not learned words. [16a] In the same way, if I were to think, 'I will teach the immeasurable mode of being of the self-existent sole lord himself, who is inexpressible and inconceivable,' I would be no different from such a child. However, in order to satisfy your mind, I will clarify this article of faith just briefly. For example, when a person looks in a mirror, he sees in the mirror his reflection, which resembles him. In the same way, because the self-existent jewel, the sole lord, is an omniscient being free of limitations and impediments, he knows himself eternally, without beginning, middle, or end. Because of this self-knowledge, he creates a reflection of his unsurpassed wisdom, which is similar to himself in all ways without beginning. Now, the difference between the reflection of a person who looks in a mirror and the reflection of the self-existent jewel, the sole lord who knows himself, is this. The reflection of the person who looks in the mirror cannot be the same continuum as the person, yet the reflection of the self-existent jewel, the sole lord who knows himself, is inseparable, not different, and one with the continuum of the self-existent jewel who knows himself. There is no way for an object that is known and the reflection of an object that is known to become the same nature. Yet the self-existent jewel knows himself. Meditating on this, understand that the self-existent jewel is established as two with a slight difference in nature.

[16b] "Furthermore, the self-existent jewel, through the very act of knowing himself, creates a reflection that is similar to himself in all ways without beginning and is the same entity. The nature that creates is determined by the name 'father,' and the nature that is created is determined by the name 'son.' As was explained here, the creator father and the created son are an inseparable continuum, identical without any difference in entity. Therefore, please understand that the two of them are not two self-existent jewels and that they are a single self-existent jewel that have a slight difference in their unsurpassed nature. Furthermore, the self-existent jewel, the sole lord, knows himself eternally, without beginning, middle, or end, and the father and son have a slight difference in nature. The father takes immeasurable joy in the unsurpassed qualities and immeasurable greatness of his son, who is completely similar to him, and the son takes immeasurable joy in the unsurpassed qualities and immeasurable greatness of his father, who is completely similar to him. For example, the father creates the nature of the son through the act of knowing himself. In this way, due to the two, father and son, rejoicing in each other, another unexcelled nature is established from both father and son. For example, although the son created by the father has a slightly different nature than the father, yet his continuum is indivisibly one with the father with no difference in entity. [17a] In the same way, the third nature which is established from both the father and the son delighting in each other has a nature that is slightly different from the nature of the father and the nature of the son, yet its continuum is indivisibly one with both the father and the son with no difference in entity. That third nature, which is established from both father and son, is called the unsurpassed perfect mind. In the end, because the father is the jewel and the son is also the jewel, the unsurpassed perfect mind is the jewel. How-

ever, because the three—the father, son, and unsurpassed perfect mind—are established as a single indivisible unity without a difference in entity, you should generate the faith of belief in the self-existent jewel, the peerless sole lord; the father, son, and unsurpassed perfect mind are not three self-existent jewels.

"Let me give an example of something surpassable and apply it to what it means to be unsurpassed. For example, it is from springs that rivers emerge, and from rivers that lakes emerge. For example, rivers comes from springs and lakes come from rivers; spring, river, and lake mean three different things yet the water of a spring, the water of a river, and the water of a lake are the same without difference. Also, each finger of the hand has three joints, and the first joint is not the second and the third joints; the second and the third joints are separate. However, these three separate joints are not established as three separate fingers, they are one finger that is not different. Similarly, among the three, the father, son, and the unsurpassed pure mind, because the father created the son, the son is created from the father, as a river comes from a spring. [17b] The unsurpassed pure mind is established from the father and son, as a lake comes from springs and rivers. The father, son, and the unsurpassed pure mind are established as three slightly different unsurpassed natures. Just as a spring, river, and lake that come from the same undifferentiated water are established as a single indivisible continuum without a difference in entity, so the self-existent jewel, the peerless sole lord is one."

Here, the seeker of the essence of wisdom exclaimed: "O! How wonderful! For example, the mind of a child considers a lake covering four or five leagues to be vast. If at a later point in time, he sets out on a great ocean that seems to be without depths or limits, without boundaries in any direction, straight ahead, right, left, above, and below, not only will he recognize that the lake he saw before is very small, but soon forgetting his previous idea, he will contemplate only the qualities of the vast ocean, overcome with wonder, without being satisfied [by anything else]. In the same way, this mind of mine has generated a discriminating wisdom that is like a blazing fire with regard to the impure tenets of deluded faith and deceptive religion of the past. Thanks to your kindness, O paṇḍita, who is like the captain, I have set out on the great ocean of the inexpressible and inconceivable qualities of the self-existent jewel, the peerless sole lord, which are without depths or limits, without boundaries in any direction; I shall completely dispel my previous conceptions. [18a] I shall rejoice, without being satisfied [by anything else], in the qualities and greatness of the self-existent jewel, the peerless sole lord, who is unsurpassed, inexpressible, and inconceivable. With all my thoughts generating the faith of belief, I will completely submit to him.

"Now, please clarify the meaning of the words, 'The supreme guide Jesus Christ's act of kindness in being born as a human; he came into the world and died for the sake of all humans.'"

The paṇḍita clarified it, saying: "Among the three unsurpassed natures of the self-existent jewel, the peerless sole lord—the father, son, and the unsurpassed perfect mind—which are established as one inseparable continuum without a difference of entity, the son is the self-existent jewel without a beginning. Yet he took on a human mind and a human form at a point in time. Although the unsurpassed continuum of the self-existent jewel and the surpassable continuum of the human body are two and unrelated, they became one nature without duality and he was born as a human. After he was born, he served the welfare of ordinary people and his disciples through teaching the good path and performing various miracles. He remained in this world for thirty-three years. And for the welfare of all humans, from the beginning of the world to the end, those who have been born, are born, and will be born, he was nailed to the wood of the cross with iron nails and died, sacrificing his life. Therefore, leaving no deeds of the supreme guide undone, he extended limitless compassion to us. [18b]

"To summarize the points I have explained here: The self-existing jewel is the peerless sole lord; the miraculous way in which his unsurpassed nature is three; the son, the glorious and supreme guide Jesus Christ took birth as a human. He came into the world and died for the sake of all humans. These two forms of his immeasurable compassion are the two cherished special objects in which the faith of belief is produced. In order to contemplate and benefit from these two cherished special objects in which the faith of belief is produced, all Christians, whether young or old, remember this many times each day with the sign of the pure cross. What is the sign of the pure cross? I will explain. First, place the tips of the fingers of your right hand on the middle of the forehead and say 'Father'; then, placing them at the point between your chest and navel, say 'son,' and, finally, placing them on your left and right shoulder, say 'unsurpassed pure mind.' With faith, make the sign of the pure cross. Do not say, 'in the names of'; you should say 'in the name of,' cultivating the faith of belief in the self-existent jewel, the peerless sole lord. Having done so, by saying 'father, son, and unexcelled perfect mind,' cultivate the faith of belief in the self-existent jewel having three un-surpassed natures. And by making the sign of the pure cross [19a], generate the faith of belief in the glorious and supreme guide Jesus Christ who came into the world and died for the sake of all humans."

Again, the seeker of the essence of wisdom asked: "You have spoken of the need first to identify the way of generating the faith of belief before entering the good path of the Christian faith and religion. Now, please re-cite the way of generating faith?"

The paṇḍita replied: "The twelve main disciples of the glorious and su-preme guide Jesus Christ composed twelve statements as a way to generate the faith of belief. If one were to translate them into Tibetan and recite them, it would be like this:

I believe from the depths of my mind in (1) the self-existent jewel, the pre-cious father, endowed with immeasurable and unsurpassed power, who brought into being out of nothing the heavens and the earth, together with all that is; (2) in his only son, lord Jesus Christ, our venerable lord; (3) that through the miracle of the unsurpassed power of the unsurpassed pure mind, he entered and was formed in the womb of his celibate mother, without being tainted by any fault and was born from the ever good Mary, who was completely without the fault of unchastity; (4) that under the terrifying rule of Pontius Pilate, he underwent a great many powerful and harsh feelings of suffering. He was nailed to the wood of the cross with iron nails, died, and was placed in a tomb; (5) that he went to the realm of hell; that after he died, [19b] when the third day arrived, the body in which he had died, leaving nothing, came back to life, without having feelings of suffering or signs of decay; (6) that he went into the realm of the heavens and sits on the right side of the father, the self-existent jewel endowed with immeasurable and unsurpassed power; (7) that in order to carry out the law for the living and the dead, at the end time of the world, he will come from the realm and the right side of the father. I believe with all my thoughts in (8) the unsurpassed pure mind and the pure catholic church, (9) in the coming together of the roots of virtue gathered by pure beings, (10) that all infractions are rejected by the power of repair and subdued and dispelled by immeasurable compassion, (11) that at the end time of the world, all humans will encounter the physical body in which they died in the past and in that, without lacking consciousness, they will rise again,

(12) and have eternal life of perfect and complete enjoyment of the unsurpassed final aim, without reversal and without end. Amen.

I have explained the way to generate the faith of belief through recitation."

Again, the seeker of the essence of wisdom asked: "The meaning of 'self-existing jewel, the father' is clear from what you explained before. Please set forth the reasons for calling him 'endowed with immeasurable and unsurpassed power.'"

The paṇḍita replied: "The self-existent jewel, the peerless sole lord, has immeasurable power. [20a] He is able to bring everything into reality in accordance with his intention, without any exception, obstruction, impediment, or difficulty, and he is able to make what already exists utterly non-existent."

Again, the seeker of the essence of wisdom asked: "How does one understand 'brought into being out of nothing the heavens and the earth, together with all that is'?"

The paṇḍita said: "The self-existing jewel, the sole peerless lord, has no beginning, middle, or end; he is eternal without [ever] being non-existent. All impermanent things marked by production and disintegration did not exist in the beginning. Through the immeasurable compassion and unsurpassed power of the self-existent jewel, the heavens and the earth and all the types of living and nonliving beings came into existence at the beginning of time.

"Let me again explain 'out of nothing.' You must understand the difference between the self-existent jewel and impermanent things. It is thus: Conditioned things that are subject to production and disintegration arise as effects in dependence upon each other. As causes, they come to construct each other. However, if the other enabling factors of causes and conditions do not come together, a cause does not create its effect. Thus, a mason cannot build a house without having stones, earth, pillars, beams, and rafters. When a house that has already been built is destroyed, the stones, earth, and so on that are its constituents cannot be made utterly non-existent. [20b] The self-existent jewel is not of such a nature. Acting as the cause, he brings everything in the manifest world into existence out of nothing without any other factors coming together with him. If the intention arises to destroy what has already been brought into existence, he is able to make it utterly non-existent. Therefore, because the self-existent jewel knows himself without obstruction, without obstruction he created a son who resembles him and who, indivisible from his continuum, is one with him without difference. Certain of this, we say 'In the name of the Father.' Furthermore, induced by his immeasurable compassion, with his unsurpassed power he brought impermanent phenomena into existence out of nothing. What has already come into being he prolongs without making them utterly non-existent. Therefore, understand that he is [the creator of] the qualities of production, disintegration, and impermanence, our precious father."

Again, the seeker of the essence of wisdom said: "You have already set forth earlier the reasons for 'his only son.' Please clarify the meaning of the words 'Jesus Christ' and so on."

The paṇḍita replied: "With regard to the only son of the self-existent jewel, the father, it is said, 'In the name of Jesus Christ.' The etymology of 'Jesus' is guide and savior; the etymology of 'Christ' is a precious teacher who is like a crown jewel among teachers and a lord of kings who is like the sun surrounded by the planets and stars among [other] kings. I have explained the etymology. [21a] Regarding the reason for calling him our lord, due to the immeasurable power and unsurpassed strength of the father and the son, they are one and not two. The precious son of the father, Jesus Christ, brought us into existence out of nothing and, through his kindness of coming into the world and giving up his life for the sake of all humans, he freed all of us from becoming slaves of ghosts and demons. For these two reasons he is called 'our lord.'"

Again, the seeker of the essence of wisdom asked: "Please explain the statement, 'Through the miracle of the unsurpassed power of the pure unsurpassed mind, he entered the womb of his celibate mother, who was untainted by any fault and was born from the ever good Mary, who was without the fault of unchastity.'"

The paṇḍita replied: "No human is born except in dependence on the semen and blood of the father and mother, and no child is conceived and created except in the place of the lust and copulation of the father and mother. The miraculous way in which the son of the self-existent jewel was born from his ever good mother without a father who had been born into a human body was this: Through its unsurpassed power, the unsurpassed pure mind created the body of a child, adorned with the signs, from the immaculate heart blood of the ever good Mary, who was without the fault of unchastity, and placed it in her womb. At the same time, which was like an instant, [21b] it created out of nothing a sublime consciousness adorned with all auspicious qualities and adornments and then united it with the body endowed with the signs. The self-existent jewel in his nature as the son united the body and mind of that perfect child with himself. Through such a miracle, the glorious guide, peerless savior, and sole lord Jesus Christ is one with the continuum of the self-existent jewel without beginning. Yet for the sake of all humans he became a human with a beginning in time, which is held to be a beginning. For example, just as he exists as the same continuum with the self-existent jewel, being created from a father without having a mother, without a beginning, so he was born from an ever good mother without a father, being born with a beginning in time. This is how the son of the self-existent jewel entered his mother's womb. After nine months, the body of the perfect child became complete. Both the mother and the son were never stained by impurity and the mother had no feelings of pain or injuries. As a ray of the sun passes unbroken through a clear crystal, the perfect child came into this world from his mother's womb without obstruction. This explains in detail the second phrase, 'Mary, the precious mother of our glorious guide, was ever good, never having the fault of unchastity before her son was born, at the time when her son was born, and after her son was born.'" [22a]

Again, the seeker of the essence of wisdom asked: "Please clarify the statement, 'under the terrifying rule of Pontius Pilate, he underwent a great many powerful and harsh feelings of suffering. He was nailed to the wood of the cross with iron nails, died, and was placed in a tomb.'"

The paṇḍita replied: "Jesus Christ, the guide and sole lord, was born to his ever good mother. He perfected his excellent deeds and revealed the auspicious path of the faith and religion that is beneficial after death and achieves the goal. With various miracles he served the welfare of ordinary people and his disciples. After spending thirty-three years in this world, he became the object of the attachment, hatred, and envy of Pontius Pilate, the governor of a land called Judea, who tormented him with various powerful and harsh sufferings. He was nailed to the wood of the cross with iron nails. For our sake, the faultless and pure guide gave up his life and died out of great compassion. Some pure beings who had faith respectfully placed his corpse in a new tomb. I have clarified the meaning of the fourth statement."

Here, the seeker of the essence of wisdom asked: "Since Jesus Christ is without defects and without faults, completely perfect, and endowed with unsurpassed power, [22b] what is the reason he submitted to various feelings of suffering and in particular the suffering of being killed? I am in a state of doubt."

The paṇḍita replied: "As explained before, through the immeasurable compassion and unsurpassed power of the self-existent jewel, the heavens and the earth and all the types of living and nonliving beings were made to come into being at the beginning of time. He caused [the earth] to be filled with humans in the form of a man and a woman and taught them what to adopt and discard. Not long after that, deceived by a demon, the man and woman did not act as they had been instructed and displeased the sole self-existent jewel. Immediately, the self-existent jewel became unhappy with the two original humans and all the humans of their lineage. So, in keeping with that misdeed, he caused such things as suffering, unhappiness, fear, sickness, aging, and death to arise relentlessly, as punishment for not heeding his instructions. Gradually, the human race greatly increased and ordinary beings, as if led by the noose of the afflictions, acted contrary to what is fitting. Not shunning the afflictions and obstructions, without shame and regret, as if they were powerless, they fell into the abyss of hell, which has no end and from which there is no escape. The power of the heavy sins caused by displeasing the self-existent jewel, the sole lord, creates the inexhaustible sufferings of hell, which has no end and from which there is no escape. From that point on, caused by displeasing the self-existent jewel, the sole lord, the power of the misdeeds became immeasurable. [23a] No matter what good deeds humans do, they cannot defeat or reverse the power of sin that leads to the inexhaustible sufferings of hell, which has no end and from which there is no escape. There is no alternative but to descend into hell.

"For example, if a loving father or mother saw their child who could not walk by its own power going toward a dangerous place, they would instinctively, anxiously, without the laziness of procrastination, and without feeling fear, lead their only beloved child from danger, using all their energy and physical strength. They would bring about the happiness of their child with their own suffering. In the same manner, through his nature of immeasurable compassion, the self-existent jewel sees that none of the sinful humans can escape the dangers of hell. Powerful and compassionate, he acts for our welfare, considering it not a burden but a joy. And in order to save all humans from the servitude of their misdeeds, he completely defeated the power of all the misdeeds, and so on, of all humans with the unsurpassed virtuous goodness and immeasurable auspiciousness of submitting to the great suffering and terror of being nailed to the wood of the cross and the suffering of giving up his life. He perfectly fulfilled the welfare of all humans who have come and who will come. My response has removed the doubts."

Again, the seeker of the essence of wisdom asked with doubt: "Jesus Christ, the sole lord who is the peerless guide and savior, [23b] perfectly fulfilled the welfare of all humans who have come and who will come. He completely defeated the power of all the misdeeds of all humans. Yet so many humans will undergo the sufferings of hell after they die, and here in the world of the living, when the fault arises of not doing what should be adopted and not avoiding what should be discarded, one should cleanse these with such things as the power to remove and repair them with strong remorse and resolve. How are these both correct?"

The paṇḍita replied: "For example, a skilled physician prepares a precious antidote to help those who have been bitten by a poisonous snake. Some who have been bitten by a poisonous snake do not ask for the medicine, out of attachment, hatred, or pride. Some ask for the medicine but do not take it. Although the skilled physician made a potent medicine to benefit those bitten by a poisonous snake, a great many humans who have been bitten by a poisonous snake will inevitably die. In the same way, Jesus Christ, the sole lord who is the peerless guide and savior, has fulfilled the welfare of all humans who have come and who will come and has completely defeated the power of all of the negative deeds of all humans. Yet just as the sick person must take the excellent medicine prepared by the physician, [24a] so each human must make it their own and take advantage of the unsurpassed roots of virtue accumulated for our welfare by Jesus Christ, which have the power to completely defeat all negative deeds and their powers. Thus, those who do not have faith in Jesus Christ, the sole lord who is the peerless guide and savior, and in the stainless Christian faith and religion that he taught are like sick people who do not ask for medicine. Those who have faith in him and in the faith and religion he taught, yet are motivated by laziness and stupidity, not doing virtuous deeds, not having remorse and resolve for their negative deeds, are like those who have asked for the medicine but do not take the medicine after being bitten by the poisonous snake. Through not making it their own and taking advantage of the unsurpassed roots of virtue accumulated for our welfare by Jesus Christ, which have the power to completely defeat all negative deeds and their powers, they undergo the ceaseless suffering of hell, which has no end and from which there is no escape. My response has removed the doubts."

Again, the seeker of the essence of wisdom asked with doubt: "Jesus Christ, the glorious guide, is the self-existent jewel. How could he experience feelings of suffering, die, and so on?"

The paṇḍita replied: "For example, humans have a body and a mind; the mind does not disintegrate and does not die. However, because the body dies [24b], it is true to say 'humans die.' In the same way, if he is the self-existent jewel, he is intrinsically established. Therefore he is not physical and must intrinsically be an entity of all qualities and greatness, not possessing the slightest fault. Jesus Christ is the self-existent jewel, yet he consented to take on the continuum of a human; he is the self-existent jewel and he is a human. Insofar as he is the self-existing jewel, it is not appropriate to maintain that he experiences suffering and dies; however, as a human, he definitely experienced feelings of suffering and the suffering of death. Thus, through my response, I have removed the doubts."

Again, the seeker of the essence of wisdom asked: "Please clarify the statement, 'He went to the realm of hell. After he died, when the third day arrived, the body in which he had died, leaving nothing, came back to life, with no feelings of suffering or signs of decay.'"

The paṇḍita replied: "The realm of hell has four levels. The lowest level is where one experiences a great many inexhaustible sufferings as the fruition of your misdeeds. The hell called purgatory is a place where lighter evil deeds or the remnants of misdeeds that have not been completely defeated through the power of repair are purified through suffering them until [the remnants of misdeeds], overpowered by remorse and resolve, are eliminated. [25a] The hell called limbo is a neutral and temporary abode for children who died when they were young without developing the awareness to distinguish between good and bad and who have not received the blessing that purifies the root defect through the power of baptism. The hell called the limbo of the pure beings of the past is for those who have no residue of faults to be purified, yet in the past were not able to go to the place where they would attain the vision of the face of the self-existent jewel in the realm which is the highest aim; [this limbo] is the place where the minds of these pure beings abide in goodness. Jesus Christ, the sole lord who is the peerless guide and savior, went to the realm of hell called the limbo of the pure beings of the past after he died and accomplished their final aim, leading them finally to the place where they attained the vision of face of the self-existent jewel without end. After he appeared to those pure beings and accomplished their highest aim, when the third day after his death arrived, the body in which he had died came back to life, with no feelings of suffering or signs of decay. I have clarified the meaning of the fifth statement."

Again, the seeker of the essence of wisdom asked: "Please clarify the statement, 'He went into the realm of the heavens and abides on the right side of the father, the self-existent jewel endowed with immeasurable and unsurpassed power.'"

The paṇḍita replied: "The previously killed body having come back to life, [25b] Jesus Christ remained in this world for forty days. He was clearly seen by the faithful and by a great many beings with pure minds and he displayed various miracles. Finally, seen by all, through his immeasurable power and unsurpassed strength, he went to the realm of the heavens in his risen body. There is no excess or deficit, no high or low between the father, the unsurpassed pure mind, [and Jesus]; this is the reason it is said that he sits on the right side of the father, the self-existent jewel. I have clarified the meaning of the sixth statement."

Again, the seeker of the essence of wisdom asked: "Please clarify the meaning of the statement, 'In order to carry out the law for the living and the dead, at the end time of the world, he will come from the realm and the right side of the father.'"

The paṇḍita replied: "First, the reason for 'at the end time of the world' is that although the time when this world will be destroyed is not certain, it is definite that it will not remain but in the future will be burned by a terrible blazing fire, being destroyed and becoming non-existent. At the end time of the world, Jesus Christ, the sole lord who is the savior, will come from the realm of the heavens in the manner of a precious judge with such splendor that we cannot bear to look at him. The reason for 'the living and the dead' is that on the last day of the world, many children and those in the prime of life will be alive. In a single moment they will die, and as soon as they have died they will again come to life. Their bodies and souls will be reunited and they will rise. [26a] Therefore, those who died in the past and those who, although alive on the last day of the world, died must then reunite their bodies and souls and rise. I have clarified the meaning of the seventh statement 'In order to carry out the law for the living and the dead,' and so on."

Again, the seeker of the essence of wisdom asked: "You already clearly established earlier the meaning of 'the unsurpassed pure mind' in the eighth statement from the perspective of setting forth the cherished object in which the faith of belief is generated. Please clarify the meaning of the statement, 'the pure catholic church and the coming together of the roots of virtue gathered by pure beings.' "

The paṇḍita replied: "Regarding the meaning and etymology of church [*rgyas za* = *chiesa*], it is the community of people called Christians who have faith in Jesus Christ, who is the sole lord and peerless savior, and who uphold and practice as the crown jewel the stainless faith and religion that he taught. Regarding the meaning and etymology of 'catholic,' it means no difference in place or time, that is, a commonality of space or time, and oneness without a second. Regarding the reason for saying 'oneness,' for example, the land of Tibet has many different villages, towns, cities, and markets, but there is one king and one tradition. Therefore, the land of Tibet is one country. In the same way, there are inconceivable numbers of people in all parts of the world in the community of people called Christians, but their teacher is the sole lord Jesus Christ, without a second, and their faith and religion is one. [26b] For this reason, it is called 'one.' The reason for saying 'pure,' is because the precious teacher of the religion is inexpressibly and inconceivably pure, because the faith he taught is perfectly and completely stainless, owing to the absolute purity of his religion, and because within the community of people called Christians, there have been continually without interruption so many people so thoroughly adorned with various qualities of goodness. Therefore it is called pure. With regard to the meaning of 'the coming together of the roots of virtue gathered by pure beings,' for example, among the united limbs of a living and healthy body, whatever health occurs for one limb becomes a factor for the welfare and health of all the other limbs. In the same way, in the community of Christians, any good deeds performed by individual persons not only benefit themselves with the deeds they do themselves, they also benefit all the other people who are limbs of that community. I have clarified the meaning of the ninth statement."

Again, the seeker of the essence of wisdom asked: "Please clarify the meaning of the statement 'All infractions are rejected by the power of repair and subdued and dispelled by immeasurable compassion.' "

The paṇḍita replied: "All humans who belong to the lineage of the man and woman who came into existence at the beginning of time are born as though chained to the root defect. [27a] Also, inconceivably many humans accumulate negative deeds without fear, as if drawn by the noose of the afflictions. Alas and alack! Whether chained by the root defect or whether actually accumulating negative deeds, as if rising up as enemies of the self-existent jewel, they are bereft of the compassionate blessings of the self-existent jewel. As long as they remain in this state, beings will not be capable of achieving the final aim, worthy of attainment. If they knowingly and willingly accumulate faults, they must undergo the inexhaustible sufferings of hell, which has no end and from which there is no escape. There are two compassionate powers: (1) because it repairs the root defect and because it acts as a blessing that transforms you into the son of the self-existent jewel, it is called the power of baptism, and (2) because it repairs all of the misdeeds you have accumulated yourself and because it acts as a blessing that transforms you into a friend of the self-existent jewel, it is called the compassionate power of penitence. Apart from the Christian faith and religion, these two do not exist in any other faith or religion, as illustrated by the example of the sick who do not ask for medicine. Only in the faith and religion taught by Jesus Christ, the sole lord and savior, is there the blessing that repairs, powerfully defeats, overpowers with limitless great compassion, and eradicates any misdeed. This is taught as an article for generating the faith of belief. I have clarified the meaning of the tenth statement."

Again, the seeker of the essence of wisdom asked: [27b] "Please set forth the meaning of the statement 'At the end time of the world, all humans will encounter the physical body in which they died in the past and in that, without lacking consciousness, they will rise again.'"

The paṇḍita replied: "It is illogical that good deeds and misdeeds are wasted. Therefore at the time of the cause, negative and positive deeds are performed, with the body accompanying the mind. Therefore, at the time of the effect, pleasant and unpleasant effects must be felt, with the body[3] accompanying the mind. It is also illogical for one person to experience the effects [of actions] accumulated by someone else. Therefore, because at the time of the cause, this present body accompanies the mind, and positive and negative deeds are performed, then also at the time of the effect, this present body accompanies the mind and pleasant and unpleasant effects must be felt. Due to these two correct and learned reasons on the topic of cause and effect, it is taught as an article of belief that at the end time of the world, the mind arises again connected with the physical body that died earlier, without separation. I have clarified the meaning of the eleventh statement."

Again, the seeker of the essence of wisdom asked with doubt: "After death, some bodies are burned into ashes, some are eaten by creatures of the air, water, or land. At the end time of the world, how do they rise again and come back to life?" [28a]

The paṇḍita replied: "As I explained in the context of the first statement, the self-existent jewel, the peerless sole lord is endowed with limitless power and unsurpassed strength. He created all conditioned things, both the heavens and the earth, out of nothing. At the beginning of time, he created the body and mind out of nothing. What need is there to speak of his ability at the end time of the world to bring bodies that have turned into ashes and so on back to their previous forms? My response has removed the doubts."

Again, the seeker of the essence of wisdom asked: "Please clarify the statement, 'eternal life of perfect and complete enjoyment of the unsurpassed final aim, without reversal and without end.'"

The paṇḍita replied: "Regarding 'eternal life of perfect and complete enjoyment of the unsurpassed final aim, without reversal and without end,' after the destruction of the world, the bodies and minds of the pure beings, having passed beyond all fear, will achieve complete and perfect enjoyments which are marvelous, ceaseless, and unsurpassed, without disintegration or change. This is called the highest aim, the aim of definite goodness. For example, for those who have never embarked on the road to India, those who embarked but did not go there before, or those who after embarking gave up the journey, it is impossible to reach India. Similarly, those who have never entered the faith and religion taught by Jesus Christ, who is the peerless guide and sole lord, [28b] those who have entered it but do not devote themselves to what is to be adopted and what is to be discarded, or those who after having entered turn away and give up the path, will never reach the highest aim, the aim of definite goodness. Therefore, what is called the highest aim, the aim of definite goodness, is attained only by pure beings who, until their death, develop faith in Jesus Christ, the guide and sole lord, from the depths of their minds and who conform to the faith and religion that he taught. I have clarified how to generate the faith of belief by means of the twelfth statement."

Again the seeker of the essence of wisdom asked: "Now, through generating the faith of belief, on what object is my mind focused in perfect faith?"

The paṇḍita replied: "The faith of belief is generating the awareness that the valid and undeceptive words of the learned ones are true just as they are taught. Therefore, in all cases of these articles of the faith of belief, you should take as your object the fact that the self-existent jewel Jesus Christ, who is the sole lord and peerless guide, is utterly without fault or deception; things must exist as spoken by him, and [you should take as your object] the fact that he taught, revealing and describing the meanings of the greatest mysteries to us, the deluded. You should generate the unwavering faith of belief with all your thoughts."

Here, the seeker of the essence of wisdom asked: "Now, please fulfill my wish that you kindly teach me how to generate the faith capable of reliance." [29a]

The paṇḍita replied: "There are two: (1) The seven cherished objects for generating the faith capable of reliance, and (2) generating faith in dependence on these objects.

"Regarding the first. Out of compassion for deluded humans who pursue objects that create desire, anger, and obscuration and who, like children, lack the mental strength to help or harm, Jesus Christ, the sole lord and peerless guide, composed a most powerful prayer of request. It kindly gathers the milk of the faith capable of reliance for us, whom he cares for like a compassionate mother for her beloved child. What is that marvelous prayer of request? It is thus:

> O our precious father who abides in the boundless heavens, may your renowned name spread widely and become an object of praise and respect. May your realm be manifested to us. May your intention be manifested in all parts of the earth as it is in the boundless heavens. Please give us today food for each day. We ask that you destroy our debts as we do not make others repay debts. Do not allow us to fall into a place that impedes virtuous thoughts and creates non-virtuous thoughts and please protect us and free us from outer and inner harm and all fears. May this be achieved.

Because seven requests are bestowed in the palm of your hands through the excellent prayer of supplication, [29b] seven articles of the faith of reliance have been set forth."

Again, the seeker of the essence of wisdom asked: "Please clarify the meaning of the phrase, 'our precious father who abides in the boundless heavens.'"

The paṇḍita replied: "These words, which are like a prologue to the prayer, set forth both the object of the prayer and the special nature of the object. Here, the object to whom we go for refuge and to whom we pray is the self-existent jewel, the peerless sole lord. Therefore, by recalling the greatness of his abiding in the boundless heavens, we understand his ability to respond to what we want and what we need, pervaded by his immeasurable power and unsurpassed strength. By remembering that this is the great act of our precious father and that we are his children, we understand that he is endowed with great immeasurable compassion, such that, pervaded by unsurpassed qualities of love and compassion, it is impossible for him to act contrary to our wants and needs; having faith, your appeal will increase greatly."

Again, the seeker of the essence of wisdom asked: "The self-existent jewel pervades everywhere with no division anywhere; what is the reason for 'who abides in the boundless heavens'?"

The paṇḍita replied: "The self-existent jewel does pervade everywhere with no division anywhere. However, [30a] among the parts of the world, the boundless heavens are the most important; the boundless heavens accord with the boundless greatness and power of the self-existent jewel; and the boundless heavens are the place where one attains, without obstruction, without veil, and without obscuration, the vision of the face of the self-existent jewel. Therefore, it says, 'who abides in the boundless heaven.'"

The seeker of the essence of wisdom asked: "Please clarify the statement 'May your renowned name spread widely and become an object of praise and respect.'"

The paṇḍita replied: "In this world, an inconceivable number of deluded humans follow religions that are false and untrue and do not have faith in the self-existent jewel, the peerless sole lord. What need is there to mention his unsurpassed qualities? They do not know of his existence or recognize his name. Through the kindness of his immeasurable compassion, faithful Christians, who have become the children of the self-existent jewel, bow to him with all their thoughts, requesting and praying that the self-existent jewel's renowned name will spread widely and become an object of praise and respect."

Again, the seeker of the essence of wisdom asked: "Please clarify the meaning of the statement, 'May your realm be manifested to us.'"

The paṇḍita replied: "Through the blessings of his immeasurable compassion, Christians, who have become children of the self-existent jewel, [30b] seek the highest aim of definite goodness, which is the goal of the soul (*bdag*). They request and pray that after they die, they will go to the eternal and uninterrupted attainment, having—without obstruction, without veil, and without obscuration—the vision of the face of the self-existent jewel and that after the destruction of the world, they will achieve the perfect and complete attainment, without disintegration and without change, of the unsurpassed enjoyments of body and mind. I have clarified the meaning of the words of the second part of the prayer."

Again, the seeker of wisdom asked: "Please set forth the meaning of the statement, 'May your intention be manifested in all parts of the earth as it is in the boundless heavens.'"

The paṇḍita replied: "The highest aim of definite goodness, which is the goal, is, passing beyond all fear, to go to the realm where one attains the eternal vision of the face of the self-existent jewel and, after the destruction of the world, to attain the unsurpassed and inexhaustible enjoyments of body and mind. The method for achieving that aim is trusting in the stainless faith and religion taught by Jesus Christ in three ways: having faith in what he said, avoiding what is to be discarded, and achieving what needs to be adopted. Again, for example, a small child does not have the ability by itself to obtain the food, clothing, and so on it needs for survival; it must cry for its parents' kindness. In the same way, all humans large and small, bound by the fetters of the afflictions, [31a] cannot by their own power have perfect and complete faith for a long time without interruption, perfectly and completely avoid what is to be discarded, and achieve what needs to be adopted. Thus, after the Christian prays to attain the highest aim of definite goodness, which is the goal, as the method to achieve that aim, he asks from the depths of his heart for the blessing to have faith in what the self-existent jewel has said and wants, to completely avoid what is to be discarded, and to engage in virtuous deeds."

Again, the seeker of the essence of wisdom asked: "Please set forth the reason for saying, 'as it is in the boundless heavens.'"

The paṇḍita replied: "Formless and inconceivably pure minds called angels and the inconceivable mind of pure beings who have already given up this body and died enjoy the highest aim of definite goodness, which is the attainment of the vision of the face of the self-existent jewel in the realm of heaven. They rejoice and delight in the self-existent jewel eternally, without interruption and without wavering of mind, and they never violate his will. In the same way, the faithful pray, saying 'I ask to be blessed to rejoice and delight in the self-existent jewel without interruption and without wavering of mind until I die and not to violate his pure will.' [31b] I have clarified the meaning of the words of the third part of the prayer."

Again, the seeker of the essence of wisdom asked: "Please set forth the reasons for saying, 'Please give us today food for each day.'"

The paṇḍita replied: "Each human is made from the combination of body and mind. For example, if the body is not sustained with food each day, it will fall into the abyss of all the sufferings of sickness and death. In the same way, if consciousness is not strengthened through instructions on religion, focusing on objects that lead toward religion, and the blessing of the jewel that spreads the religion, it will be struck by the intense disease of the afflictions and fall into the abyss of all horrors and sufferings. Thus, here, with the word 'food,' the Christian prays to receive each day the food that nourishes the body and the blessings that strengthen the religious direction of the mind. I have clarified the meaning of the words of the fourth part of the prayer."

Again, the seeker of the essence of wisdom asked: "Please set forth the meaning of the statement, 'We ask that you destroy our debts as we do not make others repay debts.'"

The paṇḍita replied: "In the first, second, third, and fourth parts of this prayer, we have already prayed to realize the goodness of mind and body. Now in the fifth, sixth and seventh parts, we pray to be protected from the horrors of body and mind [32a] by the immeasurable compassion of the self-existent jewel. First, with the word 'debts' we ask for the compassion that frees us from the horrors of faults and completely purifies them."

Again, the seeker of the essence of wisdom asked: "What is the reason for calling negative deeds 'debts'?"

The paṇḍita replied: "For example, in any legal system of the world, for whatever debt is created, restitution must be made. In the same way, after a dark negative deed is committed, [the need] for restitution is created; the negative deed is called a debt. According to the religion taught by the self-existent jewel, the reason for restitution after either a positive deed is not performed or a negative deed is performed without mindfulness and introspection, is that, having displeased the self-existent jewel without listening to him, you must please him and be reconciled with him. If you do not please him and are not reconciled with him, after death, you must powerlessly undergo the ceaseless sufferings of hell."

Again, the seeker of the essence of wisdom asked: "Please set forth the reason for saying, 'as we do not make others repay debts.'"

The paṇḍita replied: "The word 'debt' is taken to mean what does damage to either our reputation, our body, or our possessions. [32b] For example, we have already displeased the self-existent jewel with our negative deeds; we ask him to forgive and remove all the misdeeds that have the capacity to produce their fruit, saying 'Have mercy.' In the same way, we must cultivate forbearance[4] from the depths of our thoughts, without becoming angry about harm done [to us], without seeking revenge against others. Without that, the prayer made, having no power, will not achieve its purpose. I have clarified the meaning of the words of the fifth part of the prayer."

Again, the seeker of the essence of wisdom asked: "Please set forth the meaning of the statement, 'Do not allow us to fall into a place that impedes virtuous thoughts and that creates non-virtuous thoughts.'"

The paṇḍita replied: "The things that impede virtuous thoughts and that create non-virtuous thoughts are powerful. Therefore, when you encounter either of them, fearing that you will do wrong, as if being forced, you pray with a pure mind not to encounter the things that impede virtuous thoughts and that create non-virtuous thoughts. I have clarified the meaning of the sixth part of the prayer."

Again, the seeker of the essence of wisdom asked: "Please set forth the meaning of the statement, 'Please protect us and free us from outer and inner harm and all fears.'"

The paṇḍita replied: "In the fifth and sixth parts of the prayer, you pray specifically to be led from the horrors of negative deeds and [33a] not to encounter things that impede virtuous thoughts, and so on. Here, after going for refuge in the self-existent jewel, we pray for his compassion, which protects us from all fears, outer, inner, and in general.

I have set forth the seven precious objects in which the faith capable of reliance is generated through clarifying the meaning of the words of the seven-part prayer composed by Jesus Christ, the peerless guide and sole lord, for the benefit of the faithful."

Again, the seeker of the essence of wisdom asked: "Now, having shown me the kindness of setting forth the seven precious objects on the basis of which the faith capable of reliance is generated, please establish the perfect faith in my mind."

The paṇḍita replied: "You must rely on and have faith in where you have gone for refuge. Therefore, you should generate the faith capable of reliance through remembering the qualities of the object of refuge. Here also, the object to whom you go for refuge is the self-existent jewel, who is the peerless guide and sole lord. He is the entity of all greatness and qualities, yet from the perspective of being a place of refuge, you must remember two special qualities. What are these two? The quality of being pervaded by immeasurable power and unsurpassed strength, and the quality of extending immeasurable compassion to all without bias. If we meditate again and again on these two special qualities, we conclude that [33b] it is impossible that the self-existent jewel would not protect us from all fears and would not bring about whatever goodness is appropriate. Generating unshakable faith, whatever you pray for with a powerful mind, you will undoubtedly achieve. Furthermore, the faith capable of reliance is to be generated from the perspective of remembering the promise by the self-existent jewel to bring about the highest aim, the definite goodness of the faithful, or completely fulfill whatever object that they pray for that benefits the mind, and [from the perspective of remembering that] the unsurpassed roots of virtue accumulated by Jesus Christ for the faithful have the unsurpassed power to bring about our goodness or to protect us from fear."

Again, the seeker of the essence of wisdom asked: "Except for the self-existent jewel, nothing is pervaded by immeasurable power and unsurpassed strength and extends immeasurable compassion to all without bias. Therefore, except for the self-existent jewel, nothing is worthy of going for refuge; nothing is the object for generating the faith capable of reliance. When you do not have the time to pray many times to the ever good Mary, mother of Jesus Christ, the peerless sole lord, why do you Christians pray three times a day?"

The paṇḍita replied, removing the doubt: "Due to the self-existent jewel's quality of being pervaded by immeasurable power and unsurpassed strength and his quality of extending immeasurable compassion to all without bias, [34a] he is the peerless guide and sole lord, the place of refuge who protects us from all fears and brings about whatever goodness is appropriate. However, there are formless and inconceivably pure minds called angels and the inconceivable minds of pure beings who have attained the highest aim and have attained the vision of the face of the self-existent jewel. In particular, the mother of the precious Jesus Christ, the precious ever good Mary, is like the attendant of the self-existent jewel, making kind requests for great compassion for the sake of the faithful. Thus, you should understand that she has the ability to protect the faithful from all fears and to achieve goodness.

Therefore, after the prayer composed for the sake of the faithful by Jesus Christ, the peerless guide and savior and sole lord, Christians pray to the ever good Mary, the mother of Jesus Christ."

The seeker of the essence of wisdom asked, "Please recite the prayer that is to be made to the ever good Mary, mother of Jesus Christ."

The pandita recited the prayer that is to be made to the ever good Mary, mother of Jesus Christ:

> How wondrous! Through the great immeasurable compassion of the self-existent jewel, precious Mary, you have come to have the physical marks of goodness. O, you are completely permeated by the joy of the self-existent jewel. The self-existent jewel assists you like a friend. [34b]. Among all women, you are to be praised, and the fruition of your womb, the precious Jesus Christ, is also to be worshipped and praised. O Mary, precious mother of the self-existent jewel, at all times, from now until death, kindly ask for immeasurable compassion for the sake of us sinners. May it be fulfilled now.

"Thus have I recited the prayer of supplication to the Mother of Jesus Christ, the all-good Mary."

Here, the seeker of the essence of wisdom asked: "Please set forth how to generate the faith that is clear, stainless, and joyful."

The pandita replied: "Because the object in which you generate the faith that is clear, stainless, and joyful is the self-existent jewel alone, there are many good methods for generating the faith that is clear, stainless, and joyful, one greater than the other. However, the method that all humans without discrimination can readily adopt is to directly implement what is to be adopted and abandon what is to be discarded in accordance with how the self-existent jewel taught the path."

The seeker of the essence of wisdom asked: "Please explain the commandments of the self-existent jewel that teach humans the path of what to adopt and what to discard."

The pandita replied: "There are ten commandments of the self-existent jewel that teach humans the path of what to adopt and what to discard. What are the ten? It is thus:

> The ten are: (1) Because I am the self-existent jewel who is your lord, do not take anything other than me as an object of worship and an object of

refuge. (2) Do not use my name without purpose. (3) On days that are taught to be auspicious, [35a] properly perform the rituals of the auspicious day. (4) Honor your father and your mother. (5) Do not take the lives of humans. (6) Abandon sexual misconduct. (7) Do not steal. (8) Do not make judgments and bear witness falsely. (9) Do not covet anything that belongs to another. (10) Do not generate a mind of desire for a woman who belongs to someone else."

Again, the seeker of the essence of wisdom asked: "Please comment on the intended meaning of the first commandment."

The paṇḍita replied: "If this commandment is divided there are two, one thing to be received into the palm of the hand and two things to be abandoned. What is to be adopted is to hold, without any disparity between your thoughts and your words, that the self-existent jewel is the peerless guide and sole lord and to develop the faith that he alone exists as such. The first thing to be abandoned is to abandon holding any other person or created thing apart from the self-existent jewel as an object of worship and an object of refuge. The second thing to be abandoned is to abandon holding such things as manmade images as an object of worship and an object of refuge."

Again, the seeker of the essence of wisdom asked: "Please clarify the meaning of what is to be received into the palm of the hand in this commandment."

The paṇḍita replied: "If what is to be adopted is divided, there are four supreme types of virtuous goodness to be achieved: the virtuous goodness that generates the faith of belief, the virtuous goodness that generates the faith of reliance, the virtuous goodness that generates the faith of joy, and the virtuous goodness that holds the self-existent jewel to be an object of respect with all your thoughts.

"From the perspective of the virtuous goodness that generates the faith of belief, [35b] you should view the self-existent jewel, the peerless sole lord, as an object of belief that is without error and without deception. If you believe this in accordance with how he himself taught the essential points of faith, you will generate a special type of virtuous goodness. If you view the stainless faith taught by him wrongly, you will create a misdeed that entails not abiding by this first commandment.

"From the perspective of the virtuous goodness that generates the faith of reliance, the self-existent jewel has the nature of possessing the quality of being pervaded by immeasurable power and unsurpassed strength, the quality of extending immeasurable compassion to all without bias, and the quality of being unable to ever waver in his promise. Therefore, if you have the faith that it is impossible for him not to protect you from fear and not to establish you in goodness, you will generate the supreme type of virtuous goodness. If you view him wrongly [thinking] that even if he looks on you with compassion and you go for refuge to him, he is either unable to help or although able, he does not do so, you will create a misdeed that entails not abiding by this commandment.

"From the perspective of the virtuous goodness that generates the faith of joy, through seeing the self-existent jewel as inexpressibly and inconceivably without peer and without measure, utterly without fault, and endowed with all unsurpassed virtues, you will feel joy from the depths of your heart, with all your thoughts, to the extent of your capacity and knowledge. If you completely avoid what displeases him and strive with great dedication to completely please him, then you will generate the primary form of virtuous goodness. [36a] How could there be a greater joy? If you take joy in something else that is other than the self-existent jewel, or do not take joy in or have wrong ideas about the self-existent jewel, you will create a misdeed, which is heavy, heinous, and unbearable, and entails not abiding by this first commandment.

"From the perspective of the virtuous goodness that holds the self-existent jewel to be an object of reverence, if you make unsurpassed offerings to the self-existent jewel or on his behalf, or praise him, you will generate the supreme type of virtuous goodness. If you insult him by actions, words, or gestures that are disrespectful to the self-existent jewel, the places where he is worshipped, or the offerings made to him, you will create a heinous misdeed that entails not abiding by this first commandment."

Again, the seeker of the essence of wisdom asked: "Please clarify the meaning of the first object of abandonment in the palm of your hand for this commandment."

The pandita replied: "Here, he made the commandment by saying, 'Completely abandon taking anything other than the self-existent jewel as an object of worship and an object of refuge.' Those who have faith in living persons, those who have gone from this world to the other world, or in conditioned, impermanent, and dependent things and regard them as a jewel-like object of worship and an object of refuge, those who have faith in, make offerings to, and go for refuge to any other types of demons called ghosts, demons, and *nāgas,* and those who use either mantras or sorcery [36b] create the misdeed of not abiding by this commandment as well as a heinous act of great force."

Again, the seeker of the essence of wisdom asked: "Please clarify the meaning of the second object of abandonment in the palm of your hand for this commandment."

The paṇḍita replied: "Here, holding manmade images as objects of worship and objects of refuge is to be abandoned. Such objects arise only falsely and deceptively. Those who bow down or make offerings before a statue or a painting that is devoid of the [true] object of refuge will create a misdeed that entails not abiding by this commandment as well as a heinous act of great force. Having set this forth, I have commented on the intended meaning of the first commandment."

Again, the seeker of the essence of wisdom asked: "Please kindly explain what was intended [by the self-existent jewel] when he made the commandment, 'Do not use my name without purpose.'"

The paṇḍita replied: "When divided from the perspective of this commandment, there are four kinds of non-virtuous speech to be abandoned, which are the opposite of four kinds of virtuous speech, which create faith in and perfectly honor the self-existent jewel, the peerless sole lord. What are the four kinds of virtuous speech, which create faith in and perfectly honor the self-existent jewel, the peerless sole lord? (1) The virtuous speech that, through the force of reverence for the supreme self-existent jewel himself and generating the faith of complete joy in dependence on observing the unsurpassed qualities of the self-existent jewel, [37a] mentally bows to and reveres his auspicious name; (2) the virtue of swearing an oath, with words of truth, taking the self-existent jewel himself as witness, reverently observing that the self-existent jewel has a nature endowed with the quality of omniscience, endowed with the quality of worthiness to be held as a completely valid witness, utterly lacking error and deceit, and endowed with the quality of acting as the protector and refuge on the side of the perfect truth; (3) the virtuous speech of generating the thought 'I will please the self-existent jewel' and then, motivated by this, promising 'I will achieve this or that virtue' or vowing 'I will avoid this or that non-virtuous deed'; and (4) the virtuous speech of remembering the immeasurable qualities and greatness of the self-existent jewel and offering praise.

"What are the four types of non-virtuous speech that are the opposite of these four virtues? They are (1) the non-virtuous speech of using the good name of the self-existent jewel in anger, in jest, or without purpose; (2) the non-virtuous speech of taking the self-existent jewel as witness and then breaking an oath with false words, promising with an oath 'I will do this or that non-virtuous deed,' or taking the self-existent jewel as a witness with no need or purpose whatsoever; (3) the non-virtuous speech of intending to please the self-existent jewel and then not undertaking whatever is to be done; (4) the non-virtuous speech of disparaging the self-existent jewel."

Again, the seeker of the essence of wisdom asked: [37b] "Please explain what [the self-existent jewel] intended when he made the commandment, 'On days that are taught to be auspicious, properly perform the rituals of the auspicious day.'"

The paṇḍita replied: "Regarding the rituals of the auspicious day, on days taught to be auspicious days, you should avoid difficult deeds of physical toil and activities such as making things and make prayers of unsurpassed offering to the self-existent jewel, revering and pleasing him with body and mind."

Again, the seeker of the essence of wisdom asked: "Please explain what [the self-existent jewel] intended when he made the commandment, 'Honor your father and mother.'"

The paṇḍita replied: "There are three ways to honor your father and mother: to make them an object of gratitude and serve your parents according to their needs; to obey what your parents say; and to respect them with your body and mind. Thus, in these three ways you should strive to follow this commandment given by the self-existent jewel."

Again, the seeker of the essence of wisdom asked: "Please explain what [the self-existent jewel] intended when he made the commandment, 'Do not take the lives of humans.'"

The paṇḍita replied: "When divided from the perspective of this commandment, you must avoid taking the lives of humans and such things as wounding and beating that injure the body of a human. Therefore, there are two things to be abandoned. Although this is the case, a king or a judge acting in accordance with the law and taking the life of someone like a thief does not violate this commandment because they rule their subjects and because taking the life of the guilty [38a] is aimed at the virtue of the law not being broken. What is the reason for saying 'Do not take the lives of humans' and not saying do not take life in general? For example, things such as trees, woolen fabric, and fire are simply things established to benefit humans and for the use of humans. Therefore, cutting down a tree, tearing a piece of woolen cloth, or putting out a fire does not create sin. In the same way, the self-existent jewel, the peerless sole lord who made everything that exists, made all creatures other than humans for the benefit of humans. Therefore, you should decide that the killing of wild animals, [domestic] animals, and birds for food, clothing, medicine, and so forth does not create sin."

Again, the seeker of the essence of wisdom asked: "Please explain what [the self-existent jewel] intended when he made the commandment, 'Abandon sexual misconduct.'"

The paṇḍita replied: "A woman taken as your wife is not the object to be abandoned here. It refers to women who belong to others, your relatives, women who are protecting the purity of their sexual organ because of keeping a vow of celibacy, those who have already given up the act of sex with a religious intention, and women who, although not keeping the vow of celibacy, have not become the wives of yourself or others and so are not women [suitable for sex]. Therefore, these are the basis for sexual misconduct. Also, misdeeds of sexual misconduct are committed with respect to four things: inappropriate person, inappropriate part [of the body], inappropriate time, and inappropriate place. However, because these acts are of an embarrassing nature, [38b] I shall not set these forth in detail here. In general, if simply looking at an object of desire with a lustful mind causes an unbearable non-virtue violating this commandment, what need is there to speak of anything else?"

Again, the seeker of the essence of wisdom asked: "Please explain what [the self-existent jewel] intended when he made the commandment, 'Do not steal.'"

The paṇḍita replied: "When divided from the perspective of this commandment, two non-virtues are to be abandoned: stealing and seizing. To abandon stealing is to abandon taking what is not given; tricking and deceiving others when buying and selling; damaging, burning, or destroying others' possessions without their knowledge; not paying what you owe, not paying the price or wages for what you owe; finding possessions lost by others and taking them for your own without their knowledge, despite knowing who the owner is; and taking shared possessions as your own without others knowing it. To abandon seizing is to abandon forcibly taking the gold, silver and so on, that has been left as collateral for a loan you previously made, damaging or destroying the possessions of others before their eyes, and openly taking shared possessions as your own."

Again, the seeker of the essence of wisdom asked: "Please explain what [the self-existent jewel] intended when he made the commandment, 'Do not make judgment and bear witness falsely.'"

The paṇḍita replied: "From the perspective of this commandment, lying, harsh speech, divisive speech, and wrong wishes are to be abandoned. [39a] There are three kinds of lies: (1) in a lawsuit or acting as a witness, whether in the presence of a judge or not, to intentionally lie and aim to harm another person, saying, 'He has this fault' when he does not; (2) lies intended to help others; and (3) lies that are idle gossip that neither benefits or harms others. Among these three, the latter two are light non-virtues; the first is usually very heavy. There are two kinds of divisive speech: (1) although another person is faultless, to lie, saying that he has this fault and this defect and (2) truthfully disclosing the faults of someone that are not known to others, even though the person has the faults, saying 'He has this fault and that defect,' making him an object of the anger, harmful intent, or wrong thoughts of others who did not know he had such faults. Because these damage the reputations of others, the former and latter are heavy or light non-virtues in accordance with the extent of the damage.

"What is the non-virtuous speech that requests and prayers for what is wrong? It is becoming angry at another person and saying 'May you die before your time' or cursing another person in that way. There are two: (1) remembering what you said when angry and knowingly wanting what you wished for to happen and (2) not remembering or not wanting what you wished for to happen. The latter is a light non-virtue; the former is very heavy."

[39b] Again, the seeker of the essence of wisdom asked: "Please explain what [the self-existent jewel] intended when he made the commandment, 'Do not covet anything that belongs to another. Do not generate a mind of desire for a woman who belongs to someone else.'"

The paṇḍita replied; "Virtuous and non-virtuous actions have three factors: the object, the intention, and the completion. Earlier, it was taught that the completion of stealing and sexual misconduct are to be abandoned. The tenth and the ninth commandments[5] teach that although you do not do what you think about, if you knowingly think, 'I will steal' or if you know-ingly think 'I will have sex with a woman who belongs to someone else,' you generate the misdeed of stealing and the misdeed of sexual misconduct."

Again, the seeker of the essence of wisdom asked: "Please summarize the things to adopt and discard."

The paṇḍita replied: "If I were to summarize the things to adopt and discard taught by the self-existent jewel, the peerless sole lord of all, to humans endowed with the intelligence to distinguish right and wrong, re-gardless of their status, place, or time, you should know that there are two things to adopt and two things to abandon. The two things to adopt are (1) to delight in the unsurpassed qualities of the self-existent jewel, the peerless sole lord, and to generate the faith of joy from the depths of your heart with a clear and stainless mind to your utmost capacity and knowledge, and (2) to cherish all other human beings worthy of being cherished like yourself, as if you exchanged [self and other]. The two things to abandon are the physical, verbal, and mental deeds that are the opposites of the two to be adopted."

Again, the seeker of the essence of wisdom asked: "One [40a] must make manifest and abandon in accordance with what the self-existent jewel has revealed in the commandments. Apart from these, are there are other vir-tues to be adopted and non-virtues to be abandoned that are accepted in the Christian religion? If so, please explain them."

The paṇḍita replied: "You must know six other commandments called 'the commandments of the church.' What are the six? (1) On days designated as auspicious days you bow with body and mind and listen to the rite of the offering of the sacrifice to the self-existent jewel, the peerless sole lord. (2) At the time of Quaresima [Lent], the four seasons of the year, and on the eve of the important auspicious days, you fast, and on the sixth and seventh day of each week, you do not eat meat. (3) Each year, if it has not been ex-plained [to do so] many times, then at least once, in the hearing of an object of confession, you repent whatever faults you have committed with body, speech, and mind and vow [not to commit them again]. (4) Each year you reverently receive the sacrificial substance of the unsurpassed sacrifice offered to the self-existent jewel. (5) You offer the religious tax. (6) Festivals of taking a bride are not to be celebrated from the first day of the time called Advent, the coming of the self-existent jewel into the world, until the auspicious day called Epiphany and from the first day of the great fast called Quaresima [Lent] to the eighth day of the auspicious day called Pasqua [Easter]."

Again, the seeker of the essence of wisdom asked: "Please clarify the meaning of the words of the six commandments."

The paṇḍita replied: "On each auspicious day, each priest who is followed by Christians [40b] clarifies these when he sets forth the religion (chos) and teaches the manner and the time for practicing them [i.e., the six commandments]. Fearing too many words, I will not elaborate beyond just that."

Again, the seeker of the essence of wisdom asked: "By explaining the path of what to adopt and discard, you have already explained the path of virtuous and non-virtuous deeds. Please set forth the fruits of virtuous and non-virtuous deeds that come after them."

The paṇḍita replied: "There are three fruits of doing good: (1) becoming pleasing in the eyes of the self-existent jewel and little by little becoming worthy of attaining the goal; (2) the strength and ability to achieve your purpose, and (3) the ability to purify defects. Regarding the first, according to the customs of the world, if a servant of a king does a good deed that greatly pleases the king, the king will give the servant a decree conferring high position and bestowing more and more diverting entertainments and worldly pleasures. In the same way, the self-existent jewel confers a decree of immeasurable compassion to persons endowed with faith and a pure mind as a benefit for their good deeds, becoming pleasing in the eyes of the self-existent jewel and little by little making them worthy to attain the enjoyment of unsurpassed goodness after their death in the realm where one attains the vision of his face. Having done this, he fills us with his kindness more and more. What arises from a good deed and this first fruition of immeasurable compassion is not a shared deed that can be dedicated to others; it is produced for the doer of the good deed alone.

"Regarding the second fruit, for example, if a beloved sole son repeatedly does what his parents say, with great effort, [41a] he becomes a source of great joy and contentment, not contradicting whatever his parents want and need. In the same way, if persons endowed with faith and a pure mind abandon [the bad] and bring about [the good] in accordance with the commandments given and the instructions set forth by the self-existent jewel, the compassionate lord, the self-existent jewel will delight in their good deeds and will be pleased by the good offerings they make; he will bring about the completion of whatever good purposes that the doer of the good deed seeks. Because this fruit is a shared deed that can be dedicated to others, it has the capacity to bring benefit for both oneself and others.

"Regarding the third fruit, for example, if someone who has drunk poison is not given the antidote immediately, the life of the body is lost. If they take a good antidote, although their life is not destroyed, the capacity of the poison is not completely destroyed by the antidote and discomfort and suffering are produced again and again. In the same way, if negative deeds are accumulated and are not confessed with the force of regret and resolve, you will have to undergo the ceaseless sufferings of hell, without end and without liberation. If the misdeeds are confessed without the laziness of procrastination, although the capacity to bring about hell, without end and without liberation, is destroyed, the capacity to bring about sufferings that need to be destroyed is not completely removed; you must experience a great many sufferings that need to be destroyed. [41b] Again for example, if the antidote is not sufficient and a good curing medicine and good food are repeatedly eaten, not only will the life of the body not be destroyed, the capacity of the poison will slowly be destroyed completely and all physical discomfort and suffering will be completely pacified. In the same way, not content with confession through the power of regret, resolve, and declaring the faults, if you repeatedly accumulate virtuous good deeds, it will completely destroy the capacity to bring about the ceaseless sufferings of hell, without end and without liberation. Thus, the remaining capacity to bring about sufferings that need to be destroyed will slowly be destroyed and weakened, without any residue. Because this fruit is a shared deed that can be dedicated to others, it has the capacity to bring benefit for both oneself and others."

Again, the seeker of the essence of wisdom asked: "Now, please set forth the fruits that arise from the negative actions of misdeeds."

The paṇḍita replied: "For example, different fruits come from different fruit trees. In the same way, different fruits of suffering arise from different negative deeds. Therefore, here I will set forth the general nature, the divisions, and the fruits of negative deeds. Regarding the first, a negative deed is either actively not abandoning an action that is to be abandoned or not performing a deed that is to be done, thus not acting in accordance with the commandments of the self-existent jewel and willfully casting aside the auspicious path that he taught. Regarding the second, there are two kinds of negative deeds: the root defect and faults done by oneself. Regarding the latter, there are two: heavy and light.

"What is the root defect? I will explain. [42a] The spontaneously established and self-existent jewel, eternal, undifferentiated, without beginning, is the peerless sole lord, the lord of immeasurable great compassion. Through his boundless capacity and unsurpassed power, he created out of nothing at the beginning of time the four great elements, the heavens and the earth, and in the heavens, inconceivably many great minds that are formless, as well as the sun, moon, all the stars, and innumerable types of birds. On the vast spheres of earth and water he created inanimate things and creatures other than humans without measure. After this, he created the first two humans in the form of a male and a female. The male was named Adam and the female was named Eve. At the same time that he created them, he adorned both of their bodies and minds with eight outer ornaments and inner ornaments. The eight outer ornaments and inner ornaments are: (1) their image was pleasing to the self-existent jewel and pure; (2) lacking the obstructions to omniscience, their mental power to distinguish right from wrong was very strong; (3) lacking the afflictive obstructions, they had very clear minds endowed with the mindfulness to engage in good deeds and the introspection to be frightened by misdeeds; (4) they had flexible bodies able to do worthy deeds, acting as directed by the mind, without struggle and having the quality of diligently deciding, without mental discord, to do worthy deeds; (5) with crops growing without needing to plow the earth and without inflicting harm to any animate or inanimate thing, their bodies had the quality of not being tormented by feelings of hardship, fear, or fatigue; (6) the quality of controlling creatures without being disobeyed; [42b] (7) the quality that if they avoided faults, their bodies did not decay and lacked the sufferings of sickness, aging, and death; and (8) the quality of, after remaining here for a long time, without giving up their bodies, they would go to the realm where one attains the vision of the face of the self-existent jewel and attains the inexhaustible unsurpassed enjoyments.

"Following this, because [the self-existent jewel] granted power to them, he gave them just one commandment. To set forth the benefits of acting in accordance with it and the faults of not acting in accordance with it, the self-existent jewel said, 'I have created you two here at this beginning. In the future, there will be measureless and countless generations of your descendants, your children, grandchildren, and great grandchildren. If you act in accordance with what I teach you, you and your innumerable children and grandchildren will not lack those outer and inner attributes and I will regard you as my beloved children. Later you will attain all of the aims of unsurpassed enjoyment and inexhaustible definite goodness in my realm. If you disobey me and do not accept what I have taught you, not only will you and your children and your grandchildren and your grandchildren's grand-children without number lose the outer ornaments and the inner ornaments, you will become the object of my displeasure and as long as you live in the world you will undergo a great many sufferings, such as unhappiness, displeasure, fear, sickness, aging, and death. After you die, you will not be able to go to my realm and you shall not attain the unsurpassed goodness.'

"Not long after, the first two humans were deceived by a demon [43a] and did not act in accordance with the commandment of the self-existent jewel. The first misdeed destroyed them and all of their progeny. That first misdeed touches all of us born into the lineage of the first two humans. Through its power we are born with fault, without separation from it. Thus, that defect we are born with is called the root defect. I have set forth the origin and etymology of the root defect."

Again, the seeker of the essence of wisdom asked: "Because the faults that one does oneself have differences of being heavy or light, please distinguish how they are heavy and light."

The paṇḍita replied: "As explained earlier, with regard to non-virtuous deeds, there are three: the object, the intention, and the completion. The difference of heaviness and lightness in two non-virtuous deeds arises in accordance with the difference in the object and the intention. If this is applied to the non-virtue of stealing or taking what is not given, the object of taking what is not given is the possessions of others. The intention is the thought 'I will make the possessions of another my own.' At the time when the motivation to take what is not given is produced, there are cases of thinking of that while mindfulness is not entirely clear or while that desire is not entirely complete. There are cases of thinking in that way without suffering from absentmindedness but willfully deciding with introspection. If you steal the possessions of great value of another or desire to steal without suffering from absentmindedness but decide with introspection, [43b] a heavy non-virtue arises. If you steal the possessions of another of little value, or think 'I will make the possessions of another my own' while mindfulness is not entirely clear or while that desire is not entirely complete, it produces a fault that has the quality of lightness. If those are applied to [other] non-virtues, it is very easy to understand the distinction between heavy and light non-virtues. I have set forth the difference between heavy and light faults."

Again, the seeker of the essence of wisdom asked: "I have heard that, among the heavy faults, there are some that are very powerful, destroying the pure mind like poison. Please set those forth in particular."

The paṇḍita replied: "There are seven that are called faults that destroy the pure mind and faults that are like the fountain and root of all faults. They are pride, avarice, desire for impure deeds, anger, intemperance in food and drink, envy, and the laziness of mental darkness."

Again, the seeker of the essence of wisdom asked: "Please explain the definition of pride, the faults that arise from it, as well as its antidote."[6]

The paṇḍita replied: "Pride is exaggerating your own positive attributes and acting with a sense of superiority. The faults that arise from it are arrogance, conceit, disparaging others, belligerence, and ignoring authority. The antidote is to strive to have the quality of humility, to see yourself as flawed, to see others as endowed with qualities, to contemplate the faults of pride, and to regard yourself as someone disparaged by everyone and to regard others as worthy of respect, not just in words but from the depths of your thoughts." [44a]

Again, the seeker of the essence of wisdom asked: "Please explain the definition of avarice, the faults that arise from it, and its antidotes."

The paṇḍita replied: "Avarice is coveting that wants to make the possessions of others your own, the discontent of not giving away your own possessions, protecting your possessions, and although wanting to give more, failing to serve your own [best] interests [by not giving]. It is an attitude that makes you fail to see what is ruinous or what is fulfilling. The faults that arise from it are stealing, robbing, deceit, lack of compassion, and so on. The antidote is giving gifts and viewing gold, silver, and so on as a source of many faults and much unhappiness."

Again, the seeker of the essence of wisdom asked: "Please explain the definition of the desire for impure deeds, the faults that arise from it, and its antidotes."

The paṇḍita replied: "The desire for impure deeds is becoming overjoyed by the object of copulation, obsession with physical pleasure, seeking desire, wanting to obtain it, and fearing being separated from it. The faults that arise from it are dark and thick mental obscuration, an unstable mind, deception, adultery, vulgar words, and lack of shame. The antidotes are abstinence, ascetic practice, cultivation of serenity (śamatha), meditation that things have no essence, and restraint of the senses."

Again, the seeker of the essence of wisdom asked: "Please explain the definition of anger, the faults it gives rise to, and its antidotes." [44b]

The paṇḍita replied: "Anger is impatience with obstacles and desire for revenge. The faults that arise from it are quarrels, harsh words, disparaging, insanity, and so on. The antidote is patience."

Again, the seeker of the essence of wisdom asked: "Please explain the definition of intemperance in food and drink, the faults that arise from it, and its antidotes."

The paṇḍita replied: "Intemperance in food and drink is not being satisfied with food and drink, seeking both good food and inappropriate food, eating at inappropriate times, and viewing food and drink as sources of great joy. The faults that arise from it are ignorance, self-indulgence, talking too much, and desire for impure behavior [i.e., sexual intercourse]. The antidote is to know the right amount of food and drink as well as abstinence, and contemplating the benefits of these two and the faults of not knowing the right amount of food and drink."

Again, the seeker of the essence of wisdom asked: "Please explain the definition of envy, the faults that arise from it, and its antidotes."

The paṇḍita replied: "Envy creates unhappiness about either the fame or resources of others, fearing that an increase in either the fame or resources of others will cause your own fame and resources to decrease. The faults that arise from it are divisive speech, slander, taking human life, and so on. The antidote is love, altruism, and respect for others."

Again, the seeker of the essence of wisdom asked: "Please explain the definition of the laziness of mental darkness, the faults it gives rise to, and its antidotes."

The paṇḍita replied: "The laziness of mental darkness is regarding virtuous deeds that are to be done as a burden, causing sadness; [45a] coming under the power of the laziness of procrastination, you do not do what is to be done now, putting it off to a later time. The faults that arise from it are misunderstanding virtuous deeds, having no shame and no regret for non-virtuous deeds, not seeking the final aim, and not confessing non-virtues even at the point of death. The antidote is effort."

Again, the seeker of the essence of wisdom asked: "You have set forth the root defect and the heavy and light faults done by each of us. Please explain their specific fruits."

The paṇḍita replied: "The fruit of the root defect is to be displeasing in the eyes of the self-existent jewel, thick mental darkness, not delighting in the forces of light and delighting in the forces of darkness, [planting] the seeds of the afflictions, having difficulty acquiring food and drink, fears, and the sufferings of sickness, aging, and death. If the root defect is not cleansed before death, you will not attain the final aim. The fruit of heavy faults [committed by yourself] are to be displeasing in the eyes of the self-existent jewel, discomfort, and unhappiness. If they are not properly confessed and properly stopped, after death you will undergo the ceaseless sufferings of hell, without end and without liberation. The fruit of light faults are a weakening of the efforts of a virtuous mind, a strengthening in the power of the seeds of afflictions, and having to experience ceaseless suffering."

Again, the seeker of the essence of wisdom asked: "You have set forth the fruit of virtuous and non-virtuous deeds. Please explain the power to create joy in virtue and to cause it to increase without interruption, like a flowing river, [45b] and the power that creates fear of the forces of darkness and avoids faults, and the power to cleanse faults that have been accumulated."

The paṇḍita replied: "For example, without the external eye organ, the eye consciousness is incapable of seeing forms. In the same way, without the blessings bestowed through the immeasurable great compassion of the self-existent jewel, the peerless sole lord, the minds of humans will not be worthy of attaining the final aim to be achieved nor will they be capable of the virtue that has the capacity to attain it. Again, for example, a newly born child, lacking physical strength, cannot sit up and not fall down without being held by its mother, nor, after falling down, is it capable of getting up without being led by [her] hands. In the same way, without being seen, held, and led by the compassion of the self-existent jewel, this mind of humans, bereft of strength, is not capable of avoiding non-virtuous deeds for a long time and in every way, nor is it capable of turning away from non-virtuous deeds and moving forward. Therefore it is of great importance to set forth here the actual method for increasing the blessings of immeasurable great compassion of the self-existent jewel.

"Regarding this, there are three: (1) the general name of the actual methods for increasing the blessings of great immeasurable compassion of the self-existent jewel, (2) their number and individual names, and (3) showing [who] set them forth and gave them their capacity. With regard to the first: the actual methods for increasing the blessings of great immeasurable compassion of the self-existent jewel are called sacraments. The translation of 'sacrament' is: [46a] the proof of the blessings of great immeasurable compassion of the self-existent jewel, who is not apprehended through characteristics. If their number is explained, there are seven. If each of their names is explained, they are: *battesimo* [baptism], *cresima* [confirmation], *eucharistia* [eucharist], *penitenza* [penance], *olio santo* [holy oil], *ordine sacro* [holy orders], and *matrimonio* [marriage]. Who set them forth and gave them their capacity? Jesus Christ, the peerless guide and savior and sole lord."

Again, the seeker of the essence of wisdom asked: "Please explain the translation of baptism."

The paṇḍita replied: "The translation of *battesimo* is the offering of washing. The reason it is called that is because it is actual washing with water. How does one offer this washing? Washing, having [this] meaning, has three elements: (1) to actually wash the person to be washed with real water; (2) at the same time, to say 'I baptize you in the name of the father, the son, and the unsurpassed mind'; and (3) for the washer to think 'with this washing, I fulfill the wish of Jesus Christ, the guide, savior, and sole lord, and the tradition of the holy church.' If washing is done without all three of these characteristics, not only will it become meaningless, but the person being washed will not benefit and the washer will commit a misdeed.

"What blessing of great immeasurable compassion of the self-existent jewel is brought forth by baptism? If baptism is received properly, [46b] there is the blessing of completely dispelling the types of defects: purifying from the root the root defect and all the heavy and light defects committed by yourself and their capacity. There is the blessing that the mind will become pure in every way, you will become pleasing in the eyes of the self-existent jewel, you will be accepted as a child of the self-existent jewel so that, after death, you become worthy of attaining the final aim. There is the blessing that you will come into the community of Christians, children of the self-existent jewel, and will benefit together in all the roots of virtues of that community.

"Who performs the washing? Washing the recipient of washing is an activity of the priest. However, when there is no priest, representatives of the priest called deacons and sub-deacons perform the washing. If there is no priest or representative of a priest, any human male performs the washing; if there are none, any woman performs the washing. Therefore, if all Christians, regardless of whether they are men or women, large or small, learn, without error, how to perform washing, it is very good. Who is an appropriate vessel for receiving washing? If you die without actually receiving washing or not having a genuine wish to receive it, you cannot attain the final aim and go to the realm where you will have a vision of the face of the self-existent jewel. Therefore, Christians bestow washing on small children, who can easily die and do not have the capacity to wish to receive washing. Also, if those, young or old, who have developed faith in the pure Christian faith and religion from the depths of their thoughts [47a], have a strong awareness of the difference between right and wrong, learn this religion well, completely forsake without wavering all the evil paths of other impure religions, regret their faults and develop resolve, they are suitable vessels to receive washing."

Again, the seeker of the essence of wisdom asked: "Please explain the translation of the sacrament called *cresima*."

The paṇḍita replied, "The etymology of *cresima* can be expressed because the translation of *cresima* is 'making stable.' Thus, the sacrament of *cresima* makes the mind of the faithful person very stable upon the object of faith. Or, the etymology of *cresima* can be expressed because the translation of *cresima* is 'anoint with oil.' Thus, when this sacrament is performed, the great priest anoints the forehead of the recipient with oil. What blessing of the self-existent jewel is brought forth by *cresima*? It makes the mind of the faithful person very stable upon the object of faith and it brings forth the blessing of not being afraid to give up their life for the sake of the religion."

Again, the seeker of the essence of wisdom asked: "Please explain the translation of the sacrament called Eucharist."

The paṇḍita replied: "The translation of Eucharist is remembering kindness and expressing gratitude. Through offering this sacrament, you remember the kindness of Jesus Christ, the peerless guide and savior and the sole lord, [47b] who underwent many painful, harsh, and unbearable sufferings and gave up his life for the sake of all humans, and you praise him and express gratitude with a pure and unstained mind. Through displaying this sacrament, Jesus Christ transformed his body and blood to restore the mental power of the faithful. Through receiving this sacrament, the faithful remember his immeasurable kindness and express gratitude, with thoughts of reverence and respect."

Again, the seeker of the essence of wisdom asked: "Please set forth the reason for the statement, 'Through displaying this sacrament, Jesus Christ transformed his body and blood to restore the mental power of the faithful.'"

The paṇḍita replied; "On the day before Jesus Christ, the peerless guide and savior and the sole lord, gave up his life and died for the sake of all humans, he had his last meal with his twelve disciples during the first part of the night. At that time, he held a piece of bread made from flour in his hand, divided it, and gave some to each of his disciples. He told them the following: 'This bread is my actual body that I will soon deliver into the hands of the sinful enemy for your sake. Eat it and, remembering what I have done, act in that way.' He then held a vessel filled with grape wine, blessed it, and said: 'Because this is my blood, you should drink it and, remembering what I have done, act in that way.' [48a] To clarify the meaning of the statement, in the past, people who had faith in the self-existent jewel, the peerless sole lord, made ordinary offerings like flowers and gems. When Jesus Christ died, he gave his own body, blood, and life to completely purify our sins, making an unsurpassed offering to the self-existent jewel, the precious father. If we offer those [ordinary things] to the self-existent jewel, who is the master of all impermanent things that have arisen and will arise, he is not pleased by them. Thus, just as Jesus Christ made the unsurpassed offering to the self-existent jewel, the precious father, with his own blood and life, he revealed to the faithful the method of making the unsurpassed offering, his blood, body, and mind in which the human and the self-existent jewel are the same essence. He revealed the method in which the essence of bread made from flour is transformed into his body and the essence of grape wine is transformed into his blood.

"For example, just as he offered his body and blood to his twelve great disciples, so, remembering his kindness, the faithful should make the unsurpassed offering to the self-existent jewel of the body of precious Jesus Christ beneath the offering substance which is not real bread but just appears to have the form of bread, and the blood of the precious Jesus Christ beneath the offering substance that is not real grape wine but just appears to have the form, smell, and flavor of grape wine. [48b] [Then], reinforcing their mental power and virtuous power, they make fervent supplications and reverently eat them. In brief, through the offering substance that is not real bread but just appears to have the shape of bread, and the offering substance that is not real grape wine but just appears to have the smell, flavor, and shape of grape wine, they make the unsurpassed offering of the body and blood of precious Jesus Christ to the self-existent jewel, and, raising their mental power and virtuous power, they make fervent supplications and reverently eat them. These two are called the sacrament of Eucharist."

Again, the seeker of the essence of wisdom asked: "Please explain how to reverently eat this unsurpassed offering."

The paṇḍita replied: "There are three: (1) to perfectly confess the three: regretting all faults, having resolve, and explaining your faults; (2) not to eat or drink anything from midnight until you receive the unexcelled offering; and (3) to understand well the definition and meaning of how this sacrament becomes the unsurpassed offering and to develop mental clarity, the faith of belief, and reverence and respect."

Again, the seeker of the essence of wisdom asked: "What blessing of the self-existent jewel is brought forth by the sacrament of Eucharist?"

The paṇḍita replied: "Through this sacrament being an unsurpassed offering, it brings about the blessing that the self-existent jewel is reconciled with those who have faults and he views them with great immeasurable compassion, weakening and exhausting the power of their faults to bear the fruit of suffering. [49a] It also brings about the blessing of increasing the happiness that benefits life in this world and the definite goodness of the final aim. Through raising your mental power and virtuous power and making fervent supplications, it brings out the blessing of greatly strengthening and increasing qualities, such as the attitude of delighting in the forces of light and not delighting in the forces of darkness, and the faith of belief, the faith capable of reliance, and the faith of delight, and it greatly decreases all afflictions and defects."

Again, the seeker of the essence of wisdom asked: "Please define what is called *penitenza*."

The paṇḍita replied: "The power to repair defects that was granted through the immeasurable great compassion of Jesus Christ, the peerless guide and savior and sole lord, is the sacrament called *penitenza*. How do you attain the power to repair faults? For that, there are two elements: (1) properly describing the faults by the person confessing their sins, and (2) actually reciting the words that have the capacity to free him from the bonds of fault by the priest who is the object of the confession. Therefore, regarding the definition of the sacrament called *penitenza*, for example, experienced by the external sense consciousnesses, a person confessing their sins describes the faults they have committed beginning from the time of receiving baptism, and the object of confession recites the words that have the capacity to repair the faults. [49b] In the same way, without being experienced by the external senses consciousnesses, the self-existent jewel, the lord of immeasurable great compassion, through the power of the words of the object of confession, frees the mind of the person confessing their sins from the bonds of all their faults, and reverses the capacity of those faults to bring about the sufferings of hell.

"From the perspective of repairing faults, what are the elements of repair that must be achieved by the person confessing their sins? There are five. What are the five? (1) To remember all the paths of action committed through body, speech, and mind and to examine your mind without feeble effort; (2) to generate regret, not just in words but from the depths of your heart, with an attitude of not delighting in and of condemning whatever faults you have done; (3) to generate uncontrived resolve [not to commit them again]; (4) to describe to the object of confession the faults that you have committed, their number, and their weight, without omission; and (5) to undertake and complete the penalties of confession as they were set forth by the object of confession.

"What blessings of the self-existent jewel are brought forth by the sacrament called *penitenza*? The blessing of reversing the faults of the person confessing their sins through the immeasurable great compassion of the self-existent lord; the blessing of exchanging the inexhaustible sufferings of hell, without end and without liberation, for other sufferings that can be exhausted; and the blessing of restoring the benefits of roots of virtue destroyed earlier by faulty deeds, as if they had returned."

Again, the seeker of the essence of wisdom asked: "Please explain the definition of the sacrament called *olio santo*." [50a]

The paṇḍita replied: "This sacrament is placing blessed oil on the sense organs of a faithful person who is afflicted by a grave sickness and is at the point of death, and at the same time, saying prayers for his benefit. What blessing of the self-existent jewel is brought out by this sacrament? The blessing of reversing faults, the blessing of creating feelings of happiness in the body and mind of the person afflicted by great illness and by the obstacles of demons, and the blessing of curing the physical disease, if it does not oppose the benefits to the mind of the sick person."

Again, the seeker of the essence of wisdom asked: "Please explain the definition of the sacrament called *ordine sacro*."

The paṇḍita replied: "This sacrament, through seven stages of initiation, makes the unsurpassed offering to the self-existent jewel and it enables one to perform other sacraments for persons who are suitable vessels. Except for persons well trained in the things to be known, [others] are not suitable vessels to receive this sacrament. Thus, I will not say more than this here."

Again, the seeker of the essence of wisdom asked: "Please explain the translation of the sacrament called *matrimonio*."

The paṇḍita replied: "The translation of *matrimonio* is sending or receiving a bride so that the family lineage does not end. The blessings of the self-existent jewel brought forth by this sacrament are: the blessing of both the bride and her recipient loving each other without discord; the blessing of [50b] setting a good example for the children born to the couple; and making them suitable vessels for practicing the points of faith and religion.

"Thus, as explained earlier, bringing about [virtue] and abandoning [non-virtue] in accordance with how the path of what to adopt and discard was taught by the self-existent jewel, the peerless sole lord is the way to generate the faith that takes delight in the self-existent jewel. If you can repair faulty deeds and accomplish virtuous deeds through relying on excellent methods such as the sacraments, you will generate a wondrous faith that takes delight in the self-existent jewel. You should generate the faith of belief, the faith capable of reliance, and the faith that is clear, stainless, and joyful, not just in words, but with all of your understanding and capacity. If those do not weaken before you die, you will have already embarked on the path without turning back. It is impossible that you will not reach the end of the path; after you die you will attain the highest aim of attaining the vision of the face of the self-existent jewel."

A Final Thought

❧

According to traditional Tibetan sources, in the late eighth century a momentous debate took place at Samye, the first Buddhist monastery in Tibet. There were two factions at court, one Chinese, led by the Chan monk Moheyan, and the other Indian, whose champion was the renowned Indian scholar Kamalaśīla, who had been invited from India. The issue at hand was whether the achievement of enlightenment is sudden or gradual, with the Chinese holding the sudden view and the Indians the gradual view. The king of Tibet, Trisong Detsen, organized a debate between Moheyan and Kamalaśīla. At its conclusion, he declared Kamalaśīla the victor and banished Moheyan and his views from Tibet.

Scholars have called into question many elements of the traditional account, including whether there actually was a formal debate (rather than an exchange of documents), what precisely was at stake, and who won. Yet the story plays an important role in the Tibetans' narrative of the history of Buddhism in their land. Regardless of what actually happened, it appears that from this point, Tibetans came to regard India, rather than China, as their primary source of the dharma.

Desideri reports that in March 1717 he was summoned to court, where Lhazang Khan told him that he had read the book he had written for him, was impressed by it, but found it to be completely at odds with the doctrines of the Tibetan religion. However, he did not want to pass judgment on Desideri's religion without full consideration. "To that end he had decided to hold a debate, with myself on the one side and the lamas and doctors of religion of that country and its universities on the other."[1] Desideri's studies at Shidé and Sera were intended as his preparation.

Like so many things in Desideri's *Historical Notices,* we have no confirmation that such a conversation took place. Indeed, Desideri's view of Lhazang Khan as a just and wise king is a minority opinion; in Tibetan sources he is remembered for the assassination of the regent of the Fifth Dalai Lama, the murder of the abbot of one of the colleges of Sera Monastery, the demise of the true Sixth Dalai Lama, and the selection of a false Sixth Dalai Lama. For many Tibetans, he was a tyrant who deserved his bloody demise.

Yet Lhazang Khan considered himself to be the king of Tibet, and a pious Buddhist king, in the tradition of Trisong Detsen. We might imagine, therefore, that he had suggested a debate between Buddhists and Christians. Had he done so, and had such a debate taken place, it would have been a remarkable event, even if it did not result in the conversion of the Land of Snows to the Christian faith. It seems that Desideri believed that such a debate would take place; we can regard the extensive notes that he took beginning in July as preparations for this portentous moment. However, on November 21 a large army of Dzungar Mongols encamped outside Lhasa. They attacked the city on November 30. Lhazang was killed, his sword in his hand, on December 3, 1717. With his hopes for a debate, with his patron serving as the judge, now dashed, Desideri set to work on the *Inquiry,* a work that is presented in the traditional debate format. It is, perhaps, a record of what he would have said, if anyone had listened. During his time in Tibet, Desideri did not seem to attract the attention of the leading lamas of the day, such famous figures as Jamyang Shepa (1648–1721), who was the tutor of Lhazang Khan, or the Second Panchen Lama, Losang Yeshé (1663–1737). Both were great scholars and both would have sought to counter Desideri's arguments.

Yet as he began the text, he had not given up hope. His patron was dead and he sought a new one. The Seventh Dalai Lama arrived in Lhasa in autumn of 1720. It was on January 10, 1721, that Desideri received the official order to leave Tibet. Although he was in Lhasa in April of that year, he did not have an audience with the Seventh Dalai Lama. On December 15, 1721, he left Tibet, never to return. He took his refutation of rebirth and emptiness with him back to the Vatican.

One can only speculate what might have occurred if Desideri had remained in Tibet, completed his *Inquiry,* and had it printed (assuming that he could find a patron to provide the substantial funds to print a book of that length). It would have caused a sensation. Even the shorter and more manageable critique of emptiness in the *Essence of Christianity* would have attracted the attention, and the contestation, of the scholars of the monasteries of Lhasa. Instead, Desideri was thwarted by politics: the politics of Tibet and the politics of Rome.

We are left to wonder what Desideri would have thought if he could have known that in 1973 another Dalai Lama, the Fourteenth, would come to the Vatican for an audience with the pope; that in 1997 that Dalai Lama would publish *The Good Heart: A Buddhist Perspective on the Teachings of Jesus,* in which he offered a commentary on passages from the Gospels; and that in his 2010 *Towards a True Kinship of Faiths,* the Dalai Lama would mention Desideri, saying, "Although he came originally as a missionary, intent to convert the Tibetans to Christianity, Desideri's experience of immersion in Tibetan culture produced a remarkable and very early testament to inter-religious dialogue. . . . I hope that one day a translation and careful study of this important document [the *Inquiry*] will be undertaken to make it available to the wider world."[2] Desideri's work, or at least word of his work, finally reached the Dalai Lama.

Topical Outline (*sa bcad*) of the *Inquiry*

☙

[Salutation] [1a3]
[Preamble] [1b17]

1. The benefits of studying others' religions [2b26]
   A. The benefit of becoming thoroughly learned in religion [2b30]
   B. The benefit of creating an entirely firm mind in order to directly experience religion [3a2]
   C. The benefit of creating a strong and powerful sense of joy in religion by engaging in appropriate religious deeds and infusing one's mind with religion [3a23]

2. How to see the other's religion in a wise way [5b20]
   A. Generating the three recognitions
      1. Having the recognition of religion as a seed [5b22]
      2. Having the recognition of oneself as the soil [5b33]
      3. Generating the recognition that the benefits of living in accordance with religion and doing good deeds is unique to humans compared to beasts, and that the highest reality of definite goodness, far superior to all worldly happiness, is like the fruit [6a5]
   B. Abandoning the three defects of a soil [6a30]
   C. Cultivating all three conditions of listening [6b26]

3. Demonstrating how, having studied the other's religion, there is benefit in debating about one's own religion [7a26]

4. Actual debates on the essential points of the so-called previous births [9a7]
   A. Engaging in debates on the essential points of the so-called previous births
      1. Refuting the other's position
         a. Refuting that birth is beginningless [9a11]
         b. Demonstrating that the birth of sentient beings does not come into being through the power of deeds [71b16]¹
            1. General thoughts on the birth of sentient beings [71b18]
            2. Specific thoughts on the birth of sentient beings as presented in the opponent's system [94a6]
               a. The birth of humans [94a9]
                  1. Identification of human birth itself [94b14]
                     a. Consideration of the external continuum of humans [94a15]
                     b. Consideration of the internal continuum of humans [97b18]
                  2. Explanation of the sufferings associated with human birth [107b5]
                  3. Analysis of the factors of happiness associated with human birth [109b7]
                  4. Having considered virtuous deeds and human birth next to each other, demonstrating that it is unsuitable for human birth to be the effect of virtuous deeds [112b16]
                  5. As an aside, stating damaging objections to the opponent's system by analyzing the birth of gods and demigods [142b16]
               b. Demonstrating how the birth of sentient beings does not come into being through the power of deeds, on the basis of analyzing the births as animals or ghosts [153b7]
                  1. Describing the opponent's system [154b9]
                  2. Stating damaging objections to it [158b5]
               c. The birth of so-called hell beings [189b32]
                  1. Describing the system and assertion of the opponent [189b34]
                     a. The number and sufferings of the hells described in their system [190a2]
                        1. The great hells of sentient beings [190a3]
                        2. The neighboring hells [190b7]

        3. The cold hells [190b32]

        4. The hot hells [191a12]

    b. Discussion of the life span [in the hells] [191a18]

    c. Demonstrating how their system engages in senseless contradictory talk concerning whether or not one can accumulate deeds while undergoing the sufferings of hell [192a18]

        1. Showing how their system makes contradictory statements, by asserting that a being can accumulate non-virtuous deeds that send one into a lower realm while experiencing the sufferings of hell, when they have already admitted that the life span in hell is of a definite length and that the sufferings of hell will come to an end [192a24]

        2. Showing how their system makes contradictory statements by asserting that while undergoing the sufferings of hell, virtuous deeds cannot be accumulated and that they can be accumulated [194a14]

  2. Refuting that system [196a15]

    a. Stating damaging objections that refute the assertions of that system [196a16]

        1. Stating damaging objections that refute the assertion that birth in hell comes through the power of deeds, the position that is specifically being analyzed in this context [196a20]

        2. Conclusion of the refutation of the other's system on the topic of former and later lives, showing that a great many points in the texts of the opponent are unreliable and impure, like the collapsed relying on the collapsed. Specifically, there are twenty [such points] [232b16] [*The book ends with this heading. This and the remainder of the sections are missing.*]

    b. Dispelling objections

  2. Presenting one's position thoroughly

  3. Dispelling objections [to one's own position]

B. Engaging in debates pertaining to the view of emptiness

Subjects of the *Inquiry*

੧੭

1. If you Tibetans employ from your own tradition a correct inferential reasoning familiar to the other party [the opponent], then it follows that no birth of any sentient being has the quality of being beginningless, because the birth of any sentient being that has already been born does not have the quality of being beginningless. [9a]

2. Furthermore, as stated in the commentary on [Āryadeva's] *Four Hundred,* "Nonetheless for a given thing, / That which is produced has no coming / And that which has ceased has no going; / It definitely lacks intrinsic existence." [9a]

3. Furthermore, if, in general, it is tenable that coming exists, there must exist an end point to which it comes. Not only that, the end point to which it will come later must exist on the opposite side of where it comes from as something newly arisen that did not exist before. [9b]

4. Furthermore, for example, just as water does not have the capacity to become hot through its own character or through its own entity, no sentient being has a capacity to come to birth through a nature established by its own character or own entity. [10a]

5. Furthermore, for example, if one asserts that the sky above has no limit in the upward direction, then one will have to assert that the sky above has no farthest

limit in the upward direction. In the same way, if one asserts that the birth of any sentient being does not have a starting point in the past, one will have to admit that the birth of any sentient being does not have a farthest limit in the past. [11b]

6. Furthermore, you assert the sky above to be established as something that has parts. And if you assert that it is other than and separate from the assemblage and collection of its parts, then there would be such faults as that the physical body would be other than and separate from the collection of its limbs, without being incomplete. [12a]

7. Furthermore, one must understand that the existence of impermanent things can be of only three types, nothing else. What are these three? They are (1) those that did not exist earlier but exist later, (2) those that existed earlier and remain uninterrupted without ceasing, and (3) those that exist earlier and do not remain uninterrupted without ceasing. [14a]

8. Furthermore, for example, if you assert that the birth of sentient beings is limitless, then you must assert that it lacks an end limit [as well]. In the same way, if you assert that the birth of sentient beings has no beginning, then you must assert that it lacks a limit that is a beginning point. [14b]

9. Furthermore, for example, although the great ocean is difficult to measure, it is not the case that its depths are measureless; it has a deepest point. In the same way, even in the scriptures of you Tibetans, although it is asserted that the birth of sentient beings, like the ocean, is difficult to measure, it is concluded that it is not the case that it lacks an end limit; it has an end point. [15b]

10 and 11 missing

12. Furthermore, for example, women make cotton threads of different lengths and stop their spinning when it is complete, and diligently rolling them, they gather whatever cotton yarn they have created. In the same way, in the opponent's own system, all sentient beings are tormented by suffering and accumulate deeds; whatever deeds that are done cannot be lost. Through the fruition of those, [sentient beings] undergo suffering in immeasurable births in succession without beginning. [17a]

13. Furthermore, with regard to what are called the sources (āyatana, skye mched), one must understand there are twelve sources: the internal eye source and the ex-

ternal form source, the internal ear source and the external sound source, the internal nose source and the external odor source, the internal tongue source and the external flavor source, the internal body source and the external tangible object source, and the internal mind source and the external phenomena source. [20b]

14. Furthermore, with regard to a flower growing from the stalk of a flower plant, the many parts [that make it] emerge in stages. . . . In the same way, in the scriptures of the opponent, the birth of sentient beings relies on causes and conditions and arises in dependence on them. [26a]

15. Furthermore, it is not feasible for a single sentient being, who is not multiple, to have different former and later births because even the opponent does not assert that a single sentient being who is not multiple has different births that exist at the same time. [32a]

16. Furthermore, the birth of sentient beings does not have the quality of being beginningless because it depends on causes and conditions. If you say that this does not follow, it does follow because it must be asserted that if the birth of sentient beings relies on causes and conditions, the coming into being of sentient beings depends on causes and conditions. [35a]

17. Up to this point, I have analyzed what the nature of birth is and what the mode of being of sentient beings are like and have demonstrated from those two perspectives how the birth of sentient beings does not have the quality of being beginningless. At this point, through analyzing the mode of being of the minds of sentient beings, I shall demonstrate how the birth of sentient beings does not have the quality of being beginningless. This has three parts: (1) that what is called "mind" or "intellect" or "consciousness" is not material and does not possess form, (2) that it does not have the quality of disintegration, and (3) that, although it does not have the quality of disintegration, it does not have the quality of beginningless birth. [37a]

18. From the perspective of [analyzing] what is called "mind" or "intellect" or "consciousness" of a sentient being, it has been proven that the birth of sentient beings does not have the quality of being beginningless. Now, one should understand this in the following way. For example, a powerful and confident king destroyed and killed an opposing army. And at the time of staging a [victory] celebration for his subjects, if he is unable to directly show the terrifying body of the enemy, which had such splendor that one could not bear to view it, he would display the robes, armor, helmet, and weapons of the enemy. The subjects who had gathered for the

celebration would take the robes, weapons, and so on, as proofs of what the unbearable splendor and so forth of the body of the enemy must have been like before. In the same way, when analyzing whether or not what the scriptures of the
opponent call "sentient beings' former births" has a beginning time or not, they
are not able to directly show such things as sentient beings who have already arisen
at a time in the past. I have analyzed whether or not such births have the quality of
having no beginning at an earlier time, which is like the robes of those at a time in
the past. By doing so, from the experience of the former time, such as the limits of
what is called "previous birth," which the eyes of the opponent cannot see, I imagined
well and took them as proof; it must be concluded that what is called "sentient beings' former births" do not have a time that is beginningless. [53a]

19. Furthermore, for example, one must assert that without parts, the bearer of the
parts [the whole] does not exist. In the same way, one must assert that without more
and still more and a great many, there cannot be that which is innumerable. [55a]

20. I have investigated from the perspective of the essential points of the character
of birth or the nature of birth or the attributes of birth, and I have analyzed in detail the subtle points for determining how birth occurs. At this point, having analyzed the tenets and scriptures of the opponent, I will demonstrate that it must be
untenable even in that system [of the opponent] that the birth of sentient beings
has the quality of being beginningless. [56a]

21. Furthermore, from the perspective of the twelve links of dependent origination,
it must be untenable in the opponent's scriptures that the birth of sentient beings
lacks a beginning and is beginningless. [61a]

22. Furthermore, because the scriptures of the opponent assert that the birth of sentient beings comes into being through the power of deeds, I will demonstrate that the
birth of sentient beings does not lack a beginning and is not beginningless from
the perspective of deeds. It is very important, therefore, [first] to present from the
scriptures of the opponent virtuous and non-virtuous deeds and their effects in general, as well as how the various types and divisions of deeds are presented. [63a]

23. Furthermore, given that [for you] the birth of sentient beings has no existence,
you must assert that no deeds of sentient beings exist [as well]. [66a]

24. Furthermore, from the perspective of virtuous and non-virtuous deeds, one must
understand the following. In the opponent's scriptures, one will have to admit that

it is untenable that the birth of sentient beings lacks a beginning and is beginning-less. This is because in the opponent's scriptures the birth of sentient beings comes into being through the power of either a virtuous or non-virtuous deed. [67b]

25. Demonstrating that the birth of sentient beings does not come into being through the power of deeds. [71b]

26. Furthermore, it is illogical to assert that the birth of sentient beings arises through the power of deeds because it is illogical to assert for any sentient being that different births arise many times in sequence. [73a]

27. Furthermore, it is illogical to assert that the birth of sentient beings arises through the power of deeds, because if you assert that the birth of sentient beings arises through the power of deeds, you must assert that for any sentient being different births arise many times in sequence and to assert that is illogical. [75a]

28. Furthermore, it is illogical to assert that the birth of sentient beings arises through the power of deeds, because if you assert that the birth of sentient beings arises through the power of deeds, you must assert that for any sentient being different births arise many times in sequence and to assert that is illogical. [77a] [This is identical to #27.]

29. Furthermore, it is illogical to assert that the birth of sentient beings arises through the power of deeds, because if you assert that the birth of sentient beings arises through the power of deeds, you must maintain that for any sentient being many different former and later births arise. [84b]

30. Furthermore, on the basis of [using] inferences familiar to others in the opponent's own scriptures or through parity of reasoning, one should understand the following. For the opponent such things as the fire of hell do not exist; because they do not exist, it must follow that being born in hell is meaningless. [86b]

31. Furthermore, on the basis of identifying the meaning of birth, one should understand the following. Earlier, using the example of a flower, the need to distinguish between the mere existence of a sentient being and in what forms sentient beings exist has already been demonstrated. Here, one must understand that the birth of sentient beings is the mere existence of a sentient being and that it is neither the happiness nor suffering of the forms in which sentient beings exist. [89b]

32. Furthermore, in the opponent's scriptures, for the cause that establishes the birth of a sentient being, deeds and afflictions are necessary. However, afflictions are primary because as presented in that system, without the afflictions, even if there are previously accumulated deeds beyond number, just as a sprout does not come into being from a seed that is deprived of such things as moisture and earth, so the sprout of suffering does not come into being without the cooperative conditions for the deed. [92a]

33. Furthermore, in the opponent's scriptures, for the cause that establishes the birth of a sentient being, deeds and afflictions are necessary. However, afflictions are presented as primary. This should be understood in the following manner. There is no possibility for the well-being of a sentient being to emerge from the afflictions. So if the opponent possesses the strength of mind to distinguish good from bad he would have to admit that it is illogical to assert that any birth of a sentient being comes through the power of the afflictions. [93b]

34. Furthermore, even within the opponent's own system it becomes untenable for the afflictions to be the cause from which the birth of sentient beings arises, because in the opponent's scriptures, the afflictions are [said to be] the cause that shorten the lifespan. [93b]

35. Specific contemplations on how the birth of sentient beings is presented in the opponent's scriptures. [94a]

36. Consideration of the inside of humans. [97b]

37. Furthermore, for example, just as the spring season is the time for plowing and cultivation, this state of birth must be understood as a time of accumulating deeds that bear fruit in the future. Here at the time of birth, the mind of the human can abandon non-virtuous deeds and, without laziness and with great effort, can accumulate deeds of perfect virtue. However, if the inside of a human in such a state is carefully investigated with the wisdom of discriminative awareness, one must decide that this time of birth is a time in which the mind of a human lacks happiness and undergoes various sufferings. [102b]

38. Furthermore, at the time of the cause, the time of birth, the mental continuum of a human can abandon non-virtuous deeds and, without laziness and with great effort, can accumulate deeds of perfect virtue. However, in the meantime, there exist no means of preventing the occurrence of unbearable, harsh, and great sufferings. [104a]

39. If one were to look at the mind of a human who, at this time of the cause, the time of birth, turns further and further away from white deeds and enters evil paths of darkness, then this [alleged] time of the cause for such things as being reborn as a human and so on must be utterly troubled by suffering, torment, and unhappiness. Therefore, it is untenable that this state is the fruition that arises from virtuous deeds. [104b]

40. Second, the explanation of the sufferings associated with human birth. If the opponent's assertion that human birth has various sufferings is tenable, then it must be unsuitable for human birth to be called a happy realm or the fruition of virtue even according to the opponent's scriptures. Therefore, here, I will avoid stating damaging objections to the opponent from our own system and will explain the sufferings of human birth according to the opponent's own scriptures. [107b]

41. Third, the analysis of the factors of happiness associated with the human birth. If, from the perspective of the factors of happiness and prosperity associated with human birth, one thinks that human birth is a happy realm and the fruition of perfect virtue, this is untenable, because all of those pleasures and wealth are never suitable to be the fruitions of perfect virtue. [109b]

42. Furthermore, given that the assertion that the fruitions that arise from deeds of perfect virtue cannot be experienced and the assertion that their attainment becomes meaningless are illogical, human birth itself as well as the factors of happiness associated with human birth cannot be experienced [at all]. [110a]

43. Furthermore, given that it is illogical to assert that the fruitions that arise from deeds of perfect virtue cannot be experienced and that their attainment becomes meaningless, the presentation that human birth and all of the factors of happiness associated with human birth are the fruition of perfect virtue becomes untenable because they cannot be experienced. [111a]

44. Furthermore, given that it is illogical to assert that the fruitions that arise from deeds of perfect virtue cannot be experienced and that their attainment becomes meaningless, the presentation that human birth and all of the factors of happiness associated with human birth are the fruition of perfect virtue becomes untenable because they cannot be experienced. [111b] (This is identical to #43)

45. Fourth, having considered virtuous deeds and human birth next to each other, demonstrating how it is unsuitable for human birth to be the fruition of virtuous deeds. [112b]

46. Furthermore, the assertion that after death, the doer of deeds of perfect virtue will be born as a human through the fruition of those deeds is illogical, because it is illogical that the well-being of the doer of deeds of perfect virtue will decay and decline through attaining the fruition of deeds of perfect virtue. Therefore, if you assert that the doer of deeds of perfect virtue will be born as a human through the fruition of those deeds, then you must assert that through attaining the fruition of deeds of perfect virtue, his well-being will decay and decline. [116a]

47. Furthermore, I have already demonstrated extensively above how it is illogical for the fruition of deeds done by a body that existed in the past to be experienced by another body that emerged later. It is illogical to assert that, because of thorough dependence upon and connection to the body of the past and the familiarity developed during the previous body through its efforts at cultivating good deeds and completely protecting them, they become linked to the subsequent body as if accompanying it. [119a]

48. For example, a most courageous and confident minister had a large retinue, a good horse, and the best weapons. With those, he protected the body of the precious king and benefited the king's subjects. Having prepared the powerful army with four branches, if there are those who are dissatisfied with [the size of] their own kingdom and come to seize other's land to conquer and plunder it, the minister would seek the means to completely defeat and utterly destroy those enemies. In return for his good deeds and benefits he had brought to others, if he were to be deprived of a large retinue, good horses, and best weapons, this would be most unsuitable. A scholar endowed with eloquence set this forth well in a letter praising the qualities of the precious king, describing it extensively and poetically. Now, if the precious king, extending his kindness and filled with benevolence, were to command that the hands and tongue of this person be cut off, a person who sought the means to honor the king and offer praise to him, this would be most inappropriate. In the same way, at the time of the cause, the doer of good deeds accumulates the collection of conditions favorable to the nature [of good deeds] and seeks the means and strength to make even small virtues become larger. Yet at the time of attaining the fruition, those things completely decay and the person becomes completely bereft of those. One must conclude that this is illogical. [119b]

49. Furthermore, for example, it is illogical for a healthy body that good food and drink serve as the cause of being afflicted by a severe illness. In the same way, it must be decided with regard to the doer of deeds of perfect virtue that the fruition of his deeds of perfect virtue are not things that serve as the cause of great faults and his undergoing unbearable and immeasurable suffering. [120a]

50. Furthermore, in the scriptures of the opponent, not only does fruition arise from deeds of virtue, one maintains that very large fruitions arise from small deeds of virtue. [120b]

51. Furthermore, in the scriptures of the opponent, not only does fruition arise from deeds of virtue, it must be asserted that it is illogical for the fruition that arises from deeds of virtue to be occasions for the arising of unpleasantness and mental suffering. [123a]

52. To speak in that way is most illogical because it is illogical to conceive and to say that what is uncertain is certain; to speak in that way is a case of conceiving and saying that what is uncertain is certain. That follows because to speak in that way is a case of conceiving and saying that it is certain that [the person] will attain a pleasant fruition after their death; until the final moment of death has passed, it is uncertain whether they will attain a pleasant fruition or if they will attain an unpleasant fruition. [132a]

53. While appealing to those lamas who describe without error and without confusion all of the possessions that were owned by the previous lama, I shall ask them questions in the following way. [136a]

54. To respond to that objection, by understanding that a reflection [of a face in a mirror] lacks a [real] face, there is no contradiction whatsoever in not conceiving it to be true as a face but conceiving it to be true as a reflection. In the same way, there is no contradiction whatsoever in not conceiving it to be true that a later lama or person remembers all of the possessions that were owned by the lama or person of the previous lifetime, but conceiving it to be true that a later lama or person describes without confusion all of the possessions that were owned by the lama or person of the previous lifetime. [137b]

55. Furthermore, we assert that it is untenable that our later lamas or persons remember all the possessions owned by the previous lama or person. Therefore, we assert that it is untenable that our later lamas or persons describe all the possessions owned by the previous lama or person. But does that violate conventional valid cognition? [138a]

56. Furthermore, with regard to the position that asserts that those who perform deeds of perfect virtue are born as humans through the fruition of those deeds after they die, it is asserted that at the time of the later lifetime, the person born as a human does not remember the scriptures that he memorized and learned at the

time of his previous life, but at the time of the later lifetime he remembers all of the possessions that he owned at the time of his previous lifetime. This is to be understood and its faults presented. [139a]

57. Furthermore, for example, the sprout that arises from a rice seed is rice, the sprout that grows from a barley seed is barley, the sprout that grows from a wheat seed is wheat, and the sprout that arises from a pea seed is peas. In the same way, you must assert that the fruition that arises from the seed of perfect virtue has the character of perfect virtue because, if a sprout does not grow from a seed at a place where it is tenable for the seed to exist, then dense darkness would arise from the tongues of a flame and it would not be possible to avoid anything that is or is not an effect being produced from anything that is or is not its cause. [139b]

58. Here, an impartial and capable person, led and guided by the rope of various perfect tenets and solid and irrefutable reasons, who is unclouded by the darkness of prejudice, said: "In this world there are many different types of humans, such as foolish common beings, the wise, and the superior. Therefore, it is illogical that all of the different types of humans, wherever they are, completely lack the power of mind to distinguish the logical and the illogical, coming under the power of external and internal causes of error, lacking the path that leads to the supreme aim of persons, the goal." [140a]

59. Furthermore, for example, although the feet of a dove that lives on the thatched roof of a house that has a vessel filled with yogurt do not step in the vessel of yogurt, its footprints are seen there. In the same way, it is asserted in the scriptures of the opponent that although a person of this life did not go to a previous birth, the previous experiences are remembered here. One must understand how the feasibility of the memory for previous experiences is inferred in the scriptures of the opponent. [141b]

60. Furthermore, it is not established by the valid cognition of a conventional consciousness that those who perform deeds of perfect virtue are born as humans through the fruition of those deeds after they die and that, being born there, they remember their past experiences, because those who perform deeds of perfect virtue being born as humans through the fruition of those deeds and, being born there, their remembering their past experiences is not an object of a conventional consciousness. [142a]

61. Fifth, having analyzed the birth of gods and demigods, stating the damaging objections to the opponent's system. [142b]

62. From the perspective of happiness, the assertion that the fruitions that arise from deeds of perfect virtue are not to be enjoyed and that their attainment becomes meaningless is illogical. Therefore, one must assert that all the joyful bliss, qualities of the Realm of Desire, and marvels of birth as either a demigod or god are not suitable as the fruition of virtue because they are not to be enjoyed. [143b]

63. Furthermore, the enjoyment of happiness is for the sake of mental satisfaction and contentment. Therefore, the joyful bliss that accompanies either birth as a demigod or birth as a god is merely the creation of minds of happiness to counteract suffering; it is not happiness intrinsically, without depending on the removal of suffering. [143b]

64. Furthermore, in the opponent's scriptures, meditating on suffering and ugliness are antidotes to conceiving the joyful bliss and marvels of heaven as happiness and growing accustomed to their exaggerated beauty. If one cultivates those, one turns away from them. If one does not cultivate those, obscuration, desire, and so forth will increase and one must undergo immeasurable suffering. Therefore, in the opponent's own system, conceiving the joyful bliss and marvels of heaven as happiness and growing accustomed to their exaggerated beauty are to be abandoned; one must feel disgust toward them and create discontent, the wish to discard them, and fear. [143b]

65. Furthermore, the *Stories of the Collections (Sambhāraparikathā)* says:[1] . . . It is asserted that the gods of the Realm of Form and the gods of the Formless Realm, after experiencing pleasure for a long time, are tormented by the suffering of conditioning and fall into the unbearable sufferings of the bad realms. Thus, although the gods of the Realm of Form and the gods of the Formless Realm are able to find pleasure, it must be asserted that they do not enjoy the pleasure that they find because they do not create a mind that is joyful there. [143b]

66. Furthermore, the *Stories of the Collections (Sambhāraparikathā)* says:[2] . . . It must follow that even in the scriptures of the opponent, birth as a god of the Realm of Desire is not suitable as the fruition that arises from virtuous deeds because in that scripture of the opponent the fruition that arises from virtuous actions must have a nature of happiness, and birth as a god of the Realm of Desire does not have a nature of happiness. [144a]

67. Furthermore, it is stated that gods of the Realm of Desire are burned by an inner fire sparked by desire for the Realm of Desire; because their minds are not undistracted and controlled even for a moment, they have the nature of being distracted

and agitated. It is very important to grasp here the definition of distraction and the definition of an undistracted mind. [144a]

66. [Desideri repeats the number] Furthermore, as was demonstrated earlier from the perspective of the need for the method of sowing and planting the seed that bears the fruition of perfect virtue and the method for enjoying the fruition of perfect virtue to be the same, the time for attaining the fruition of perfect virtue must be the time that the mental continuum is tied to what does not contradict perfect virtue and its object and [must be] the time that the mind does not scatter toward an object that is an obstacle to perfect virtue. Therefore, if one asserts that after death the doer of deeds of perfect virtue is born as a god of the Realm of Desire through the fruition of those deeds, then one must assert that after death, the time that the doer of deeds of perfect virtue is born as a god of the Realm of Desire through the fruition of those deeds is the time that he attains and enjoys the fruition of perfect virtue. [145a]

67. [Desideri repeats the number] Now, from the perspective of considering deeds of perfect virtue and birth as a demigod or god next to each other, one should understand the following. The assertion that after death, the doer of deeds of perfect virtue will be born as a demigod or god through the fruition of those deeds is illogical because it is illogical that the well being of the doer of deeds of perfect virtue will decay and decline through attaining the fruition of deeds of perfect virtue. Therefore, if you assert that the doer of deeds of perfect virtue will be born as a demigod or god through the fruition of those deeds, then you must assert that through attaining the fruition of deeds of perfect virtue, his well-being will decay and decline. [145a]

68. Furthermore, as was demonstrated in the section stating the damaging objections [to the assertions about] human birth, it is logical that a [true] deed of virtue exists as something that has aspects of higher quality, greatness, and goodness, and a quality of beauty, without there being discordance or disharmony between the deed and its effect. One must assert that the fruition that arises in dependence on a deed of perfect virtue is also established with similar characteristics of higher quality, greatness, and goodness, and a quality of beauty. Therefore, it is illogical that after death the doer of deeds of perfect virtue is born as a god through the fruition of those deeds because one must assert that the fruition that arises in dependence on deeds of perfect virtue is established as pleasant, a basis for being pleased, powerlessly captivating the mind, producing mental ease, and something to delight in. Therefore, one must assert that the birth of a god is not established in

any way with characteristics of quality, greatness, and goodness, and a quality of beauty. [145b]

69. Furthermore, the happiness, qualities of the Realm of Desire, and marvels found by gods of the Realm of Desire are not happiness by their own nature and are false, and have the quality of deception, and are like illusions. Therefore, one must assert that whatever they find does not establish satisfaction and contentment, are not suitable to be enjoyed, and are merely sufferings that increase grasping. [146a]

70. Furthermore, in general, the quality of goodness has such [levels] as high, middling, and weak. Therefore, one must assert that in general the goodness of a sentient being is something to be analyzed, such as existing in terms of high, middling, or just low. Therefore, specifically, although the birth of a god of the Realm of Desire, its happiness, qualities of the Realm of Desire, and marvels can be qualities of goodness of sentient beings, one must assert that those are something to be analyzed, such as existing in terms of high, middling, or just low as qualities of goodness. [146a]

71. If one analyzes the birth of demigods and the gods of the higher Realm of Form and Formless Realm, they are sufferings because they have afflictions, have obstructions, and they lead to lower states of existence. [147b]

72. Furthermore, the *Stories of the Collections (Sambhāraparikathā)* says:[3] ... Gods of the higher Realm of Form and Formless Realm are not suitable as bases of definite liberation. And the *Friendly Letter (Suhṛllekha)* says:[4] ... Demigods also are not suitable bases for seeing the truth. If one is born in the world of the demigods, or the higher Realm of Form and Formless Realm, reverting again and again from those [divine] abodes, one must go to many dangerous places that are abodes of discomfort, such as the unfortunate realms, and suffering will continually arise. [147b]

73. Furthermore, in the opponent's scriptures, in general, there are three types of deeds: virtuous, non-virtuous, and neutral. From the two kinds of virtuous deeds— contaminated and uncontaminated—here, the contaminated [are being considered, of which there are two]: meritorious deeds and unwavering deeds. [148a]

74. Therefore, it must be concluded that whether it is birth as a god in the higher Realm of Form and Formless Realm, it is illogical to assert that it is a fruition that arises from deeds of perfect virtue. [151a]

75. In the assertion of the opponent it is maintained that the birth of animals and ghosts is necessarily the fruition of non-virtuous deeds. [154b]

76. Second, demonstrating that in general if something is suffering it is not tenable that in general it is the fruition of non-virtuous deeds. [158b]

A Latin Version of the *Inquiry*

To the Greater Glory of God

Explanation of the Book Written in the Tibetan Language in Refutation of the Pythagorean Doctrine of the Transmigration of Souls according to the Tibetans' System

In these times of ours, those who set themselves the task of understanding the sciences that are most worthy of being known, labor, for the most part, under the error of thinking that knowledge can be procured by themselves with little or hardly any effort. Thus they apply only one ear to listening to the sciences, and only one eye to reading and examining them. Hence it follows that even when they have already completed their course of studies they appear puffed up and inflated, and if you should gently poke them you will find nothing substantial and everything hollow. How can he who has but one ear inclined and attentive to just one part distinguish the false from the true? How can he who has but one eye fixed and focused on just one part distinguish white from black? How can land that is fallow, never disturbed and turned over, up and down, by anyone, produce crops? Stagnant water, which has known nothing of being raised, lowered, conveyed here and there and led back again, necessarily putrefies. If the body should always lie on one and the same side it will of necessity sicken, weaken and die. Over a long time and with much work the attentive farmer tills, turns over, and stirs up the ground with the plow, the hoe, and other agricultural implements in order to gather an abundant harvest and rich and plentiful crops from his small field. Over a long time and with much work the industrious artisan rubs and polishes in order to render gold and gemstones even more precious and brilliant. The careful pilot, in order to avoid whirlpools and rocks and bring his own and others' lives safe and sound to the chosen port and safe harbor, turns the ship's prow now to this side, now to that, scanning everywhere, near and far, wherever he fears shipwreck, and he cautiously takes refuge in whatever direction the safe hope of life draws him, and with swelling sails carefully changes course. For which reason, you who are wonderfully endowed with talent and good sense and are utterly free from every vice of bias, turn your mind to this thing alone, that you avoid the rocks of error and accusation, which are most dangerous not to the body, which would be very much to be feared, but to your souls, and so arrive at the most blessed port of blessed eternal salvation, safe and sound. Under the present circumstances, with all my prayers, I pray, I beseech, and implore all of you to eagerly and freely receive with ears alert and mind intent that which I, for your own good, am about to tell you.

Surely there is nothing that contributes to the dignity of human society to such a degree as a correct rule for thinking and acting, and there is no one among you who does not know that indeed such has been inherited from our ancestors in the name of our Faith. Truly, given the flaw of human mutability and inconstancy . . .

LATIN TEXT

[1] A. M. D. G. [2] Explicatio Libri Thibetensi idiomate conscripti in [3] confutationem Pïthagoricae sententiae de Transmigra=[4] tione Animarum juxta Thibetanorum sistema. [New Para:] [5] Quicumque nostris hisce temporibus scientiarum [6] quae maximè scitu dignae sunt intelligendarum studio incumbunt, hoc ple=[7] rumque vitio Laborant, ut, siquidem parvo ac pene nullo labore sapienti=[8] am sibi comparandam existimant, scientiis audiendis unaṁ tantuṁ au=[9] rem, iisque inspiciendis rimandisque unum tantum^2 oculum adhibeant. Hinc [10] fit, ut quamvis, emenso jam studiorum curriculo, tumidi inflatique appa=[11] reant, si digitos admoveas, solidum nihil, inania omnia reperias. Qui=[12] cumque unam tantum^2 habeat aurem, et hanc quidem in unam tantum^2 partem [13] propensam, arrectamque, quînam mendacium a veritate secernat? Qui=[14] cumque unum tantum^2 habeat oculum, et hunc quidem in unam tantum^2 partem [15] apertum, haerentemque, quînam album a nigro secernat? Immota, nunquam [16] agitata, et a nullo sus deque versa tellus, quînam segetes producat? Attolli, [17] deprimique, huc atque illuc ferri , reducique nescia, ac semper immobilis aqua, [18] putrescat

necesse est. Si uno eodemque semper Latere decumbat corpus, [19] aegrotet, tab-escat, pereat necesse est. Ut uberes segetes, dulcemque fructum [20] copiam ex ag-ello colligat, vomere, ligone, aliisque agrestibus instrumentis [21] diù multumque terram exercet, invertit, exagitat sedulus agricola. Aurum [22] gemmasque ut longè pretiosiores, nitidioresque reddat industrius artifex, diù [23] multumque perfricat, expolitque. Ut sirtes, et scopulos effugiat, suamque, [24] et aliorum vitam optatum in portum, fidamque in stationem sarctam tectamque [25] reducat solicitus nauta, navis proram modò in hanc, modò in illam partem [26] inflectit, cuncta hinc, atque inde circumspicit, unde naufragium metuit, cau=[27] tus refugit, quàque tuta spes vitae allicit, tumidis velis pronus, anxiusque [153v] [1] deflectit. Quamobrèm qui-cumque ingenio, ac prudentia mirificè praediti, et [2] omni prorsus tenacitatis vitio immunes, in id unum animum intenditis vestrum [3] ut, non corpori, quod vel maximè esset pertimescendum sed animis intensissimos [4] errorum criminumque scopulos devitetis, et ad beatissimum aeternae salutis, beatitatis=[5] que portum tuti atque incolumes appellatis, vos omnes in praesentiarum votis om=[6] nibus oro, atque obtestor, ut arrectis auribus, intentisque animis ea quae pro ves=[7] tra utilitate dicturus sum avidè libenterque excipiatis. [8] [New para:] Nihil profectò est, quod humanae reipublicae dignitatem tantopere [9] commendet, quàm recta sentiendi, agendique norma, quam quidem a proavis [10] nostris Religionis nomine nuncupatam esse, nemo vestrum est, qui ignoret. Verum, g[11]cùm humanae volu-bilitatis, atque inconstantiae vitio factum sit . . . [1]

Notes

۶۶

At the Jesuit Archives in Rome, the Archivum Romanum Societatus Iesu (ARSI), documents are organized according to the headquarters of the mission for which they were produced. Because the Tibet mission was launched from the Jesuit headquarters in Goa, Desideri's manuscripts held at ARSI are designated as "Goa," followed by a number. Hence, the *Inquiry* is ARSI Goa 75 and the *Essence of the Christian Religion* is ARSI Goa 76a. In the notes that follow, passages from Desideri's Tibetan manuscripts are identified by their ARSI designation, their number, and their folio number. Following the conventions of Tibetan studies, recto is designated by the letter *a* and verso is designated by the letter *b*. In the translations in Chapter 2 and Chapter 4 and in Appendix 2, the page numbers are included in brackets in the body of the translation. For example, [12b] means the verso of the twelfth page. In Appendix 1, the line number is also given; [1a3] means the third line of the recto of the first page.

INTRODUCTION

1. On the death of Andrade, see Michael J. Sweet, "Murder in the Refectory: The Death of António de Andrade, S.J.," *Catholic Historical Review,* 102, no. 1 (Winter 2016): 26–45.

2. Regarding Father Toscano's translation style, if Desideri's *Essence of the Christian Religion* is taken as an example, one notes that he translates the catechism section literally and accurately, but in the section refuting emptiness he often sacrifices the complexity of Desideri's text by deleting entire sentences and paraphrasing others, translating into Italian only what he seems to have regarded as representative of Desideri's argument. We are grateful to Martino Dibeltulo for this observation.

3. Richard F. Sherburne, "A Christian-Buddhist Dialog? Some Notes on Desideri's Tibetan Manuscripts," in *Reflections on Tibetan Culture: Essays in Memory of Turrell V. Wylie,* ed. Lawrence Epstein and Richard F. Sherburne (Lewiston, NY: Edwin Mellen Press, 1990): 295–305.

4. Here, the most important work is Trent Pomplun, *Jesuit on the Roof of the World: Ippolito Desideri's Mission to Tibet, 1716–1721* (New York: Oxford University Press, 2010).

5. See Michael J. Sweet, trans., *Mission to Tibet: The Extraordinary Eighteenth-Century Account of Father Ippolito Desideri, S.J.,* ed. Leonard Zwilling (Boston: Wisdom Publications, 2010), 14–62; Trent Pomplun, *Jesuit on the Roof of the World: Ippolito Desideri's Mission to Tibet, 1716–1721* (New York: Oxford University Press, 2010); and Enzo G. Bargiacchi, *A Bridge across Two Cultures: Ippolito Desideri S.J. (1684–1733); A Brief Biography* (Firenze: Istituto Geografico Militare, 2008). The most comprehensive bibliography on Desideri is Enzo Gualtiero Bargiacchi, *Ippolito Desideri, S.J.: Opera e Bibliografia* (Roma: Institutum Historicum, S. I., 2007). The most useful biography of Desideri is Enzo Gualtiero Bargiacchi, *Ippolito Desideri S.J.: Alla Scoperta del Tibet e del Buddismo* (Pistoia: Brigata del Leoncino, 2006). The definitive work on the Italian missions to Tibet remains Luciano Petech, *I missionari italiani nel Tibet e nel Nepal* (Roma: Libreria dello Stato, 1952–1957). Desideri is discussed especially in volumes 5–7 of this seven-volume study.

6. Both Desideri and Freyre wrote detailed, and sometimes divergent, accounts of their journey. See Sweet, *Mission to Tibet,* 165–175 for Desideri and 611–624 for Freyre.

7. See ibid., 182.

8. In a personal communication Michael Sweet and Leonard Zwilling suggest that this identification might be mistaken. Desideri describes this first book as "a small book on the unity of the true Law of salvation in which the belief that everyone can find salvation in his own law is shown to be false" (see ibid., 573). However, *Dawn* is a relatively lengthy text of 128 Tibetan pages. Furthermore, it is written in verse, with a skill and a vocabulary that would have been difficult for Desideri to acquire after just nine and a half months in Tibet. Sweet and Zwilling suggest that the "small book" may have been something much shorter and much less impressive than Desideri's other Tibetan compositions and therefore a work that he may not have brought back to Rome.

9. Sweet, *Mission to Tibet,* 639.

10. For a translation of the decree and the accompanying letter to Desideri from Michelangelo Tamburini, General of the Society of Jesus, see ibid., 625–626.

11. For a useful discussion of the various rites controversies, see Pomplun, *Jesuit on the Roof of the World,* 135–140.

12. For a study of early European encounters with Buddhism, see, for example, Donald S. Lopez Jr., *From Stone to Flesh: A Short History of the Buddha* (Chicago: University of Chicago Press, 2013).

13. See Urs App, *The Cult of Emptiness: The Western Discovery of Buddhist Thought and the Invention of Oriental Philosophy* (Rorschach / Kyoto: UniversityMedia, 2012), 25.

14. Ibid., 26. For the Jesuit presentation and critique of this doctrine, App's study is highly recommended.

15. Desideri's catechism might be profitably compared to those of other Jesuit missionaries, including that of Henrique Henriques and Roberto de Nobili, composed in the Tamil language of South India, as well as *The Truth-Reflecting Mirror* by Jerónimo Xavier, composed in Persian (which Desideri read in India). On the former, see Roberto de Nobili, SJ, *Preaching Wisdom to the Wise,* trans. Anand Amaladass, SJ, and Francis X. Clooney, SJ (Chestnut Hill, MA: Institute of Jesuit Sources, 2000). On the latter, see Sweet, *Mission to Tibet,* 679, notes 431–433.

16. For a useful discussion of the evolution of the text, see Matteo Ricci, SJ, *The True Meaning of the Lord of Heaven (T'ien-chu Shih-i),* trans. Douglas Lancashire and Peter Hu Kuo-chen, SJ (St. Louis: Institute of Jesuit Sources, 1985), 10–21. See also App, *The Cult of Emptiness,* 92–96.

17. Ricci, *The True Meaning,* 69.

18. Ibid., 67.

19. Ibid., 103.

20. Ibid., 241.

21. Ibid.

22. Christopher (Cristoforo) Borri (1583–1632), "An Account of Cochin-China in Two Parts: The First Treats of the Temporal State of that Kingdom; The Second, of What Concerns the Spiritual," in John Pinkerton, *A General Collection of the Best and Most Interesting Voyages and Travels in All Parts of the World: Many of Which Are Now First Translated into English; Digested on a New Plan,* vol. 9 (London, 1811), 821.

23. Father Borri's source for his description of the Buddha's teaching is not clear. However, it is possible that he received it not from a Buddhist source but from a report of his fellow Jesuits in Japan. See App, *The Cult of Emptiness,* 44–46.

24. Sweet, *Mission to Tibet,* 364.

25. In a letter of August 16, 1626, he wrote, "The peoples of this great Thibeth are not idolaters: for we have found that they acknowledge the adorable Unity and Trinity of the true God; they know there are three Hierarchies of Angelic Spirits, divided into nine Choirs, according to the differences of their excellencies

and dignities; that there is a Hell which awaits the wicked, and a Paradise for the reward of the good." See H. Hosten, SJ, "A Letter of Father Francisco Godinho, SJ, from Western Tibet," *Journal of the Asiatic Society of Bengal,* n.s., 21 (1925): 66. The "trinity" likely derives from what he may have learned of the three jewels; the "hierarchies" and "choirs" are likely the three realms and nine levels *(khams gsum sa dgu)* of the Buddhist cosmos.

26. See Sweet, *Mission to Tibet,* 429.

27. Ibid., 638.

28. Ibid., 640.

29. Cited in Ippolito Desideri, SJ, *Il T'o-rans (L'Aurora),* Introduzione, traduzione e note di Giuseppe Toscano S.X. (Rome: IsMEO, 1981), 39.

30. Among Desideri's Italian writings, there is a short work refuting rebirth, found at ARSI Goa 73, fols. 285–308. Toscano speculates that this is the second work to which Desideri refers in his letter to the pope. The first part of the text (285–295) deals with the impossibility of rebirth being a punishment for the wicked, and the second part (296–308) deals with the impossibility of rebirth being a reward for the good. See Ippolito Desideri, SJ, *Il T'o-rans (L'Aurora),* Introduzione, traduzione e note di Giuseppe Toscano S.X. (Rome: IsMEO, 1981), 39.

31. Desideri seems to have first written his works in Italian and then translated them himself into Tibetan. He then had his Tibetan text copied by a Tibetan scribe. In the case of the *Inquiry,* neither his Italian text nor his original Tibetan draft has been located. Desideri's account book from the period indicates payments for ink and paper during this period. There are no notations for payments to a scribe (as there are for his first work in Tibetan). We are grateful to Leonard Zwilling (personal communication) for this information. The absence of a notation of payment to a scribe does not in itself mean that the surviving manuscript of the *Inquiry* was not the work of a scribe. However, until a careful forensic analysis is made of the *Inquiry,* comparing it to *dbu can* passages in Desideri's own hand (found, for example, in ARSI Goa 74), the question cannot be answered with certainty.

32. Those dates with their respective Tibetan page numbers and the number of days between each signature are:

Tibetan Page	Date	Days Between
1	24 June 1718	
9	6 July 1718	12
17	5 August 1718	30
25	22 August 1718	17
33	7 September 1718	16
41	24 September 1718	17
49	2 October 1718	8
57	18 October 1718	16
65	2 November 1718	15

73	21 November 1718	19
81	3 December 1718	12
89	26 December 1718	23
97	25 January 1719	30
105	22 February 1719	28
113	25 March 1719	31
121	16 April 1719	22
129	3 May 1719	17
137	18 May 1719	15
145	24 June 1719	37

Some further insight into the process of composition is found in a letter that Desideri sent to the Cardinals of the Propaganda, dated December 21, 1719. There he writes, "I began a work in this language divided in two tomes, in the first of which, with natural reasons and not without great erudition of their principles and authors, I refute, by means of their same principles and authors, the error whereby the birth of the living is *ab aeterno* and the fruit of their own actions, and the transmigration of souls; and in the second I show the necessity of a primal cause, from which all other things depend, and I refute their awful mistake, in which they say that there is not, nor there can be, any entity in itself, uncaused and independent; and in this second tome I similarly proceed with both natural reasons and reasons deduced from their same principles and authors; and although one of these tomes has not yet been revised and copied, it has indeed come to an end, and the other one has arrived to a bit before [the end]." As Toscano notes, the second work is likely *Origin of Sentient Beings, Phenomena, and So Forth*. The first and incomplete work is presumably the *Inquiry;* the date of the letter is six months after the last date above. As we know, the work remained unfinished. See Ippolito Desideri, SJ, *Il T'o-rans (L'Aurora),* Introduzione, traduzione e note di Giuseppe Toscano S.X. (Rome: IsMEO, 1981), 42–43. Our thanks to Martino Dibeltulo for translating the passage from the Italian.

33. Sweet, *Mission to Tibet,* 192–193.

34. Ibid., 573.

35. For a discussion of each of Desideri's Tibetan works and speculation on the order of their composition, see Trent Pomplun, "Natural Reason and Buddhist Philosophy: The Tibetan Studies of Ippolito Desideri, S. J.," *History of Religions* 50, no. 4 (May 2011): 384–419.

36. Sweet, *Mission to Tibet,* 193.

37. Ibid., 461.

38. Ibid., 568.

39. *Explicatio Libri Thibetensi idiomate conscripti in confutationem Pithagoricae sententiae de Transmigratione Animarum juxta Thibetanorum sistema (Explanation of the Book Written in the Tibetan Language in Refutation of the Pythagorean Doctrine of the Transmigration of Souls according to the Tibetans' System).* The extant text (presented

in Latin and English in Appendix 3) is only a side and a half long. It begins with what is clearly a paraphrase of the opening prayer of Tsong kha pa's *Lam rim chen mo,* making it the first extant translation of Tsong kha pa into a European language. The text goes on to reproduce some of the metaphors that appear in what we call the fourth poem at the beginning of the *Inquiry.* Although the text does not carry a date, circumstantial evidence suggests that it was written when Desideri was in Tibet. We are grateful to Leonard Zwilling for making us aware of its existence and providing a translation from the Latin.

40. These works are found in ARSI Goa 74.

41. See Sweet, *Mission to Tibet,* 393–394; ARSI Goa 75, 195b. For a helpful list of all the Tibetan texts cited in Desideri's works, see Pomplun, "Natural Reason and Buddhist Philosophy," 415–419.

42. See, for example, ARSI Goa 75, 12b–13a.

43. On the notes Desideri took from various sūtras, as found in ARSI Goa 74, see Pomplun, "Natural Reason and Buddhist Philosophy," 395.

44. Tsong-kha-pa, *The Great Treatise on the Stages of the Path to Enlightenment,* 3 vols. (Ithaca, NY: Snow Lion Publications, 2000–2004),1:259.

45. For a variety of reasons, the Capuchin mission to Tibet has not received extensive study in English-language scholarship. For a fascinating brief history of the Capuchin mission to Tibet (which both predated and extended long beyond the mission of Desideri), see Isrun Engelhardt, "Between Tolerance and Dogmatism: Tibetan Reactions to the Capuchin Missionaries in Lhasa, 1707–1745," *Zentral-Asiatische Studien* 34 (2005): 55–97.

46. We are grateful to Michael Sweet and Leonard Zwilling for pointing this out.

47. On the critical importance of this Sanskrit work on poetics for the Tibetan literary tradition, see Thupten Jinpa and Jas Elsner, *Songs of Spiritual Experience* (Boston: Shambhala, 2000), introduction.

48. To provide some examples, in the title itself, Desideri writes *I po li do zhes bya ba yis* instead of using the standard instrumental form *zhes bya bas.* In the opening prose of the preamble (2b.2), we find the phrase "among all the fields of knowledge," which Desideri renders as *shes bya thams bcad rnams kyi nang nas.* No trained Tibetan author would commit the redundancy of using both *thams cad* ("all") and *rnams,* a plural marker. Desideri also makes a somewhat strange use of the verb *zhu ba,* which can mean "appeal," "plead," "say," "question," or "inquire," in contexts where it is inappropriate. Immediately after his preamble, Desideri opens the body of the text with the awkward phrase *zhu zhus bzhin du chos kyi don la rtsod pa dngos su brgyab pa,* containing the unusual word combination *zhu zhus bzhin du.* In the refutation of emptiness in the *Essence of Christianity,* Desideri seems to often use *stong pa nyid* ("emptiness"), when he should use *stong pa* ("empty"), an important distinction. Finally, Desideri frequently uses the wrong verb tense. One of his key terms is *dgag pa,* which means to "refute," "reject," or "stop." Desideri often uses the past tense, *bkag*

pa, not when referring to something that has already been refuted but when embarking on the refutation itself.

49. After completing our translation of the text, we learned that the *Essence of Christianity* had been translated by Elaine M. Robson as part of her 2014 University of Bristol doctoral dissertation, entitled "A Christian Catechism in Tibetan: An English translation and study of Ippolito Desideri's Tibetan manuscript, *The Essence of the Christian Faith.*" In addition to a full translation, Dr. Robson's dissertation provides a useful commentary on the text. In the section on emptiness, she provides references to passages in Desideri's *'Byung khung* and *Nges legs* where he makes similar arguments. She also notes relevant passages in Aquinas. In the section on the catechism, she provides passages from other Roman Catholic catechisms.

50. Sweet, *Mission to Tibet,* 584.

51. See Pomplun, *Jesuit on the Roof of the World,* 145–151.

1. INTRODUCTION TO *INQUIRY CONCERNING THE DOCTRINES OF PREVIOUS LIVES AND EMPTINESS*

1. On the term *sgo skar,* or "star head," see Trent Pomplun, *Jesuit on the Roof of the World: Ippolito Desideri's Mission to Tibet, 1716–1721* (New York: Oxford University Press, 2010), 264n107, which includes references to the range of scholarship on the term *sgo dkar (white head).* Desideri's Italian translator, the Xaverian Missionary Father Giuseppe Toscano (who died before he was able to complete a translation of this text) renders the term simply as "Christian."

2. For a discussion of the importance of syllable stress in various genres of Tibetan poetry, see the introduction in Thupten Jinpa and Jas Elsner, *Songs of Spiritual Experience* (Boston: Shambhala, 2000).

3. For a translation of the *Jātakamālā* in two volumes, see Justin Meiland, trans., *Garland of the Buddha's Past Lives by Āryaśūra* (New York: NYU Press, 2009).

4. For the legend of the Sixth Dalai Lama's escape, see Michael Aris, *Hidden Treasures and Secret Lives* (New York: Routledge, 1989).

5. Richard F. Sherburne argues that it is a poem to God. See "A Christian-Buddhist Dialog? Some Notes on Desideri's Tibetan Manuscripts," in *Reflections on Tibetan Culture: Essays in Memory of Turrell V. Wylie,* ed. Lawrence Epstein and Richard F. Sherburne (Lewiston, NY: Edwin Mellen Press, 1990), 304; Desideri's translator Giuseppe Toscano thought that the poem was dedicated to Lhazang Khan. See Ippolito Desideri, SJ, *Il T'o-rans (L'Aurora),* Introduzione, traduzione e note di Giuseppe Toscano S.X. (Rome: IsMEO, 1981), 42.

In a personal communication, Michael Sweet and Leonard Zwilling considered four possibilities. First, the reference could indeed be to the Dalai Lama. However, at the time of the composition of the text (or at least of the manuscript), the Seventh

Dalai Lama was only ten years old and had not yet been brought to Lhasa. Furthermore, Desideri suggests that the object of the poem is someone he has met ("you have held me with love and compassion"). The second possibility, therefore, is that the referent is Lhazang Khan. He had already been killed at the time of the manuscript, but Desideri may have composed the poem at an earlier date. The third possibility is the Panchen Lama, Losang Yeshé (1663–1737), whom Desideri admired and whom he may have met. Finally, Sweet and Zwilling suggest the possibility that Desideri was writing of some future scholar whom he would convert to Christianity and who would aid him in spreading the Gospel. Among these options, Sweet and Zwilling consider Lhazang Khan as the most likely choice.

6. Tsong-kha-pa, *The Great Treatise on the Stages of the Path to Enlightenment*, 3 vols. (Ithaca, NY: Snow Lion Publications, 2000–2004), 1:33–34.

7. F. Max Müller, *Lectures on the Science of Religion* (New York: C. Scribner and Co., 1872), 11.

8. In this text and in his *Historical Notices,* Desideri consistently refers to Tibet as "this Tibet" (*bod 'di* in Tibetan). At the time of his mission, the Europeans in India, following Muslim writers, referred to Baltistan (an ethnically Tibetan region of modern Pakistan) as "Little Tibet" and Ladakh as "Great Tibet." When he learned of the existence of Central Tibet, Desideri referred to it as a third Tibet. Likely learning that such a term was incomprehensible to Tibetans, he nonetheless felt compelled, even when writing in Tibetan, to refer to Tibet as "this Tibet."

9. See Michael J. Sweet, trans., *Mission to Tibet: The Extraordinary Eighteenth-Century Account of Father Ippolito Desideri, S.J.,* ed. Leonard Zwilling (Boston: Wisdom Publications, 2010), 573.

10. Ibid., 343.

11. See Donald S. Lopez Jr., *A Study of Svātantrika* (Ithaca, NY: Snow Lion Publications, 1987), 105.

12. For a translation of the original, see Tsong-kha-pa, *The Great Treatise,* 3:306–307.

13. Cited in ibid., 1:76.

14. Ibid., 60.

15. Ibid., 56. The *Udānavarga* stanza reads: "Through hearing, one understands phenomena. / Through hearing, one overcomes sins. / Through hearing, one discards the meaningless. / Through hearing, one attains nirvāṇa."

16. For a discussion of Desideri's views of Tibetan idolatry, see Donald S. Lopez Jr., *From Stone to Flesh: A Short History of the Buddha* (Chicago: University of Chicago Press, 2013).

17. See Tsong-kha-pa, *The Great Treatise,* 3:50, where he cites Kamalaśīla as a source for this image.

18. See *The Middle Length Discourses of the Buddha,* trans. Bhikkhu Ñāṇamoli and Bhikkhu Bodhi (Boston: Wisdom Publications, 1995), 591.

19. Thomas Aquinas, *On the Eternity of the World (De Aeternitate Mundi)*, in Robert T. Miller, *Internet Medieval Sourcebook*, http://legacy.fordham.edu/halsall/basis/aquinas-eternity.asp.

20. See H. Hosten, SJ, ed., *A Missionary in Tibet: Letters and Other Papers of Fr. Ippolito Desideri, S.J. (1713–21)* (New Delhi: Cosmo Publications, 1998), 77.

21. See Sweet, *Mission to Tibet*, 342–343. These nine points are followed by three additional points by Desideri, dealing with gods, demigods, and humans, respectively. The lengthy discussion of gods deserves particular attention. For example, Desideri writes, "From the cosmology described in the Tibetans' books, one is led to the obvious conclusion that the ancient people and pagans of Hindustan, from whom the Tibetans took most of their books, had adopted in its entirety, or nearly so, the system propounded and explained by the fifth-century Alexandria author Cosmas the Egyptian" (see 346).

22. Sweet, *Mission to Tibet*, 299. Desideri's argument is discussed at length in Michael J. Sweet, "The Devil's Stratagem or Human Fraud: Ippolito Desideri on the Reincarnate Succession of the Dalai Lama," *Buddhist-Christian Studies* 29 (2009): 131–140.

23. Sweet, *Mission to Tibet*, 304.

24. Ibid., 301.

25. Ibid., 304.

26. Ibid., 306. It is noteworthy that Desideri's traveling companion and fellow priest, Manoel Freyre, held a similar opinion. Freyre wrote, "When one of their superiors migrates, not into another body as they falsely believe, but truly to the pit of Hell, another is elected, though not through a search but actually with the help of the Devil. This is how it happens: the Evil Demon enters into someone, usually one of the relatives of the deceased, and informs him about some small possessions. . . . In such and other ways the Devil triumphs, ensnaring souls by swaying them to believing in a new resurrection. And finally the one who is possessed by the Devil is elected lama of the whole monastery." See Sweet, *Mission to Tibet*, 618–619.

27. Matteo Ricci, SJ, *The True Meaning of the Lord of Heaven (T'ien-chu Shih-i)*, trans. Douglas Lancashire and Peter Hu Kuo-chen, SJ (St. Louis: Institute of Jesuit Sources, 1985), 241.

28. At *Bodhicaryāvatāra* 7:14, Śāntideva writes, "Fool, there is no time to sleep. / It is hard to catch this boat again."

2. SELECTIONS FROM *INQUIRY CONCERNING THE DOCTRINES OF PREVIOUS LIVES AND EMPTINESS*

1. This stanza and the next two are adaptations from the opening verses of Tsong kha pa's *Great Treatise*. See Tsong-kha-pa, *The Great Treatise on the Stages of*

the Path to Enlightenment, 3 vols. (Ithaca, NY: Snow Lion Publications, 2000–2004), 1:32, for the original verses as they appear in Tsong kha pa's text. As noted in the Introduction to the present volume, Desideri draws the great majority of his citations of Indian works from Tsong kha pa's *Lam rim chen mo.* We have sought to locate these passages in the three-volume translation just cited. For those interested in the Tibetan text (which Desideri sometimes adapts for his own purposes), this translation is based on *Byang chub lam rim che ba* (Dharamsala, India: Tibetan Cultural Printing Press, 1991), with references to the Tibetan pages included in the translation. The annotations to the three-volume translation also provide references to the canonical sources of the Indian citations. In many cases, our translation of the passages from *Lam rim chen mo* differs from that in the three-volume translation from Snow Lion Publications.

2. Based on his reading of Desideri's Latin version of this passage (see Appendix 3), Leonard Zwilling (personal communication) suggests that Desideri intended the verb *phyag* ("polish") here rather than *phyug.* We have followed his suggestion.

3. This stanza is adapted from Tsong kha pa, *The Great Treatise,* 1:34.

4. As explained in the previous chapter, this final section, which constitutes most of the text, is not translated here.

5. Here and throughout, we have translated Tibetan technical terms and proper names into Sanskrit. Although Desideri did not know Sanskrit, he understood the technical vocabulary of Buddhism; we have therefore rendered these terms in the technical vocabulary of modern Buddhist Studies. For example, we have translated *byang chub sems* here as *bodhicitta,* rather than as "aspiration to enlightenment." Elsewhere, we have rendered *'khor ba* as "saṃsāra" rather than "cyclic existence," etc. For the names of Indian authors, Zla ba grags pa is Candrakīrti, Klu sgrub is Nāgārjuna, etc.

6. Desideri's *nyon mongs pa'i gnod kyis brlams pa* is an unusual phrase. This phrase appears customarily as "possessed by the demon of afflictions" *(nyon mongs pa'i gdon gyis brlams pa);* he may have written *gnod* while intending *gdon.*

7. Desideri adapts this passage from Śāntideva's *Bodhicaryāvatāra* 4.23. It is found in *The Great Treatise,* 1:122.

8. This and the next four verses are adaptations from the *Samādhirāja Sūtra,* with the final line changed to suit Desideri's own purpose here. He also places these stanzas in a different order than in the sūtra. These citations are found in *The Great Treatise,* 3:306, where the final line reads, "Know all phenomena are this way."

9. The text mistakenly reads *ma ngan* instead of *mya ngan.*

10. The text reads *phyir bcos* ("repair"). Desideri likely intended *phyir phyogs.*

11. Desideri draws this passage from the *Udānavarga* from Tsong kha pa, *The Great Treatise,* 1:155.

12. Desideri here adapts two lines from Āryadeva's *Four Hundred (Catuḥśataka* 12.1) as cited by Tsong kha pa, *The Great Treatise,* 1:75.

13. Desideri draws these two lines from Bhāviveka's *Essence of the Middle Way* *(Madhyamakahṛdaya)* as cited by Tsong kha pa, *The Great Treatise,* 1:76.

14. This is an adaptation of a verse from Nāgārjuna's *Friendly Letter,* cited in Tsong kha pa's *Great Treatise,* 1:126. Desideri changes two lines of the stanza that appear as the following in the original, "One who is born as a human, / And then becomes involved in wrongdoing / . . ."

15. This stanza is adapted from Śāntideva's *Bodhicaryāvatāra,* 5:109, which reads, "Through my body I shall engage in these deeds; / What point is there in saying it with words alone? / Will the mere reading of medical treatment / Help the person who is ill?"

16. We have not been able to locate the source for Desideri's list of the sixteen benefits of giving the gift of dharma.

17. Desideri draws this and the next three stanzas from Āryaśura's *Jātakamālā* as cited in *The Great Treatise,* 1:56–57.

18. These passages, except for the third stanza, are adaptations of verses from the *Ratnatālala Sūtra* extolling the virtues of faith *(dad pa),* as found in Kangyur, mdo sde *ba,* 63b7–64a4.

19. Desideri draws this passage from *The Great Treatise,* 1:56, where it is cited from the *Udānavarga,* 23:6.

20. This and the next two passages are from adapted the *Udānavarga,* 23:3–5.

21. This stanza appears to be Desideri's own composition.

22. This and the subsequent stanzas in this section appear to be Desideri's own composition.

23. All the stanzas in this section pertaining to the fourth quality of debate appear to be Desideri's own composition.

24. Desideri omits short passages from the sūtra at the end of each of the three types of karma, where examples, such as Devadatta and King Ajātaśatru, are provided.

25. *Las rnam par 'byed pa,* Kangyur, mdo sde *sa,* 282a7. This sūtra is not cited in Tsong kha pa's *Great Treatise.* For an edition of the Sanskrit and Tibetan texts, see Sylvain Lévi, *Mahā-karmavibhaṅga (La grande classification des actes) et Karmavibhaṅgopadeśa (Discussion sur le Mahā Karmavibhaṅga)* (Paris: Librairie Ernest Leroux, 1932). The Sanskrit of the quoted passage occurs on p. 22; the Tibetan occurs on p. 191.

26. Desideri draws this passage from *The Great Treatise,* 1:254–255, omitting parts of it.

27. Desideri draws this passage from ibid., 1:255.

28. Ibid.

29. The text mistakenly reads *bskyod* instead of *bskyed.*

30. Desideri draws this passage from *The Great Treatise,* 3:291–292.

31. Kangyur, mdo sde *ha,* 117b5. The full title of this sūtra is *Thabs mkhas pa chen po sangs rgyas drin lan bsab pa'i mdo;* no Sanskrit title is provided in the Sde dge canon. This is one of the rare works cited by Desideri that Tsong kha pa does not cite in *Lam*

rim chen mo, although this is a text well-known in Geluk circles on the topic of *bodhicitta.* In ARSI Goa 74, 21*r,* we see that Desideri copied a long passage from the fourth chapter of this sūtra. The passage here is found on the last two lines of 21*r.*

32. Kangyur, mdo sde *ha,* 198b6. This is a rare quotation that Desideri did not draw from *Lam rim chen mo.* However, Tsong kha pa mentions this text without quoting from it. In Goa ARSI 74 27*r,* we see that Desideri copied a long passage from this sūtra.

33. Desideri draws this entire passage, beginning with "For example" and ending here, from *The Great Treatise,* 3:292.

34. Desideri draws this entire passage, beginning with "For example" and ending here, from ibid., 3:303.

35. Ibid.

36. The negative particle *ma* is missing in Desideri's manuscript here, a scribal error.

37. Desideri draws this entire passage, beginning with "For example" and ending here, from *The Great Treatise,* 3:293.

38. *Mūlamadhyamakakārikā* 27:10–11 as translated by Mark Siderits and Shōryū Katsura in *Nāgārjuna's Middle Way* (Boston: Wisdom Publications, 2013), 323–324.

39. Ibid., 27:16cd, 327.

40. Desideri draws this passage from *The Great Treatise,* 1:277–278, but omits part of the passage.

41. The text mistakenly reads *nang* for *gnang.*

42. Desideri draws this entire passage, beginning with "For example" and ending here, from *The Great Treatise,* 3:294–295. A pigeon on a thatched roof leaving its footprints on yogurt inside the hut is well known among monastic scholars as an example of an inexplicable phenomenon.

43. *Prasannapadā,* Tengyur, dbu ma *'a,* 118a3. Desideri draws this passage from *The Great Treatise,* 3:152.

44. The text mistakenly reads *smon sran* instead of *mon sran.*

3. INTRODUCTION TO *ESSENCE OF THE CHRISTIAN RELIGION*

1. See Michael J. Sweet, trans., *Mission to Tibet: The Extraordinary Eighteenth-Century Account of Father Ippolito Desideri, S.J.,* ed. Leonard Zwilling (Boston: Wisdom Publications, 2010), 192.

2. Ibid., 192–193.

3. Ibid., 573.

4. For a recent translation, see *Nāgārjuna's Middle Way* by Mark Siderits and Shōryū Katsura (Boston: Wisdom Publications, 2013), which contains brief commentaries on the verses drawn from key Indian commentaries.

5. Sweet, *Mission to Tibet*, 371–372. As Sweet notes, Desideri draws the discussion of fire from the tenth chapter ("Analysis of Fire and Fuel") of Nāgārjuna's *Mūlamadhyamakakārikā*.

6. Ibid., 190–191.

7. Translation by Thupten Jinpa; the translation of the full text is available at http://tibetanclassics.org/en/media-resources/text/other-texts-translated-by-thupten -jinpa-phd.

8. Anton C. Pegis, ed., *Basic Writings of St. Thomas Aquinas*, vol. 1 (Indianapolis: Hackett, 1997), 23.

9. Sweet, *Mission to Tibet*, 371.

10. Ibid., 374.

11. There is an extensive secondary literature on Buddhist critiques of the existence of God. See, for example, Ernst Steinkellner, "Hindu Doctrines of Creation and Their Buddhist Critiques," in *Buddhism, Christianity and the Question of Creation: Karmic or Divine*, ed. Perry Schmidt-Leukel (London: Ashgate, 2006), 15–32. On Dharmakīrti's critique, see, for example, Roger Jackson, "Dharmakīrti's Refutation of Theism," *Philosophy East and West* 36, no. 4 (1986): 315–348.

12. For speculations on the Greek and Latin terms that Desideri was rendering into Tibetan, see Trent Pomplun, *Jesuit on the Roof of the World: Ippolito Desideri's Mission to Tibet, 1716–1721* (New York: Oxford University Press, 2010), 157.

13. George E. Ganns, trans., *The Spiritual Exercises of Saint Ignatius: A Translation and Commentary* (Chicago: Loyola Press, 1992), 27–28.

14. For a discussion of the theological background to Desideri's presentation of the Trinity, and a somewhat different reading of the Tibetan than that which appears in our translation, see Trent Pomplun, "The Holy Trinity in Ippolito Desideri's *Ke ri se sti yan gyi chos lugs kyi snying po*," *Buddhist Christian Studies* 29 (2009): 117–129.

15. There is a Tibetan story about a toad living in a small pond who does not believe tales of a vast ocean. When he finally sees it, he dies of shock.

16. Sweet, *Mission to Tibet*, 394–396.

17. On *délok*, see Bryan J. Cuevas, *Travels in the Netherworld: Popular Narratives of Death and Afterlife in Tibet* (New York: Oxford University Press, 2011).

18. The term translated here as "heinous" is *'tsham med* in Tibetan, literally "without interruption," a term used to describe those deeds that lead directly to rebirth in hell in the next lifetime, without another lifetime intervening.

19. Sweet, *Mission to Tibet*, 391.

20. For Tsong kha pa's exposition of the four powers, see Tsong-kha-pa, *The Great Treatise on the Stages of the Path to Enlightenment*, 3 vols. (Ithaca, NY: Snow Lion Publications, 2000–2004), 1:251–259.

4. *ESSENCE OF THE CHRISTIAN RELIGION*

1. Desideri's Tibetan text reads, *mdor na tha snyad pa'i shes pa la grub pa'i dngos 'di rnams blang bar bya ste.* This last syllable, *ste,* is a scribal error and should be *na,* a conditional.

2. Reading *ni* as *na.*

3. In the Tibetan text the term "body" (*lus*) is missing; we have added it here.

4. "Forbearance" (*bzod pa*), which is the Tibetan equivalent of the Sanskrit term *kṣanti,* is the closest word in the Tibetan Buddhist lexicon that Desideri would have found to convey the Christian concept of forgiveness. We have retained Desideri's use of the Tibetan term, rather than translate it as "forgiveness." There is an extensive discussion of the Buddhist concept of forbearance in the exposition of the six perfections (*pāramitā*) in Tsong kha pa's *Great Treatise.*

5. The text includes the number two above "tenth" and the number one above "ninth," suggesting that their order was to be reversed when the text was printed.

6. Throughout this section the Tibetan text reads *snying po* (essence) but should read *gnyen po* (antidote).

A FINAL THOUGHT

1. Michael J. Sweet, trans., *Mission to Tibet: The Extraordinary Eighteenth-Century Account of Father Ippolito Desideri, S.J.,* ed. Leonard Zwilling (Boston: Wisdom Publications, 2010), 187.

2. The Dalai Lama, *Towards a True Kinship of Faiths: How the World's Religions Can Come Together* (New York: Random House, 2011), 12.

APPENDIX 1. TOPICAL OUTLINE *(SA BCAD)* OF THE *INQUIRY*

1. On page 9a11, Desideri writes this heading as "Refuting that the birth of sentient beings comes into being through the power of deeds" when he first lists this in the broader outline above.

APPENDIX 2. SUBJECTS OF THE *INQUIRY*

1. For a translation of this passage, see Tsong-kha-pa, *The Great Treatise on the Stages of the Path to Enlightenment,* 3 vols. (Ithaca, NY: Snow Lion Publications, 2000–2004), 1:295.

2. Ibid., 294.
3. Ibid., 295.
4. Ibid., 292–293.

APPENDIX 3. A LATIN VERSION OF THE *INQUIRY*

1. ARSI Goa 73, *f.* 153*r* and *v.* Transcription and translation of the Latin text by Leonard Zwilling.

Acknowledgments

ᘔ

We are grateful to the Archivum Romanum Societatis Iesu (ARSI) in Rome for granting us permission to translate Desideri's works and for providing us with copies of the Tibetan texts, as well as with the pages from Desideri's manuscripts that are reproduced on the cover and the frontispiece. We are also grateful to the American Council of Learned Societies (ACLS) for a Collaborative Research Fellowship that supported this project. We would also like to thank Enzo Bargiacchi for encouraging us to pursue this project, as well as Michael Sweet and Leonard Zwilling for their deep knowledge of Desideriana.

Index

❦

Abhidharmakośa (Vasubandhu), 169

abhiṣeka, 189

ācāryas, 75

Adam and Eve, 186; afflictive obstructions, 187; disobedience of, 241; inner ornaments, 240; obstructions to omniscience, 187; outer ornaments, 240

Advent, 237

Africa, 75, 142

Aggañña Sutta, 59

America, 75, 142

Analects (Confucius), 8

Andrade, Antonio de, 1

Aquinas, Thomas, 13, 29, 60, 170, 283n49; argument from design, 169; first argument of, 166; five proofs, 164–165

Archivum Romanun Societatis Iesu (ARSI), 3

arhat, 34, 49, 51–52, 187

Aristotle, 11, 60; efficient cause, 13; final cause, 13; formal cause, 13; four causes, 13; material cause, 13

Āryaśūra, 32–33, 54

Asia, 7, 10–11, 13, 58, 61, 75–76, 142–143, 157

Atiśa, 51

Augustine, Saint, 174

avarice, 242

avyākata, 59

baptism, 222, 245–246, 248

Bellarmino, Roberto, 170–171

Bengal, 1

Bhāviveka, 52, 169

Bhutan, 1

Blaze of Reasoning (*Tarkajvālā*) (Bhāviveka), 116, 169

Bodh Gayā, 179

Bodhicaryāvatāra (Śāntideva). See *Engaging in the Bodhisattva Deeds*

bodhicitta, 90, 94, 184

Bodhipathapradīpa (Atiśa). See *Lamp for the Path to Enlightenment*

bodhisattvas, 129, 184, 187

Book of Changes, 8

Book of Documents, 8

Book of Rites, 8

Borri, Cristoforo, 6, 11–13

Brahmajāla Sutta, 169

Bruno, 170–171

Buddha, 9, 10, 11, 13, 32, 36, 38, 42, 47, 57–58, 70–71, 155, 157–158, 169, 172, 179; conception of, and Virgin Mary, 176–177; first sermon of, 153–154; fourteen questions, 59; Jesus, contrast with, 34; knowledge of extinction, 34; knowledge of non-arising, 34; noble silence of, 59; second sermon of, 152; two bodies of, 33

buddha field (*buddhakṣetra*), 32

buddha nature (*tathāgatagarbha*), 157

Buddhapālita, 47

Buddhism, 18–19, 26–27, 39, 42, 64, 69, 151, 161, 167, 184, 251; causation, theory of, 66, 168; creation myth of, 59; doctrines, refutation of, 5, 8–9; eighteen elements, 72; ethical theory of, 188; hells, system of in, 179–180; inferential reasoning, 65; as false religion, 14, 20, 29, 43, 48–49, 52; flaws in, 45; illusion in, 46–47; and Jesuits, 5–9, 29; magician's illusion, 73; non-virtues, 75–76; no self doctrine of, 152–154; original sin, as foreign to, 173; other religions, comparisons to, 51; past virtues, 75–76; rebirth, doctrine of, 30, 74, 166, 179–180; root afflictions, 188; secondary afflictions, 188; six consciousnesses, 72; six objects, 72; six organs, 72; theism, critiques of, 169; three jewels, 160, 170, 175; transfer of merit, 186. *See also* Indian Buddhism; Tibetan Buddhism

Byang chub lam rim che ba. See *Great Treatise on the Stages of the Path to Enlightenment* (Tsong kha pa)

Cabral, João, 1, 2

Cacella, Estavão, 1–2

Candragomin, 53

Candrakīrti, 66, 71–73, 124–125, 130, 135, 156

Canisius, Peter, 170

Capuchins, 2, 5, 23, 36, 37, 170–171; lawsuit against, 29

Castiglione, Giuseppe, 6

catechism, 8, 19, 28, 64, 152, 160–161, 170–172, 180–181

Catechismus Minor (Peter Canisius), 170

Catholic Church, 171

Catuḥśataka (Āryadeva). See *Four Hundred*

Chapa Chökyi Sengé (Phyva pa chos kyi seng ge), 53

Chenrezik (Spyan ras gzigs), 20

China, 5, 6–10, 37, 44, 75, 94, 142, 157, 184, 251

China Illustrata (Kircher), 2

Chinese Rites Controversy, 5

"A Christian-Buddhist Dialog? Some Notes on Desideri's Tibetan Manuscripts" (Sherburne), 3

Classic of Poetry, 8

Clear Words (*Prasannapadā*) (Candrakīrti), 135

Clement XI, 3

Cochin China, 11. *See also* Vietnam

comparative religion, 40, 42–45, 49

confession, 186, 190; of sins, 248–249

Confucianism, 10–11

Confucius, 8

Cosimo III de' Medici, 3

Cosmas the Egyptian, 285n21

Council of Chalcedon, 33

creatio ex nihilo, 178

cresima, 246

Dalai Lama, 20, 37, 67–68, 178, 283–284n5

Daodejing, 9

Daoism, 9

Dawn, Signaling the Rise of the Sun That Dispels the Darkness (*Tho rangs mun sel nyi ma shar ba'i brda*) (Desideri), 4, 16, 18, 150–151, 278n8 definite goodness (*nges legs*), 42, 49, 89–90, 223, 225–226, 229, 240

Definite Goodness (Nges legs) (Desideri), 18, 150, 152

Democritus, 62

dependent origination (*pratītyasamutpāda*), 32, 163

Desideri, Ippolito, 1, 13–15, 17–19, 22, 26, 32–37, 39–41, 46–48, 51, 60–61, 66, 76–77, 150–151, 173, 251, 278n2, 278n8, 279n15, 280n30, 280n31, 280–281n32, 282n48, 283n49, 283–284n5, 284n8, 285n21, 285n26, 285–286n1, 286n5, 287–288n31; Adam and Eve, description of, 186–187; analytical consciousness, 165–166; Apostles' Creed, commentary on, 176, 178, 181, 183, 185; background of, 3–5; on baptism, 189–190; on beginningless rebirth, 166–167; Buddhism, flaws in, 45, 52; Buddhist doctrines, refutation of, 5, 8–10, 16; Capuchins, lawsuit against, 29; catechism, use of, 152, 170–172, 180–181; on causation theory, 168; comparative religion, case for, 42–45, 49; on confession, 186, 190; conventional consciousness, 165–166; debate, benefits of, 53–57; Devil, work of, 68, 73; on doctrine of dependent origination, 163; doctrine of emptiness, explanation of, 155–158; doctrine of emptiness, refutation of, 28–31, 74, 152, 162, 164, 167–169; doctrine of rebirth, explanation of, 61–63; doctrine of rebirth, refutation of, 21, 27, 30–31, 53, 58, 63–65, 67, 75, 162; on Eucharist, 189–190; as failure, 5–6, 29; faith of belief, 181; faith of clarity, 181–182; faith of reliance, 181; fame of, 2, 6–7, 29; and first cause, 170; on Garden of Eden, 186–188; on incarnate lamas, 67–68, 71–73; intrinsic existence, 165, 166, 167, 168, 169, 170; Lord's Prayer, 185; original sin, 179; on past lives, 68–75; on penitence, 189–191; reflection of moon metaphor, 161–162; and resurrection, 177; seed and soil, imagery use of, 49–50, 52; on self-existence, 160; on seven sacraments, 189–190; on Ten Commandments, 182–185; Tibet, order to leave from, 252–253; Tibetan Buddhism, knowledge of, 20–21; Tibetan prose style of, 23–25; Tibetan scholars, criticism of, 38; Tibetan Studies, as forefather of, 28; and trinity, 174–175; Tsong kha pa, influence on, 158–159; two truths doctrine, 162; virgin birth, discussion of, 178; and Virgin Mary, 176–177; on virtuous deeds, 185–186; whole and its parts, relationship between, 167; work, defense of, 5. *See also individual works of*

dharma, 39, 129, 172, 251

dharmakāya (truth body), 33

Dharmakīrti, 169–170

Diamond Sūtra (Vajracchedikā), 46, 153

Dibeltulo, Martino, 278n2

Differentiations of Actions (Karmavibhaṅga), 22, 115

Dīgha Nikāya, 169

Doctrine of the Mean (Confucius), 8

D'Orville, Albert, 2

La Dottrina Cristiana (Bellarmino), 171

Dzungar Mongols, 36

Early Jesuit Travellers in Central Asia (Wessels), 2

Easter, 237

Elements (Euclid), 6

emptiness (*śūnyatā*), 9, 14–15, 18–19, 30, 49, 161, 163, 171, 173; and catechism, 170; explanation of, 153–158; origins of, 11–13; refutation of, 1, 8–10, 28–31, 74, 152, 164, 167–170, 180, 253

Engaging in the Bodhisattva Deeds (Bodhicaryāvatāra) (Śāntideva), 47, 53, 184, 285n28, 286n7, 287n15

Entrance to the Middle Way (*Madhyama-kāvatāra*) (Candrakīrti), 66, 72, 124–125, 130–131, 156

Epiphany, 237

Essence of the Christian Religion (Desideri), 3, 16, 24, 28–29, 40–41, 64, 150, 152, 166, 194, 216–222, 235–250, 253, 282n48, 283n49; Apostles' Creed, 185, 205–206; catechism, style of in, 160–161, 170–172, 180, 278n2; as Christian *upāya*, 173; circle analogy, 204–205; conventional consciousness, 197–200, 202–204, 206; doctrine of emptiness, refutation of in, 27, 170, 180; doctrine of rebirth, refutation of in, 180, 199–200, 206; faith capable of reliance, 207, 224–229, 231–232; faith of belief, 207–214, 223–224, 231; faith that is clear, stainless, and joyful, 207, 226, 230–232; false religion, 169, 172; immeasurable power of Jesus, 214–215; intrinsic nature, emptiness of, 193, 195–198, 200–205, 207–208; Lord's Prayer, 185; peerless lord, meaning of, 208–212; preamble of, 160–161; precious jewel, meaning of, 208; reflection of moon metaphor in, 161–162, 200–201, 207; seven sacraments, 189–191; Six Commandments, 185; Ten Commandments, 185; three natures, 209–213; Tibet, philosophical system of, as false, 192–193; translation of, 191

Eucharist, 189–190, 246–248

Euclid, 6

Europe, 8, 44, 75, 142

Explanation of the Book Written in the Tibetan Language in Refutation of the Pythagorean Doctrine of the Transmigration of Souls according to the Tibetans' System (Desideri), 20, 273–275

Extensive Sport (*Lalitavistara*), 71, 128

Fernández, Juan, 7

Fifth Dalai Lama, 157, 252

Filippi, Filippo de, 2

First Council of Nicaea, 33

Formless Realm, 51

Four Hundred (*Catuḥśataka*) (Āryadeva), 130

Fourteenth Dalai Lama, 253

Freyre, Manoel, 4, 285n26

Galileo, 170–171

Garden of Eden, 10, 178–179, 186–188

Garland of Birth Stories (*Jātakamālā*) (Āryaśūra), 32–33, 54

Geluk sect, 4–5, 66, 156, 169; political ascendancy of, 157

Gervaise, Nicolas, 6

Godinho, Francisco, 14

Gomes, Piero, 7–8

The Good Heart: A Buddhist Perspective on the Teachings of Jesus (Dalai Lama), 253

Great Learning (Confucius), 8

Great Treatise on the Stages of the Path to Enlightenment (*Byang chub lam rim che ba*) (Tsong kha pa), 5, 21–22, 25, 38, 47, 49, 51–52, 54, 56, 77, 158, 169, 184, 188, 281–282n39, 285–286n1, 287–288n31, 290n4; "insight" section of, 173

Groups of Utterances (*Udānavarga*), 45, 284n15, 286n11, 287n19, 287n20

Grueber, Johann, 1–2

Haribhadra, 116

Harrowing of Hell, 179

Heart Sūtra, 151, 153

hell: in Buddhism, 179–180; in Christianity, 179–180, 219; and limbo, 179, 219; limbo of pure, 219; and purgatory, 179, 219; realms of, 219; root defect, 179–180, 221–222

Henriques, Henrique, 279n15

Hinduism, 75

Hindu schools, 154

Hindustan, 55, 61, 169, 285n21

Historical Notices (Desideri), 5, 17–20, 22, 28, 45, 55, 61–64, 67–68, 73, 151–152, 155, 157, 169, 177, 188, 252, 284n8
Hundred Actions Sūtra (*Karmaśataka*), 23, 120

immaculate conception, 176
India, 3–5, 7, 9–10, 16, 42, 61, 94, 142, 152, 163, 169, 194, 199, 223, 251, 279n15, 284n8
Indian Buddhism, 55, 56, 59–60, 153, 158. *See also* Buddhism
Indochina, 6
In Praise of Dependent Origination (*Rten 'brel bstod pa*) (Tsong kha pa), 157–158
Inquiry concerning the Doctrines of Previous Lives and of Emptiness (Desideri), 3, 8, 15, 18–24, 29, 60–61, 63–64, 67–68, 73, 76, 121, 131–133, 137, 149, 150–151, 159, 166, 180, 191, 252–253, 280n31, 280–281n32, 281–282n39; comparative religion, case for in, 40–41, 99–106; false religions, 79, 93, 104; invocation of, 78–82; one's own religion, benefits of debating, 106–114; opening poem of, 31–35; preamble of, 57–58, 82–87; signatures, use of in, 16–17; studying religion of others, benefits of, 87–89; translation of, 25–27; as unfinished work, 27
Italy, 8–9

Jamyang Shepa ('Jam dbyangs bzhed pa), 252
Japan, 6–7, 157
Jātakamālā (Āryaśūra). See *Garland of Birth Stories*
jātaka stories, 32
Jesuit Archives, 3, 158
Jesuits, 4–9, 29, 170, 173
Jesus Christ, 32, 35–36, 41, 172, 175, 180, 207, 221–222, 224–229; Adam and Eve, 240–241; auspicious days, rituals of, 234;

Buddha, contrast with, 34; conception of, 176–178; dual nature of, 33; immeasurable power of, 214; Last Supper, 190, 247; limbo of pure, 219; Lord's Prayer, 181; miraculous birth of, 215–216; misdeeds against, 232–233; resurrection of, 179, 219–220, 223; and sacraments, 244–250; sign of cross, 212; spear wound of, 34; suffering of, 216–219; Ten Commandments, 230–237; three natures of, 212–213; twelve disciples of, 213, 247
Judaism, 75–76, 143
Judgment Day, 178, 180

Kamalaśīla, 251
Kangxi emperor, 6
karma, 21, 52, 58, 70, 115–116, 180; and afflictions (*kleśa*), 22; and rebirth, 61–63
Karmaśataka. See *Hundred Actions Sūtra*
Karmavibhaṅga. See *Differentiations of Actions*
Kashmir, 44, 94, 142
Kircher, Athanasius, 2
kleśa, 34
kṣānti, 290n4

Lalitavistara, 71, 128
Lamp for the Path to Enlightenment (*Bodhipathapradīpa*) (Atiśa), 51
Lam rim chen mo. See *Great Treatise on the Stages of the Path to Enlightenment*
Lent, 237
Lhasa (Tibet), 2, 4–5, 19, 33, 163, 194, 199, 253; sacking of, 36–37
Lhazang Khan, 4–5, 20, 36, 37, 71, 151, 251–252, 283–284n5
Lokāyata, 59
Lord's Prayer, 181, 183
Losang Yeshé, 252, 283–284n5
Lotus Sūtra, 34
Lower Mongolia, 142
Loyola, Ignatius, 173

Madhyamakakārikā (Nāgārjuna). See *Verses on the Middle Way*

Madhyamaka school, 9–10, 46–47, 56, 65–66, 153, 168, 170; analytical consciousness, 164–165; chariot metaphor, 167; conventional truth, 161, 163–165; and self-existence, 160; two truths doctrine, 161–162; ultimate truth, 161; whole and its parts, relationship between, 167

Madhyamakāvatāra (Candrakīrti). See *Entrance to the Middle Way*

Mahāvibhāṣa, 169

Mahāyāna, doctrines, 28, 33, 58, 154

Maitreya, 125

Malabar Rites Controversy, 5

Mandhātṛ, King, 120

Māra, 54, 179

Marpa, 190–191

Materialists, 59

matrimony, 250

Māyā, 177

Mencius (Confucius), 8

mental consciousness (*manovijāna*), 50

metempsychosis, 61

Milarepa, 190–191

mindfulness, 48, 50, 56, 97, 186, 227, 240–241

Mirror of Poetics (*Kāvyādarśa*) 24

Mission to Tibet: The Extraordinary Eighteenth-Century Account of Father Ippolito Desideri, S. J. (Sweet and Zwilling), 2

Moheyan, 251

mtha' dpyod (critical analysis), 24, 63–64, 74

Müller, Friedrich Max, 40

Muslims, 75–76, 143

Nāgārjuna, 70–71, 153–156, 120, 124–125, 168

Nangsa, Lady, 178

negative deeds, 22, 69, 90, 98, 152–153, 179–180, 187, 218, 222, 228; accumulation of, 220–221, 239; as debts, 227; effects of, 188; kinds of, 186, 239; misdeeds by oneself, 186, 188, 239; root defect, 186, 239–240. See also non-virtuous deeds

Nepal, 44, 75, 94, 142

neyārtha, 21

nirvāṇa, 34, 38, 129, 187

nītārtha, 21

Nobili, Roberto de, 279n15

non-virtuous deeds, 238, 244; and anger, 242–243; and avarice, 242; and completion, 236, 241; and envy, 242–243; food and drink, intemperance of, 242–243; heavy faults of, 241–242; impure deeds, 242; and intention, 236, 241; light faults of, 241; mental darkness, laziness of, 242–243; and object, 236, 241; and pride, 242. See also negative deeds

no self, 47, 59, 152

nothingness (*wu*), 9

Notizie Istoriche del Thibet (*Historical Notices of Tibet*) (Desideri), 2–3

olio santo, 249

On the Eternity of the World (Aquinas), 60

ordine sacro, 249–50

Orazio della Penna, Francesco, 4, 6, 20, 170

original sin, 176, 179–180, 186, 189, 219, 221–222, 239, 245; 245; fruit of, 243–244; origin of, 240–241

Origin of Sentient Beings, Phenomena, and So Forth (*Sems can dang chos la sogs pa rnams kyi 'byung khungs*) (Desideri), 18, 150, 152, 280–281n32

Pāli, 32, 59

paṇḍita (scholar), 28, 171

penitence, 222, 248–249

Pereira, Tomás, 6

perfection of giving (*dānapāramitā*), 54

Perfection of Wisdom in Eight Thousand Stanzas, 22, 116

perfection of wisdom sūtras, 153

Petech, Luciano, 2

polygamy, 61
Pontius Pilate, 213, 216
Pramāṇavārttika (Dharmakīrti), 169
Prasannapadā. See Clear Words
pratītyasamutpāda (dependent origination),
    154–156
pride, 242
Propaganda Fide, 2, 5, 29
Pythagoras, 10

Qianlong emperor, 6
Qing court, 6
Qing emperor, 37

rebirth, 15, 18, 22, 49, 71, 74, 170, 179, 187;
    as absurd, 60; Christian doctrine,
    problem of, 60; as eternal, 60; explana-
    tion of, 58–60; as inherited, 59–60; no
    beginning, 59, 65–67, 166, 168, 214;
    refutation of, 1, 8–9, 16, 21, 27, 30–31,
    53, 58, 63–65, 180, 253
resurrection, 180–81
Rhodes, Alexandre de, 6
Ricci, Matteo, 6–7, 58, 75, 184; Buddhist
    doctrines, refutation of, 8–9; reincarna-
    tion, attack on, 10–11
Robson, Elaine M., 283n49
Roman Catholic Church, 191
Roman Catholic missions, 6–7, 10, 14.
    See also Capuchins; Jesuits
Rome (Italy), 253
Rten 'brel bstod pa (Tsong kha pa). See In
    Praise of Dependent Origination
Ruggieri, Michele, 7–8
rūpakāya (form body), 33

sacraments, 244–250
samādhi, 110
Samādhirāja Sūtra, 47, 53, 121
Samantabhadra, 177
śamatha (serenity), 56, 110, 242
saṃgha, 172
Sāṃkhya, 66–67

saṃsāra, 34, 51–52, 56, 58, 76, 154, 206
Samye monastery, debate at, 251–252
Śāntarakṣita, 169
Śāntideva, 47, 53, 76, 184
Sera Monastery, 252
seven deadly sins, 188
seven sacraments, 190–191; Tibetan
    Buddhism, analogues in, 189
Seventh Dalai Lama, 37, 252, 283–284n5
Sherburne, Richard, 3
Shigatse (Tibet), 1
Siam, 6, 11
siṃhanāda (lion's roar), 57
Six Commandments, 185
six perfections (pāramitā), 54, 290n4; of
    giving (dānapāramitā), 54
Sixth Dalai Lama, 37, 71; false vs. true, 252
Society of Jesus. See Jesuits
Spiritual Exercises (Loyola), 173
Spring and Autumn Annals, 8
star heads, 31
Summa Theologica (Aquinas), 29, 164
summum bonum, 18–19
śūnyatā. See emptiness
Sūtra on the Flowering of the Bhagavan's
    Wisdom, 22
Sūtra on Limitless Lives, 22
Sūtra on Repaying Kindness, 22, 120
Sūtra Setting Forth the Causes and Effects of
    Good and Evil, 22
Sūtra of the Wise and the Foolish, 23
svabhāva (intrinsic nature), 154
Sweet, Michael, 2, 278n8, 283–284n5

Tachard, Guy, 6
Tarkajvālā (Bhāviveka). See Blaze of
    Reasoning
Tattvasaṃgraha (Śāntarakṣita), 169
Ten Commandments, 182, 185; against
    killing, 183–184; Tibetan analogue to, 183
Thailand, 6
Tibet, 1–2, 4–6, 9, 14–15, 18–19, 23,
    28–29, 33, 35–36, 38, 42, 44, 47, 55, 58,

Tibet *(continued)*
68, 75, 82–83, 85, 87, 88, 94, 141,
143–147, 152, 156–157, 169, 173, 178,
221, 251–253, 278n8, 284n8
Tibetan Buddhism, 2, 6–7, 15, 18–22,
25–29, 35, 47, 55–56, 171, 178, 191;
bodhisattva in, 43; confession, analogue
in, 190; faith of belief, 172, 176; faith of
clear admiration, 172; faith of emulation,
172; four powers, 190; Geluk sect of, 156;
Nyingma sect of, 177; philosophical
system of, as false, 192–193; seven-
branched service, 72; seven sacraments,
analogues in, 189; texts of, 16, 31–32,
38–39. *See also* Buddhism
Tibetan Studies, 28
Tokugawa shoguns, 6
Toscano, Giuseppe, 3, 278n2, 280n30,
280–281n32, 283n1, 283–284n5
Towards a True Kinship of Faith (Dalai
Lama), 253
transubstantiation, 35
Trigault, Nicolas, 6
trinity, 41, 174
Trisong Detsen, 251–52
The True Meaning of the Lord of Heaven
(*Tianzhu shiyi*) (Ricci), 7–11, 75
*The True Record of the Lord of Heaven, A New
Compilation from India* (*Xinbian xizhuguo
tianzhu shilu*) (Ruggieri and Gomes), 7
The Truth-Reflecting Mirror (Xavier), 279n15
Tsaparang (Tibet), 1

Tsong kha pa, 5, 21–23, 25, 33, 38–39, 47,
51–54, 77, 156, 158–59, 161, 163–165,
169, 173–174, 183–184, 188, 281–282n39,
285–286n1, 287–288n31; critique of, 157;
intrinsic existence, 166; serenity
meditation, instructions on, 56

Udānavarga. See *Groups of Utterances*
Upagupta, 125
upāya, 173
Upper Mongolia, 142

Valignano, Alessandro, 6
Vasubandhu, 169
Vatican, 253
Verses on the Middle Way (*Madhya-
makakārikā*) (Nāgārjuna), 70, 120–121,
124–125, 153, 155–156, 168
Vietnam, 6, 11
Virgin Mary, 171, 176–178, 182, 213,
215–216, 229–230

Wessels, Cornelius, 2–3

Xavier, Francis, 6–7, 170
Xavier, Jerómino, 279n15

Yogācāra school, 46

zin bris (notes), 24
Zwilling, Leonard, 2, 278n8, 280n31,
281–282n39, 283–284n5